IBM PC

An Introduction to the Operating System, BASIC Programming, and Applications

Third Edition

Dr. Larry Joel Goldstein

A Brady Book
Published by Prentice Hall Press
New York, NY 10023

IBM PC: An introduction to the Operating System, BASIC Programming, and Applications—Third Edition

Copyright © 1986 by Brady Communications Company, Inc.
All rights reserved
including the right of reproduction
in whole or in part in any form.

A Brady Book
Published by Prentice Hall Press
A Division of Simon & Schuster, Inc.
Gulf + Western Building
One Gulf + Western Plaza
New York, New York 10023

Library of Congress Cataloging in Publication Data

Goldstein, Larry Joel.

　IBM PC: An Introduction to the Operating System, BASIC Programming, and Applications—Third Edition

　Includes index.
　　1. IBM Personal Computer—Programming.
2. BASIC (Computer program language)　I. Title.
QA76.8.I2594G64　1985　　　　005.265　　　　　85-31391
ISBN 0-89303-620-X

Printed in the United States of America

86 87 88 89 90 91 92 93 94 95 96　1 2 3 4 5 6 7 8 9 10

Limits of Liability and Disclaimer of Warranty

The author and publisher of this book have used their best efforts in preparing this book and the programs in it. These efforts include the development, research, and testing of the theories and programs to determine their effectiveness. The author and publisher make no warranty of any kind, expressed or implied, with regard to these programs or the documentation contained in this book. The author and publisher shall not be liable in any event for incidental or consequential damages in connection with, or arising out of, the furnishing, performance, or use of these programs.

Contents

Preface to the Third Edition

I have been most gratified by the reception accorded the first two editions of this book, which found their way into the hands of several hundred thousand readers. Many of them took the time to write me with suggestions for improvements and additions. This correspondence has been very helpful and greatly appreciated. Many reader suggestions have found their way into this new edition.

Our fundamental goals for this edition have remained the same as for the preceding ones: to provide an introduction to the MS-DOS operating system and BASIC programming for beginners with one of the IBM family of personal computers. In this edition, I have made the following changes and additions:

1. The description of the IBM family of computers has been expanded to reflect the latest machines, and the most recent versions of the operating system and the Microsoft BASIC language.

2. The description of BASIC has been expanded to provide more detailed coverage of various topics and to include various new topics.

3. I have added extensive discussions on program design and planning. These discussions occur throughout the book. Moreover, in Chapter 18, I have included a case study to show how a complex program is planned and coded.

4. I have added chapters on memory management and use of printer graphics.

5. All programs have been rewritten to emphasize detailed commenting and structured style. Moreover, the program header comments now connect the programs with the corresponding files on the optional program diskette.

6. I have added a detailed discussion of flowcharting, using the ANSI standard flowcharting symbols.

This edition has grown considerably over its predecessor. As it stands, it contains more than ample material for learning BASIC programming in a self-study style.

The world of personal computing being what it is, we can expect further changes which will require future revisions of this book. With these in mind, please keep your suggestions and comments coming.

I would like to thank Terry Anderson, Computer Science Editor for his conscientious work on behalf of this edition and Charles Siegel, President of the Brady Communications Company, for his support of this book and of my writing projects in general.

Larry Joel Goldstein

Registered Trademarks

IBM PC, XT, AT, ProPrinter, Matrix Printer, Graphics Printer, and Color Printer are registered trademarks of International Business Machines Corporation.

MS-DOS is a registered trademark of Microsoft Corp.

Epson, MX/80, MX/100, LQ 1500, LX/80, FX/80, GRAFTRAX-80, and GRAFTRAX-PLUS are trademarks of Epson America, Inc.

Part One
Introduction

1

A First Look at Computers

1.0 Chapter Objectives

IN THIS CHAPTER, WE:

- Define personal computing and describe its wide range of applications.

- Describe the main components of a computer: CPU, input, output, and memory units, and the functions of each.

- Describe the various members of the IBM family of personal computers.

- Describe the possible systems which can be designed around IBM-compatible personal computers.

1.1 Introduction—What is a Computer?

In the past decade, personal computers have become common tools on the job, in schools, and in the home. They allow their users to perform a tremendous variety of tasks more efficiently than they could previously be performed, if they could be accomplished at all. These personal computers are changing the way we think, work, and learn. To help you appreciate the all-pervasive nature of personal computers, let me cite a single statistic. By 1984, less than a decade after the invention of the first personal computer, more than 60 percent of all office workers had access to a personal computer.

In 1981, IBM introduced its first entry into the personal computer market. The original IBM PC has enjoyed extraordinary popularity and is in use in millions of homes, schools, and businesses. IBM has responded to the success of its PC by introducing an entire line of personal computers, varying in accessories, computing power, and, of course, price. IBM's personal computer line has become the *de facto* standard of microcomputing. In the last few years there have been more than 100 personal computers which are, to some degree, IBM clones. These clones are compatible with the IBM machines in the sense that they can run most IBM PC programs unaltered. As of this writing, more than half of all personal computers are either IBMs or are compatible with the IBM PC.

1

This book is an introduction to personal computing on the IBM personal computers. It is divided into two parts. They first is an introduction to the operating system MS-DOS, the control program that manages IBM personal computers. This part will teach you enough to run applications programs and to perform the rudimentary tasks necessary to personal computing, such as making copies of files and formatting diskettes.

The second part of the book is an introduction to programming in BASIC on the IBM personal computers. In this part, I teach you to write programs in BASIC. Moreover, this part contains many interesting applications programs which you can use on your own computer. These programs are useful as well as instructional. You may study them as they appear in the text and type them into your computer to run them. Alternatively, you may purchase these programs on diskette and thereby save yourself the trouble of typing them in and dealing with the inevitable typographical errors that will arise.

This book is designed as a text, to be used either for self-study or in a classroom setting. Accordingly, it contains questions for you to answer. You should attempt to answer these questions and test your answers on your computer. It is only by being an active learner that you will get the most from this text.

What is Personal Computing?

The personal computer is not a toy. It is a genuine computer with most of the features of its big brothers, the so-called "main-frame" computers, which still cost several million dollars. A personal computer can be equipped with enough capacity to handle the accounting and inventory control tasks of most small businesses. It can also perform computations for engineers and scientists, and it can even be used to keep track of home finances and personal clerical chores. It would be quite impossible to give a complete list of the possible applications of personal computers. However, the following list can suggest the range of possibilities:

For the business person

Accounting

Record keeping

Clerical chores

Inventory

Cash management

Payroll

Graph and chart preparation

Word processing

Data analysis

Networking

For the home

Record keeping

Budget management

Investment analysis

Correspondence

Energy conservation

Home security

On-line information retrieval

Tax return preparation

For the student

Computer literacy

Preparation of term papers

Analysis of experiments

Preparation of graphs and charts

Project schedules

Storage and organization of notes

For the professional

Billing

Analysis of data

Report generation

Correspondence

Stock market data access

Scientific/engineering calculations

For Recreation

Computer games

Computer graphics

Computer art

As you can see, the list is quite extensive. If your interests aren't listed, don't worry! There's plenty of room for those of you who are just plain curious about computers and wish to learn about them as a hobby.

1.2 What is a Computer?

At the heart of every computer is a **central processing unit** (or **CPU**), which performs the commands you specify. This unit carries out arithmetic, makes

Figure 1-1. **The main components of a computer.**

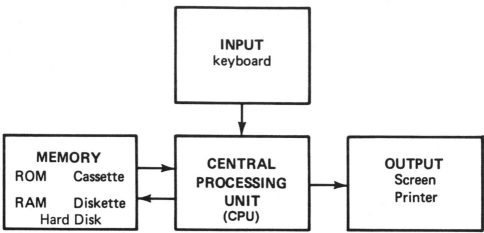

logical decisions, and so forth. In essence, the CPU is the "brain" of the computer. The **memory** of a computer allows it to "remember" numbers, words, and paragraphs, as well as the list of commands you wish the computer to perform. The **input unit** allows you to send information to the computer; the **output unit** allows the computer to send information to you. The relationship of these four basic components of a computer are shown in Figure 1-1.

In a personal computer, the CPU is contained in a single semiconductor chip, about an inch long. The CPUs used in the IBM personal computers are manufactured by Intel Corporation. The CPU of the IBM PC, PC/XT, and IBM Portable computers is an **8088 microprocessor.** In the IBM PC AT, the CPU is a more powerful chip, then **80286 microprocessor.** As a computer novice, it is not necessary for you to know anything about the electronics of the CPU. You may view the CPU as a magical device which somehow manages to carry out instructions that direct the computer to do certain things.

The main input device of the IBM Personal Computer is the computer keyboard. We will discuss the special features of the keyboard in Section 2.5. For now, think of the keyboard as a typewriter. By typing symbols on the keyboard, you are inputting them to the computer.

The IBM Personal Computer has a number of output devices. The most basic is the "TV screen" (sometimes called the video monitor or **video display**). You may also use a printer to provide output on paper. In computer jargon, printed output is called **hard copy.**

There are five possible types of memory in an IBM Personal Computer: **ROM, RAM, cassette, diskette,** and **hard disk** (or **fixed disk**). Each of these types of memory has its own advantages and disadvantages. Microcomputers attempt to make memory as versatile as possible by using several kinds of memory, thereby allowing them to take advantage of the good features of each.

ROM

ROM stands for "read-only memory." The computer can read ROM but cannot write anything in it. ROM is reserved for certain very important programs necessary to the operation of the machine. For example, every time you turn on the computer, it automatically runs a series of programs to test the operations of the various components of the system. These diagnostic programs (as well as others) are recorded in ROM at the factory and you cannot change them.

RAM

RAM stands for "random-access memory." This is the memory which you can read and write. If you type characters on the keyboard, they are then stored in RAM. Similarly, results of calculations are kept in RAM awaiting output to you. As we shall see, RAM even holds the instructions which perform the calculations!

There is an extremely important feature of RAM which you should remember:

If the computer is turned off, then RAM is erased.

Therefore, RAM may not be used to store data in permanent form. Nevertheless, it is used as the computer's main working storage because of its great speed. (It takes about a millionth of a second to store or retrieve a piece of data from RAM.)

The size of RAM is measured in bytes. Essentially, a **byte** is a single character (such as "A" or "!"). You will often hear statements such as: "This PC/XT is equipped with 256K of RAM." The abbreviation "K" stands for the number 1024. For example, 256K stands for 256 times 1024 or 263,144 bytes. Each model of the IBM PC comes with a certain standard amount of RAM. However, this memory may be expanded by adding memory chips to an optional memory circuit card that is inserted into an expansion slot within the system unit of the computer.

To make permanent copies of programs and data, we may use either a diskette drive or a hard disk.

Diskette Drives

A diskette drive (see Figure 1-2) records information on flexible diskettes that resemble phonograph records. The diskettes are often called "floppy disks," and they can store several hundred thousand characters each! (A double-spaced typed page contains about 2,000 characters.) (See Figure 1-3.)

Figure 1-2. **A diskette drive.**

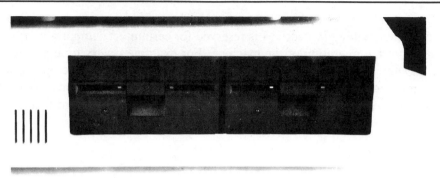

Winchester disks

A **hard disk** (or **fixed disk**), also called a **Winchester disk,** stores information on a hard platter that is sealed within either the drive unit itself or a hard plastic cartridge (see Figure 1-4). Winchester disks are the most costly storage medium for your computer. However, they allow the most rapid access to your data and can store from five million to 100 million characters.

In this book, we will assume that your system contains at least one diskette drive.

1.3   A Grand Tour of The IBM Family of Computers

Before we turn on the computer, let's get acquainted with the various parts of the PC. (For a discussion of the PC/XT and the AT, see the end of this section.) In Figure 1-5, we have shown the three basic components: the monitor, the keyboard, and the system unit. We assume that you have followed IBM's instructions and have properly connected the various cables between these units. Note that computer cables are designed to be inserted in only one direction. Note that the end of the cable is not square, but trapezoidal in shape (see Figure 1-6). This odd shape guarantees that the many pins plug properly into the various holes in the mating plug. In turn, this guarantees that the various signals carried by the cable are directed to their proper places.

Note that we place the monitor on top of the system unit for convenient viewing. If you wish, you may place your monitor beside the system unit. The choice is yours, but by all means arrange your system for comfort and convenience. You will be using your system for many hours at a time and these little convenience features will lessen eyestrain and fatigue.

Figure 1-3.   **A floppy diskette.**

Figure 1-4.   **A Winchester disk drive.**

Figure 1-5.   **The IBM PC.**

Figure 1-6.   **A computer cable.**

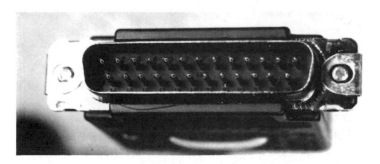

The keyboard is attached to the system unit via a coiled cord, which allows you to situate the keyboard in a comfortable position. Note also the retractable legs that tilt the keyboard at an angle with the table. This is also a "human factors" feature that is designed to minimize fatigue. We will discuss the various other features of the keyboard in Section 2.5.

Of all the basic components, the system unit is the most mysterious so let's explore its contents. At the front of the unit are the diskette drives. Each drive has a slot in which to insert a diskette. Put your fingers in the groove in the center of the left drive and gently pull forward. (See Figure 1-7.) Note how the door lifts. This is the position of the door for diskette insertion. (More about that later.) For now, just push the door down to its original position.

Figure 1-7.   **Opening the door of a diskette drive.**

In Figure 1-8, we show the rear of the system unit on an IBM PC. Note that there are many places to plug in cables of various sizes and shapes. (Your system unit may look somewhat different, depending on the boards installed.) The system unit shown has plugs for a printer, a color display, and a communications interface. (More about each of these later.)

Figure 1-9 shows the interior of an IBM PC. (If you are a novice, please don't remove the case of your computer; just settle for looking at the picture.) The large unit in the corner is the power source and a cooling fan. Also note the speaker in the lower left corner. The system board, which is the main electronic circuit of the computer, is situated horizontally at the bottom of the computer. The 8088 chip is on this board. The vertical boards are optional and are inserted in sockets called **expansion slots,** located on the system board. You may choose from a veritable

Figure 1-8.   **The rear of the IBM PC system unit.**

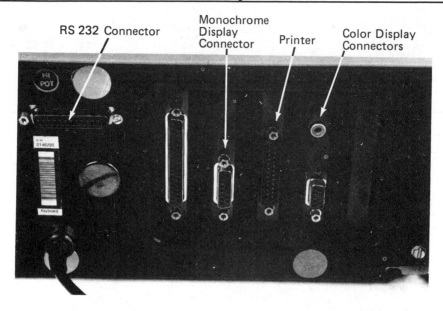

Figure 1-9.   **The interior of the IBM Personal Computer.**

smorgasbord of circuit boards to expand the capabilities of your computer. The boards in Figure 1-9 are, from left to right, a monochrome display interface, a memory expansion board, a diskette controller board, and a color/graphics interface. To give you a feel for the complexity of these boards, we have shown a close-up of the color/graphics interface in Figure 1-10. In Figure 1-11, we show a close-up of a ROM chip, next to a paper clip for size comparison.

Figure 1-10.   **The color/graphics interface.**

Don't be intimidated by the sight of the electronic circuitry. In order to use your computer, you won't need to know how it works.

The IBM PC/XT

Figure 1-12 is a picture of the IBM PC/XT. This computer is an upgraded model of the PC. The main difference is the hard disk on the right side of the system unit, instead of a second diskette drive. The hard-disk system allows for as much storage as 25 diskettes used by the floppy diskette drive on its left.

Figure 1-11.   **A ROM chip.**

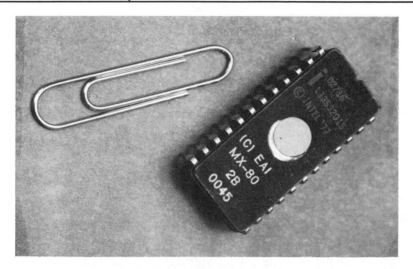

Figure 1-12.   **The IBM PC/XT.**

Figure 1-13. **The PC AT.**

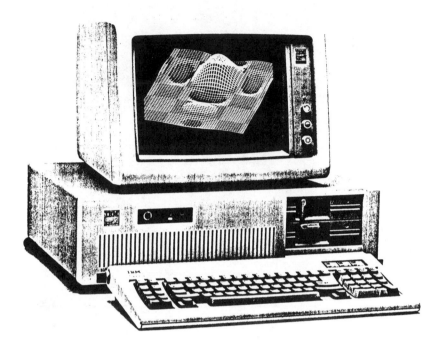

The PC AT

As of this writing, IBM's most powerful personal computer is the PC AT. Its 80286 CPU makes it run approximately four times as fast as the 8088-based PC. Moreover, the PC AT can be equipped with an optional 20-megabyte high-performance hard disk that allows access to data in about one-third the time of the PC/XT hard disk. The PC AT comes with a high-capacity diskette drive that allows storage of 1.2 megabytes on a floppy diskette. However, in order to achieve this storage density, it is necessary to use special high-quality diskettes.

IBM PC Compatibles

Manufacturers have produced machines that are compatibles of each of the IBM personal computer models. The standard and optional features vary from machine to machine. However, as far as running programs in BASIC is concerned, they all function similarly when using the same version of BASIC.

1.4 Typical PC Components and Systems

In Section 1.3 we surveyed your IBM PC, both from the outside and from within. However, your system may differ quite a bit from the ones shown. Indeed, the IBM PC allows (requires?) you to customize your system in very much the same way that you build a stereo system from individual components. In this section, we will discuss the main component types and the various choices you have.

The typical PC system contains the following five components:

1. System unit
2. Keyboard
3. Disk storage
4. Monitor
5. Printer

The interconnection of these units is illustrated in Figure 1-14.

System Unit

There are four system units—the IBM PC, IBM PC Portable, the IBM PC/XT, and the PC AT. The PC/XT and PC AT come with a number of standard features that are optional on the PC. Moreover, the PC/XT and PC AT have eight expansion slots, as compared to five for the PC and PC Portable.

Keyboard

There is no choice here. All IBM PCs have the same keyboard.

Disk Storage

You may choose among three types of disk storage:

1. Single-sided diskette drives. These drives write on only one side of a floppy diskette.
2. Double-sided diskette drives. These drives can write on both sides of a floppy diskette.
3. Winchester, or hard disk, drives.

The PC does not come with any diskette drives as standard equipment. However, the system unit has space for either one or two such drives. The PC/XT comes with a double-sided diskette drive and a Winchester drive as standard

Figure 1-14.   **Connection of a typical PC system.**

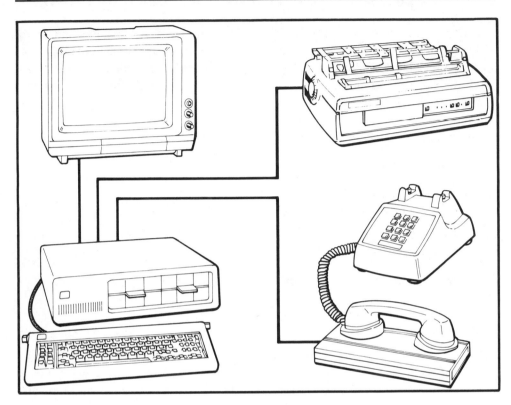

equipment. In order to use diskette drives, you must have a diskette interface card in one of the expansion slots inside the machine. Moreover, a Winchester drive requires its own interface card.

In addition to disk storage in the system unit, you may connect additional drives in external cabinets. Such drives are connected to an appropriate interface adapter card (usually the one supplied by the drive manufacturer) in one of the expansion slots.

Monitor

You have a wide variety of monitors from which to choose. They include:

- *Monochrome Display*. This type of screen displays letters in a single color, usually green or amber. It features exceptionally crisp letters. This display must be connected to an IBM monochrome or equivalent adapter, plugged into one of the expansion slots. Whether or not a monochrome display can display graphics depends on the particular adapter used. The IBM monochrome display adapter can display text only. However, a number of other monochrome adapters allow display of both text and graphics.

- *IBM Color Display or equivalent*. This type of display can provide color displays and can display text and graphics. It must be connencted to a color/graphics adapter (IBM or equivalent) plugged into one of the expansion slots.

- *Home television set*. You may use your home television set as a monitor. However, you must equip the cable with a special adapter. (This is the same sort of adapter required to connect a video game to your television.) A home television set must be plugged into a color/graphics adapter. A home television set will provide only a 40-character screen width.

- *IBM Enhanced Color Display and IBM Professional Color Display*. These displays provide higher quality color images and are especially useful for graphics applications. Each of these displays requires a special adapter card.

Printer

There are three basic types of printers:

1. *Dot-matrix printers*. These printers print letters as a collection of dots. They are distinguished by their speed. In this category are several IBM printers, namely:

   IBM 80 CPS Dot Matrix Printer
   IBM Graphics Printer
   IBM Color Printer
   IBM ProPrinter

   In addition, there are scores of other fine dot-matrix printers that may be used with IBM PCs. The least capable dot-matrix printers produce fair to medium print quality. However, many dot-matrix printers have a ''near letter quality'' mode in which letters are printed with a very dense array of dots. In this mode, it is very hard to distinguish the individual dots, so that the print quality approximates that of a typewriter.

2. *Daisy-wheel printers*. These printers print fully-formed letters, such as those printed by an electric typewriter. They are distinguished by the high quality of their printing, although they generally print more slowly than the dot-matrix printers.

3. *Laser printers*. These printers, the most expensive, combine high-quality printing with great speed. A laser printer can produce from eight to more than 50 pages a minute. The print quality rivals that of typeset text.

Your printer must be connected to the system unit. The exact nature of this connection will depend on the printer. Some printers are equipped with a **parallel interface** and some with a **serial interface**. (Don't worry about what these terms mean.) For a parallel interface, you must connect the printer to a **parallel printer adapter**; for a serial interface, you must connect the printer to an **asynchronous communications adapter** (also called an **RS-232 interface**).

The parallel printer adapter and the asynchronous communications adapter may each be purchased as expansion boards. However, the monochrome display adapter already includes a parallel printer adapter. Furthermore, there are many "combination" boards that include both a parallel printer adapter and an asynchronous communications adapter yet they occupy only a single expansion slot.

Other Expansion Boards

There are many other boards that may be used to expand the capabilities of your PC. Here are a few of the possibilities:

- *Game adapter*—allows your PC to use both game joysticks and a light pen.
- *Memory boards*—allow you to expand the RAM of your PC.
- *Clock/calendar*—allows your PC to keep track of the time and date, even with the machine turned off.
- *Multi-function boards*—allow various combinations of functions, such as printer adapter, game adapter, serial communications adapter, memory expansion, or monochrome or color/graphics display adapter. These boards are a popular way to have many functions in your PC and still save precious expansion slots.

Congratulations
on a smart purchase!

Now — turn your book into an
even more powerful learning tool!

(And eliminate hours of frustrating
programming errors as well.)

See other side for details . . .

BUSINESS REPLY MAIL
FIRST CLASS   PERMIT NO. 17   WEST NYACK, NY

POSTAGE WILL BE PAID BY ADDRESSEE

NO POSTAGE
NECESSARY
IF MAILED
IN THE
UNITED STATES

**PRENTICE-HALL, INC.
P.O. Box 462
West Nyack, NY 10994**

With the addition of the book's companion diskette —

You'll save time, energy (and some sanity!) when you're ready to get down to serious PC programming!

Developed by the same author, the diskette is designed for easy use. You'll work through, modify, and examine programs at your own pace. Without the annoyance of keystroke or programming errors.

Incorporating all the programs from the text (more than 100 in all!), it includes word processing . . . bar generation . . . form letter generation . . . list management . . . computer games . . . and more.

You get all that for only $25.00!

To order, use this handy, postage-paid envelope. Enclose a check or money order for $25.00, plus local sales tax. Or charge it to your VISA or MasterCard.

Why not do it today?

☐**YES!** I want to make learning to use my PC as fast and easy as possible. Please rush me **Diskette to Accompany IBM PC: An Introduction to the Operating System, BASIC Programming, and Applications - Third Edition** /D6358-8. I have enclosed payment of $25.00 plus sales tax.

Name _____

Address _____

City _____ State_____ Zip_____

Charge my Credit Card Instead
☐ VISA   ☐ MasterCard

_____
Account Number

_____
Expiration Date

_____
Signature as it appears on Card

Brady Brady Communications Co., Inc., New York, NY 10020
A Simon & Schuster Publishing Company

2

Using Your PC for the First Time

2.0   Chapter Objectives

IN THIS CHAPTER, WE PRESENT the information you need to know to use your computer for the first time. In particular, we:

- Describe the operation and use of diskette drives and hard disks.
- Learn to start the computer.
- Learn the naming system for diskette drives and hard disks.
- Learn to make a copy of a diskette.
- Learn to back up the DOS diskette.
- Learn the layout of the keyboard.

2.1   On Diskettes, Diskette Drives, and Fixed Disks

Your floppy diskette drives are a critical part of your computer system. They allow you to store and retrieve both programs and data. Even on systems with a hard disk, the floppy diskette drive(s) are important for loading new software onto the hard disk and for backing up the contents of the hard disk. Before we proceed any further, let's get acquainted with these remarkable devices.

The Anatomy of a Diskette

To store information, the diskette drives use 5 1/4-inch floppy diskettes. Diskettes come in single-sided and double-sided versions. A single-sided diskette may be written on only one side, a double-sided diskette on both sides. A single-sided diskette can accommodate approximately 163,000 characters (about 50 double-spaced typed pages), a double-sided diskette approximately twice as many. DOS 2.0 introduced a 9-sector per track format that allows approximately 360K per diskette. Finally, the high-density drives of the PC AT can accommodate approximately 1200K per diskette.

Diskette drives come in single-sided and double-sided models. A double-sided drive can read single-sided and double-sided diskettes. However, a single-sided drive can read only single-sided diskettes. Although the first IBM PCs sported only single-sided drives, they have increasingly given way to higher-density storage devices in the last few years.

Figure 2-1 illustrates the essential parts of a diskette. The diskette itself is a magnetically-coated circular piece of mylar plastic that rotates freely within a stiff jacket. The jacket is designed to protect the diskette. The interior of the jacket contains a lubricant that helps the diskette rotate freely within the jacket. The diskette is sealed inside. *Never* attempt to open the protective jacket. The labels on the jacket identify the contents of the diskette.

The diskette drive reads and writes on the diskette through the **read-write** window. Never, under any circumstances, touch the surface of the diskette. Diskettes are very fragile. A small piece of dust or even oil from a fingerprint could damage the diskette and render parts of the information on it totally useless.

The **write-protect notch** allows you to prevent changes to information on the diskette. When this notch is covered with one of the metallic labels provided with the diskettes, the computer may read the diskette, but it will not write or change any information on the diskette. To write on a diskette, the write-protect notch must be uncovered.

You should have a few blank diskettes on hand. Why not take a moment to inspect one of them and locate the various parts of the diskette described above. (The labeling on your diskettes may differ from that shown in Figure 2-1.)

Cautions in Handling Diskettes

Diskettes are sensitive and should be treated with some care. Here are some tips in using diskettes:

1. Always keep a diskette in its paper envelope when it is not in use.

2. Store diskettes in a vertical position just like you would a phonograph record.

3. Never touch the surface of a diskette or try to wipe the surface of a diskette with a rag, handkerchief, or other piece of cloth.

4. Keep diskettes away from extreme heat, such as that produced from radiators or direct sun.

5. Never bend a diskette.

6. When writing on a diskette label, use only a felt-tipped pen. Never use any sort of instrument with a sharp point.

Figure 2-1. **A diskette.**

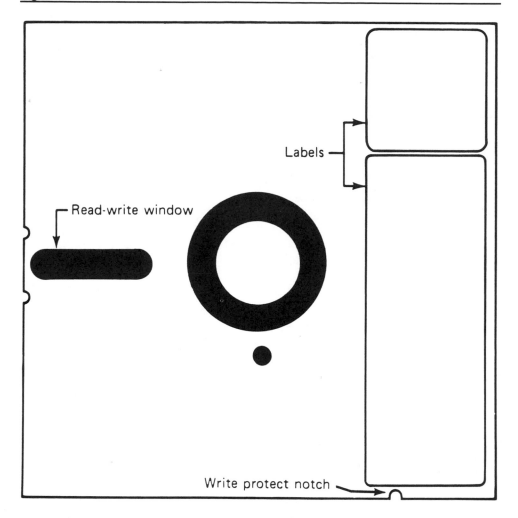

7. Keep diskettes away from magnetic fields, such as those generated by electrical motors, radios, televisions, tape recorders, telephones, and other electrical devices. A strong magnetic field may erase data on a diskette.

8. Never remove a diskette while the drive is running. (You can tell if a drive is running by the sound of the motor and the ''in use'' light on the front of the drive.) Doing so may cause permanent damage to the diskette.

The above list of precautions may seem overwhelming if you are just starting out. However, once you set up a suitable set of procedures for handling and storing diskettes, you will find that they are a reliable, long-lasting storage medium.

Using Diskettes

To insert a diskette into a diskette drive, open the door of the drive. Turn the diskette so that the label side is facing up and the read-write window is closest to the computer. Gently push the diskette into the drive until you hear a click. Close the drive door. The diskette may now be read by the computer.

To remove a diskette from a drive, first be sure that the light to the left of the drive door is off. Lift the drive door and gently pull the diskette forward and out of the drive.

TEST YOUR UNDERSTANDING 1
Take a blank diskette and practice inserting it in the diskette drive on the left. Remove the diskette from the drive.

Fixed Disks

A **fixed disk** (also called a **hard disk**) is a magnetic storage medium in the form of a circular platter (the size varies) that rotates within a sealed enclosure. A fixed disk can hold much more data than a diskette. Depending on the particular fixed disk, the capacity may be anywhere from 10 million to 100 million characters. Moreover, fixed disks rotate much more rapidly than do diskettes and therefore can access their data much more rapidly.

In recent years, the price of fixed disks has plunged and they have become quite common equipment on personal computers.

2.2   Starting Your PC

To control the flow of information to and from the diskette drives (and between just about any two points within the computer system), we need a program called an **operating system**. Such a program acts as a manager for all the activities that go on in the computer. More specifically, it coordinates the flow of information between the keyboard, video display, RAM, ROM, diskette files, and any other peripheral devices that you may have added to your computer system.

The official operating system of the IBM PC is called **IBM DOS** (IBM Disk Operating System—pronounced IBM-doss), also called **MS-DOS**[1] or **PC-DOS**, or just **DOS** for short. Actually, DOS has undergone several revisions since its original version. As of this moment, the latest version is DOS 3.1. All of our discussions will apply (unless we specifically tell you otherwise) to all versions of DOS from 2.00 on.

---

[1]MS stands for Microsoft Corporation, the company that designed DOS.

Starting a System without a Fixed Disk

When you purchased your system, you should have also purchased a copy of a manual called *Disk Operating System.* Just inside the rear cover of the DOS manual is a plastic jacket containing a diskette labeled **DOS**. This diskette is your master copy of the programs necessary to operate your diskette drives. This diskette is extremely important. So important, in fact, that it does not have a write-protect notch. This means that you can never write on this diskette. (No chance for accidentally altering its programs!) We refer to this diskette as the **master DOS diskette**.

In order to start your computer, it is necessary to first read DOS into the computer. Ordinarily, this would be done with a copy of the master DOS diskette rather than with the original itself. On your first pass through, however, you don't yet have any extra copies of the DOS diskette, so we must use the master. Here's the procedure to follow.

Starting Your Computer
(for Systems without a Fixed Disk)

1. Insert the DOS diskette into the diskette drive on the left (or your only diskette drive if you have only one). The label side should be up. Push the diskette to the rear of the drive until you hear a click. Close the drive door.

2. Turn on your monitor. (If you have the IBM Monochrome display, it will turn on automatically when you turn on the system unit.)

3. Turn on the printer (if one is connected).

4. On the rear of the right side of the system unit (the box in which the diskette drives sit) you will find the computer On-Off switch. (See Figure 2-2.) Flick it to the up position. For about 30-45 seconds the computer does diagnostic testing, to determine if all its components are working properly. When the tests are complete the computer should respond with a beep and the display[2]:

   `Enter today's date (mm-dd-yy):`

   The computer will respond with a display similar to:

   `Enter correct time (mm:hh:ss):`

5. Type in the correct time (in the format 14:03:00 for 2:03 PM, as the PC uses a 24-hour clock). The computer will respond with a display similar to:

---

[2]Depending on your version of DOS, the displays you see may be somewhat different from those described. Also, if your computer is equipped with a battery-operated clock-calendar, DOS will not request the time or date.

Figure 2-2.

```
The IBM Personal Computer DOS
Version 2.10 Copyright IBM Corp. 1981,1982,1983,1984
A>_
```

The symbol *A >* is called the **DOS prompt** and it tells you that DOS is loaded and ready to accept commands.

6. In this chapter, we'll learn to use many of the DOS commands. At this point, let's give the command to read the BASIC programming language from the DOS diskette into RAM. Type:

```
basica
```

Press the **ENTER** key (this is the key indicated with ⏎). The computer will respond with a display similar to:

```
The IBM Personal Computer Basic
Version A2.10 Copyright IBM Corp. 1981,1982,1983,1984
xxxxx Bytes Free
Ok
_
```

Note the letters *Ok* in the last line of the display. These letters are the **BASIC prompt**. They indicate that the computer language (BASIC) is ready to accept instructions. The small blinking box is called the **cursor**. It indicates the place on the screen where the next typed character will appear.

7. To return from BASIC to DOS, type:

```
system
```

and press ENTER. The computer will display the DOS prompt *A >*.

TEST YOUR UNDERSTANDING 1[3] (answers on page 25)

a. Turn on your computer and load DOS.

b. Load BASIC.

c. Return to DOS.

Turning Off the Computer

Here is the procedure to turn off your computer:

1. Turn off the system unit.

2. Turn off the monitor. (This step is not necessary if you are using the IBM Monochrome display.)

3. Remove any diskettes from the drives.

ANSWERS TO TEST YOUR UNDERSTANDING 1

1. a. Follow the instructions 1-7 for Starting Your Computer.
    b. Follow instruction 6.
    c. Follow instruction 7.

---

[3]Answers to TEST YOUR UNDERSTANDING questions are located at the end of each section

Starting Your Computer
(for Systems with a Fixed Disk)

In a system with a fixed disk, DOS is usually stored on the fixed disk so no DOS diskette is needed. In fact, if you wish the computer to start up using DOS on a fixed disk, no diskette may be present in the first diskette drive.

In this book, we will not discuss the mechanics of organizing a fixed disk. For the details of this process, consult your DOS manual.

2.3   More About Diskette Drives

Some diskette drives and fixed disks are placed within the system unit. These are called **internal drives**. Others may be placed in separate cabinets, connected to the system unit by means of a cable. These are called **external drives**.

The drives are given the names A:, B:, C:, and D: (note the colons). The drive names are used to refer to a drive within a command. In most cases, the names are used to refer to a drive within a command. In most cases, the names A: and B: are reserved for diskette drives. The name of the main hard disk is C:.

At any given moment, one of your drives is designated as the **current drive**. If you give a command without mentioning the drive label, the computer assumes that you mean the current drive. When the computer is first turned on, the current drive is set equal to A: in the case of a diskette-based system and set equal to C: for a system started from a hard disk. Another name for the current drive is the **default drive**.

The DOS prompt always indicates the current drive. If you see the prompt $A>$, then the current drive is A:. If you see the prompt $B>$, then the current drive is B:.

To change the current drive:

1.   Obtain the DOS prompt A> or B>.

2.   Type the name of the new current drive (remember the colon). Press **ENTER**.

TEST YOUR UNDERSTANDING 1 (answers on page 26)

a.   Turn on your computer and change the current drive from A: to B:.

b.   Change the current drive back to A:.

ANSWERS TO TEST YOUR UNDERSTANDING 1

1:   a. After turning on the computer and obtaining the DOS prompt, type B: and press **ENTER**.

b. Type A: and press **ENTER**.

2.4 Backing Up Your DOS Diskette

Good programming practice dictates that you keep duplicate copies of all your diskettes. In computer language, a copy is called a **backup**. Making backups reduces the chance that you will lose your programs and data due to accidents (power blackout, coffee spilled on a diskette, and so forth). It is an especially good idea to make a copy of the master DOS diskette the first time you use it. Later, you should use only the copy. Store the original DOS diskette in a safe place so that yet another copy can be made if the first copy is damaged. Here is the procedure for making a backup copy of a diskette. (The instructions are for single-drive systems. For systems with two drives, see the comment below.)

Copying One Diskette Onto Another

We must copy the contents of the master DOS diskette onto a blank diskette.

1. Obtain the DOS prompt *A*>. Insert the DOS diskette into drive A:. Type

    ```
    DISKCOPY
    ```

    then press the **ENTER** key. The computer will respond with the display:

    ```
    Insert source diskette in drive A
    Strike any key when ready
    ```

2. The source diskette, namely the DOS diskette, is already in drive A:, so strike any key. The computer will copy a portion of DOS into RAM. When it has copied as much as it can, it will display

    ```
    Insert target diskette in drive A
    Strike any key when ready
    ```

    Remove the DOS diskette and insert a blank diskette. Next, press any key. The computer will now copy the data in RAM onto the diskette. If there is more data to be copied from the DOS diskette, you will be directed to reinsert the DOS diskette. Steps 1 and 2 will then be repeated a number of times. After all the data has been copied, the computer will display something like:

    ```
    Copy complete
    Copy another? (Y/N)
    ```

    Answer *N* to indicate that we do not wish to copy another diskette. The computer will now display the DOS prompt:

    ```
    A>
    ```

3. Your blank diskette is now an exact copy of the original. At this point, you may give another DOS command or request BASIC.

Two-Drive Systems.   To copy the contents of the diskette in A: onto the diskette in B:, proceed as above, but use the command

```
DISKCOPY A: B:
```

Notice that the source drive (the one you are copying from) is listed first and the target drive (the one you are copying to) is listed second.

TEST YOUR UNDERSTANDING 1 (answer on page 28)
Make a copy of the DOS system diskette supplied with your diskette operating system.

From now on you should use only the copy of the master DOS diskette, **not** the original. Put the original in a safe place, so that it may be used to make yet another copy if the current copy is damaged.

A Word to the Wise
The backup procedure just described may be used to copy the contents of any diskette onto any other. Because diskettes are fragile, it is strongly recommended that you maintain duplicate copies of all your diskettes. A good procedure is to update your copies at the end of each session with the computer. This may seem like a big bother, but it will prevent untold grief if, by some mishap, a diskette with critical programs or data is erased or damaged.

TEST YOUR UNDERSTANDING 2 (answer on page 28)
Use your copy of the master DOS diskette to make another copy. (A copy of a copy is just as good as the original!)

ANSWERS TO TEST YOUR UNDERSTANDINGS 1 AND 2
1: Follow instructions 1-3 on page 27.

2: Follow instructions 1-3 on page 27, except start with the copy DOS diskette in drive A:.

2.5 The Keyboard

Let us examine the PC keyboard (see Figure 2-3). This keyboard looks complex, but can be understood if we examine it a section at a time. Let's begin with the central section (see Figure 2-4).

Figure 2-3. **The IBM Personal Computer keyboard.**

Figure 2-4. **The central section of the keyboard.**

The central section is very much like a typewriter keyboard. There are a few symbols that are not present on a typewriter, such as:

<

>

^

~

[

]

\

{

}

Also, you should note the following important differences from a typewriter keyboard:

1. There are separate keys for 1 (one) and l (el). (Many typewriters use the lowercase l to do double duty as a one.)

2. The number **0** (zero) has a slash through it on screen. This is to distinguish it from the letter **o**.

Here are the functions of the other keys in the central portion of the keyboard:

 Space bar. Generates a blank space just like the space bar on a typewriter.

 Shift key. Shifts keys to their uppercase meanings. For keys with two symbols, the upper symbol takes effect. The uppercase meanings are in effect only as long as the Shift key is held down. Releasing the Shift key causes keys to assume their lowercase meanings. Note that there are two Shift keys, one on each side of the keyboard.

 Caps Lock key. See the discussion on page 34.

 Backspace key. Moves the cursor back one space. Erases any letter it backs over.

 ENTER key. Similar to a carriage return key on a typewriter. Used to end a line and to place the cursor at the beginning of the next line. A line may be corrected with backspaces until the ENTER key is pressed.

 Tab key. Works like the tab key on a typewriter. Moves the cursor to the next tab stop.

 Control key. Used in combination with other keys. For example, the key combination Ctrl-A means to simultaneously press

Ctrl and A. Such combinations are used to generate control codes for the screen and printer.

 Escape key. Used to indicate that certain sequences of letters are to be interpreted as control codes.

 Alternate key. Used in combination with other keys in a manner similar to the Ctrl key.

 PrtSc key. Used to print the screen. (See the discussion below.)

Turn on your PC and obtain the DOS prompt A>. Strike a few keys to get the feel of the keyboard. Note that as you type, the corresponding characters will appear on the screen. Note, also, how the cursor travels along the typing line. It always sits at the location where the next typed character will appear.

As you type, you should notice the similarities between the IBM Personal Computer keyboard and that of a typewriter. However, you should also note the differences. At the end of a typewriter line, you return the carriage, either manually or, on an electric typewriter, with a carriage return key. Of course, your screen has no carriage return. However, you still must tell the computer that you are ready to move on to the next line. This is accomplished by hitting the ENTER key. If you depress the ENTER key, the cursor then returns to the next line and positions itself at the extreme left side of the screen. The ENTER key also has another function. It signals the computer to accept the line just typed. Until you hit the ENTER key, you may add to the line, change portions, or even erase it. (We'll learn to do these editing procedures shortly.)

Keep typing until you are at the bottom of the screen. If you hit ENTER, the entire contents of the screen will move up by one line and the line at the top of the screen will disappear. This movement of lines on and off the screen is called **scrolling**.

As you may have already noticed, the computer will respond to some of your typed lines with error messages. Don't worry about these now. The computer has been taught to respond only to certain typed commands. If it encounters a command that it doesn't recognize, it announces this fact with an error message. It is extremely important for you to realize that these errors in no way harm the computer. In fact, there is little you can do to hurt your computer (except by means of physical abuse, of course). Don't be intimidated by the occasional slaps on the wrist handed out by your computer. Whatever happens, don't let these ''slaps'' stop you from experimenting. The worst that can happen is that you might have to turn your computer off and start all over!

System Reset

You may restart the computer from the keyboard by pressing the **Ctrl, Alt,** and **Del** keys simultaneously. This key sequence returns the computer to the state it was in just after being turned on. Both RAM and the screen will be erased.

Printing the Screen

The PC provides several features that allow you to print what appears on the screen. Obtain the DOS prompt A> and press the key combination Ctrl-PrtSc. (Also make sure your printer is turned on.) All subsequent text that appears on your screen will also be printed. This provides you with a written record of a session at the computer. To turn off the printing, press Ctrl-PrtSc again.

You may obtain a printed copy of the current screen by pressing the key combination Shift-PrtSc. If you are in BASIC, this will work only using DOS 2.00 or later versions.

TEST YOUR UNDERSTANDING 1 (answer on page 37)
Print the current contents of the screen.

Keyboard Usage in BASIC

Many of the keys have special meanings while BASIC is running. To illustrate this keyboard usage, let's load BASIC by obtaining the DOS prompt and typing

```
basica
```

followed by **ENTER**. When you obtain the BASIC prompt, begin typing. Notice that if you neglect to end a line, it spills over onto the next. However, after almost three lines (255 characters) BASIC automatically terminates the line, just as if you had pressed **ENTER**.

Scrolling and corrections using the backspace key work pretty much the same in BASIC as they do in DOS.

Fill your screen with 8 or 10 lines of text. To erase the screen, use this key combination:

Ctrl-Home

All characters on the screen will be erased and only the cursor will remain. The cursor is positioned in the upper left corner of the screen, its so-called "home" position.

Numeric Keypad

Let us now turn our attention to the right side of the keyboard. Note that each of the digits 0-9 appears twice: once in the usual place at the top of the keyboard and a second time at the right-hand side. (See Figure 2-5.) The numeric keys on

Figure 2-5. **The numeric keypad.**

the right side are arranged like the keys of a calculator and are designed to make typing numbers easier. It makes no difference which set of numerical keys you use. In fact, you may alternate them in any manner, entering a 1 from the top set, then a 5 from the right set, and so forth. The right set of keys is called the **numeric keypad**.

Actually, the keys of the numeric keypad do double duty. They are also used in BASIC for editing (for altering text that has already been typed). For now just remember that the Num Lock key controls which function the keys of the numeric keypad assume. When the Num Lock key is engaged, the numeric keypad functions like a calculator keyboard. With the Num Lock key disengaged, the numeric keypad is used for editing. When the computer is first turned on, the keypad is set for editing. So for your first use of the numeric keypad, it will be necessary to disengage the Num Lock key.

Editing Keys.   Let's now describe the functions of the keys on the numeric keypad when used for editing. (the Num Lock key must be engaged.)

Cursor Motion Keys.   These four arrow keys are used to move the cursor in the indicated directions. Note that these keys move the cursor only in BASIC. Don't confuse the up arrow with the Shift key.

Insert Key.   When this key is pressed, you may insert text at the current cursor position. As text is inserted, existing text is moved to the right to accommodate the new letters. The effect of the **Ins** key is cancelled either by pressing **Ins** again, by pressing **Del**, or by pressing ENTER, or by using the cursor motion keys.

Delete Key.   When this key is pressed, one letter is deleted at the cursor position.

Using the Caps Lock Key.   In most computer work, it is convenient to type using only uppercase letters. For one thing, capitals are larger and easier to read on the screen. You may turn off the lowercase letters by depressing the Caps Lock key. In this mode, the letter keys are automatically typed as capitals. *Note, however, that the non-letter keys (such as 1 and !) still have two meanings. To type the upper symbol, you must still use the Shift key.* To exit from the uppercase mode, once again depress the Caps Lock key. With the Caps Lock key engaged, if you press the Shift key and a letter key, a lowercase letter is displayed.

TEST YOUR UNDERSTANDING 2 (answers on page 36)

a.   Type your name on the screen.

b.   Erase the screen.

c.   Repeat a. using uppercase letters. (Don't worry about the computer's response to your typing!)

Line Width.   The IBM Personal Computer allows lines to contain either 40 characters or 80 characters per line. To switch from one line width to the other, we use the **WIDTH** command. To switch to 40 characters per line, type

`WIDTH 40`

followed by ENTER. To return to 80 characters per line, type

WIDTH 80

followed by ENTER. In the rest of this test, we assume that the lines are 80 characters wide. If you use a 40-character line width, your displays may look somewhat different than those indicated.

Note that if you are using the IBM Monochrome Display, then the *WIDTH 40* command will cause the characters to be displayed 40 across, only on the left half of the screen.

Function Key Display.   Note that the last line of the screen is filled with data that does not change as you type. This data displays the assignment of certain user-programmable keys, F1-F10 at the left side of the keyboard. (See Figure 2-6.) If your screen is set to display a 40-character wide display, then only

Figure 2-6. **Function keys.**

the definitions of keys F1-F5 are displayed. The function keys F1-F10 may be programmed to generate certain often-used key sequences or words. Figure 2-7 shows the initial function key display.

You may turn off the function key display by typing

KEY OFF

followed by ENTER. If you wish to turn on the display, type

KEY ON

By keeping the display line off, you make the last screen line available for program use.

Figure 2-7. **Function key display.**

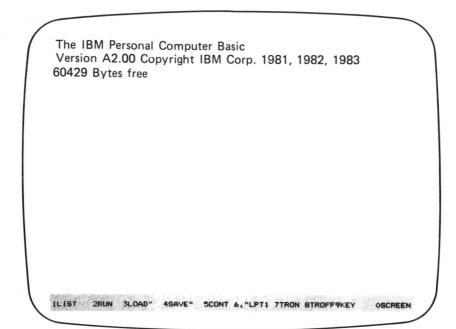

The IBM Personal Computer Basic
Version A2.00 Copyright IBM Corp. 1981, 1982, 1983
60429 Bytes free

1LIST   2RUN   3LOAD"   4SAVE"   5CONT 6,"LPT1 7TRON 8TROFF9KEY   0SCREEN

ANSWERS TO TEST YOUR UNDERSTANDINGS 1 and 2

1: Press Shift-PrtSc simultaneously.

2: a. Type your name, ending the line with ENTER.
    b. Press Ctrl and Home simultaneously.
    c. Press Caps Lock and repeat part a.

Part Two
An Introduction to MS-DOS

3

An Introduction to DOS

3.0   Chapter Objectives

THE DISK OPERATING SYSTEM (DOS) intrudes into every aspect of PC use. It is no exaggeration to say that every time you sit down at your computer, you are using DOS. In this chapter, you will learn to use some of the most essential aspects of DOS. In particular, we learn about:

- Files and file-naming rules.
- The directory of a diskette or hard disk.
- PC device names and file specifications.
- Executing commands and programs from DOS.
- Copying files.
- Formatting diskettes.
- The most basic internal and external DOS commands.

3.1   Files and Filenames

The contents of a diskette are broken into units called **files**. For our present purposes, think of a file as a collection of characters. For example, the characters comprising Section 3.1 of this book, when stored on diskette, might comprise one file. (In fact, as this book was being written, the sections were stored on diskette in exactly that way.)

A diskette may contain many files. (The maximum number depends on which version of DOS you are using, as well as on the type of drives your computer has.) However, diskette files may be classified into two broad categories: **programs** and **data files**.

Programs.   A program is a sequence of computer instructions. Throughout this book, we will be discussing programs of one sort or another—programs to compute loan interest, to play tic tac toe, and to print form letters, to mention but a few.

Data files.   A data file contains data, such as payroll information, personnel data, recipes, train and airline schedules, appointment calendars, and so forth. Programs often make use of data files. This is done by including instructions within the program for reading (or writing) particular data files. In this way, you may, for example, look up appointments and let the computer make decisions based on data in the file.

Filenames

Each file is identified by a **filename**. Here are some examples of valid filenames:

```
BASIC.COM
FORMAT.COM
PAYROLL
GAME.001
```

A filename consists of two parts—the main filename (*BASIC,FORMAT, PAYROLL,GAME*) and an optional extension (*COM, no extension, 001*). The main filename may contain as many as eight characters, the extension as many as three. The two parts of the filename are separated by a period.

The following characters are allowed in a filename:

The letters *A-Z*

The digits *0-9*

Any of these characters:

   ! @ # $ % & ( ) - _ { } ' `

Note that a filename cannot include any of the following characters:

   | \ < > , / ? ' ~ : + = * ^

The only period allowed in a filename is the one separating the two parts of the filename. Moreover, a filename cannot contain any spaces.

A filename may be spelled with either upper- or lowercase letters. However, DOS will convert the filename into uppercase. For example, the filenames:

   JOHN   John

refer to the same file.

TEST YOUR UNDERSTANDING 1 (answers on page 42)
What is wrong with the following filenames?

   a. *ALICE 01*   b. *#2324/1*   c. *alphabetical*

A particular diskette can have only one file with a particular name. However, there is nothing to stop you from using the same filename to refer to different files on **different** diskettes, although this is not a very good idea because you (not the computer) may get confused about where a particular file is located.

When you name a file, choose a name that somehow suggests the contents. For example, if you generate a monthly payroll file, you may name the various monthly files:

PAYROLL.JAN, PAYROLL.FEB, PAYROLL.MAR,...

and so forth.

The Directory

Each diskette has a directory listing the name of each file on the diskette as well as some descriptive information about the file. Let's analyze one directory entry, the one for the file named *DISKCOPY.COM*. This file is actually a program we've already used, namely the program for copying the contents of one diskette onto another. We used this program to back up our master DOS diskette. The directory entry for *DISKCOPY.COM* reads[1]:

```
DISKCOPY    2444  3-08-83  12:00p
```

The first two parts of the entry, namely *DISKCOPY* and *COM*, give the filename and the extension. The next part of the entry gives the size of the file in bytes. *DISKCOPY.COM* is 2444 bytes long. The final two parts of the directory entry give the date and time the file was last changed. In this example, *DISK-COPY.COM* was last altered on *3-08-83* at *12:00PM*.

DOS maintains the directory automatically. Each time a file is added or changed, DOS makes the appropriate changes in the directory, so that it always accurately reflects the contents of the diskette.

You may examine the directory of a diskette using the DOS command *DIR*. For example, to examine the directory of the diskette in drive A:, type

```
DIR A:
```

and press ENTER. The directory of drive *A:* is then displayed on the screen.

To display the directory of the diskette in drive *B:*, use the command

```
DIR B:
```

If you wish to display the directory of the current drive, omit the drive name. That is, the command

```
DIR
```

---

[1]This display corresponds to DOS 2.00. In DOS 1.1, DISKCOPY is 2008 bytes and was created 5-07-82, 12:00pm.

displays the directory of the diskette in the current drive.

TEST YOUR UNDERSTANDING 2 (answer on page 42)
Display the directory of your DOS diskette.

TEST YOUR UNDERSTANDING 3 (answer on page 42)
Suppose that a diskette contains too many files to be displayed on the screen at one time. How can you determine the entire directory?

ANSWERS TO TEST YOUR UNDERSTANDINGS 1, 2, and 3

1: a. Illegal space
   b. Illegal character (/)
   c. Too many characters

2: Place the DOS diskette in the current drive, type *DIR* and press ENTER.

3: Use Ctrl-PrtSc to print the contents of the screen as they are displayed.

3.2 File Specifications

As we mentioned in Section 3.1, two different files may have the same name as long as they are on separate diskettes. But what happens when you put one of the diskettes in drive *A:* and one in drive *B:*? Clearly, there is potential for dangerous confusion here. In order to specify a file without ambiguity, you must give, in addition to the filename, the location of the file.

PC Device Names

DOS specifies the various components of the PC using the following abbreviations:

A:, B:, C:, D: disk drives

(diskette drives or hard disks)

CON: the console (or keyboard)

SCRN: the screen

LPT1: printer #1

LPT2: printer #2

COM1: communications adapter #1

COM2: communications adapter #2

(Most systems will have only one printer and one communications adapter attached. However, DOS allows for expansion.)

File Specifications

The combination of a device name and a filename is called a **file specification**. Here are some examples:

```
A:ACCOUNTING
COM1:XYZ.01
LPT1:PRINT.2
```

Each file has an associated file specification that tells the location of the file and the filename. The file specification contains enough information to find the file without any ambiguities.

In order for a file specification to be valid, both the device name and the filename must be valid.

You may omit the device name from a file specification. In this case, DOS assumes that the device is the current diskette drive. For example, if the current drive is B:, then the file specification *ARITH.ADD* stands for

```
B:ARITH.ADD
```

Wild Card Characters

The characters * and ? in a filename have a special meaning for DOS.

The character * may be used as either the main filename or the extension. The portion of the filename replaced by * may be anything at all. For example, consider this filename:

```
*.COM
```

This filename stands for any file with the extension COM. Similarly, the filename

```
WS.*
```

stands for any file with the main name WS. Finally, the filename

.

stands for any file.

Such "ambiguous" filenames can shorten various DOS commands. For example, we may copy a file from one diskette to another using the COPY command (see Section 3.4). To copy all files from the diskette in drive *A:* to the diskette in drive *B:*, use the simple command

COPY A:*.* B:

Similarly, to copy all files on the diskette in drive *A:* with a *COM* extension onto the diskette in drive *B:*, use the command

COPY A:*.COM B:

The character ? in a filename allows a single character to be ambiguous. For example, consider this filename:

EXAMPLE.00?

The third letter in the extension may be anything. Similarly, consider this filename:

N??.000

The main filename has three letters, begins with N, and the last two letters of the main filename may be anything.

Filenames using * and ? may be used in file specifications.

3.3 Executing Commands and Programs

DOS has many commands that perform "housekeeping" functions for the PC. For example, we have already met the command *DISKCOPY*, which allows you to copy the contents of one diskette onto another, and the command DIR, which allows you to display a diskette directory. In the remainder of this chapter, we will discuss the various DOS commands and how to use them. First, let's make some general comments about DOS commands.

To execute a DOS command, the DOS prompt must be displayed. Then do the following:

1. Type the DOS command.

2. Press ENTER.

DOS will execute the command. When execution is complete, DOS will redisplay the DOS prompt.

We saw this procedure in our discussions of the DOS commands *DIR* and *DISKCOPY*.

Before you press ENTER, you may use the backspace key to correct mistakes. If you make an error in a command, DOS is quite tolerant. For example, give the command *XXXXXX*. (There is no such command.) DOS will respond with

```
Bad Command or File Name
A>
```

You may now give another command.

Before you press ENTER, you may press the Esc key. This erases the current line and allows you to retype the command.

Here's another type of error that can occur. Remove the DOS diskette and type the command *DISKCOPY A: B:*. DOS will attempt to read the *DISKCOPY* program from the non-existent diskette. After a few seconds, DOS will respond with the prompt:

```
Error reading drive A:
Repeat(R), Ignore(I), or Abort(A)
```

Type *R* to repeat the command (presumably after you have replaced the diskette), *I* to ignore the error (in this case, you will generate the same error message), or *A* (in which case the command will be cancelled and the DOS prompt redisplayed). Note that in typing *R, I,* or *A,* you don't need to press ENTER.

Internal Versus External DOS Commands

We have already noted that the command *DISKCOPY* is contained in the file *DISKCOPY.COM* on the DOS diskette. However, if you inspect the directory of the DOS diskette, you will not find a file named anything like *DIR.COM*. So where does DOS obtain the program corresponding to the command *DIR*? The answer lies in the way DOS works.

When you start your computer system, you read part of DOS into RAM. This portion of DOS stays in RAM throughout your session with the computer. The most important DOS commands are contained in this portion of DOS so that they can be available without fetching them from diskette. Such commands are called **internal commands** and DIR is an example. You may remove the DOS diskette from the current drive and still have the internal DOS commands available.

It would be nice to have all of DOS' commands in RAM all the time. For one thing, they would execute more quickly. However, this gain must be balanced against the permanent decrease in the amount of RAM. Any decrease in RAM lowers the allowable size of application programs. As a compromise, the least frequently-used DOS commands are stored on diskette. These commands are called **external commands**. When you request an external command, the corresponding diskette file is read into memory and is executed. Upon completion, however, the memory is made available for the next program or command.

TEST YOUR UNDERSTANDING 1 (answer on page 46)
Remove the DOS diskette from drive A:. Give the command

`DISKCOPY A: B:`

What happens? Why?

Running Programs Under DOS

We have described the procedure for executing DOS commands. However, the same procedure may be used for programs. Many programs you purchase are stored in files with the extensions *COM* or *EXE*. To run such a program, just type the filename without the extension, and press ENTER. For example, the BASIC language is one of the programs on the DOS diskette and its filename is *BASICA.COM*. To run BASIC, type *BASICA* and press ENTER.

Programs on Diskettes in Other Drives

So far, we have restricted our discussion to programs or commands contained on the diskette in the current drive. However, you may run a program or execute a command located anywhere. Just precede the command name by the drive designation. For example, suppose that *BASICA* is on the diskette in drive *B:*. To run this program, type

`B:BASICA`

and press ENTER.

ANSWER TO TEST YOUR UNDERSTANDING 1
1: DOS reports an error reading drive A:, since it cannot find the file DISKCOPY.COM to read.

3.4 The COPY Command

You may move a file from one place to another within the computer using the **COPY** command. This command is very important. Here is how to use it.

1. Obtain the DOS prompt *A >*. (If you are in BASIC, type *SYSTEM* and press ENTER to obtain this prompt.)

2. To copy file specification *<filespec1>* to file specification *<filespec2>*, type

    `COPY <filespec1> <filespec2>`

    and press ENTER. (Note that there is a space between the two file specifications.)

For example, to copy *A:BASICA.COM* (this is the copy of the BASIC language *BASICA.COM* located on the diskette in drive *A:*) to drive *B:*, type

`COPY A:BASICA.COM B:BASICA.COM`

and press ENTER. The computer makes a copy of *BASICA.COM* on the diskette in drive *B:*.

Actually, if you wish to leave the filename the same in the copy, you may include only the device name in the second file specification. For example, the above copying operation can also be accomplished by typing

`COPY A:BASICA.COM B:`

followed by ENTER.

Creating a Diskette File

We may use the *COPY* command to copy from the keyboard (device name *CON:*) directly to a diskette file. Here's how. Sit down at your computer and obtain the DOS prompt *A >*. Type

`COPY CON: A:TEST`

and press ENTER.

We have just told DOS that we wish to copy a file from the console (keyboard) to drive *A:* and give the resulting file the name *TEST*. Now type

`This is a test.`
`We are creating the file TEST on drive A:`

End each line with ENTER. Note that the above lines are displayed on the screen. Moreover, DOS temporarily stores input lines in RAM. To indicate that we are done inputting data, press function key *F6* followed by ENTER. DOS will now copy the input lines from RAM to a diskette file, as you requested. You will see the drive light on drive A: go on. This means that the writing operation is in progress. The computer will finally respond with the message:

`1 File(s) copied`

You have just created the file *TEST*. If you are not convinced, list the directory of drive *A:* by typing

`DIR A:`

followed by ENTER. Among the data appearing on the screen will be a line in this form:

```
TEST      62      2/25/83    11:15a
```

This **directory entry** tells you that the name of the file is TEST, that it contains 62 bytes (62 characters, counting spaces, ENTERs, and so forth), and that the file was created on 2/25/83 at 11:15AM. (The computer computes the date and time from the data you specified when you turned the computer on.)

If you are still not convinced that you have created a file, let's copy the file back to the screen. Type

```
COPY TEST CON:
```

and press ENTER. We have just requested that DOS copy *TEST* from the current drive (*A:*) to the console. (To the computer's way of thinking, the console consists of both the keyboard and screen.) Note that the contents of the file will be displayed on the screen.

Finally, let's copy the file *TEST* to the printer with the command

```
COPY TEST LPT1:
```

followed by ENTER. (Before giving the command, check that the printer is on.) The printer will print the contents of the file.

TEST YOUR UNDERSTANDING 1 (answer on page 49)
Create a file *TEST2* on drive *B:* containing the following data:

```
This line is part of TEST2 on drive B:
```

TEST YOUR UNDERSTANDING 2 (answer on page 49)
Redisplay *TEST2* on the screen.

Using Wild Card Characters with COPY

The wild card characters ? and * are very useful in describing COPY operations. Recall that the character * replaces any sequence of characters within a main filename or an extension. For example, the filename *.001* refers to all files with an extension of *001*. Some examples of filenames that qualify are:

```
JANE.001 HOWARD.001  MONEY.001 A.001
```

A command of the form

```
COPY A:*.001 B:
```

copies all files on *A:* with extension *001* onto *B:*.

To copy all the files on *A:* to *B:*, use this command:

```
COPY A:*.* B:
```

Recall that the wild card character ? stands for a single character. For example, the filename *??ME.001* can stand for the filenames *FAME.001* and *HOME.001*, as well as *LIME.001*.

TEST YOUR UNDERSTANDING 3 (answer on page 49)
Write a command that copies all files on B: with an extension *BAS* to *A:*.

ANSWERS TO TEST YOUR UNDERSTANDINGS 1, 2, and 3
1: Obtain the DOS prompt *A >* . Type *COPY CON: B:TEST* followed by ENTER. Type the line followed by ENTER. Press F6 followed by ENTER.

2: Obtain the DOS prompt. Type *COPY B:TEST2 CON:*

3: *COPY B:*.BAS A:*

3.5   COPYing and FORMATting Diskettes

In Chapter 2 we made several copies of the DOS master diskette. However, this diskette, important as it is, is not the only diskette we will need. Indeed, the DOS diskette has very little unused space. We need a diskette with plenty of room to write our own programs and data files. In this section, we will learn to prepare such diskettes.

Formatting a Diskette

When DOS writes on a diskette, it does so in a very orderly fashion. Data is written in circular rings called **tracks**. (See Figure 3-1.) Each track is divided into a number of sectors (eight or nine depending on your version of DOS). (See Figure 3-2.)

For DOS to write on a diskette, the track and sector boundaries must be written on the diskette. The IBM PC uses **soft-sectored diskettes**, which means that the tracks and sector boundaries are not prerecorded at the factory. Rather, it is your job to prepare a diskette for use by first writing these boundaries on it. This task is called **formatting** and is carried out by the DOS command **FORMAT**.

Figure 3-1. **The tracks of a diskette.**

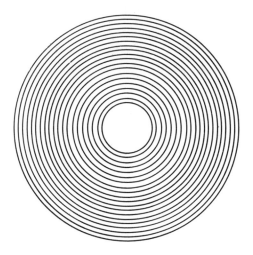

Figure 3-2. **The sectors of a diskette track.**

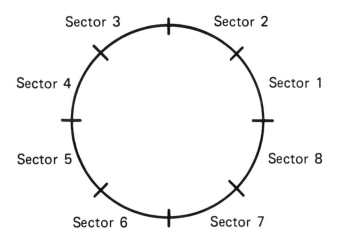

The FORMAT command is an external command. To use it, you must start with a DOS diskette in the current drive. Type

```
FORMAT <drive>
```

Here, *<drive>* is the name of the drive containing the diskette to be formatted. For example, to format a diskette in drive *A:*, type

`FORMAT A:`

DOS will respond with the prompt:

```
Insert new diskette for drive A:
and strike any key when ready
```

Place a blank diskette into drive *A:*. Press any key. The computer will proceed to format the diskette. Eventually, the display will look something like this (this display is correct for a single-sided drive):

```
Formatting...Format Complete

160,256 bytes on diskette
160,256 bytes available
```

```
Format another (Y/N)?
```

At this point, you may answer the question *Y*(= YES) and format another diskette or *N*(= NO), in which case DOS will terminate the *FORMAT* operation and redisplay the DOS prompt, awaiting your next command.

The above procedure has been designed so that you may format diskettes one after another. It's a good idea to format an entire box of diskettes when you first buy it. By doing this, you know that all the blank diskettes you have lying around are ready for writing.

The numbers displayed in your final FORMAT prompt may be different from those above. First of all, the number of bytes on diskette depends on the type of diskette drive (one-sided or two-sided, standard or high-density). It also depends on which version of DOS you are using. DOS 2.00 and later versions can record nine sectors per track; DOS 1.1 records eight.

If you are using version DOS 1.1 or later in a two-sided drive, the FORMAT command automatically formats your diskette as a two-sided diskette. If the drive is one-sided, then the formatted diskette will also be one-sided. If, however, you are formatting a diskette on a two-sided drive but wish to subsequently use it on a one-sided drive, you must instruct DOS to format the diskette as single-sided. This is done using the */1* option. For example, to format the diskette in drive *A:* as a single-sided diskette, use the command:

`FORMAT A: /1`

NOTE: You may reformat a diskette that has already been formatted. This erases all data on the diskette. (This is a sure way of destroying sensitive information you don't want lying around.)

TEST YOUR UNDERSTANDING 1 (answer on page 52)
Format a blank diskette.

The number of bytes available is usually the same as the number of bytes on the diskette. Occasionally, a diskette will contain microscopic flaws that prevent DOS from formatting some sectors. DOS hides these sectors in an invisible file called **BADTRACK**. You never need to worry about these sectors being used in one of your files and ruining your data! However, if any sectors are placed in BADTRACK, the number of bytes available on the diskette is reduced.

The diskettes produced by the above procedure are totally blank. They do not contain the DOS files necessary to start the computer. You may include the DOS internal commands on the formatted diskette by using this command:

```
FORMAT A:  /S
```

A diskette produced by this command may be used to start the computer. The DOS internal commands occupy a rather small portion of the diskette. Therefore, most of the diskette is available for your use. When you format a diskette with the /S option, the final display looks something like this:

```
Formatting...Format Complete

160256 bytes on diskette
 39936 bytes used by system
120320 bytes available

Format another (Y/N)?
```

TEST YOUR UNDERSTANDING 2 (answers on page 52)
Format a blank diskette with the /S option.

    a.   Use this diskette to restart the computer.

    b.   Display the directory of A:. Can you explain what you see?

In Chapter 2, we learned to copy a diskette using the DISKCOPY command. We used this command to make a copy of the master DOS diskette. However, we did not mention FORMATing in that discussion. The reason is that the DISKCOPY command automatically formats the diskette onto which it is copying (the **target diskette**). This formatting is performed only if necessary.

ANSWERS TO TEST YOUR UNDERSTANDINGS 1 and 2
1:   Place a DOS diskette in drive A: and the disk to be formatted in drive B:. Type FORMAT B: followed by ENTER.

2:   a.   Place the formatted diskette in drive *A:* and press Ctrl-Alt-Del simultaneously.

       b.   The only file in the directory is *COMMAND.COM*, which occupies 17,664 bytes (in DOS 2.00). The system occupies 39,936 bytes. The remaining bytes are contained in the main DOS files, called IBMBIOS.COM and IBMDOS.COM, which are invisible as far as the directory is concerned.

3.6   Other DOS Internal Commands

In this section we present a brief survey of the most commonly used DOS internal commands. Remember that these commands may be used whenever the DOS prompt is displayed. They do not require any information from the DOS diskette.

ERASE allows you to erase a file. For example, to erase the file *EXAMPLE.TXT* on the diskette in drive *A:*, use the command

```
ERASE A:EXAMPLE.TXT
```

If the drive designation is omitted, then the current drive is assumed. For example,

```
ERASE EXAMPLE.TXT
```

erases *EXAMPLE.TXT* on the diskette in the current drive. The ERASE command may be used with the wild card characters * and ?. For example, to erase all files on the diskette in drive *A:*, use the command

```
ERASE A:*.*
```

TEST YOUR UNDERSTANDING 1 (answer on page 54)
Write a command that erases all files on the current drive with a five-character main name and an extension of *COM*.

RENAME allows you to rename a file. For example, to rename *A:OLDFILE* with the name *NEWFILE*, use the command

```
RENAME A:OLDFILE NEWFILE
```

Note that the current filename comes first and then the new filename. If you do not give a drive designation with the current filename, then the current drive is assumed.

TEST YOUR UNDERSTANDING 2 (answer on page 54)
Write a command that renames *A:TEST.COM* to *A:T.COM*.

DATE allows you to set the date. For example, to set the date to *4-12-83*, use the command

`DATE 4-12-83`

TEST YOUR UNDERSTANDING 3 (answer on page 54)
Write a command that sets the date to Dec. 12, 1984.

TIME allows you to set the time. For example, to set the time to 1:04:00 PM, use the command

`TIME 13:04:00`

TEST YOUR UNDERSTANDING 4 (answer on page 54)
Write a command to set the time to 12:00:00 AM.

TYPE allows you to display the contents of a file. For example, to display the contents of the file *A:TEST1*, use the command

`TYPE A:TEST1`

If you try to display a program, it will usually look like a bunch of gibberish. Program files are designed for the convenience of the computer, not for humans. However, a text file will be displayed in readable form.

To obtain a written copy of a file, you may first press Ctrl-PrtSc then give the TYPE command. The file will be displayed on the screen and also printed on your printer.

COMP allows you to compare two files to determine whether they are identical. For example, suppose that we wish to compare *FILE1* on the diskette in drive *A:* with *FILE2* on the diskette in drive *B:*. Give the command

`COMP A:FILE1 B:FILE2`

This command may be used to check on the results of a COPY operation to determine whether the copy is identical to the original. Note that the COMP command does not give you a chance to change diskettes. Therefore, the diskettes with the files needed for comparison must be on the diskettes prior to giving the COMP command.

ANSWERS TO TEST YOUR UNDERSTANDINGS 1, 2, 3, and 4
1: `ERASE ?????.COM`
2: `RENAME A:TEST.COM A:T.COM`
3: `DATE 12-12-84`
4: `TIME 00:00:00`

3.7   Other DOS External Commands

In this section, we summarize some of the most commonly used DOS external commands. Note that in order to use any of these commands, DOS must obtain the appropriate program from the DOS diskette.

DISKCOMP allows you to compare the contents of two diskettes, byte by byte. For example, to compare the diskettes in drives *A:* and *B:*, use the command

```
DISKCOMP A: B:
```

If your system has only one drive, you would also use this command for diskette comparison, even though you don't have a drive *B:*. DOS will prompt you to swap the diskettes in your single drive so that a comparison may be made.

CHKDSK allows you to check the number of bytes remaining on a diskette. It also performs a check to determine if any inconsistencies exist in the way the files are stored. To perform a CHKDSK operation on the diskette in drive *B:*, use the command

```
CHKDSK B:
```

The result of this command is a display of the form:

```
160256 bytes total disk space
 22272 bytes in 2 hidden files
 45455 in 4 user files
 92529 bytes available on disk

 65536 bytes total memory
 52785 bytes free
```

As usual, your numbers may vary, depending on your system, version of DOS, and so forth.

You should execute a CHKDSK every so often for each of your diskettes, in order to assure the integrity of your files and to determine the space remaining on the diskette.

TEST YOUR UNDERSTANDING 1 (answer on page 55)
Suppose that the DOS diskette is in drive *B:* and that drive *A:* is the current drive. Write a command for performing *CHKDSK* on the diskette in drive *A:*.

ANSWER TO TEST YOUR UNDERSTANDING 1
1: `B:CHKDSK A:`

4

Further Topics in DOS

4.0 Chapter Objectives

THIS CHAPTER PRESENTS FURTHER topics in DOS. You may omit this chapter on a first reading, especially if your system does not use a hard disk. In this chapter we discuss:

- Paths, directories, and subdirectories.
- The root and current directories.
- DOS commands using paths.
- Batch files.
- The AUTOEXEC.BAT file.
- The CONFIG.SYS file.

4.1 Paths, Directories, and Subdirectories

Directories and Subdirectories

DOS allows you to manipulate files contained on either a floppy diskette or a hard disk drive. A hard disk functions much like a floppy disk, except for its greater storage capacity and its higher speed. However, a hard disk may contain thousands of files at one time. A single directory can be unwieldy. It can be difficult for you to look at, and it can be slow for the computer to search for a particular file. To combat this problem, DOS allows you to organize your directory in a "tree structure."

The concept of a tree-structured directory is most useful for systems equipped with a hard disk, since it is a hard disk that most needs a tree-structured directory's organization. But what if you don't have a hard disk? In this case, you have two choices. You may use the tree-structured directories as if your diskette were a hard disk, or you may ignore them completely.

To explain what we mean, consider the typical DOS directory shown in Figure 4-1.

Figure 4-1. **A DOS directory.**

```
Volume in drive C is DOS
Directory of C:\Midwest


.                    <DIR>        4-17-83     7:49p
..                   <DIR>        4-17-83     7:49p
PAYROLL     83       <DIR>        4-30-83    10:09a
PERSON      83       <DIR>        5-12-83    11:00a
INVENTRY    83       <DIR>        5-12-83     3:45p
MEMO       518       5847         5-18-83     1:12p
MEMO       520       4850         5-20-83     3:24p
```

The first line of the directory gives the volume title. DOS allows you to assign a title to a disk. In this case, the contents of the hard disk are named ''DOS'' (drive *C*: is the hard disk). A typical DOS directory has two sorts of entries, files and directories. A file entry is exactly the same sort of entry described in Chapter 3. For example, the directory of Figure 4-1 lists the files *MEMO.518* and *MEMO.520*. The notations *<DIR>* indicate that all of the other entries are directories: *PAYROLL.83, PERSON.83, INVENTRY.83*. Each of the subdirectories of the directory shown may contain files and directories of its own. (Don't worry about the directories ''.'' and ''..'' for now. They serve a purely technical role.)

In DOS, each directory has a name, which may consist of a main part and an extension. The rules for directory names are the same as for filenames. (See the beginning of Chapter 3.) For example, the directory shown in Figure 4-1 has the name *MIDWEST*. The organization of files into directories may be described as a tree. For example, Figure 4-2 shows the relationship of the directory of Figure 4-1 with other directories on the same disk. The main directory *RECORDS* has three subdirectories: *MIDWEST, SOUTH,* and *NORTHEAST*. Each of these subdirectories has several subdirectories as well as several files.

Note that a file or directory name may be repeated in various parts of a tree. For example, each of the directories *MIDWEST, SOUTH,* and *NORTHEAST* has a subdirectory named *PERSON*. However, each directory named *PERSON* is independent; their respective contents need have nothing to do with one another.

The Root Directory

When a diskette or hard disk is formatted, DOS creates a master directory called the **root directory**, designated by the symbol \. (This symbol is called a **backslash**. You may type it from the keyboard using the key just to the right of the left Shift key.) All directories are subdirectories of the root directory. Note the root directory at the bottom of the tree in Figure 4-2.

Figure 4-2.   **The directory of C:.**

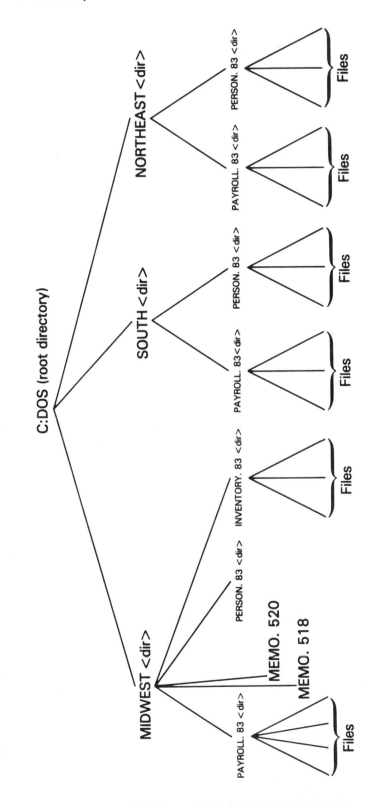

The Current Directory

At any given moment, each disk drive has a directory designated as the current directory. If you give DOS a command without specifying a directory, then the current directory is assumed. When DOS is started, the current directory is the root directory for each drive.

Here are some examples of DOS commands that refer to the current directory. The first command changes the current drive to *C:* and the directory to the current directory of *C:*. The second command lists the contents of the current directory of the diskette in drive *A:*.

```
C:
DIR A:
```

Paths

To completely specify a file for use in a DOS command, you must give the drive, the filename, and the path to the file starting from the current directory. For example, suppose that the current directory is *MIDWEST* and you wish to refer to *FILE.1*. You specify the file with the path

```
INVENTRY\FILE.1
```

This sequence of names is called a **path**. It tells DOS that to find the file, start from the current directory, go to the subdirectory *INVENTRY*, and then go to *FILE.1*. As a second example, suppose that the current directory is the root directory. Then the path to *FILE.1* is

```
MIDWEST\INVENTRY\FILE.1
```

As a third example, suppose that the current drive is *A:*. The path to *FILE.1* is now

```
C:\MIDWEST\INVENTRY\FILE.1
```

(The path begins with \ to indicate that the search should begin with the root directory.)

Most DOS commands use paths instead of filenames. For example, suppose that the current directory is *MIDWEST*. Then the command

```
DIR INVENTRY
```

will list the contents of the subdirectory *INVENTRY*. Similarly, suppose that the current drive is *A:*. Then the command

```
COPY C:\MIDWEST\INVENTRY\*.* A:
```

will copy all files in the subdirectory *C:\MIDWEST\INVENTRY* to the current directory of the diskette in drive *A:*.

Any missing parameters in a path mean that the current value of the parameter is to be assumed. For example, if the drive designation is omitted, then the current drive is assumed. If the path is omitted, then the current directory is assumed.

TEST YOUR UNDERSTANDING 1 (answers on page 63)

    a.   Write a command to list the directory of *NORTH\PERSON*.

    b.   Write a command to copy all files in *NORTH\PERSON* to *SOUTH\INVENT*.

TEST YOUR UNDERSTANDING 2 (answer on page 63)

What does this command do?

```
COPY A:*.* C:
```

TEST YOUR UNDERSTANDING 3 (answer on page 63)

What does this command do?

```
COPY *.* A:
```

The symbol .. may be used in a path to indicate a move one level down the tree, from a subdirectory to its "parent directory." For example, suppose that the current directory is *MIDWEST*. Then the path

```
..
```

refers to the root directory. Similarly, if the current directory is the subdirectory *INVENTRY* of *MIDWEST*, then the path

```
..\..
```

describes a move two steps down the tree, to the root directory. As yet another example, suppose that we wish to get to the subdirectory *PERSON* of *SOUTH* from the subdirectory *INVENTRY* of *MIDWEST*. We must go down to the root directory and back up to *PERSON*. Here is a path that describes these moves.

```
..\..\SOUTH\PERSON
```

NOTE: DOS limits path lengths to 63 characters.

Changing the Current Directory

You may change the current directory by using the DOS command **CHDIR**. For example, suppose that the current directory is *MIDWEST* and you wish to change to the subdirectory *PERSON*. The proper command is

```
CHDIR PERSON
```

The general format of the *CHDIR* command is

```
CHDIR <path>
```

Here, *<path>* is a path from the current directory to the desired current directory.

If a drive designation is included in the path, then *CHDIR* will change the current directory on the indicated drive. However, the current drive is not changed. For example, suppose that you wish to perform the directory change "`..`" for drive *A:* and the current drive is *C:*. The command

```
CHDIR A:..
```

changes the current directory on *A:* but leaves the current drive as *C:*.

Directory changes occur so often that DOS allows you to use the shorthand *CD* instead of *CHDIR*.

TEST YOUR UNDERSTANDING 4 (answers on page 63)

a. Suppose that the current directory is *MIDWEST*. Write a command that changes the current directory to the root directory.

b. Suppose that the current directory is *MIDWEST*. Write a command that changes the current directory to the subdirectory *PERSON* of *SOUTH*.

c. Suppose that the current directory is *MIDWEST* and the current drive is *C:*. Change the current drive to *A:* and perform the directory change .. on *C:*.

Creating and Deleting Directories

You may create directories using the *MKDIR* command. For example, suppose that the current directory is the root directory. To create the subdirectory *MID-WEST*, use the command

```
MKDIR \MIDWEST
```

Still assuming that the current directory is the root directory, we may create the subdirectory *INVENTRY* of *MIDWEST* using the command

```
MKDIR\MIDWEST\INVENTRY
```

The general form of the *MKDIR* command is

```
MKDIR [drive:]path
```

If the drive is omitted, then the current drive is assumed. DOS allows you to use the shorthand *MD* instead of *MKDIR*.

TEST YOUR UNDERSTANDING 5 (answer on page 63)

Suppose that the current directory is *MIDWEST*. Write a command to create the directory *SOUTH* in the root directory.

Note that you cannot copy files into a directory until the directory is created by the MKDIR command. BASIC and DOS respond to any attempt to reference a non-existent directory with an *Invalid Directory* or *Filename error*.

The MKDIR command creates the specified directory and enters it in two files: the . and .. files. The first of these contains the names of all files and subdirectories contained within the particular directory. Initially, the . file contains no entries. The .. file specifies the directory to which this subdirectory belongs. That is, the .. file contains the information necessary to descend one level in the tree.

The root directory may contain as many as 64 entries in case of a single-sided diskette or 112 entries in case of a double-sided diskette or a hard disk. However, there are no limitations on the number of entries in a subdirectory.

You may delete a directory using the **RMDIR** command. To remove a directory, it must contain only the . and .. files. (This is a safety feature so that you will not accidentally delete files by mistake.) The *RMDIR* command works similarly to the command MKDIR. It has the format

```
RMDIR [drive:] path
```

For example, if the current directory is the root directory, then you may remove the subdirectory *PERSON* of *MIDWEST* using the command

```
RMDIR \MIDWEST\PERSON
```

If you attempt to remove a directory containing files other than . and . . , then DOS reports an error.

DOS allows the shorthand of *RM* instead of *RMDIR*.

COPY and ERASE Using Paths

You may add files to a directory in the usual ways, using the COPY command, for instance. Similarly, you may erase files using the ERASE command. Both COPY and ERASE may use paths to describe the files involved. Of course, you may omit the paths if you wish to refer to files in the current directory.

For example, to copy *FILE1* to the current directory of drive *C:*, use the command

```
COPY FILE1 C:
```

As a second example, suppose that the current directory is the root directory and we wish to copy *FILE1* into the subdirectory *MIDWEST\PERSON*. We use the command

```
COPY FILE1 MIDWEST\PERSON
```

After performing this command, we can erase *FILE1* using the command

```
ERASE FILE1
```

NOTE: The COPY and ERASE commands refer only to files and not to directories. To copy the contents of a directory, you must first use MKDIR to create a directory with the proper name, then use the COPY command to copy the desired files into the new directory.

TEST YOUR UNDERSTANDING 6 (answers on page 63)

a.   Write a command to copy all files in the current directory on *A:* to the directory *MIDWEST\INVENTRY*.

b.   Write a command to erase all files in the root directory of drive *A:*.

ANSWERS TO TEST YOUR UNDERSTANDINGS 1, 2, 3, 4, 5, and 6

1:   a.   `DIR NORTH\PERSON`
     b.   `COPY NORTH\PERSON\*.* SOUTH\INVENT`

2:   It copies all files on the diskette in drive *A:* onto the current directory.

3:   It copies all files in the current directory onto the diskette in drive *A:*.

4:   a.   `CD ..`
     b.   `CD .. \SOUTH\PERSON`
     c.   `A:`
          `CD C:..`

5:   `MD ..\SOUTH`

6:   a.   `COPY A:*.* C:MIDWEST\INVENTRY`
     b.   `ERASE A:*.*`

4.2　Creating Your Own DOS Commands—Batch Files

In the preceding sections, we learned about the most useful DOS commands. Most often, you will execute DOS commands by typing them directly from the keyboard, as described earlier in the chapter. In many applications, however, it is necessary to execute the same sequence of DOS commands repeatedly. For example, consider the following situation.

Suppose that you have a diskette containing four files named *ACCOUNTS.MAY, PROFIT.MAY, PAYABLE.MAY,* and *SALES.MAY.* Your business is computerized and every one of your 10 managers has an IBM PC. Rather than distribute the contents of the files via paper copies, in the traditional manner, you wish to send each manager a copy of the files on diskette.

A simple solution is to use *DISKCOPY* to make 10 copies of the diskette containing the files. Suppose, however, that your diskette also contains some sensitive information that you do not wish to circulate. In this case, you may prepare the duplicate diskettes by copying the files one at a time. This may be done via the *COPY* command. Here are the DOS commands required to prepare one duplicate diskette, starting from an unformatted diskette:

```
FORMAT B: \S
COPY A:ACCOUNTS.MAY B:
COPY A:PROFIT.MAY B:
COPY A:PAYABLE.MAY B:
COPY A:SALES.MAY B:
```

Assume that your files are contained on the same diskette as FORMAT.COM and that this diskette is in drive *A:.* The duplicate diskette is in drive *B:.*

It is possible to prepare the 10 duplicates by typing these commands in manually. But what a chore! And it is easy to make a mistake in typing, especially as the afternoon draws to a close. There is, fortunately, a much better way to proceed: using a batch file.

A **batch file** is a diskette file consisting of a list of DOS commands. A batch file must have a filename with the extension *BAT*. In our case, let's name the batch file *C.BAT*, and let's store it on the diskette in drive *A:.* In order to create the batch file, use the *COPY* command. Type

```
COPY CON: A:C.BAT
```

and press ENTER. Now type in the DOS commands exactly as they appear in the above list. At the end of each line, press ENTER. After typing the last line and pressing ENTER, press function key F6 and then ENTER. DOS responds with the message

```
1 file(s) copied
```

The file *C.BAT* is now on the diskette in drive *A:*.

To execute the list of DOS commands, we now merely type the letter *C* and press ENTER. (It is just as if we created a new DOS command with the name *C.*) DOS then searches the current diskette (*A:*), finds the batch file, and executes the various commands, in the order specified.

TEST YOUR UNDERSTANDING 1 (answer on page 66)

Modify the above list of DOS commands so that they include a check that the copies of the files are identical to the originals.

Now our copying job is cut down to size:

1. Insert a blank diskette into drive *B:*.

2. Type *C* and press ENTER.

3. Wait for the commands to be executed.

4. Repeat operations 1-3 until all 10 copies are made.

Parameters

Let's stick with our fictitious company. Suppose that the 10 diskettes are to be prepared and sent every month. The filenames are always the same, but the month abbreviations, as given in the filename extensions, vary. You can prepare a new batch file *C.BAT* every month. However, there is a better way. Designate the month abbreviation by the symbol *%1*. (% is an abbreviation for parameter and 1 is the number of the parameter.) The commands of the batch file are then written:

```
FORMAT B:\S
COPY A:ACCOUNTS.%1 B:
COPY A:PROFIT.%1 B:
COPY A:PAYABLE.%1 B:
COPY A:SALES.%1 B:
```

For the month of *MAY*, give the batch command

```
C MAY
```

For the month of *JUNE*, give the batch command

```
C JUN
```

and so forth.

You may use up to nine parameters, *%1, %2, . . . ,%9*. You specify the values of these parameters when you give the batch command, with consecutive parameter values separated by spaces. For example, if a batch file *D* uses the two parameters *%1* and *%2*, then to execute the batch file with *%1 = JAN* and *%2 = FEB*, we use the command

D JAN FEB

ANSWER TO TEST YOUR UNDERSTANDING 1
1:   Add the DOS commands

```
COMP A:ACCOUNTS.MAY B:
COMP A:PROFIT.MAY B:
COMP A:PAYABLE.MAY B:
COMP A:SALES.MAY B:
```

4.3   The AUTOEXEC.BAT and CONFIG.SYS Files

Let's now discuss two files that can be used to customize your PC.

The AUTOEXEC.BAT File

The **AUTOEXEC.BAT** file is a batch file that is automatically executed whenever DOS is started. If a diskette contains a file with the name AUTOEXEC.BAT, then it is executed on DOS start-up without any operator action. For example, suppose that you want your PC to start BASIC automatically whenever DOS is started. Just create a diskette file called AUTOEXEC.BAT containing the command

```
BASICA
```

The AUTOEXEC.BAT file can contain any number of commands to initialize your system exactly as you find convenient. For example, your AUTOEXEC.BAT file may initialize a desktop manager program that gives you access to a calendar, notepad, and calculator to be used even while a program is running. Or, the AUTOEXEC.BAT file may contain commands that set the screen width or directs output so that the printer is properly connected. And so forth. The AUTOEXEC.BAT file can save you from manually executing a large number of commands required on machine start-up.

Note that you may have only one AUTOEXEC.BAT file on a given diskette or hard disk. On the other hand, you may have many ordinary batch files (but these are not executed automatically).

TEST YOUR UNDERSTANDING 1 (answer on page 67)
Modify your DOS diskette so that BASIC is started whenever you start DOS.

The AUTOEXEC.BAT file may be used for some clever purposes. For example, let's return to our company with 10 managers. Suppose that you wish to include a covering memo that reads:

```
TO:MANAGERS
HERE ARE THE STATEMENTS FOR MAY.
WE'LL MEET TO DISCUSS THEM ON 6/4
AT 5:30 pm.

JR
```

Here is how the message can be automatically displayed:

1. Create a file on your diskette that contains the text of the message. Call the file *MSSG*.

2. Create a file AUTOEXEC.BAT containing the DOS command
   `TYPE MSSG`

3. Modify the batch file *C.BAT* so that it copies *MSSG* and AUTOEXEC.BAT onto each of the 10 copies.

Each manager will start his or her PC using a duplicate diskette. The AUTOEXEC.BAT file will cause the file MSSG to be displayed on the screen.

The CONFIG.SYS File

The **CONFIG.SYS** file is another file that is read by DOS automatically on system start-up. It allows you to tell DOS to recognize additional devices other than those specified by DOS device names. For example, to include a Microsoft mouse as a device in your system, it is necessary to include a line:

`device = MOUSE.SYS`

within the CONFIG.SYS file. Here *MOUSE.SYS* is the name of a file that tells DOS the characteristics of the mouse device and how to access it. This file is supplied when you purchase the mouse.

There are many different devices that can be added to the list of DOS devices using the CONFIG.SYS file, including mice, joysticks, light pens, special-purpose monitors, and graphics boards. Once you set up the CONFIG.SYS file, you need do nothing further. Each time the system is started, the devices specified in CONFIG.SYS are installed. Make sure, however, that the files referenced in CONFIG.SYS are contained on the disk you use to start the computer.

ANSWER TO TEST YOUR UNDERSTANDING 1

1: Add the file *AUTOEXEC.BAT* consisting of the single DOS command

`BASICA`

4.4 More About DOS

In Chapters 3 and 4, we have given only a beginner's sketch of the features of DOS. There are many features that we haven't even mentioned. For example, the **ASSIGN** command allows you to redirect all input and output for one disk drive to another drive. There are other batch file commands that allow for elaborate decision-making in executing a batch file. And beginning in DOS version 3.1, there is networking, which allows DOS to control a system consisting of multiple computers and assorted peripheral devices.

To go further into DOS takes us beyond the introductory level of this book. If you would like to learn more, however, there are several books you can go to:

- *Inside the IBM PC, Revised and Enlarged* by Peter Norton, 2nd edition, Brady Communications Company, Inc., 1986.
- *The Peter Norton Programmer's Guide to the IBM PC*, Microsoft Press, 1985.

Part Three

An Introduction to IBM PC BASIC Programming

5

Getting Started in BASIC

5.0 Chapter Objectives

THIS CHAPTER PRESENTS THE most elementary concepts of BASIC programming, including:

- A history of the BASIC language.

- Executing BASIC statements in immediate mode.

- Numbers and text in BASIC.

- How to run a BASIC program.

- Interrupting and LISTing BASIC programs.

- Writing elementary BASIC programs.

- PRINTing numbers and text.

- Using variables.

- The LET statement.

- Single- and double-precision variables, string variables.

- The SWAP statement.

- Using remarks in programs.

- Using a printer.

- BASIC commands, including NEW, LIST, LLIST, DELETE, RUN, SAVE, and KILL.

- Saving, recalling, and erasing programs from a diskette or hard disk.

- Automatically generating line numbers.

- Renumbering program lines.

- Programming tips.

- Using the BASIC full-screen editor.

5.1   Beginning BASIC

In Chapter 2, we learned to manipulate the keyboard and display screen of an IBM PC. Now we'll learn how to give instructions to the computer.

Just as humans use languages to communicate with one another, computers use languages to communicate with other electronic devices (such as printers), human operators, and even other computers. There are hundreds of computer languages in use today, and your IBM PC is capable of ''speaking'' quite a few of them. Among these languages, BASIC is both versatile and very easy to learn. It was developed especially for computer novices by John Kemeny and Thomas Kurtz at Dartmouth College in the mid 1960s. During the late 1970s, BASIC became the standard language of microcomputers. In the next few chapters, we will concentrate on teaching the fundamentals of BASIC. In the process, you will learn a great deal about the way in which a computer may be used to solve problems.

The IBM PC actually comes with three different versions of the BASIC language. The least powerful version of BASIC is called **Cassette BASIC.** This is the BASIC version that is supplied with all IBM PCs and is stored in ROM. The other two versions of BASIC are called **BASIC** and **BASICA,** or **Advanced BASIC.** These versions are contained on the DOS diskette supplied when you purchase DOS. BASICA is a much more comprehensive version of BASIC and includes all the commands included in both Cassette BASIC and BASIC. In this book, we will ignore the latter two versions of BASIC and concentrate on BASICA.

So remember: All of our statements apply to BASICA, but may not apply to Cassette BASIC and BASIC. Moreover, when we refer to BASIC, we mean the BASICA version.

5.2   BASIC Statements
in Immediate Mode

Assume that you have loaded BASIC and have obtained the BASIC prompt. Now give the computer some instructions in BASIC. Type

```
PRINT 3+2
```

and press ENTER. The computer immediately fires back the answer:

```
 5
Ok
```

The *Ok* prompt indicates that BASIC is awaiting another instruction. Type

`CLS`

and press ENTER. The screen is erased and the cursor is positioned in the upper left corner (the so-called **home position**).

Now try some other BASIC instructions. Here is an interesting instruction to try if you have a color monitor attached to a color graphics adapter. Type

`SCREEN 1,0`

and press ENTER. This instruction tells BASIC to enter medium-resolution graphics mode (*SCREEN 1*). The *0* portion of the command enables color. Next, set the background and text colors by typing the statement

`COLOR 1,2 <ENTER>`

(From now on, we will write *<ENTER>* to mean "and press the ENTER key".) Notice that the screen turns blue and the *Ok* prompt is displayed in yellow.

TEST YOUR UNDERSTANDING 1

Try this statement:

`COLOR 2,4 <ENTER>`

What does it do?

TEST YOUR UNDERSTANDING 2

Try this statement:

`COLOR n <ENTER>`

and replace n with 0,1,2,3,4, ... How many different background colors are possible?

BASIC is equipped with an incredible array of statements that perform a variety of tasks. As just a hint of things to come, try out a few graphics and music statements.

Type the statement

`PLAY "CDEF" <ENTER>`

The computer plays four notes. These notes are C, D, E, and F. Next, clear the screen and type the statement

`CIRCLE (100,100),75 <ENTER>`

BASIC will draw a circle as shown in Figure 5-1.

Figure 5-1.   **A circle centered at (100,100) with radius 75.**

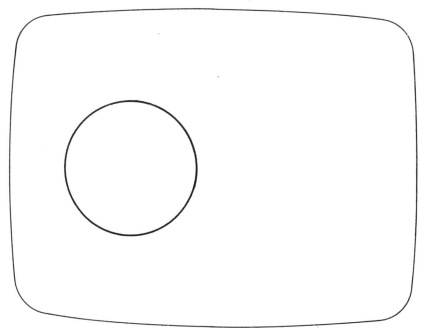

Actually, BASIC has an extensive repertoire of graphics statements that you will learn shortly.

The exercises below give you an opportunity to explore a few more of BASIC's instructions.

5.3   BASIC Constants and Arithmetic

In learning to use a language, you first must learn the alphabet of the language. Next, you must learn the vocabulary of the language. Finally, you must study the way in which words are put together into sentences. In learning the BASIC language, we will follow the progression just described. In Chapter 2, you learned about the characters of the IBM PC keyboard. These characters are the alphabet of BASIC. Next, you'll learn some vocabulary words. The simplest "words" are the so-called **constants.**

BASIC Constants

BASIC allows you to manipulate numbers and text. The rules for manipulating numeric data differ from those for handling text, however. In BASIC, we distinguish between these two types of data as follows: a **numeric constant** is a number, and a **string constant** is a sequence of keyboard characters that may include letters, numbers, or any other keyboard symbols. The following are examples of numeric constants:

5

−2

3.145

23456

456.7834

27134000000000

The following are examples of string constants:

"John",

"Accounts Receivable"

"$234.45 Due"

"Dec. 4,1981"

Note that string constants are always enclosed in quotation marks. In order to avoid vagueness, quotation marks may not appear as part of a string constant. (In practice, use an apostrophe (') as a substitute for a quotation mark (") within a string constant.) Numbers may appear within a string constant, such as "$45.30". However, you cannot use such numbers in arithmetic. Only numbers not enclosed by quotation marks may be used for arithmetic.

In many applications, it is necessary to refer to a string constant that has no characters within its quotation marks, namely the string "". This string constant is called the **null string.**

Arithmetic in BASIC

BASIC allows you to perform all the usual arithmetic operations. Addition and subtraction are written in the usual way:

5 + 4

9 − 8

Multiplication, however, is typed using the asterisk (*), which shares the "8" key. As an example, the product of 5 and 3 is typed as:

5*3

Division is typed using the slash (/). For example, 8.2 divided by 15 is typed as

8.2/15

All elementary arithmetic operations (addition, subtraction, multiplication, and division) are carried out to seven decimal places. For example, the result of the statement

PRINT 8.2/15

is the display

```
 .5466666
Ok
```

Example 1.   Write a BASIC statement to calculate the sum of 54.75, 78.83, and 548.

Solution.   The sum is indicated by typing

54.75 + 78.83 + 548

The BASIC instruction for printing data on the screen is *PRINT,* so the instruction is as follows:

PRINT 54.75 + 78.83 + 548

The Order of Operations and Parentheses

BASIC carries out arithmetic operations in a special order. It scans an expression and carries out all multiplication and division, proceeding in left-to-right order. It then returns to the left side of the expression and performs addition and subtraction proceeding left-to-right.

For example, consider this expression:

2*3 + 4*5 + 3*3

BASIC first scans the expression from left to right and performs all multiplications and divisions in the order in which they are encountered. It simplifies the expression to

6 + 20 + 9

BASIC then starts again at the left and performs all addition and subtraction operations in the order encountered. This gives the result:

35

The order of operations is extremely important. Let's try another example:

1 − 3/2*5

BASIC first performs the division 3/2. This simplifies the expression to

1 − 1.5*5

Next, it performs the multiplication 1.5*5 to obtain

$1 - 7.5$

Finally, it starts from the left again and performs addition and subtraction to obtain

-6.5

Knowing the order of operations helps you to correctly translate familiar arithmetic procedures into computer language. For example, consider this fraction:

$$\frac{5 + 3/2}{5*8}$$

According to the rules of arithmetic, you simplify this fraction by first simplifying the numerator and denominator to obtain

$$\frac{6.5}{40}$$

Note that you must perform the operations specified in the numerator and denominator **before** performing the division indicated in the fraction. You may indicate this in BASIC (as in algebra) by using parentheses:

$(5 + 3/2)/(5*8)$

BASIC does all the math inside the parentheses first, following the precedence rules given above. For example, in the above expression, the parentheses $(5 + 3/2)$ and $(5*8)$ are evaluated first, to give

6.5/40

BASIC then performs the division.

TEST YOUR UNDERSTANDING 1 (answer on page 82)
Evaluate this expression:

$3*5 - 4*3/2 + 4 - 8/2$

In evaluating parentheses, BASIC uses the same rules stated above: First perform all multiplications and divisions in left-to-right order. Then perform all additions and subtractions in left-to-right order.

What about parentheses within parentheses? Well, you have enough knowledge to figure out what BASIC does. Work out this example:

$(1 + 3*(4 + 5))*(1 + 4)$

BASIC looks at the expression and decides it must first evaluate the left-most parenthesis $(1 + 3*(4 + 5))$. When it attempts to evaluate it, however, it encounters a parenthesis within, namely (4+5), which must be evaluated first. So the first simplification is

(1+3*9)*(1+4)

Now BASIC begins all over. It evaluates the left-most parenthesis to get

28*(1+4)

Next, it evaluates the right parenthesis to get

28*5

Finally, it performs the multiplication to obtain the answer:

140

Example 2.   What numeric values will BASIC calculate from these expressions?

   a.   (5 + 7)/2

   b.   5 + 7/2

   c.   5 + 7*3/2

   d.   (5 + 7*3)/2

Solution.

   a.   The computer first applies its rules for the order of calculation to determine the value in the parentheses, namely 12. It then divides 12 by 2 to obtain 6.

   b.   The computer scans the expression from left to right performing all multiplication and division in the order encountered. First it divides 7 by 2 to obtain 3.5. It then rescans the line and performs all additions and subtractions in order. This gives us

       5 + 3.5 = 8.5

   c.   The computer first performs all multiplication and division in order:

       5 + 10.5

       It then performs addition to obtain 15.5.

   d.   The computer calculates the value of all parentheses first. In this case, it computes 5 + 7*3 = 26. (Note that it does the multiplication first!) Next, it rescans the line which now looks like this:

       26/2

       It performs the division to obtain 13.

TEST YOUR UNDERSTANDING 2 (answer on page 82)
Calculate $5 + 3/2 + 2$ and $(5 + 3)/(2 + 2)$. What is the result?

Example 3. Write a BASIC instruction to calculate the quantity

$$\frac{22 \times 18 + 34 \times 11 - 12.5 \times 8}{27.8 + 42.1}$$

Solution. Here is the instruction:

```
10 PRINT (22*18 + 34*11 - 12.5*8)/(27.8+42.1)
```

The parentheses in line 10 tell BASIC to calculate the values of the numerator and denominator before doing the division implied by the fraction. First calculate (22*18 + 34*11 − 12.5*8) and (27.8 + 42.1) before performing the division.

TEST YOUR UNDERSTANDING 3 (answers on page 82)
Write BASIC programs to calculate:

a. $((4 \times 3 + 5 \times 8 + 7 \times 9)/(7 \times 9 + 4 \times 3 + 8 \times 7)) \times 48.7$

b. 27.8 percent of $(112 + 38 + 42)$

c. The average of the numbers 88, 78, 84, 49, and 63

Scientific Notation

For certain applications, you may wish to specify your numeric constants in **exponential format** (also called **scientific notation**). This is especially helpful in the case of very large and very small numbers. Consider the number 15,300,000,000. You can type this number as:

15300000000

However, it is very inconvenient to type all the zeros, but it can be written more easily as 1.53E10. The 1.53 indicates the first three digits of the number. E10 means that you move the decimal point in the 1.53 to the right 10 places. Similarly, the number −237,000 may be written in the exponential format as −2.37E5. Exponential format also may be used for very small numbers. For example, the number 0.00000000054 may be written in exponential format as 5.4E-10. The -10 indicates that the decimal point in 5.4 is to be moved 10 places to the *left*.

TEST YOUR UNDERSTANDING 4 (answers on page 82)
a. Write these numbers in exponential format: .00048 and −1374.5
b. Write these numbers in decimal format: −9.7E3, 9.7E-3 and −9.7E-3

BASIC can display at most seven significant digits of a number. (At least for the single-precision numbers we are dealing with for most of this book. You'll learn how to get more precision later.) If you ask it to display a number with more than seven significant digits, BASIC automatically shifts to scientific notation. For example, the statement

`PRINT 123456789`

produces the display

`1.234568E+08`

Note that the initial seven digits are obtained by rounding the given 10 digits.

Exponentiation

Suppose that A is a number and N is a positive whole number (this means that N is one of the numbers 1, 2, 3, 4, ...) . Therefore, **A raised to the Nth power** is the product of A times itself N times. This quantity usually is denoted A^N, and the process of calculating it is called exponentiation. For example,

$$2^3 = 2*2*2 = 8, \quad 5^7 = 5*5*5*5*5*5*5 = 78125$$

$$A^N = A*A*A*...*A \text{ (N times)}$$

It is possible to calculate A^N by repeated multiplication. However, if N is large, this can be tiresome to type. BASIC provides a shortcut for typing this function. Exponentiation is denoted by the symbol ^, which is produced by hitting the key with the upward-pointing arrow (this symbol shares the ''6'' key at the top of the keyboard). For example, 2^3 is denoted 2^3. The operation of exponentiation is done before multiplication and division. This is illustrated in the following example.

Example 4.
Determine the value that BASIC assigns to this expression:

20*3 - 5*2^3

Solution. The exponentiation is performed first to yield

20*3 - 5*8 = 60 - 40
= 20

TEST YOUR UNDERSTANDING 5 (answers on page 82)
Evaluate the following, first manually and then using BASIC.

a. $2^4 \times 3^3$

b. $2^2 \times 3^3 - 12^2/3^2 \times 2$

Integer Division

Recall the days when you first learned division. Your first problems involved dividing one whole number by another. You were taught to express the answer as a quotient and a remainder. For example, the result of dividing 14 by 5 is the quotient 2 and the remainder 4. This type of division may be performed in BASIC using the operations \ and *mod*. For example:

14\5 = 2

and

14 mod 5 = 4

That is, 14\5 equals the (whole number) quotient of 14 divided by 5; 14 mod 5 equals the remainder. The symbol \ is called a backslash and should not be confused with the ordinary slash (/).

Here is a table showing the order in which \ and *mod* are performed in relationship to the other operations. The operations that are higher in the list are performed first.

^

*, /

\

mod

+ , −

Consider this expression:

5*3\2*2 mod 2

The multiplications are performed first to obtain

15\4 mod 2

Next, the \ is performed, to obtain

3 mod 2

Finally, this last expression is simplified to obtain

1

ANSWERS TO TEST YOUR UNDERSTANDINGS 1, 2, 3, 4, and 5

1: 9

2: 8.5 and 2

3: a. `PRINT ((4*3 + 5*8 + 7*9)/(7*9 + 4*3 + 8*7))*48.7`
    b. `PRINT .278*(112+38+42)`
    c. `PRINT (88+78+84+49+63)/5`

4: a. 4.8E-4, -1.3745E3
    b. -9700, .0097, -.0097

5: a. 432
    b. 76

5.4   Running BASIC Programs

Sections 5.2 and 5.3 gave examples of several BASIC statements. You told BASIC to execute a statement by typing it and then pressing the ENTER key. This method of executing statements is called the **immediate mode.** It is used for executing a single instruction at a time.

In order to make BASIC do anything really complex, it's necessary to string together many instructions (sometimes as many as several thousand). A sequence of instructions is called a **program.** You will learn to write programs that do arithmetic, draw charts, and even play tic tac toe. Before that, however, let's look at one that IBM has prepared especially to demonstrate the power of its computer.

IBM has included many interesting programs on the DOS Supplementary diskette. Let's examine some of them.

Start BASICA using your DOS diskette and then remove the DOS diskette and insert the DOS Supplementary diskette into the drive. To obtain a list of the programs on this diskette, type

FILES <ENTER>

The names of the programs on the diskette will be displayed on the screen.

One of the most impressive programs is *MUSIC*. (Note that it is listed under the name *MUSIC.BAS*. The extension BAS indicates that the program is written in BASIC.) To load the program *MUSIC* from the diskette into RAM, type

LOAD "MUSIC" <ENTER>

(Note the quotation marks.) The diskette drive light will go on, you will hear the drive at work, and the program *MUSIC* will be loaded into RAM. The drive light will then go out and the drive will stop.

Now let's make the computer perform the instructions in the program. (In computer jargon, we **run the program.**) Type

```
RUN <ENTER>
```

The computer draws a piano keyboard on the screen and displays the names of some songs. To play a song, press the key indicated. Spend a few minutes enjoying the computer-generated music. Note also how the computer "animates" the keyboard by displaying a moving note, which indicates the key being played.

Sooner or later, you will want to interrupt a computer program while it is running. This is done by pressing the Ctrl-Break key combination. It's a two-handed operation for good reason. The keys are arranged so that you won't interrupt programs accidentally. To illustrate how you may interrupt a program, run MUSIC and play a song. In the middle of the song, simultaneously hit Ctrl and Break. The program will stop and the screen will display a message like this:

```
Break in line xxxx
Ok
-
```

The line *xxxx* gives the place in the program at which you stopped the computer. (You'll learn about line numbers in Section 5.5.) The BASIC prompt *Ok* indicates that BASIC is awaiting another command. Interrupting a program does not erase it from RAM. To run the program again, just type *RUN* and press ENTER.

Well, enough music for now! Let's end the program. According to the instructions on the screen, you may "EXIT" the program by pressing Esc, a key located on the upper left side of the keyboard. Press this key. Note that the BASIC prompt *Ok* is displayed, indicating that BASIC is awaiting a command.

You probably are curious to see the set of instructions for *MUSIC*. Nothing could be easier. Type

```
LIST <ENTER>
```

You will see the instructions of the program displayed on the screen. Of course, they are going by too quickly for you to read them. Later, you'll learn how to stop the display where you want or to obtain a written copy on the printer.

TEST YOUR UNDERSTANDING 1 (answer on page 84)
Pick out a program on the DOS Supplementary diskette, load it into memory, and run it. (Some programs may require the color/graphics adapter. Don't worry. If you don't have this circuit board installed, the computer will tell you that it can't run the program and will redisplay the BASIC prompt.)

You will find many interesting programs on the optional program diskette which accompanies this book. In particular, you may wish to play some computer games, such as TICTACTOE, SHOOT, and TARGET. Just start BASIC, insert the program diskette, and follow the above instructions for loading and running a program.

ANSWER TO TEST YOUR UNDERSTANDING 1

1: Start from the BASIC prompt. Type *LOAD* <*program name*> and press ENTER. Here <*program name*> is the name of the program you wish to run. Omit the extension *BAS*. Now type *RUN* and press ENTER.

5.5 Writing BASIC Programs

You may be intimidated by the number of instructions in the program *MUSIC*. Don't be. In no time at all, you will be writing programs just as complicated. Take one step at a time and first learn to write some simple BASIC programs.

Assume that you have started BASICA and the computer shows that it is ready to accept further instructions by displaying the BASIC prompt *Ok*.

From this point on, a typical session with your computer might go like this:

1. Type in a program.

2. Locate and correct any errors in the program.

3. SAVE the program.

4. Run the program.

5. Obtain the output requested by the program.

6. Either run the program again, or repeat steps 1-4 for a new program, or end the programming session (turn off the computer and go have lunch).

To fully understand what is involved in these five steps, consider a particular example, namely a program to add 5 and 7. First, type the following instructions:

```
10 PRINT 5 + 7
20 END
```

This sequence of two instructions constitutes a program to calculate 5 + 7.

As you type the program, the computer records your instructions, **but does not carry them out.** (The line numbers 10 and 20 tell BASIC that the instructions are not to be carried out immediately.) As you are typing a program, the computer provides you with an opportunity to change, delete, and correct instruction lines.

(More on how to do this later.) Once you are content with your program, tell the computer to run it (that is, to execute the instructions) by typing the command[1]:

`RUN`

The computer will run the program and display the desired answer:

```
 12
Ok
```

If you wish the computer to run the program a second time, type *RUN* again.

Running a program does not erase it from RAM. Therefore, if you wish to add instructions to the program or change the program, you may continue typing just as if the RUN command had not intervened. For example, if you wish to include in your program the problem of calculating 5 - 7, type the additional line

`15 PRINT 5 - 7`

To see the program currently in memory, type LIST (no line number) and then hit the ENTER key. The program consists of the following three lines, now displayed on the screen:

```
LIST
10 PRINT 5 + 7
15 PRINT 5 - 7
20 END
```

Note how the computer puts line 15 in proper sequence. If you type *RUN* again, the computer displays the two answers:

```
RUN
 12
 -2

Ok
```

Note that line numbers need not be consecutive. For example, it is perfectly acceptable to have a program with line numbers 10, 23, 47, 55, or 100. Also note that it is not necessary to type instructions in numerical order. You could type line 20 and then go back and type line 10. The computer sorts out the lines and rearranges them according to increasing line numbers. This feature is especially helpful in case you accidentally omit a line while typing your program.

Here is another important fact about line numbering. If you type two lines with the same line number, the computer erases the first version and remembers the second version. This feature is very useful for correcting errors: If a line has an error, just retype it and press ENTER.

---

[1]Don't forget to follow the command with ENTER. The computer will not recognize a line unless it has been sent to it by hitting the ENTER key. In the rest of the book, we will omit the statement "Press the ENTER key" after a command.

Let's go on to another program by typing the command

NEW

NEW erases the previous program from RAM and prepares the computer to accept a new program. Remember this important fact:

RAM can contain only one of your programs at a time.

TEST YOUR UNDERSTANDING 1 (answers on page 89)

a.   Write and type in a BASIC program to calculate 12.1 + 98 + 5.32.

b.   Run the program of a.

c.   Erase the program of a. from RAM.

d.   Write a program to calculate 48.75 - 1.674.

e.   Type in and run the program of d.

Immediate Mode and Execute Mode

BASIC operates in two distinct modes. In **immediate mode,** also called **command mode,** the computer accepts typed program lines and commands (like *RUN* and *NEW*) used to manipulate programs. The computer identifies a program line by its line number. Program lines are not immediately executed. Rather, they are stored in RAM until you tell the computer what to do with them. On the other hand, commands with no line number are executed as soon as they are given.

While BASIC is running a program, it is in **execute mode.**

When you first start BASIC, it is automatically in immediate mode, indicated by the presence of the *Ok* prompt on the screen. The *RUN* command puts the computer into execute mode. After the computer finishes running a program, it redisplays the *Ok* prompt indicating that it is back in immediate mode.

Uppercase Versus Lowercase and Extra Spaces

The computer is a stern taskmaster! It has a very limited vocabulary (BASIC), and this vocabulary must be used according to very specific rules concerning the order of words, punctuation, and so forth. However, BASIC allows for some freedom of expression. For example, BASIC commands may be typed in uppercase, lowercase, or a mixture of the two. Also, any extra spaces are ignored. Thus, BASIC will interpret all of the following instructions as the same:

```
10 PRINT A
10 print a
```

```
10 Print A
10 print    A
10               print A
```

Note, however, that BASIC expects spaces in certain places. For example, there must be a space separating PRINT and *A* in the above command. Otherwise, BASIC will read the command as *PRINTA,* which is not in its vocabulary!

A Word of Warning

Many people think of a computer as an "electronic brain" that somehow has the power of human thought. This is very far from the truth. The electronics of the computer and the rules of the BASIC language allow it to recognize a very limited vocabulary, and to take various actions based on the data that is given to it. It is very important to realize that the computer does not have "common sense." The computer attempts to interpret whatever data you input. If what you input is a recognizable command, the computer performs it. It does not matter that the command makes no sense in a particular context. The computer has no way to make such judgments. It can only do what you instruct it to do.

Because of the computer's inflexibility in interpreting commands, you must tell the computer *exactly* what you want it to do. Don't worry about confusing the computer. If you communicate a command in an incorrect form, you won't damage the machine in any way! However, in order to make the machine do our bidding, it is necessary to learn to speak its language precisely.

Printing Words

So far, you have used the PRINT statement only to display the answers to numeric problems. However, this instruction is very versatile. It also allows you to display string constants. For example, consider this instruction:

```
10 PRINT "Patient History"
```

During program execution, this statement creates the following display:

```
Patient History
```

In order to display several string constants on the same line, separate them by commas in a single PRINT statement. For example, consider the instruction:

```
10 PRINT "AGE", "SEX", "ADDRESS"
```

It causes three words to be printed as follows:

```
AGE           SEX            ADDRESS
```

Both numeric constants and string constants may be included in a single PRINT statement. For example:

```
100 PRINT "AGE", 65.43, 65000
```

Here is how the computer determines the spacing on a line. Each line is divided into **print zones**. In 80-character width, the first five print zones each have 14 spaces and the sixth 10 spaces. In 40-character width, there are three print zones, the first two with 14 characters and the third with 12 characters.

By placing a comma in a PRINT statement, you are telling the computer to start the next string of text at the beginning of the next print zone. For example, the four words above begin in columns 1, 15, 29, 44 respectively, assuming an 80-character width. (See Figure 5-2.) If a PRINT statement requests a print zone beyond the current line, printing will automatically move to the first print zone of the next line.

Henceforth, we will assume that the line width is 80 characters, unless we explicitly say otherwise.

TEST YOUR UNDERSTANDING 2 (answer on page 89)
Write a program to print the following display.

```
                NAME

LAST            FIRST           GRADE

SMITH           JOHN            87
```

TEST YOUR UNDERSTANDING 3 (answer on page 89)
Write a computer program that creates the following display.

```
        BUDGET-APRIL


FOOD            387.50

CAR             475.00

GAS             123.71

UTILITIES       146.00

ENTERTAINMENT   100.00

                _____

TOTAL           (Calculate total)
```

Figure 5-2.   **Print zones in 80-column mode.**

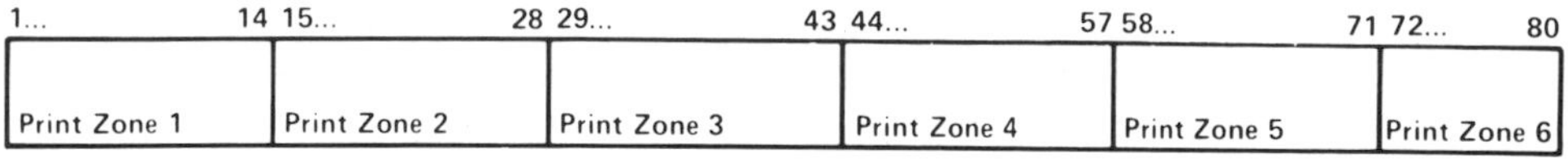

1...	14 15...	28 29...	43 44...	57 58...	71 72...	80
Print Zone 1	Print Zone 2	Print Zone 3	Print Zone 4	Print Zone 5	Print Zone 6	

ANSWERS TO TEST YOUR UNDERSTANDING 1, 2, and 3

1:   a.   ```
10 PRINT 12.1 + 98 + 5.32
20 END
```

   b.   Type *RUN* and press ENTER.

   c.   Type *NEW* and press ENTER.

   d.   ```
10 PRINT 48.75 - 1.674
20 END
```

   e.   Type in the program. Type *RUN* and press ENTER.

2:   ```
10 PRINT ,"NAME"
20 PRINT
30 PRINT "LAST","FIRST","GRADE"
40 PRINT
50 PRINT "SMITH","JOHN",87
60 END
```

3:   ```
10 PRINT ,"   BUDGET-APRIL"
20 PRINT "FOOD",,387.50
30 PRINT "CAR",, 475.00
40 PRINT "GAS",, 123.71
50 PRINT "UTILITIES",, 146.00
60 PRINT "ENTERTAINMENT",, 100.00
70 PRINT , "_____"
80 PRINT "TOTAL",
387.50+475.00+123.71+146.00+100.00
90 END
```

5.6   Giving Names to Numbers and Words

In the examples and exercises of the preceding section, you probably noticed that you wasted a considerable amount of time retyping certain numbers over and over. Not only does this retyping waste time, it also is a likely source of errors. Fortunately, such retyping is unnecessary if you use variables.

A **variable** is a collection of characters used to represent a number. A variable name must begin with a letter and can contain as many as 40 characters. Therefore, you may use variables named *PAYROLL, TAX, REFUND,* and *BALANCE*. Note, however, that not every sequence of characters is a legal variable name.

You must avoid any sequences of characters that are reserved by BASIC for special meanings. Examples of such words are:

IF, ON, OR, TO, THEN, GOTO

Once you become familiar with BASIC, it will be second nature to avoid using these and other reserved words as variable names.

A variable name *cannot* begin with a number. For example, *1A* is *not* a legal variable name. If you attempt to use a variable name that begins with a number, BASIC provides an error message.

At any given moment, a variable has a particular value. For example, the variable *A* might have the value 5 while B might have the value -2.137845. One method for changing the value of a variable is through use of the **LET** statement. The statement

```
10 LET A = 7
```

sets the value of *A* equal to 7. Any previous value of *A* is erased.

Once the value of a variable has been set, the variable may be used throughout the program. The computer inserts the appropriate value wherever the variable occurs. For instance, if *A* has the value 7, then the expression

$A + 5$

is evaluated as $7 + 5$ or 12. The expression

$3*A - 10$

is evaluated as $3*7 - 10 = 21 - 10 = 11$. The expression $2*A^2$ is evaluated as

$2*7^2 = 2*49 = 98$

TEST YOUR UNDERSTANDING 1 (answer on page 97)

Suppose that A has the value 4 and B has the value 3. What is the value of the expression $A^2/2*B^2$?

Note the following important fact:

> **If you do not specify a value for a variable,**
> **BASIC assigns it the value zero.**

Three Shortcuts

1. The word *LET* is optional. For example, the statement
    ```
    10 LET A=5
    ```
    may be abbreviated as:
    ```
    10 A=5
    ```

2. Several statements may be included on one line. To do so, just separate the various statements by colons. In particular, a single line may be used to assign values to several variables. For instance, the instruction

    `100 LET C = 18: LET D = 23: LET E = 2.718`

    assigns *C* the value *18*, *D* the value *23*, and *E* the value *2.718*. Using shortcut 1 above, you may write this instruction in the simpler form

    `100 C=18:D=23:E=2.718`

3. You may use statements that extend beyond a single line. This is especially useful when assigning values to many variables as in shortcut 2 above. When you reach the end of the physical line (40 or 80 characters wide) just keep on typing. Press ENTER when you are finished the material to be included with the current line number. An extended line may contain as many as 255 characters. When an extended line reaches 255 characters, BASIC automatically terminates it just as if you had pressed ENTER.

Variables in PRINT Statements

Variables also may be used in PRINT statements. For example, the statement

`10 PRINT A`

causes the computer to print the current value of *A* (in the first print zone, of course). The statement

`20 PRINT A,B,C`

results in printing the current values of *A*, *B*, and *C* in print zones 1, 2 and 3, respectively.

TEST YOUR UNDERSTANDING 2 (answer on page 97)
Suppose that A has the value 5. What is the result of the instruction

`10 PRINT A,A^2,2*A^2`

Example 1.   Consider the three numbers 5.71, 3.23, and 4.05. Calculate their sum, their product, and the sum of their squares (i.e., the sum of their second powers; such a sum is often used in statistics).

Solution.   Introduce the variables *A*, *B*, and *C* and set them equal, respectively, to the three numbers. Then compute the desired quantities:

```
10 LET A = 5.71: B = 3.23: C = 4.05
20 PRINT "THE SUM IS",, A+B+C
30 PRINT "THE PRODUCT IS", A*B*C
40 PRINT "THE SUM OF SQUARES IS", A^2+B^2+C^2
50 END
```

TEST YOUR UNDERSTANDING 3 (answer on page 97)
Consider the numbers 101, 102, 103, 104, 105, and 106. Write a program that calculates the product of the first two, the first three, the first four, the first five, and then all six numbers.

   The following mental imagery is often helpful in understanding how BASIC handles variables. When BASIC first encounters a variable, say A, it sets up a box (actually a memory location) that it labels "A". (See Figure 5-3.) It stores the current value of A in this box. When you request a change in the value of A, the computer throws out the current contents of the box and inserts the new value.
   Note that the value of a variable need not remain the same throughout a program. At any point in the program, you may change the value of a variable (with a LET statement, for example). If a program is called on to evaluate an expression involving a variable, it always uses the current value of the variable, ignoring any previous values the variable may have had at earlier points in the program.

TEST YOUR UNDERSTANDING 4 (answer on page 97)
Suppose that a loan for $5,000 has an interest rate of 1.5 percent on the unpaid balance at the end of each month. Write a program to calculate the interest at the end of the first month. Suppose that at the end of the first month, you make a payment of $150 (after the interest is added). Design your program to calculate the balance after the payment. (Begin by letting B = the loan balance, I = the interest, and P = the payment. After the payment, the new balance is B+I-P.)

Example 2.   What will be the output of the following computer program?

```
10 LET A = 10: B = 20
20 LET A = 5
```

Figure 5-3.   **The variable A.**

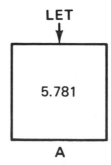

LET

5.781

A

```
30 PRINT A + B + C, A*B*C
40 END
```

Solution.   Note that no value for *C* is specified, so *C* is equal to zero. Also note that the value of *A* initially is set to 10. However, in line 20, this value is changed to 5. So in line 30, *A, B,* and *C* have the respective values 5, 20, and 0. Therefore, the output will be

```
25                    0
```

To the computer, the statement

```
LET A =
```

means that the current value of *A* is to be replaced with whatever appears to the right of the equal sign. Therefore, if you write

```
LET A = A + 1
```

you are asking the computer to replace the current value of *A* with *A + 1*. So if the current value of *A* is 4, the value of *A* after performing the instruction is 4 + 1, or 5.

TEST YOUR UNDERSTANDING 5 (answer on page 97)
What is the output of the following program?

```
10 LET A = 5.3
20 LET A = A+1
30 LET A = 2*A
40 LET A = A+B
50 PRINT A
60 END
```

The following example provides an interesting application of variable assignment and the arithmetic operations \ and *mod*.

The variables you have been using are called **single-precision numeric variables**, which are capable of holding up to seven significant digits of information. (Later on, I'll talk about double-precision numeric variables, which can hold more than seven significant digits.) If you set a single-precision variable equal to a number with more than seven significant digits, BASIC automatically rounds the number to seven significant digits. Moreover, if displaying the value of a number requires more than seven digits due to zeros before or after the decimal place, BASIC automatically shifts to scientific notation. For example, the statement

```
PRINT 123456789
```

produces the display

```
1.234568E+08
```

Note that the initial seven digits are obtained by rounding the given 10 digits. Scientific notation is used because the rounded number, namely 123456800, requires more than seven digits to display.

String Variables

So far, all of the variables discussed have represented numeric values. However, BASIC also allows variables to assume string constants (sequences of characters) as values. The variables for doing this are called **string variables.** They are denoted by a variable name followed by a dollar sign ($). Thus, *A$*, *B1$*, and *ZZ$* are all valid names of string variables. To assign a value to a string variable, use the LET statement with the desired value inserted in quotation marks after the equal sign. To set *A$* equal to the string *"Balance Sheet"*, use the statement

```
LET A$ = "Balance Sheet"
```

You may print the value of a string variable just as you print the value of a numeric variable. For example, if *A$* has the value just assigned, the statement

```
PRINT A$
```

results in the screen output

```
Balance Sheet
```

Example 3.   What will be the output of the following program:

```
10 LET A$ = "MONTHLY RECEIPTS":B$ = "MONTHLY EXPENSES"
20 LET A = 20373.1: B = 17584.31
30 PRINT A$,B$
40 PRINT A,,B
50 END
```

Solution.   Line 30 prints the values of the two string variables *A$* and *B$*, namely, *"RECEIPTS"* and *"EXPENSES"*, at the beginning of two print zones. Line 40 displays the values of *A* and *B*. Here is the output of the program:

```
RECEIPTS        EXPENSES
 20373.10        17584.31
```

Note that we have used the variables *A* and *A$* (as well as *B* and *B$*) in the same program. The variables *A* and *A$* are considered *different* by the computer. One further comment about spacing: note that the numbers do not exactly align with the headings, but are offset by one space. This is because BASIC allows room for a sign (+ or -) in front of a number. In the case of positive numbers, the sign is left out, but the space remains.

The SWAP Statement

Suppose that your program involves the two variables *A* and *B* and that you wish to reassign the values of these variables so that *A* assumes the value of *B*, and *B* the value of *A*. This may be accomplished using the BASIC statement

```
10 SWAP A, B
```

For example, if *A* currently has the value 1.8 and *B* the value 7.5, then after the above statement is executed, *A* will have the value 7.5 and *B* the value 1.8.

Note that SWAP also may be used to exchange the values of two string variables, as in the statement

```
20 SWAP A$, B$
```

However, you may never SWAP values between a string variable and a numeric variable. BASIC will report an error if you try this.

TEST YOUR UNDERSTANDING 6 (answer on page 97)

Write a BASIC program to exchange the values of the variables A and B without using the SWAP statement. (It's tricky. That's why BASIC includes the SWAP statement.)

Remarks in Programs

It is very convenient to explain programs using remarks. For one thing, remarks make programs easier to be read by a human being. Remarks also assist in finding errors and making modifications in a program. To insert a remark in a program, you may use the **REM** statement. For example, consider the line

```
520 REM X DENOTES THE STARSHIP POSITION
```

Since the line starts with *REM,* it is ignored during program execution. As a substitute for *REM,* you may use an apostrophe, as in the following example:

```
1040 ' Y IS THE LASER FORCE
```

To insert a remark on the same line as a program statement, use a colon followed by an apostrophe (or *REM*), as in this example:

```
10 LET A = PI*R^2 : ' A IS THE AREA, R IS THE RADIUS
```

Note, however, that everything after an apostrophe is ignored. Therefore, you cannot put an instruction after a remark. In the line

```
20 LET B=A^2: 'B is the area: C=B+8
```

the instruction C = B + 8 will be ignored.

The importance of remarks cannot be overemphasized. In writing BASIC programs, it is all too easy to write programs that no one (you included) can decipher. You should aim at writing programs that can be read like text. And the most significant step in this direction is to include many remarks in your programs. In what follows, we will be generous in our use of remarks, not only to make the programs easier to read, but also to set an example of good programming style.

TEST YOUR UNDERSTANDING 7 (answer on page 97)

What is the result of the following program line?

```
10 LET A=7:B$="COST":C$="TOTAL":PRINT C$,B$,"=",A
```

Example 4.   Write a program to convert *CHANGE* cents into an equivalent number of quarters, dimes, nickels, and pennies.

Solution.   Integer division may be used to compute change in terms of the number of quarters, dimes, nickels, and pennies. Indeed, suppose that change of *CHANGE* cents is due. The number of quarters in this amount is

```
CHANGE \ 25
```

Moreover, the amount left after subtracting the equivalent of the quarters is

```
CHANGE MOD 25
```

Integer dividing this amount by 10 gives the number of dimes and performing MOD 10 gives the amount left for conversion to smaller coins, and so forth. Here is the program.

```
10 '****************************************
20 'This program computes the change in
30 ' terms of dollar bills and coins due
40 ' if the total is CHANGE cents.
50 '****************************************
60 INPUT "HOW MUCH CHANGE IS DUE";CHANGE
70 QUARTERS = CHANGE \ 25
80 CHANGE = CHANGE MOD 25
90 DIMES = CHANGE \10
100 CHANGE = CHANGE MOD 10
110 NICKELS = CHANGE \ 5
120 CHANGE = CHANGE MOD 5
130 PENNIES = CHANGE
140 PRINT CHANGE;"CENTS EQUALS"
150 PRINT QUARTERS;"QUARTERS"
160 PRINT DIMES;"DIMES"
170 PRINT NICKELS;"NICKELS"
180 PRINT PENNIES;"PENNIES"
190 END
```

Using a Printer

In writing programs and analyzing their output, it is often easier to rely on written output rather than output on the screen. In computer terminology, written output is called **hard copy** and may be provided by a wide variety of printers, ranging from a dot-matrix printer costing only a few hundred dollars to a daisy-wheel printer costing several thousand dollars. As you begin to make serious use of your computer, you will find it difficult to do without hard copy. Indeed, writing programs is much easier if you can consult a hard copy listing of your program at various stages of program development. (One reason is that in printed output you are not confined to looking at your program in 25-line ''snapshots.'') Also, you will want to use the printer to produce output of programs, ranging from tables of numeric data to address lists and text files.

You may produce hard copy on your printer by using the BASIC statement **LPRINT**. For example, the statement

```
10 LPRINT A,A$
```

prints the current values of A and $A\$$ on the printer, in print zones 1 and 2. (As is the case with the screen, BASIC divides the printer line into print zones that are 14 columns wide.) Moreover, the statement

```
20 LPRINT "Customer","Credit Limit","Most Recent Pchs"
```

results in printing three headings in the first three print zones, namely:

```
Customer        Credit Limit    Most Recent Pchs
```

Printing on the printer proceeds very much like printing on the screen. It is important to realize, however, that in order to print on both the screen and the printer, it is necessary to use *both* statements PRINT and LPRINT. For example, to print the values of A and $A\$$ on both the screen and the printer, we must give two instructions, as follows:

```
10 PRINT A,A$
20 LPRINT A,A$
```

ANSWERS TO TEST YOUR UNDERSTANDINGS 1, 2, 3, 4, 5, 6, and 7

1: 72

2: It prints the display:

```
52550
```

3:
```
10 LET A=101:B=102:C=103:D=104:E=105:F=106
20 PRINT A*B
30 PRINT A*B*C
40 PRINT A*B*C*D
```

```
50 PRINT A*B*C*D*E
60 PRINT A*B*C*D*E*F
70 END
```

4:
```
10 LET B = 5000: I = .015: P = 150.00
20 IN = I*B
30 PRINT "INTEREST EQUALS", IN
40 B = B+IN
50 PRINT " BALANCE WITH INTEREST EQUALS", B
60 B = B - P
70 PRINT "BALANCE AFTER PAYMENT EQUALS", B
80 END
```

5:    12.6

6:
```
10 TEMPORARY=A
20 A=B
30 B=TEMPORARY
```

7:    It creates the display

```
TOTAL COST= 7
```

5.7   Some BASIC Commands

So far, most of our attention has been focused on learning statements to insert **inside** programs. Now let's learn a few of the commands available for **manipulating** programs and the computer. The **NEW** command, previously discussed, is in this category. Remember the following facts about BASIC commands.

BASIC Commands

1. Commands are typed *without* using a line number.
2. You must press the ENTER key after typing a command.
3. A command may be given whenever the computer is in the command mode. (Recall that whenever the computer enters the command mode, it displays the *Ok* message. The computer remains in the command mode until a *RUN* command is given.)
4. The computer executes commands as soon as they are received.

Listing a Program

To obtain a list of all program lines of the current program in RAM, type the command

```
LIST<ENTER>
```

For example, suppose RAM contains the following program:

```
10 PRINT 5+7,5-7
20 PRINT 5*7,5/7
30 END
```

(This program may or may not be currently displayed on the screen.) If you type *LIST,* then the above three instruction lines are displayed, followed by the *Ok* message.

In developing a program, you will often find that it is necessary to add program lines to sections of the program already written. This requires you to input lines in nonconsecutive order. Also, it may be necessary to correct lines already input. In either event, the screen often will not indicate the current version of the program. Typing *LIST* every so often will assist in keeping track of what has been changed. *LIST*ing is particularly helpful in checking a program or determining why a program won't run.

Note that you may display up to 25 lines of text on the screen at one time. This means you can display only 23 program statements at one time. (The *Ok* prompt takes one line, as does the cursor.) Therefore, it is often necessary to list only selected program lines rather than the entire program. To *LIST* only those statements with line numbers from 1 to 20, use the command

```
LIST 1-20 <ENTER>
```

In a similar fashion, list any collection of consecutive program lines.

There are several other variations of the LIST command. To list the program lines from the beginning of the program to line 75, use the command

```
LIST  -75 <ENTER>
```

Similarly, to list the program lines from 100 to the end of the program, use the command

```
LIST 100- <ENTER>
```

To list line 100, use the command

```
LIST 100 <ENTER>
```

TEST YOUR UNDERSTANDING 1 (answers on page 104)
Write a command to:

    a.   List line 200

    b.   List lines 300 to 330

    c.   List lines 300 to the end

Test these commands with a program.

Helpful Shortcut

If you press function key F1 and then ENTER, IBM PC BASIC displays a listing of the current program.

Printed Listings

You will find that it is difficult to write a long program relying only on screen listings. For more complex programs, a printed listing is essential. You may generate such a listing using your printer. To list the program currently in RAM, type

```
LLIST <ENTER>
```

All the variations of the LIST command also apply to the **LLIST** command. For example, you may list only those lines with line numbers in a certain range, lines from the beginning of the program to a given line number, and so forth.

Deleting Program Lines

When typing a program or revising an existing program, it is often necessary to delete lines that are already part of the program. One simple way is to type the line number followed by ENTER. For example, typing

```
275 <ENTER>
```

deletes line 275. The **DELETE** command may also be used for the same purpose. For example, you may delete line 275 using the command

```
DELETE 275 <ENTER>
```

The DELETE command has a number of variations which make it quite flexible. For example, to delete lines 200 to 500 inclusive, use the command

```
DELETE 200-500 <ENTER>
```

To delete all lines from the beginning of the program to 350, inclusive, use the command

```
DELETE  -350 <ENTER>
```

TEST YOUR UNDERSTANDING 2 (answers on page 104)

What is wrong with the following commands?

   a.   `DELETE -450`

   b.   `LIST 450-`

   c.   `DELETE 300-200`

Saving a Program

Diskette or Hard Disk.   Once you have typed a program into RAM, you may save a copy on diskette or hard disk. At any future time, you may read the saved copy back into RAM. At that point, you may re-execute the program, modify it, or add to it. For the sake of concreteness, suppose that the following program is in RAM:

```
10 PRINT 5+7
20 END
```

Program Names.   In order to save a program, you must first assign the program a name. A program name is just a filename so it may have up to eight characters, followed by a period and an extension having as many as three characters. For example:

```
ACCOUNTING1 , GAMES.JOE , STORY.003
```

The first program name is equivalent to

```
ACCOUNTI.NG1
```

If you do not specify an extension in a program name, BASIC automatically adds the extension .BAS.

Saving Programs.   Suppose that you choose the name *RETAIN* for your program. You may save this program on the diskette in either disk drive. To save *RETAIN* on drive *B:,* for example, use the command

```
SAVE "B:RETAIN"
```

This program will be saved under the name *RETAIN.BAS*. When the computer finishes writing a copy of the program onto the designated diskette, it will display the *Ok* prompt. Saving a program does not alter the copy of the program in RAM.

Cassette.   The name of a program on cassette is limited to eight characters with no extension. To save the program *"RETAIN"* on cassette, use the command

```
SAVE "CAS1:RETAIN"
```

If your system does not have a diskette drive, omit the portion *CAS1:*.

Helpful Shortcut

To save a program, press function key F4. BASIC will display

```
SAVE "
```

You may then fill in the program name and press ENTER.

Recalling a Program

To read a program from diskette into RAM, use the **LOAD** command. For example, to read *RETAIN* from the diskette in drive *B:,* use the command

```
LOAD "B:RETAIN"
```

To recall the program *"RETAIN"* from cassette, you must position the tape at the beginning (or at least at a position so that the cassette recorder may reach the program only by going in the forward direction) and use the command

```
LOAD "CAS1:RETAIN"
```

If your system does not have a diskette drive, omit the portion *CAS1:*.

Try the above sequence of commands using the given program. After saving the program, erase the program from RAM (by typing *NEW*). Then load the program. Just to check that the program has indeed been retrieved, *LIST* it.

Helpful Shortcut

To load a program, press function key F3. BASIC will display

```
LOAD "
```

You may then fill in the program name and press ENTER.

Erasing a Program From Diskette

You may erase a program from diskette using the **KILL** command. To use this command, you must recognize that if you specified no extension in your program name when you saved it, then BASIC automatically added extension .BAS. For example, the program *RETAIN* is actually stored under the name *RETAIN.BAS*. To erase this program, use the command

```
KILL "B:RETAIN.BAS"
```

The only way to erase a program from cassette is to record over it.

Manipulating Line Numbers

BASIC provides several commands that can ease your burden in dealing with line numbers.

The **AUTO** command may be used to automatically generate line numbers. To use this feature, type

```
AUTO
```

and press ENTER. BASIC will generate line numbers 10, 20, 30, 40, ... A line number will be displayed and the cursor moved to the second space after the line number. In response, type the corresponding program line. As usual, end the line by pressing ENTER. The computer will then automatically display the next line number.

To disable the AUTO feature, simultaneously press the Ctrl and Break keys. The BASIC prompt will then be displayed.

You may have noticed that we always use line numbers that are multiples of 10. There is a good reason for this seeming waste of line numbers. It is often necessary to add instructions between program lines. Our numbering scheme leaves room for up to nine such additions. (In between lines 40 and 50, for instance, you can add instruction lines 41, 42, . . . , 49.)

There are several useful variations of the AUTO command. You may start the automatic line number generation from any point. For example, to generate the line numbers

```
55, 65, 75, 85, ... ,
```

use the command

```
AUTO 55
```

You may also adjust the spacing between line numbers. For example, to generate the sequence of line numbers

```
38, 43, 48, 53, 58, ...,
```

which begins with 38 and has a spacing sequence of 5, just use the command

```
AUTO 38,5
```

BASIC also provides for automatic renumbering of lines. This is helpful, for example, when it is necessary to **MERGE** two programs whose line numbers overlap. The command

```
RENUM
```

causes BASIC to renumber all line numbers. The renumbered program will start with line 10 and use a spacing of 10. As with AUTO, the **RENUM** command has several useful variations. To renumber a program so that the line numbers begin with 1000, use the command

```
RENUM 1000
```

Renumbering may be restricted to a portion of the current program. To renumber lines 200 onward with the new line numbers beginning with 1000, use the command

```
RENUM 1000,200
```

All lines with numbers below 200 are not renumbered. You may even vary the spacing of the renumbered lines. To renumber lines 200 onward with the new line numbers beginning with 1000 and having a spacing sequence of 100, use the command

```
RENUM 1000,200,100
```

To summarize, the general form of the RENUM command is

```
RENUM <new line> <,old line> <,increment>
```

ANSWERS TO TEST YOUR UNDERSTANDINGS 1 and 2

1: a.   `LIST 200`
    b.   `LIST 300-330`
    c.   `LIST 300-`

2: a.   Nothing wrong.
    b.   Nothing wrong.
    c.   The lower line number must come first. The command should read
         `DELETE 200-300`

5.8   Some Programming Tips

Writing programs in BASIC is not difficult. However, it does require a certain amount of care and meticulous attention to detail. Each person must develop an individual programming style.

Here are a few tips that may help you over some of the rough spots of writing those first few programs.

Programming Tips

1.   Carefully think your program through. Break up the computation into steps. Describe each step in clear English. (If you can't tell yourself what you want the computer to do, it is unlikely that you can tell the computer.)

2.   Write a set of instructions corresponding to each step. Check your instructions carefully, with an eagle eye for misspellings, missing parentheses, and other errors.

3.   Pepper your work with remarks. Next week (or next month), you may wish to modify your program. It's embarrassing not to be able to figure out how your own program works!

4.   Type your program so that you can read it like a story. (More on how to do this in Chapter 6.)

5. Work through your program by hand, pretending that you are the computer. Don't rush. Go through your program one step at a time and check that it does what you want it to do.

6. Have you given all variables the values you want? Remember, if you do not specify the value of a variable, BASIC automatically assigns it the value zero. This may not be the value you intend!

In the upcoming chapters, we will not only teach you how to program in BASIC, but also encourage you to develop good programming habits and a useful programming style. In the process, we will add to the above list of programming tips.

5.9   Using the BASIC Editor

Suppose that you discover a program line with an error in it. How can you correct it? Up to now, the only way was to retype the line. There is a much better way. The IBM PC BASIC has a powerful **full-screen editor.** This editor allows you to add, delete, or change text in existing program lines. This section is designed to teach you to use the editor.

The editing process (the process of changing or correcting characters already typed) consists of three steps:

1. Indicate the location of the change.

2. Input the change.

3. Send the change to the computer by using the ENTER key.

These steps use a number of special editing keys. Most of these keys are found on the right side of the keyboard.

The best way to understand the editing process is to work through several examples. If at all possible, follow these examples by typing them out on your keyboard. Suppose that you have typed the following program lines:

```
10 PRIMT X,Y,Z
20 IF A = 5 THN 50 ELSE 30
—
```

The third line indicates the cursor position. There are two spelling errors: *PRIMT* and *THN*. (If the computer had any common sense, it would have known what you meant.) In addition, suppose that you wish to change X, Y, and Z in the first line to read *A, X, Y, Z*. Finally, suppose you wish to delete the *ELSE 30* on the second line. Let's use the editing process to correct them. The first step is to position the cursor at the first character to be corrected. To do this, use the various keys on the numeric keypad which move the cursor like this:

↑ Cursor up one line

↓ Cursor down one line

← Cursor left one character

→ Cursor right one character

(There are other cursor motion keys, but let's study only these for now.) To correct the *PRIMT* error, position the cursor at the *M*. To do this, we first hit the cursor up key twice. This moves the cursor up two lines. The display now looks like this:

```
10 PRIMT X,Y,Z
20 IF A = 5 THN 50 ELSE 30
```

Next we hit the cursor right key six times to move the cursor to the right six spaces. (Note that the space between *0* and *P* counts.) The display now looks like this:

```
10 PRIMT X,Y,Z
20 IF A = 5 THN 50 ELSE 30
```

We have now accomplished step 1: the cursor is at the character to be corrected. Now we execute step 2: we type in the change. In this case, we type *N*. Note that the *N* replaces the *M*. Here is the display:

```
10 PRINT X,Y,Z
20 IF A = 5 THN 50 ELSE 30
```

The first error has now been corrected. Note, however, that the correction has not yet been sent to the computer via the ENTER key. We could do so at this point, but it wouldn't make much sense since there is another error to correct on the same line. Let's tend to that error now. To do so, we must insert the characters *A* and *,* before the *X*. Move the cursor two spaces to the right. Here is the display:

```
10 PRINT X,Y,Z
20 IF A = 5 THN 50 ELSE 30
```

To insert text at the cursor position, we hit the Ins key and type the material to be inserted: *A,*. The Ins key puts the computer in **insert mode.** In this mode, typed text is inserted at the current position and all other text moves to the right. Here is the current display:

```
10 PRINT A,X,Y,Z
20 IF A = 5 THN 50 ELSE 30
```

Since we have finished the insertion, we cancel the insert mode. This may be done in several ways. One method is to press the Ins key again. This allows us to continue to make further corrections on the same line. Another method (in this case the preferred one) is to press the ENTER key. This cancels the insert mode and sends the corrected line to the computer. Note that the cursor may be in any position on the line when the ENTER command is given. Here is the display after pressing ENTER:

```
10 PRINT A,X,Y,Z
20 IF A = 5 THN 50 ELSE 30
```

Note that the cursor is now at the first character of line 20. We correct the misspelling of *THEN* by moving the cursor to the *N* (14 spaces to the right), pressing Ins followed by *E,* followed by Ins. Here is how the display looks now:

```
10 PRINT A,X,Y,Z
20 IF A = 5 THEN 50 ELSE 30
```

The final correction is to delete *ELSE 30*. This is done using the Del key. First we position the cursor on the *E* in *ELSE*. Then we hit the Del key seven times. Each repetition of the Del key deletes the character at the current cursor position and moves the remaining text to the left. For example, after hitting Del the first time, the display looks like this:

```
10 PRINT A,X,Y,Z
20 IF A = 5 THEN 50 LSE 30
```

After seven repetitions of the Del key, the display looks like this:

```
10 PRINT A,X,Y,Z
20 IF A = 5 THEN 50 _
```

The corrections are now complete. We send the line to the computer via the ENTER key.

The above example illustrates various editing features of the IBM PC. We may use the editing keys in the same way to alter any line on the screen. If you wish to alter a program line that is not currently on the screen, you may display the desired line using the LIST command. Editing then takes place as shown.

There are a number of other keys that make editing faster. For example, to speed up cursor movement, we have the following keys and key combinations:

- **Home** This key moves the cursor to the upper left corner of the screen (the so-called "home" position).

- **Ctrl-Home** This key combination clears the screen and brings the cursor to the home position.

- **End** This key moves the cursor to the end of the current line.

- **Ctrl-End** This key combination erases from the current cursor position to the end of the line.

- **Ctrl-Cursor Right** This key combination moves the cursor to the space to the right of the beginning of the next word. (Think of a word as any sequence of characters not containing spaces. This is not exactly correct, but is close enough for practical purposes.)

- **Ctrl-Cursor Left**   This key combination moves the cursor to the space to the left of the beginning of the next word.
- **End**   This key moves the cursor to the end of the current line.
- **Ctrl-Break**   This key combination cancels all editing changes in the current line.

IMPORTANT NOTE: Editing changes occur only in the copy of the program in RAM. In order for changes to be reflected in copies of the program on cassette or diskette, it is necessary to save the edited copy of the program. The moral:

AFTER MAKING CORRECTIONS, SAVE YOUR PROGRAM!

6

Controlling the Flow of Your Program

6.0   Chapter Objectives

IN THIS CHAPTER, WE DISCUSS statements that can be used to control the order of statement execution within a BASIC program. In particular, we discuss:

- Doing repetitive operations (loops).

- Letting your computer make decisions (conditional statements).

- Inputting information to a program while it is running.

In addition, we discuss problem-solving using BASIC programs and how to structure solutions to problems so that they may be easily programmed. As one structuue, we discuss subroutines.

6.1   Doing Repetitive Operations

Suppose that we wish to solve 50 similar multiplication problems. It is certainly possible to type in the 50 problems one at a time and let the computer solve them. However, this is a very clumsy way to proceed. Suppose that instead of 50 problems there were 500, or even 5000. Typing the problems one at a time is not practical. If, however, we can describe to the computer the entire class of problems we want solved, then we can instruct the computer to solve them using only a few BASIC statements. Let us consider a concrete problem. Suppose that we wish to calculate the quantities

$1^2, 2^2, 3^2, \ldots, 10^2$

That is, we wish to calculate a table of squares of integers from 1 to 10. This calculation can be described to the computer as calculating N^2, where the variable N is allowed to assume, one at a time, each of the values 1,2,3,...,10. Here is a sequence of BASIC statements that accomplishes the calculations:

```
1  ' ***********************************
2  ' This program lists the squares of
3  '    all the numbers from 1 to 10
4  ' ***********************************
10 FOR N=1 TO 10
20    PRINT N^2
30 NEXT N
40 END
```

The sequence of statements 10,20,30 is called a **loop**. When the computer encounters the FOR statement, it sets N equal to 1 and continues executing the statements. Statement 20 calls for printing N^2. Since N is equal to 1, we have $N^2 = 1^2 = 1$. So the computer prints a 1. After that, the computer executes statement 30, which calls for the next N. This instructs the computer to return to the FOR statement in 10, increase N to 2, and to repeat instructions 20 and 30. This time, $N^2 = 2^2 = 4$. Line 20 then prints a 4. Line 30 says go back to line 10 and increase N to 3 and so forth. Lines 10, 20, and 30 are repeated 10 times! After the computer executes lines 10, 20, and 30 with $N = 10$, it will leave the loop and execute line 40.

Type in the above program and give the RUN command. The output will look like this:

```
RUN
 1
 4
 9
 16
 25
 36
 49
 64
 81
 100
Ok
```

The variable N is called the **loop variable**. It may be used inside the loop just like you would any other variable. For example, it may be used in algebraic calculations and PRINT statements.

TEST YOUR UNDERSTANDING 1 (answers on page 119)

    a.   Devise a loop allowing N to assume the values 3 to 77.

    b.   Write a program that calculates N^2 for N = 3 to 77.

Making Loops More Readable

Note that we have indented the textual portion of line 20. This allows us to clearly see the beginning and end of the loop. It is good programming practice to always indent loops in this way since it increases program readability. The **TAB** key (the key with the two symbols ⊢ and ⊣) may be used to indent. BASIC sets up tab stops every five spaces. These are just like the tab stops on a typewriter. Whenever you press the TAB key, the cursor moves over to the next tab stop.

Let's modify the above program to include on each line of output not only N^2, but also the value of N. To make the table easier to read, let's also add two column headings. The new program reads:

```
10 ' ******************************************
20 ' This program prints all the numbers from
30 '    1 to 10 along with their squares
40 ' ******************************************
50 PRINT " N","N^2"
60 FOR N=1 TO 10
70    PRINT N,N^2
80 NEXT N
90 END
```

The output now looks like this:

```
N                    N^2
1                     1
2                     4
3                     9
4                    16
5                    25
6                    36
7                    49
8                    64
9                    81
10                  100
Ok
```

TEST YOUR UNDERSTANDING 2 (answer on page 119)
What happens if we change the number of line 10 to 25?

Let us now illustrate some of the many uses loops have by means of some examples.

Example 1.   Write a BASIC program to calculate $1+2+3+\ldots+100$.

Solution.   Let us use a variable S (for sum) to contain the sum. Let us start S at 0 and use a loop to successively add to S the numbers $1,2,3,\ldots,100$. Here is the program.

```
1 '*****************************
2 ' This program calculates the
3 ' sum of all the integers from
4 ' 1 to 100.
5 '*****************************
10 LET S = 0
```

```
20 FOR N = 1 TO 100
30   LET S = S + N
40 NEXT  N
50 PRINT S
60 END
```

When we enter the loop the first time, $S = 0$ and $N = 1$. Line 30 then replaces S by $S + N$, or $0 + 1$. Line 40 sends us back to line 20, where the value of N is now set equal to 2. In line 30, S (which is now $0 + 1$) is replaced by $S + N$, or $0 + 1 + 2$. Line 40 now sends us back to line 20, where N is now set equal to 3. Line 30 then sets S equal to $0 + 1 + 2 + 3$. Finally, on the 100th time through the loop, S is replaced by $0 + 1 + 2 + \ldots + 100$, the desired sum. If we run the program, we derive the output

```
 5050
Ok
```

TEST YOUR UNDERSTANDING 3 (answer on page 119)
Write a BASIC program to calculate $101 + 102 + \ldots + 110$.

TEST YOUR UNDERSTANDING 4 (answer on page 119)
Write a BASIC program to calculate and display the numbers $2, 2^2, 2^3, \ldots, 2^{20}$.

Example 2.   Write a program to calculate this sum:

$$1 \times 2 + 2 \times 3 + 3 \times 4 + \ldots + 49 \times 50$$

Solution.   We let the sum be contained in the variable S, as we did in the preceding example. The quantities to be added are just the numbers $N*(N+1)$ for $N = 1, 2, 3, \ldots, 49$. Here is our program:

```
10 ' *********************************
20 ' This program calculates the sum:
30 '    1x2 + 2x3 + 3x4 + ... + 49x50
40 ' *********************************
50 LET S = 0
60 FOR N = 1 TO 49
70   LET S = S + N*(N+1)
80 NEXT N
90 PRINT S
100 END
```

Some Cautions Concerning Loops

Here are two of the errors you are most likely to make in dealing with loops.

1. Every *FOR* statement must have a corresponding *NEXT*. Otherwise, BASIC will halt your program and display the error message

    `FOR without NEXT in line xxxxx`

2. Be sure that the loop variable is not already used with some other meaning. For example, suppose that the loop variable *N* is used before the loop begins. Then the loop will destroy the old value of *N* and there is no way to get it back after the loop is over.

3. Don't modify the loop variable within the loop.

Nested Loops

In many applications, it is necessary to execute a loop within a loop. For example, suppose that we wish to compute the following series of numbers:

```
1^2, 2^2, 3^2,..., 10^2,
101^2, 102^2, 103^2,..., 110^2,
...
...
2001^2, 2002^2, 2003^2,..., 2010^2
```

There are 21 groups of 10 numbers each. Each line may be computed using a loop. For example, the first line may be computed using

```
100 FOR I=1 TO 10
110   PRINT I^2
120 NEXT I
```

The second line may be computed using

```
100 FOR I=1 TO 10
110   PRINT (100+I)^2
120 NEXT I
```

And the last line may be computed using

```
100 FOR I=1 TO 10
110   PRINT (2000+I)^2
120 NEXT I
```

We can compute the desired numbers by repeating essentially the same instructions 21 times. However, it is much easier to do the repetition using a loop. The numbers to be added to *I* range from 0 (which is 0*100) for the first line, to 100 (which is 1*100) for the second line, to 2000 (which is 20*100) for the last line. This suggests that we represent these numbers as *J*100*, where *J* is a loop variable that runs from 0 to 20. We may then compute our desired table of numbers using this program:

```
10 ' ************************************************
20 ' This program displays the following numbers:
30 '     1^2, 2^2, 3^2, . . . , 10^2
```

```
40 '      101^2, 102^2, 103^2, . . . , 110^2
50 '        . . .
60 '        . . .
70 '      2001^2, 2002^2, 2003^2, . . . , 2010^2
80 ' ***********************************************
100 FOR J=0 TO 20
110   FOR I=1 TO 10
120     PRINT (100*J+I)^2;
130   NEXT I
140   PRINT
150 NEXT J
160 END
```

The instructions that are indented one level are repeated 21 times, corresponding to the values $J=0$ through $J=20$. On the first repetition ($J=0$), lines 100-120 print the numbers in the first line; on the second repetition ($J=1$), lines 100-120 print the numbers in the second line, and so forth. Note how the indentations help one to read the program. This is an example of good programming style.

If a loop is contained within a loop, then we say that the loops are **nested**. BASIC allows you to have nesting in as many layers as you wish (a loop within a loop within a loop, and so forth.)

TEST YOUR UNDERSTANDING 5 (answer on page 119)
Write a BASIC program to print the following table of numbers.

```
1  11  21  31
2  12  22  32
   .
   .
   .
9  19  29  39
```

Warning: Nested loops may not "overlap." That is, the following sequence is not allowed:

```
10 FOR J=1 TO 100
20   FOR K=1 TO 50
   .
   .
   .
80 NEXT J
90   NEXT K
```

Rather, the *NEXT K* statement must precede the *NEXT J*, so that the *K* loop is "completely inside" the *J* loop.

Applications of Loops

Example 3.   You borrow $7000 to buy a car. You finance the balance for 36 months at an interest rate of one percent per month. Your monthly payments are $232.50. Write a program to compute the amount of interest each month, the amount of the loan repaid, and the balance owed.

Solution.   Let B denote the balance owed. Initially we have B equal to 7000 dollars. At the end of each month let us compute the interest (I) owed for that month, namely *.01*B*. For example, at the end of the first month, the interest owed is *.01*7000.00 = $70.00*. Let *P = 232.50* to denote the monthly payment, and let *R* denote the amount repaid out of the current payment. Then *R = P - I*. For example, at the end of the first month, the amount of the loan repaid is *232.50 -70.00 = 162.50*. The balance owed may then be calculated as *B - R*. At the end of the first month, the balance owed is *7000.00 - 162.50 = 6837.50*. Here is a program to perform these calculations:

```
10  ' *********************************************
20  ' This program computes the monthly interest,
30  '   amount repaid, and balance owed on a loan
40  ' *********************************************
100 PRINT "MONTH","INTEREST","PAYMENT","BALANCE"
110 LET B = 7000            :'B=initial balance
120 LET P = 232.5           :'P=monthly payment
130 FOR M = 1 TO 36         :'M is month number
140    LET I = .01*B        :'Calculate interest for month
150    LET R = P - I        :'Calculate repayment
160    LET B = B - R        :'Calculate new balance
170    PRINT M,I,R,B        :'Print out data for month
180 NEXT M
190 END
```

Try to run this program. Notice that it runs, but it is pretty useless because the screen cannot contain all of the output. Most of the output goes flying by before you can read it. One method for remedying this situation is to press Ctrl and Num Lock simultaneously as the output scrolls by on the screen. This will pause execution of the program and freeze the contents of the screen. To resume execution and unfreeze the screen, press any key. The output will begin to scroll again. To use this technique requires some manual dexterity. Moreover, it is not possible to guarantee where the scrolling will stop.

TEST YOUR UNDERSTANDING 6

RUN the program of Example 3 and practice freezing the output on the screen. It may take several runs before you are comfortable with the procedure.

Let us now describe another method of adapting the output to our screen size by printing only 12 months of data at one time. This amount of data will fit since the screen contains 24 lines. We will use a second loop to keep track of 12-month periods. The variable for the new loop will be Y (for "years"), and Y will go from 0 to 2. The month variable will be *M* as before, but now *M* will go only from 1 to 12. The month number will now be *12*Y + M* (12 times the number of years plus the number of months). Here is the revised program.

```
1  ' **********************************************
2  ' This program computes the monthly interest,
3  ' amount repaid, and balance owed on a loan.
4  ' The data is displayed 12 months at a time.
5  ' The user types CONT<ENTER> to see the next
6  ' year's display.
7  ' **********************************************
10 LET B=7000
20 LET P =232.50
30 FOR Y = 0 TO 2    :'Y=year number
40    PRINT "MONTH","INTEREST","PAYMENT","BALANCE"
50    FOR M = 1 TO 12 :'Run through the months of year Y
60    LET I = .01*B:'Calculate interest for month
70    LET R = P - I:'Calculate repayment for month
80    LET B = B - R:'Calculate balance for month
90    PRINT 12*Y+M,I,R,B:'Print data for month
100   NEXT M
110 STOP  :' Halts execution
120 CLS   :' Clears Screen
130 NEXT Y:' Goes to next 12 months
140 END
```

This program utilizes several new statements. In line 110, we use the **STOP** statement. This causes the computer to stop execution of the program. The computer remembers where it stops, however, and all values of the variables are preserved. The *STOP* statement also leaves unchanged the contents of the screen. You can take as long as you wish to examine the data on the screen. When you are ready for the program to continue, type *CONT* and press ENTER. The computer will resume where it left off. The first instruction it encounters is in line 120. *CLS* clears the screen. So, after being told to continue, the computer clears the screen and goes on to the next value of *Y* — the next 12 months of data. Here is a copy of the output. The underlined statements are those you type.

MONTH	INTEREST	PAYMENT	BALANCE
1	70	162.5	6837.5
2	68.375	164.125	6673.375
3	66.73375	165.7763	6507.609
4	65.07609	167.4239	6340.185
5	63.40185	169.0982	6171.087
6	61.71086	170.7891	6000.298
7	60.00297	172.497	5827.8
8	58.278	174.222	5653.578
9	56.53578	175.9642	5477.614
10	54.77614	177.7239	5299.89
11	52.9989	179.5011	5120.389
12	51.20389	181.2961	4939.93

```
Break in 100
Ok
CONT
```

MONTH	INTEREST	PAYMENT	BALANCE
13	49.39093	183.1091	4755.984
14	47.55984	184.9402	4571.044
15	45.71044	186.7896	4384.255
16	43.84255	188.6575	4195.597
17	41.95597	190.544	4005.053
18	40.05053	192.4495	3812.603
19	38.12603	194.374	3618.229
20	36.18229	196.3177	3421.912
21	34.21912	198.2809	3223.631
22	32.23631	200.2637	3023.367
23	30.23367	202.2663	2821.101
24	28.21101	204.289	2616.812

```
Break in 100
Ok
CONT
```

MONTH	INTEREST	PAYMENT	BALANCE
25	26.16812	206.33219	2410.48
26	24.1048	208.3952	2202.085
27	22.02085	210.4792	1991.606
28	19.91606	212.584	1779.022
29	17.79022	214.7098	1564.312
30	15.64312	216.8569	1347.455
31	13.47455	219.025	1128.43
32	11.28429	221.2157	907.2138
33	9.072137	223.4279	683.7859
34	6.837859	225.6622	458.1238
35	4.58126	227.9188	230.205
36	2.30205	230.198	

```
7.034302E-03
Break in 100
CONT
Ok
```

Note that the data in the output is carried out to seven figures, even though the problem deals with dollars and cents. We will look at the problem of rounding numbers later. Also note the balance listed at the end of month 36. It is in scientific notation. The -03 indicates that the decimal point is to be moved three places to the left. The number listed is .007034302 or about .70 cents (less than one cent)! The computer shifted to scientific notation since the usual notation (.007034302) requires more than seven digits. The computer made the choice of which form of the number to display.

Using Loops to Create Delays

By using a loop we can create a delay inside the computer. Consider the following sequence of instructions:

```
10 FOR N = 1 TO 3000
20 NEXT N
```

This loop doesn't do anything! However, the computer repeats instructions 10 and 20 three thousand times! This may seem like a lot of work. But not for a computer. To obtain a feel for the speed at which the computer works, you should time this sequence of instructions. Such a loop may be used as a delay. For example, when you wish to keep some data on the screen without stopping the program, just build in a delay. Here is a program that prints two screens of text. A delay is imposed to give a person time to read the first screen.

```
10 ' ******************************************
20 ' This program demonstrates the use of a
30 '      delay loop between pages of text
40 ' ******************************************
50 PRINT "THIS IS A GRAPHICS PROGRAM TO DISPLAY SALES"
60 PRINT "FOR THE YEAR TO DATE"
70 FOR N = 1 TO 5000
80 NEXT N:'Delay Loop
90 CLS
100 PRINT "YOU MUST SUPPLY THE FOLLOWING PARAMETERS:"
110 PRINT "PRODUCT, TERRITORY, SALESPERSON"
120 END
```

Example 4.   Use a loop to produce a blinking display for a security system.

Solution.   Suppose that your security system is tied in with your computer and the system detects that an intruder is in your warehouse. Let us print out the message

```
SECURITY SYSTEM DETECTS INTRUDER - ZONE 2
```

For attention, let us blink this message on and off by alternately printing the message and clearing the screen.

```
10 FOR N = 1 TO 2000
20    PRINT "SECURITY SYSTEM DETECTS INTRUDER - ZONE 2"
30 FOR K = 1 TO 50
40 NEXT K
50    CLS
60 NEXT N
70 END
```

The loop in lines 30-40 is a delay loop to keep the message on the screen a moment. Line 50 turns the message off, but the PRINT statement in line 20 turns it back on. The message will blink 2000 times.

TEST YOUR UNDERSTANDING 7 (answer on page 119)
Write a program that blinks your name on the screen 500 times, leaving your name on the screen for a loop of length 50 each time.

More About Loops

In all of our loop examples, the loop variable increased by one with each repetition of the loop. However, it is possible to have the loop variable change by any amount. For example, the instructions

```
10 FOR N = 1 TO 5000 STEP 2
    •
    •
    •
1000 NEXT N
```

define a loop in which *N* jumps by 2 for each repetition, so *N* assumes the values

```
1,3,5,7,9,...,4999
```

Similarly, using *STEP .5* in the above loop causes N to advance by .5 and assume the values

```
1, 1.5, 2, 2.5, 3, 3.5, 4, 4.5, ... , 5000
```

It is even possible to have a negative step. In this case, the loop variable will run backwards. For example, the instructions

```
10 FOR N = 100 TO 1 STEP -1
    •
    •
    •
100 NEXT N
```

will "count down" from N = 100 to N = 1 one unit at a time. We will give some applications of such instructions in the Exercises.

TEST YOUR UNDERSTANDING 8 (answers on page 119)

Write instructions allowing N to assume the following sequences of values:

   a.   95,96.7,98.4,...,112
   b.   200,199.5,199,...,100

ANSWERS TO TEST YOUR UNDERSTANDINGS 1, 2, 3, 4, 5, 7, and 8

```
1: a.  10 FOR N=3 TO 77        b.  10 FOR N=3 TO 77
           •                       20    PRINT N^2
           •                       30 NEXT N
       100 NEXT N                  40 END
```

2:   The heading

```
N              N^2
```

is printed before each entry of the table.

```
3:  10  S=0
    20  FOR N=101 TO 110
    30      S=S+N
    40  NEXT N
    50  PRINT S
    60  END

4:  10  FOR N=1 TO 20
    20      PRINT 2^N
    30  NEXT N
    40  END

5:  10  FOR J=1 TO 9
    20      FOR I=0 TO 3
    30          PRINT 10*I+J;
    40      NEXT I
    50      PRINT
    60  NEXT J
    70  END

7:  10  FOR N=1 TO 500
    20      PRINT "<YOUR NAME>"
    30      FOR K=1 TO 50
    40      NEXT K
    50      CLS
    60  NEXT N
    70  END

8:  a.  10 FOR N=95 TO 112 STEP 1.7
    b.  20 FOR N=200 TO 100 STEP -.5
```

6.2   Letting Your Computer Make Decisions

One of the principal features that makes computers useful as problem-solving tools is their ability to make decisions. BASIC contains instructions that allow you to ask a question. The computer will determine the answer and take an action, which depends on the answer. Here are some examples of questions that the computer can answer:

IS A GREATER THAN ZERO?

IS A^2 AT LEAST 200?

DOES THE STRING LABEL$ BEGIN WITH A "Z" ?

IS AT LEAST ONE OF THE VARIABLES A, B, OR C NEGATIVE?

Here are two BASIC statements that allow you to ask such questions: The *IF...THEN* statement and the *IF...THEN...ELSE* statement. The *IF...THEN* statement has the form:

```
IF <question> THEN <statement or line number>
```

Here is how this statement works:

1. The "question" part of an *IF...THEN* statement allows you to ask questions like those above.

2. If the answer to the question is *YES*, the program executes the portion of the statement following *THEN*.

    a. If a statement follows *THEN*, this statement is executed.

    b. If a line number follows *THEN*, the program continues execution with this line number.

3. If the answer to the question is *NO*, the program continues with the next program instruction, ignoring the *THEN*.

For example, consider this instruction:

```
500 IF N = 0 THEN PRINT "CALCULATION DONE"
```

The question portion of this instruction is $N=0$; the portion following *THEN* is the statement: *PRINT "CALCULATION DONE"*. When the computer encounters this statement, it first determines if N is equal to zero. If so, it prints *"CALCULATION DONE"* and proceeds with the next instruction after line 500. However, if N is not zero, the program immediately goes to the next instruction line after 500. (It ignores the statement after *THEN*.)

Here is another example:

```
600 IF A^2 < 1 THEN 300
```

When the program reaches this instruction, it examines the value of A^2. If A^2 is less than 1, the program goes to line 300. Otherwise, the program will go on to the next instruction.

The IF...THEN...ELSE Statement

The *IF...THEN...ELSE* statement is similar to an *IF...THEN* statement, but it offers added flexibility in case the answer to the question is *NO*. The form of the *IF...THEN...ELSE* statement is:

```
IF <question> THEN <statement or line number>
    ELSE <statement or line number>
```

This statement works as follows: The computer asks the given question. If the answer is *YES*, the program executes the *THEN* portion; if the answer is *NO*, the program executes the *ELSE* portion.

Here is an example:

```
500 IF N = 0 THEN PRINT "CALCULATION DONE" ELSE 250
```

The computer first determines if N equals 0. If so, it prints *"CALCULATION DONE"*. If N is not equal to 0, the program continues execution at line 250.

Another possibility is for both *THEN* and *ELSE* to be followed by instructions, as in this example:

```
600 IF A + B >= 100 THEN PRINT A + B ELSE PRINT A
```

In executing this instruction, the computer determines whether $A+B$ is greater than or equal to 100. If so, it prints the value of $A+B$; if not, it prints the value of A. In both cases, execution continues with the next instruction after line 600.

After IF, you may insert any expression that the computer may test for truth or falsity. Here are some examples:

$N = 0$

$N > 5$ *(N is greater than 5)*

$N < 12.9$ *(N is less than 12.9)*

$N >= 0$ *(N is greater than or equal to 0)*

$N <= -1$ *(N is less than or equal to -1)*

$N <> 0$ *(N is not equal to 0)*

$A + B <> C$ *(A + B is not equal to C)*

$A\char`\^2 + B\char`\^2 <= C\char`\^2$ *($A^2 + B^2$ is less than equal to C^2)*

You may even combine statements using the words *AND* and *OR*, as in the following examples:

$N = 0$ *OR* $A > B$ *(Either N = 0 or A > B or both)*

$N > M$ *AND* $I = 0$ *(Both N > M and I = 0)*

For clarity, it's advisable to put the individual statements within parentheses. For example, the last two statements would be clearer if written in the form

(N=0) OR (A>B)

(N>M) AND (I=0)

TEST YOUR UNDERSTANDING 1 (answers on page 133)
Write instructions that do the following:

    a.   If A is less than B, then print the value of A plus B; if not, then end.

    b.   If $A^2 + D$ is at least 5000 then go to line 300; if not, go to line 500.

    c.   If N is larger than the sum of I and K, set N equal to the sum of I and K; otherwise, let N equal K.

Important: Note that if the condition of an *IF...THEN* statement is false, then the program goes to the next **line number**. If there are other statements on the same line as the *IF...THEN*, they are executed only if the condition is true. Consider, for example, the following statements:

```
200 IF X>0 THEN X=X+1: GOTO 300
210 X=0
```

If *X* is greater than 0, then *X* is replaced by *X + 1* and the program goes to the next statement, *GOTO 300*. On the other hand, if *X* is not greater than 0, then the program skips the statement *GOTO 300* and proceeds to line 210.

The *IF . . . THEN* and *IF . . . THEN . . . ELSE* statements may be used to interrupt the normal sequence of executing program lines, based on the truth or falsity of some condition. In many applications, however, we will want to perform instructions out of the normal sequence, independent of any conditions. For such applications, we may use the **GOTO** instruction. (This is not a typographical error! There is no space between *GO* and *TO*.) This instruction has the form

```
GOTO < line number >
```

For example, the instruction

```
1000 GOTO 300
```

sends the computer back to line 300 for its next instruction.

The next few examples illustrate some of the uses of the *IF...THEN, IF . . . THEN . . . ELSE*, and *GOTO* statements.

Example 1.   A lumber supply house has a policy that a credit invoice may not exceed $1,000, including a 10 percent processing fee and 5 percent sales tax. A customer orders 150 2x4 studs at $1.99 each, 30 sheets of plywood at $14.00 each, 300 pounds of nails at $1.14 per pound, two double hung insulated windows at $189.75 each. Write a program that prepares an invoice and decides whether the order is over the credit limit.

Solution.   Let's use the variables *A1, A2, A3,* and *A4* to denote, respectively, the numbers of studs, sheets of plywood, pounds of nails, and windows. Let's use the variables *B1, B2, B3,* and *B4* to denote the unit costs of these four items. The cost of the order is then computed as:

```
A1*B1+A2*B2+A3*B3+A4*B4
```

We add 10 percent of this amount to cover processing and form the sum to obtain the total order. Next, we compute 5 percent of the last amount as tax and add it to the total to obtain the total amount due. Finally, we determine if the total amount due is more than $1,000. If it is, we print out the message: *ORDER EXCEEDS $1,000. CREDIT SALE NOT PERMITTED.* Here is our program.

```
10 ' ******************************************
20 ' This program prepares an invoice for a
30 '    lumber purchase and determines whether
40 '    it is within the credit limit
```

```
50  ' ********************************************
60  LET A1=150:A2=30:A3=300:A4=2:      'Assign quantities
70  LET B1=1.99:B2=14:B3=1.14:B4=189.75: 'Assign prices
80  LET T= A1*B1+A2*B2+A3*B3+A4*B4:    'T=total price
90  PRINT "TOTAL ORDER",T
100 LET P = .1*T:                      'P=processing fee
110 PRINT "PROCESSING FEE";P
120 LET TAX = .05*(P+T):               'TAX = tax
130 PRINT "SALES TAX",TAX
140 DUE = T + P + TAX:                 'DUE=Amount due
150 PRINT "AMOUNT DUE", DUE
160 IF DUE > 1000 THEN 170 ELSE 200: 'Order > $1000 ?
170 PRINT "ORDER EXCEEDS $1,000"
180 PRINT "CREDIT SALE NOT PERMITTED"
190 GOTO 210:                          'End program
200 PRINT "CREDIT SALE OK"
210 END
```

Note the decision in line 160. If the amount due exceeds $1,000 then the computer goes to line 170 where it prints out a message denying credit. On the other hand, if the amount due is less than $1,000, the computer is sent to line 200, where credit is approved.

TEST YOUR UNDERSTANDING 2 (answer on page 133)

Suppose that a credit card charges 1.5 percent per month on any unpaid balance up to $500 and 1 percent per month on any excess over $500.

a.   Write a program that computes the service charge and the new balance.

b.   Test your program on the unpaid balances of $1,300 and $275.

TEST YOUR UNDERSTANDING 3 (answer on page 133)

Consider the following sequence of instructions.

```
100 IF A>=5 THEN 200
110 IF A>=4 THEN 300
120 IF A>=3 THEN 400
130 IF A>=2 THEN 500
```

Suppose that the current value of A is 3. List the sequence of line numbers that will be executed.

Example 2.   At $20 per square yard, a family can afford up to 500 square feet of carpet for their dining room. They wish to install the carpet in a circular shape. It has been decided that the radius of the carpet is to be a whole number of feet. What is the radius of the largest carpet they can afford? (The area of a circle of radius R is *pi* times R^2, where *pi* equals approximately 3.14159.)

Solution.   Let us compute the area of the circle of radius 1,2,3,4,... and determine which of the areas are less than 500.

```
10  ' ****************************************
20  ' This program lists the affordable sizes
30  '    of carpet for a certain family
40  ' ****************************************
50  PI = 3.14159
60  R = 1 :                 ' R=radius
70  A = PI*R^2 :            ' A=area
80  'Is A>=500 ?  If so, END. Otherwise, PRINT R.
90  IF A >=  500 THEN 120 ELSE PRINT R
100 LET R = R + 1:          ' Go to next radius
110 GOTO 70:                ' Repeat
120 END
```

Note that line 90 contains an *IF ... THEN ... ELSE* statement. If *A*, as computed in line 70, is 500 or more, then the computer goes to line 120, *END*. If A is less than 500, the computer proceeds to the next line, namely 100. It then prints out the current radius, increases the radius by 1, and goes back to line 70 to repeat the entire procedure. Note that lines 70-80-90-100-110 are repeated until the area becomes at least 500. In effect, this sequence of five instructions forms a loop. However, we did not use a *FOR ... NEXT* instruction because we did not know in advance how many times we wanted to execute the loop. We let the computer decide the stopping point via the *IF ... THEN* instruction.

The WHILE ... WEND Statements

In Section 6.1 of this chapter, we discussed the notion of a loop. In this section, we have discussed decision-making. The **WHILE...WEND** pair of statements combine the two procedures. This statement pair has the form

```
WHILE <expression>
   .
   .
   .
WEND
```

The statements between *WHILE* and *WEND* are repeated so long as *<expression>* is true. Note, however, that the statements between *WHILE* and *WEND* might never be executed. If *<expression>* is initially false, the program skips to the next statement after *WEND*. The *WHILE...WEND* pair is useful in executing loops for which you cannot specify in advance the number of repetitions.

Example 3.   Rewrite the program of Example 2 using the WHILE...WEND pair of statements.

Solution.   Here is the program adaptation.

```
10  ' *****************************************
20  ' This program lists the affordable sizes
30  '    of carpet using a WHILE loop
40  ' *****************************************
100 PI = 3.14159
110 R = 1 :                    ' R=radius
120 WHILE A <= 500
130     PRINT R
140     R = R + 1 :            ' Go to next radius
150     A = PI*R^2 :           ' A=area
160 WEND :                     ' Repeat
170 END
```

Example 4.   An election for state legislature involves two candidates. The returns from the four wards of the town are as follows:

	Ward 1	Ward 2	Ward 3	Ward 4
Mr. Thompson	487	229	1540	1211
Ms. Wilson	1870	438	110	597

Calculate the total number of votes and the percentage achieved by each candidate, and decide who won the election.

Solution.   Let *A1, A2, A3*, and *A4* be the totals for Mr. Thompson in the four wards; let *B1-B4* be the corresponding numbers for Ms. Wilson. Let *TA* and *TB* denote the total votes, respectively, for Mr. Thompson and Ms. Wilson. Here is our program.

```
1   ' *******************************************
2   ' This program computes the percentages
3   ' achieved by each candidate in an election
4   ' and determines the winner.
5   ' *******************************************
10  A1 = 487: A2 = 229: A3 = 1540: A4 = 1211
20  B1 = 1870: B2 = 438: B3 = 110: B4 = 597
30  TA = A1+A2+A3+A4 :       'Total for Thompson
40  TB = B1+B2+B3+B4 :       'Total for Wilson
50  T = TA + TB :            'Total Votes Cast
60  PA = 100*TA/T :          'Percentage for Thompson
70  ' TA/T is the ratio of votes for Thompson.
80  ' Multiply by 100 to convert to a percentage.
90    PB = 100*TB/T :        'Percentage for Wilson
100   A$ = "THOMPSON"
110   B$ = "WILSON"
120 ' Print the percentages of the candidates
130   PRINT "CANDIDATE","VOTES","PERCENTAGE"
140   PRINT A$,TA,PA
150   PRINT B$,TB,PB
160 ' Decide the winner.
170   IF TA > TB THEN PRINT "THOMPSON WINS"
      ELSE IF TA < TB THEN PRINT "WILSON WINS"
          ELSE PRINT "THOMPSON AND WILSON ARE TIED"
180 END
```

Note the logic used for deciding who won. In line 170 we compare the votes *TA* and *TB*. If *TA* is larger, then Thompson is the winner. On the other hand, if *TA* > *TB* is *false*, then we ask whether *TA* is less than *TB*. If so, then Wilson wins. On the other hand, if *TA* < *TB* is also false, then the only remaining possibility is that the two are tied. You may have trouble reading the statement in line 170. If you do, then just note that the portion

```
IF TA < TB THEN PRINT "WILSON WINS"
ELSE PRINT "THOMPSON AND WILSON ARE TIED"
```

is the statement that follows the *ELSE* in the first *IF...THEN...ELSE* statement.

Infinite Loops and Ctrl-Break

As we saw above, it is very convenient to be able to execute a loop without knowing in advance how many times the loop will be executed. However, with this convenience comes a danger. It is perfectly possible to create a loop that will be repeated an infinite number of times! For example, consider this program:

```
10 N = 1
20 PRINT N
30 N = N+1
40 GOTO 20
50 END
```

The variable *N* starts off at 1. We print it and then increase *N* by 1 (to 2), print it, increase *N* by 1 (to 3), print it, and so forth. This program will go on forever! Such programs should clearly be avoided. However, even experienced programmers occasionally create infinite loops. When this happens, there is no need to panic. There is a way to stop the computer. Just press the Ctrl and Break keys simultaneously. (In the following, we will refer to this key combination of keys as Ctrl-Break.) This key sequence interrupts the program currently in progress and returns the computer to the command mode. The computer is then ready to accept a command from the keyboard. Note, however, that any program in RAM is undisturbed.

TEST YOUR UNDERSTANDING 4

Type the above program, RUN it, and stop it using Ctrl-Break. After stopping it, RUN the program again.

The INPUT Statement

It is very convenient to have the computer request information from you while the program is actually running. This can be accomplished via the **INPUT** statement. To see how, consider the statement

```
570 INPUT A
```

When the computer encounters this statement in the course of executing the program, it displays a ? and waits for you to respond by typing the desired value of A (and then pressing the ENTER key). The computer then sets A equal to the numeric value you specified and continues running the program.

You may use an INPUT statement to specify the values of several different variables at one time. These variables may be numeric or string variables. For example, suppose that the computer encounters the statement

```
50 INPUT A,B,C$
```

It will display

```
?
```

You then type in the desired values for *A, B*, and *C$*, in the same order as in the program, and separate them by commas. For example, suppose that you type

```
10.5,11.42,BEARINGS
```

followed by an ENTER. The computer then sets

```
A = 10.5, B = 11.42, C$ = "BEARINGS"
```

If you respond to the above question mark by typing only a single number, 10.5 for example, the computer responds with

```
? Redo from start
?
```

to indicate that you should repeat the input from the beginning. If you attempt to specify a string constant where you should have a numeric constant, the computer responds with the same message:

```
? Redo from start
?
```

and waits for you to repeat the INPUT operation.

It is helpful to include a prompting message that describes the input the computer is expecting. To do so, just put the message in quotation marks after the word INPUT and place a semicolon after the message (before the list of variables to be input). For example, consider the statement

```
175 INPUT "ENTER COMPANY, AMOUNT"; A$, B
```

When the computer encounters this program line, the dialog will be as follows:

```
ENTER COMPANY, AMOUNT? AJAX OFFICE SUPPLIES, 2579.48
```

The underlined portion indicates your response to the prompt. The computer will now assign these values:

```
A$ = "AJAX OFFICE SUPPLIES", B = 2579.48
```

TEST YOUR UNDERSTANDING 5 (answer on page 133)

Write a program that allows you to set variables *A* and *B* to any desired values via an *INPUT* statement. Use the program to set *A* equal to 12 and *B* equal to 17.

The next two examples illustrate the use of the *INPUT* statement, and provide further practice in using the IF ... THEN statement.

Example 5.   You are a teacher compiling semester grades. Suppose there are four grades for each student and that each grade is on the traditional 0 to 100 scale. Write a program that accepts the grades as input, computes the semester average, and assigns grades according to the following scale:

90-100	A
80-89.9	B
70-79.9	C
60-69.9	D
< 60	F

Solution.   We will use an INPUT statement to enter the grades into the computer. Our program will allow you to compute the grades of the students, one after the other, via a loop. You may terminate the loop by entering a negative grade. Here is our program.

```
1  ' ************************************************
2  ' This program calculates the semester average
3  ' of four grades and assigns a letter grade.
4  ' Grades for one student after another are
5  ' computed. The program ends when a negative
6  ' first grade is entered.
7  ' ************************************************
10 PRINT "ENTER STUDENT'S 4 GRADES."
20 PRINT "SEPARATE GRADES BY COMMAS."
30 PRINT "FOLLOW LAST GRADE WITH <ENTER>."
40 PRINT "TO END PROGRAM, INPUT A NEGATIVE"
50 PRINT "FIRST GRADE."
60 ' Enter Grades
70   INPUT "First Grade";A1
80   IF A1 < 0 THEN 200:       'Quit if grade negative
90   INPUT "Second Grade";A2
100  INPUT "Third Grade";A3
110  INPUT "Fourth Grade";A4
120 LET A = (A1+A2+A3+A4)/4:   'Compute average
130 PRINT "SEMESTER AVERAGE", A
140 ' Assign letter grade
150 IF A >= 90 THEN PRINT "SEMESTER GRADE = A"
    ELSE IF A >= 80 THEN PRINT "SEMESTER GRADE = B"
    ELSE IF A >= 70 THEN PRINT "SEMESTER GRADE = C"
    ELSE IF A >= 60 THEN PRINT "SEMESTER GRADE = D"
    ELSE PRINT "SEMESTER GRADE = F"
160 GOTO 10
200 END
```

Note the rather long statement in line 140. This statement contains the logic to assign the letter grade to the semester average A. In IBM PC BASIC, statements may contain up to 255 characters. In inputting line 140, it will be necessary to type the line continuously, rather than in the indented form given above. This is because the spaces count toward the total number of characters in the line. And with all the spaces, the line contains more than 255 characters. We have written the line in the above form so that it will be easier for you to figure out the logic.

Example 6.   Write a program to maintain your checkbook. The program should allow you to record an initial balance, enter deposits, and enter checks. It should also warn you of overdrafts.

Solution.   Let the variable *B* always contain the current balance in the checkbook. The program will ask for the type of transaction you wish to record. A *D* means that you wish to record a deposit; a *C* means that you wish to record a check; a *Q* means that you are done entering transactions and wish to terminate the program. After entering each transaction, the computer will figure your new balance, report it to you, will check for an overdraft, and report any overdraft to you. In case of an overdraft, the program will allow you to cancel the preceding check!

```
10  ' **********************************************
20  ' This program maintains a checkbook by accepting
30  '    as input initial balance, deposits, and
40  '    checks, and warning of overdrafts
50  ' **********************************************
100   INPUT "WHAT IS YOUR STARTING BALANCE"; B
110   INPUT "WHAT TRANSACTION TYPE (D,C,or Q)"; A$
120   IF A$ = "Q" THEN 600:      'End
130   IF A$ = "D" THEN 200:      'Deposit
140   IF A$ = "C" THEN 300 ELSE 110
200  'Process Deposit
210   INPUT "DEPOSIT AMOUNT"; D
220   LET B = B + D :            'Add deposit to balance
230   PRINT "YOUR NEW BALANCE IS", B
240   GOTO 110
300  'Process check
310   INPUT "CHECK AMOUNT"; C
320   LET B = B - C :            'Deduct check amount
330   IF B<0 THEN 400 :          'Test for overdraft
340   PRINT "YOUR NEW BALANCE IS", B
350   GOTO 110
400  'Process overdraft
410   PRINT "LAST CHECK CAUSES OVERDRAFT"
420   INPUT "DO YOU WISH TO CANCEL CHECK(Y/N)"; E$
430   IF E$ = "Y" THEN 500
440   PRINT "YOUR NEW BALANCE IS", B
450   GOTO 110
500  'Cancel check
510   LET B = B + C:             'Cancel last check
520   GOTO 110
600  END
```

Scan this program carefully to make sure you understand how each of the INPUT and IF … THEN statements is used. In addition, you should use this program to obtain a feel for the dialog between you and your computer when INPUT statements are used.

Note how the above program is divided into sections. For visual purposes, each section begins with a line number that is a multiple of 100. Moreover, each section begins with a comment identifying the function of the section. In order to write a complex program, you should break the program into manageable sections. Don't get caught in a maze of complexity. Work out one section at a time and carefully comment on each section. Then put the various sections together into one program.

Example 7.   Write a BASIC program that tests mastery in addition of two-digit numbers. Let the user suggest the problems, and let the program keep score of the number correct out of ten.

Solution.   Let us request that the program user suggest pairs of numbers via an INPUT statement. The sum will also be requested via an INPUT statement. An IF … THEN statement will be used to judge the correctness. The variable R will keep track of the number correct. We will use a loop to repeat the process ten times.

```
10  '  ****************************************
20  '  This program determines the number of
30  '     times out of ten problems that the
40  '     user adds two numbers correctly
50  '  ****************************************
60     FOR N = 1 TO 10 :    'Loop to give 10 problems
70        INPUT "TYPE TWO 2-DIGIT NUMBERS"; A,B
80        INPUT "WHAT IS THEIR SUM"; C
90        IF A + B = C THEN 200
100     'Respond to incorrect answer
110        PRINT "SORRY. THE CORRECT ANSWER IS",A+B
120        GOTO 300 :        'Go to the next problem
200     'Respond to correct answer
210        PRINT "YOUR ANSWER IS CORRECT! CONGRATULATIONS"
220        LET R = R+1 :     'Increase score by 1
230        GOTO 300 :        'Go to the next problem
300     NEXT N
400  'Print score for 10 problems
410     PRINT "YOUR SCORE IS",R,"CORRECT OUT OF 10"
420     PRINT "TO TRY AGAIN, TYPE RUN"
500     END
```

More About INPUTting Data

The INPUT statement, as we have seen, may be used to input one or more constants (string or numeric) to a running program. However, the INPUT statement has a serious defect. To explain this defect, consider this statement:

```
10 INPUT A$,B$
```

Suppose that you wish to set A$ equal to the string

```
"Washington,George"
```

and B$ to the string

```
"Jefferson,Thomas"
```

Suppose that you respond to the INPUT prompt by typing

```
Washington,George, Jefferson,Thomas
```

BASIC will report an error:

```
? Redo from start
?
```

Here is the reason. INPUT looks for commas to separate the data items. The first comma occurs between *"Washington"* and *"George"*. So INPUT assigns *A$* the string *"Washington"* and *B$* the string *"George"*. But this gives excess data so BASIC declares an error. There's a simple way around this. Whenever you wish to INPUT data containing a comma, surround the appropriate strings with quotation marks. In our example, the response

```
"Washington,George","Jefferson,Thomas"
```

will assign *A$* and *B$* as we wished.

It is something of a bother to surround strings in quotation marks, so BASIC provides another statement that is not sensitive to commas: *LINE INPUT*. The LINE INPUT statement may be used to assign only one variable at a time. It reads the input until it encounters ENTER. For example, suppose that we use the statement

```
30 LINE INPUT A$
```

The computer waits for a response. Suppose that we respond with the string

```
Washington,George
```

and press ENTER. LINE INPUT will then assign *A$* the string constant *"Washington,George"*. LINE INPUT may be used only to input data to a string variable.

You may use a prompt with LINE INPUT exactly as you do with INPUT. For example, the statement

```
40 LINE INPUT "Type NAME?";A$
```

results in the prompt

```
Type NAME?
```

to which you would respond. Note that LINE INPUT does not automatically display a ? like the INPUT statement. In the above example, the ? came from the prompt.

There is a third statement that you may use to input data from the keyboard, namely **INPUT$**. This statement allows you to specify an input of only a specified length. For example, consider the statement

```
10 A$=INPUT$(5)
```

This causes the program to wait for five characters from the keyboard and assigns them to *A$*. For example, if you type *ALICE*, then *A$* will be assigned the string constant *"ALICE"*. INPUT$ is a more specialized statement than either INPUT or LINE INPUT because of the following facts:

1. INPUT$ does not automatically display the input characters on the screen. If you want them displayed, it is your responsibility to display them.

2. INPUT$ accepts all keyboard characters, including Backspace and ENTER. In particular, it does not allow you to correct your input.

If you are a beginning programmer, it's probably wisest to stick to INPUT and LINE INPUT, but we mention INPUT$ mainly for completeness.

ANSWERS TO TEST YOUR UNDERSTANDINGS 1, 2, 3, and 5

1: a. IF A<B THEN PRINT A+B ELSE END
   b. IF A^2+D>=5000 THEN 300 ELSE 500
   c. IF N>I+K THEN N=I+K ELSE N=K

2:
```
10  B=<put unpaid balance here>
20  IF B<=500 THEN 200
100 LET C=B-500
110 IN=.015*500 + .01*C
120 GOTO 300
200 IN=.015*B
300 PRINT "INTEREST EQUALS";IN
310 PRINT "NEW BALANCE EQUALS";B+IN
320 END
```

3: 100-110-120-400

5:
```
10 INPUT "THE VALUES OF A AND B ARE";A,B
20 END
```

6.3 Structuring Solutions to Problems

You may have noticed our programs are getting longer. There is no way around this. In order to utilize the computer to solve real-life problems, programs often must be quite long and must employ the full range of capabilities of the computer. This poses a number of problems including:

1. Long programs are difficult to plan.

2. Long programs are difficult to write and correct.

3. Long programs are hard to read.

All three problems will confront you in programming your computer. Let's discuss some ways to deal with them.

As an example of program planning, let's take the last program of the preceding section. Recall that this is the program that tests addition. Suppose that you are given the job of building such a program. How should you proceed? Your first inclination might be to start writing BASIC statements. At all costs, resist the temptation! Your first job is to *plan* the program.

The first step in program planning is to decide on the input and output. What data does the user give and what responses does the computer give. Make a list like this:

User input: Answers to questions

Computer output: Questions to answer

Responses to answers

    a. Response to correct answer

    b. Response to incorrect answer

    c. Report of Score

Question: Another set of problems?

The next step is to organize these inputs and outputs into a sequence of steps that follow one another in logical order. Don't worry about computer instructions at this point. Rather, describe reasonably general steps which, in the end, may actually correspond to several computer instructions. Here is how our addition program might be described.

1. Computer requests question

2. User responds

3. User enters answer

4. Computer analyzes answers and responds

    a. Reports whether answer is correct

    b. Keeps score

5. Steps 1-4 are repeated 10 times

6. Computer reports score

7. Computer queries user whether to begin again.

The third step of program planning is to sketch out the structure of the program. We see from step 5 that we will need a loop to keep track of the problems. Moreover, we know that steps 1-3 are one-line computer commands. Let's lump them together into one section of the program. On the other hand, handling correct answers is different from handling wrong answers. Let's have a separate section of the program for each of these tasks. Moreover, let's have a separate section of the program for steps 6 and 7. You should write all this down (on paper) as follows:

```
10   FOR N=1 TO 10
```

(lines 20-80 reserved for steps 1 to 3.)

```
100    'Respond to incorrect answer
200    'Respond to correct answer
300 NEXT N
400 'Print score for 10 problems
500 'Run again?
600 END
```

As the fourth step, you should begin to fill in the various steps in the above outline. Here is where you may begin writing BASIC instructions, defining variables, and so forth. Each of the steps corresponds to only a few program statements. So the program becomes easy to write and our final product is something like the following program.

```
10  ' *****************************************
20  ' This program determines the number of
30  '    times out of ten problems that the
40  '    user adds two numbers correctly
50  ' *****************************************
60     FOR N = 1 TO 10 :    'Loop to give 10 problems
70        INPUT "TYPE TWO 2-DIGIT NUMBERS"; A,B
80        INPUT "WHAT IS THEIR SUM"; C
90        IF A + B = C THEN 200
100    'Respond to incorrect answer
110       PRINT "SORRY. THE CORRECT ANSWER IS",A+B
120       GOTO 300 :          'Go to the next problem
200    'Respond to correct answer
210       PRINT "YOUR ANSWER IS CORRECT! CONGRATULATIONS"
220       LET R = R+1 :     'Increase score by 1
230       GOTO 300 :          'Go to the next problem
300    NEXT N
400 'Print score for 10 problems
410    PRINT "YOUR SCORE IS",R,"CORRECT OUT OF 10"
420    PRINT "TO TRY AGAIN, TYPE RUN"
500    END
```

It is possible that some of the steps correspond to complex sequences of operations. If so, break such steps into smaller steps, just like we have done for the entire program. Eventually, you should reduce your program to an organized sequence of steps, each corresponding to no more than about a dozen statements.

(The actual number may be more or less, depending on your comfort level. But don't allow the number to be too large. This is the way errors creep into your program!)

In organizing a program, you cannot plan the various steps in total isolation from one another. Here are some pitfalls to be aware of:

1. If a variable is to be used in two steps, then it must be given by the same name in each.

2. If a step assumes that the value of a variable has been assigned in a previous step, be sure that this is done.

3. Don't mistakenly use the same variable to mean two different things. This is an easy error to make. After several hours at the keyboard, you may forget that you already used a variable name to mean something else. No harm is done if the two variables are used in two isolated sections of the program. However, you may set the variable with one meaning in mind only to have the program then use it with the other meaning. This can make your results incorrect.

4. Be sure to assign each variable its proper starting value. (This is called **variable initialization**.) Remember that if you do not assign a value to a variable, BASIC assigns it the value 0.

The procedure for program planning described above automatically incorporates your documentation into your program. This makes it easier to read your program to correct mistakes or to alter it at a later date.

The discussion of this section just scratches the surface of the subject of program planning. Hopefully, it will ease the burden of writing and understanding BASIC programs, and will lead you to develop your own approach to program planning and organization. We'll have more to say about the subject in Chapter 7.

6.4   Subroutines

In writing programs it is often necessary to use the same sequence of instructions more than once. It may not be convenient (or even feasible) to retype the set of instructions each time it is needed. Fortunately, BASIC offers a convenient alternative: the subroutine.

A **subroutine** is a program that is incorporated within another, larger program. The subroutine may be used any number of times by the larger program. Often, the lines corresponding to a subroutine are isolated toward the end of the larger program. This arrangement is illustrated in Figure 6-1. The arrow to the subroutine indicates the point in the larger program at which the subroutine is used. The arrow pointing away from the subroutine indicates that, after completion of the subroutine, execution of the main program resumes at the point at which it was interrupted.

Figure 6-1. **A subroutine.**

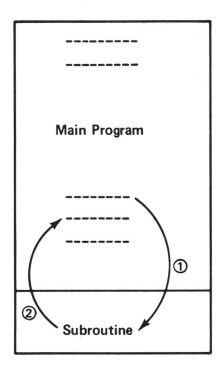

Subroutines are handled with the pair of instructions **GOSUB** and **RETURN**. The statement

```
100 GOSUB 1000
```

sends the computer to the subroutine beginning at line 1000. The computer starts at line 1000 and carries out statements in order. When a RETURN statement in the subroutine is reached, the computer goes back to the main program, starting at the first line after 100.

TEST YOUR UNDERSTANDING 1 (answer on page 142)
Consider the following program.

```
10 GOSUB 100
20 PRINT "LINE 20"
30 END
100 'Subroutine
```

```
110 PRINT "LINE 110"
120 RETURN
```

List the line numbers in order of execution.

Subroutines may serve as user-defined commands, as Example 1 illustrates.

Example 1.   Design a BASIC subroutine that erases a specified line of the screen and positions the cursor at the left end of the erased line.

Solution.   The task described is required by many programs. It is a prelude to writing on the line. In fact, it may be required many times within the same program. It would be wasteful to write separate instruction lines for each repetition. So let's write a general subroutine that can be called whenever required. Suppose that line L is to be erased. This may be accomplished in the following steps:

1.   Position the cursor at the left-most position on the line.

2.   Write 80 spaces (40 if you are in WIDTH 40).

3.   Reposition the cursor at the left-most position on the line.

To position the cursor at row r and column c, we use the statement

```
LOCATE r,c
```

We can use a loop to generate the spaces. However, there is an easier way. The string *SPACE$(n)* is a string of n spaces. By printing this string, we may "blank out" n spaces beginning at the current cursor position. Here is our subroutine:

```
5000 'Blank out line L
5010 LOCATE L,1
5020 PRINT SPACE$(80)
5030 LOCATE L,1
5040 RETURN
```

Whenever we wish to use this subroutine, we first set the value of L to the line number to be erased. Next, we execute *GOSUB 5000*. Note that the value of L must be set before the *GOSUB 5000* instruction is issued.

TEST YOUR UNDERSTANDING 2 (answer on page 142)
Write a subroutine that erases the first M columns of line L and positions the cursor in the upper left corner of the screen.

Example 2.   Write a program that turns the computer into an electronic cash register. The program should accept as entries both taxable and non-taxable amounts. It should keep track of the totals of each. On command, it should display the totals, compute the tax, and compute the grand total owed.

Solution.   A listing of the program is included below. This program illustrates some of the tricks involved in planning "user-friendly" programs. We allow the user to choose from four requests displayed on the screen. Such a display is called a **menu**. Here are the four possible requests.

1. **New Customer**. Zero all totals, clear the screen and display identifying headings as in Figure 6-2.

2. **Enter item**. Accept the amount of an item. The program asks whether the item is taxable. The amount is displayed under the appropriate heading and is added to the appropriate total (taxable or non-taxable).

3. **Compute totals**. Compute tax and display totals.

4. **Exit**. End program.

The instructions for displaying the menu are in lines 1000-1080. Note that the subroutine to blank out a particular line begins in line 6000. In many parts of the program, we will want to write on a line. We will use the subroutine beginning in line 6000 to erase that particular line.

In line 1100, the user is asked to make a choice of activity from the menu by typing one of the numbers 1-4. Based on the user response, the program goes to the subroutine at 2000, 3000, or 4000, or, in the case of choice 4, goes to line

Figure 6-2.   **Screen Layout for the PC Cash Register.**

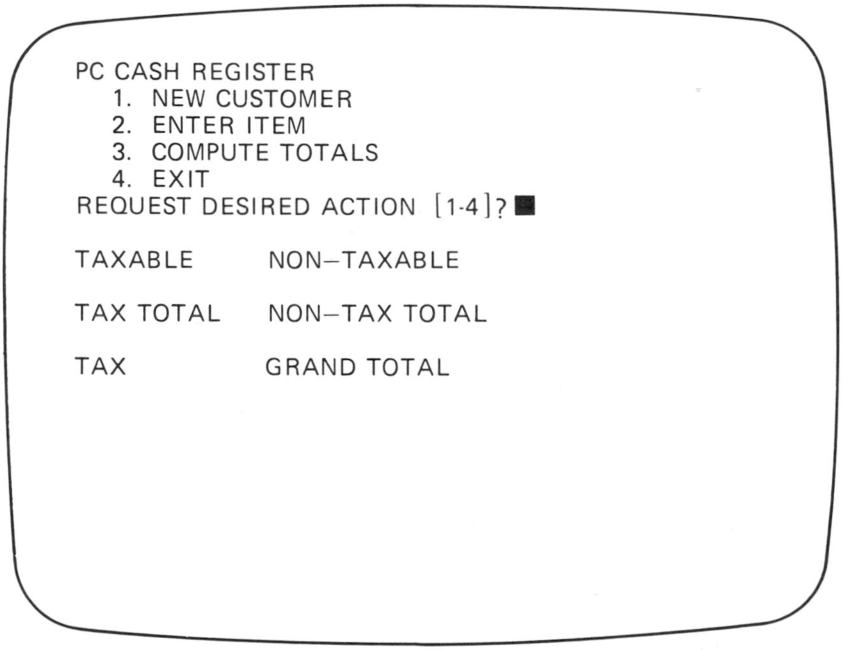

```
PC CASH REGISTER
    1. NEW CUSTOMER
    2. ENTER ITEM
    3. COMPUTE TOTALS
    4. EXIT
REQUEST DESIRED ACTION [1-4]? ■

TAXABLE      NON−TAXABLE

TAX TOTAL    NON−TAX TOTAL

TAX          GRAND TOTAL
```

1160 (no subroutine—more about that below). After the subroutine is executed, the program returns to the line after the one calling the subroutine and will make its way to line 1150. This line sends the program back to 1090, which erases the entry line and requests another activity. You may use the program all day. You may end the program by choosing option 4 on the menu.

Option 4 on the menu causes the program to go to line 1160, where the screen is cleared and the program is terminated. We did not use a subroutine to get to line 1160 since we did not expect to return. In this particular case, a *GOSUB 1160* could have been used with no harm. Since the program ends, the computer will not look for a place to return. However, it is good programming practice to use a subroutine only in instances in which the program is guaranteed to reach a *RETURN* instruction.

```
100  ' ****************************************
110  ' This program acts as a cash register,
120  '    accepting taxable and non-taxable
130  '    amounts as entries, and displaying
140  '    on command the totals, the tax,
150  '    and the grand total owed
160  ' ****************************************
1000 'Display Menu
1010     CLS
1020     LOCATE 1,1:   'Home cursor
1030     PRINT "PC CASH REGISTER"
1040     PRINT "1. NEW CUSTOMER"
1050     PRINT "2. ENTER ITEM"
1060     PRINT "3. COMPUTE TOTALS"
1070     PRINT "4. EXIT"
1080     PRINT
1090     L=7:GOSUB 5000:   'Blank out entry line
1100     INPUT "REQUEST DESIRED ACTION (1-4)";REPLY$
1110     IF REPLY$="1" THEN GOSUB 2000
1120     IF REPLY$="2" THEN GOSUB 3000
1130     IF REPLY$="3" THEN GOSUB 4000
1140     IF REPLY$="4" THEN 1160
1150     GOTO 1090
1160     CLS
1170     END
2000 'New customer subroutine
2010     'Reset totals
2020     TAXABLE=0:NONTAXABLE=0:GRANDTOTAL=0
2030     'Blank out lines 8-20 of screen
2040     FOR L=8 TO 20
2050        GOSUB 5000
2060     NEXT L
2070     'Print titles
2080     LOCATE 9,1
2090     PRINT "TAXABLE",  "NON-TAXABLE"
2100     LOCATE 12,1
2110     PRINT "TAX TOTAL", "NON-TAX TOTAL"
2120     LOCATE 15,1
2130     PRINT "TAX",  "GRAND TOTAL"
```

```
2140 RETURN
3000 'Enter item subroutine
3010    L=7:GOSUB 5000:   'Clear entry line
3020    INPUT "AMOUNT (NO DOLLAR SIGN)"; AMOUNT
3030    L=7:GOSUB 5000
3040    INPUT "TAXABLE=1,NON-TAXABLE=0";STATUS
3050    L=10:GOSUB 5000
3060    IF STATUS=1 THEN PRINT AMOUNT
3070    IF STATUS=0 THEN PRINT ,AMOUNT
3080    IF STATUS=1 THEN TAXABLE=TAXABLE+AMOUNT
3090    IF STATUS=0 THEN NONTAXABLE=NONTAXABLE+AMOUNT
3100 RETURN
4000 'Compute totals subroutine
4010    L=10:GOSUB 5000:   'Clear entry line
4020    L=13:GOSUB 5000:   'Clear first total line
4030    PRINT TAXABLE,NONTAXABLE
4040    TAX=.05*TAXABLE
4050    GRANDTOTAL=TAXABLE+TAX+NONTAXABLE
4060    L=16:GOSUB 5000
4070    PRINT TAX,GRANDTOTAL
4080 RETURN
5000 'Clear entry line L
5010    LOCATE L,1
5020    PRINT SPACE$(40);:  'Clear Entry Line
5030    LOCATE L,1
5040 RETURN
```

TEST YOUR UNDERSTANDING 3 (answer on page 142)

Enhance the program of Example 2 so that as a part of computing the totals, it asks you the amount presented ($10 bill, $20 bill, and so forth) and computes the change.

Nested Subroutines

In Example 2, we used a number of subroutines that were contained within subroutines. For example, lines 4000-4080 are a subroutine. However, on lines 4020 and 4030, we called the subroutine at 6000. Such subroutines are said to be **nested**. BASIC is able to handle such nesting. You may use nesting to any level. (A subroutine within a subroutine within a subroutine, and so forth.) However, you should be aware that a RETURN instruction always refers to the **innermost** subroutine. To put it another way, a RETURN always refers to the subroutine that was called most recently.

Caution: It is possible to accidentally create an infinite nesting of subroutines by repeatedly issuing GOSUB instructions, as in this program:

```
10 GOTO 20
20 GOSUB 10
```

The computer will eventually run out of memory to keep track of this nesting and an error will result.

The ON ... GOSUB Instruction

In Example 2, we organized the program around four main subroutines, corresponding to the four possible choices on the MENU. It took several instructions to properly channel the program to the proper subroutine. BASIC provides a convenient shortcut for use in such situations, the **ON...GOSUB** instruction. The form of this instruction is:

```
ON <expression> GOSUB <line1>,<line2>,...
```

When BASIC encounters this instruction, it evaluates *<expression>*, which should yield an integer value. If the resulting value is 1, the program executes a *GOSUB* to *<line1>*. If the value is 2, the program executes a *GOSUB* to *<line2>*, and so forth. If the value is zero or more than the number of line numbers provided, the instruction will be ignored. (If *<expression>* yields a negative value, or an integer value larger than 255, an Illegal Function Call error results.)

For example, lines 1110-1130 of Example 2 may be replaced by the single line:

```
1110 ON VAL(REPLY$) GOSUB 2000,3000,4000
```

Here, the expression *VAL(REPLY$)* converts the string *REPLY$* into its numerical equivalent (''1'' converts to 1, ''2'' to 2, and so forth) . If this value is 1, the program executes a *GOSUB 2000*, if the value is 2, a *GOSUB 3000* and if the value is 3, a *GOSUB 4000*.

ANSWERS TO TEST YOUR UNDERSTANDINGS 1, 2, and 3

1: 10-100-110-120-20-30

2:
```
5000 'Blank out 1st M columns of line L
5010 LOCATE L,1:    'Position cursor at left of line L
5020 PRINT SPACE$(M)
5030 LOCATE L,1
5040 RETURN
```

3: Add the following program lines:
```
4071 LOCATE 20,1
4072 INPUT "AMOUNT PAID";PAID
4073 PRINT "PAID","CHANGE"
4074 PRINT PAID,PAID-GRANDTOTAL
```

7
Working With Data

7.0 Chapter Objectives

IN THIS CHAPTER, WE DISCUSS ways to organize and format data, including:

- Using arrays, including the DIM and CLEAR statements.
- Inputting data using the READ, DATA, and RESTORE statements.
- Using semicolons in PRINT statements.
- Formatting output using TAB and SPC.
- Formatting output with PRINT USING.
- Using random numbers to simulate random events within programs, and applications to games of chance.

7.1 Working With Tabular Data—Arrays

In Chapter 5 we introduced the notion of a variable and used variable names like:

TAX, BALANCE, A1, TOTAL

Unfortunately, the supply of variables available to us is not sufficient for many programs. Indeed, as we shall see in this chapter, there are relatively innocent programs requiring hundreds or even thousands of variables. To meet the needs of such programs, BASIC allows for the use of so-called **subscripted variables.** Such variables are used constantly by mathematicians and are identified by numbered subscripts attached to a letter. For instance, here is a list of 1000 variables as they might appear in a mathematical work:

$A_1, A_2, A_3, \ldots, A_{1000}$

The numbers used to distinguish the variables are called **subscripts.** Likewise, the BASIC language allows definition of variables to be distinguished by subscripts. However, since the computer has difficulty placing the numbers in the traditional position, they are placed in parentheses on the same line as the letter. For example, the above list of 1000 different variables is written in BASIC as

```
A(1),A(2),A(3),...,A(1000)
```

Please note that the variable *A(1)* is not the same as the variable *A1*. You may use both of them in the same program and BASIC will interpret them as being different.

A subscripted variable is really a group of variables with a common letter identification distinguished by different integer "subscripts." For instance, the above group of variables constitute the subscripted variable *A( )*. It is often useful to view a subscripted variable as a table or array. For example, the subscripted variable *A( )* considered above can be viewed as providing the following table of information:

A(1)

A(2)

A(3)

.

.

.

A(1000)

As shown here, the subscripted variable defines a table consisting of 1000 rows. Suppose that *J* is an integer between 1 and 1000. Then row number *J* contains a single entry, namely, the value of the variable *A(J)*: the first row contains the value of *A(1)*, the second the value of *A(2)*, and so forth. Since a subscripted variable can be thought of as a table (or array), subscripted variables are often called **arrays**.

The array shown above is a table consisting of 1000 rows and a single column. BASIC allows you to consider more general arrays. For example, consider the following financial table, which records the daily income for three days from each of a chain of four computer stores:

	Store #1	*Store #2*	*Store #3*	*Store #4*
Day 1	*1258.38*	*2437.46*	*4831.90*	*987.12*
Day 2	*1107.83*	*2045.68*	*3671.86*	*1129.47*
Day 3	*1298.00*	*2136.88*	*4016.73*	*1206.34*

This table has three rows and four columns. Its entries may be stored in the computer as a set of 12 variables:

A(1,1) *A(1,2)* *A(1,3)* *A(1,4)*

A(2,1) *A(2,2)* *A(2,3)* *A(2,4)*

A(3,1) *A(3,2)* *A(3,3)* *A(3,4)*

This array of variables is very similar to a subscripted variable, except that there are now two subscripts. The first subscript indicates the row number and the second subscript indicates the column number. For example, the variable $A(3,2)$ is in the third row, second column. A collection of variables such as that given above is called a **two-dimensional array** or a **doubly-subscripted variable.** Each setting of the variables in such an array defines a tabular array. For example, if we assign the values

$$A(1,1) = 1258.38, A(1,2) = 2437.46,$$

$$A(1,3) = \quad 4831.90,$$

and so forth, then we will have the table of earnings from the computer store chain.

So far, we have only considered numeric arrays—arrays whose variables can assume only numerical values. However, it is possible to have arrays with variables that assume string values. (Recall that a string is a sequence of characters: letter, numeral, punctuation mark, or other printable keyboard symbol.) For example, here is an array that can contain string data:

$A\$(1)$

$A\$(2)$

$A\$(3)$

$A\$(4)$

The dollar signs indicate that each of the variables of the array is a string variable. If we assign the values

$A\$(1) = $ ''SLOW''

$A\$(2) = $ ''FAST''

$A\$(3) = $ ''FAST''

$A\$(4) = $ ''STOP''

then the array is this table of words:

SLOW

FAST

FAST

STOP

Similarly, the employee record table

Social Security Number	Age	Sex	Marital Status
178654775	38	M	S
345861023	29	F	M
789257958	34	F	D
375486595	42	M	M
457696064	21	F	S

may be stored in an array of the form $B\$(I,J)$, where I assumes any one of the values $1, 2, 3, 4, 5$ (I is the row), and J assumes any one of the values $1, 2, 3, 4$ (J = the column). For example, $B\$(1,1)$ has the value "178654775", $B\$(1,2)$ has the value "38", $B\$(1,3)$ has the value "M", and so forth.

BASIC allows you to have arrays that have three, four, or even more subscripts. For example, consider the computer store chain array introduced above. Suppose that we had one such array for each of ten consecutive three-day periods. This collection of data can be stored in a three-dimensional array of the form $C(I,J,K)$, where I and J represent the row and column, just as before, and K represents the year. (K can assume the values $1,2,3, \ldots, 10$.)

An array may involve any number of dimensions up to 255. The subscripts corresponding to each dimension may assume values from 0 to 32767. For all practical applications, any size array is permissible.

You must inform the computer of the sizes of the arrays you plan to use in a program. This allows the computer to allocate memory space to house all the values. To specify the size of an array, use a **DIM** (dimension) statement. For example, to define the size of the subscripted variable $A(J)$, $J=1,\ldots,1000$, we insert the statement

```
10 DIM A(1000)
```

in the program. This statement informs the computer to expect variables $A(0)$, $A(1), \ldots, A(1000)$ in the program and that it should set aside memory space for 1001 variables. Note that, in the absence of further instructions from you, BASIC begins all subscripts at 0. If you wish to use $A(0)$, fine. If not, ignore it.

You need not use all the variables defined by a DIM statement. For example, in the case of the DIM statement above, you might actually use only the variables $A(1), \ldots, A(900)$. Don't worry about it! Just make sure that you have defined enough variables. Otherwise, you could be in trouble. For example, in the case of the subscripted variable above, your program might use the variable $A(1001)$. This will create an error condition. Suppose that this variable is used first in line 570. When you attempt to run the program, the computer will report

```
Subscript out of range in 570
```

Moreover, execution of the program will be halted. To fix the error, merely redo the DIM statement to accommodate the undefined subscript.

To define the size of a two-dimensional array, use a DIM statement of the form

```
10 DIM A(5,4)
```

This statement defines an array $A(I,J)$, where I can assume the values $0, 1, 2, 3, 4, 5$ and J can assume the values $0, 1, 2, 3, 4$. Arrays with three or more subscripts are defined similarly.

TEST YOUR UNDERSTANDING 1 (answers on page 150)
Here is an array.

12   645.80

148 489.75

589 12.89

487 14.50

a.   Define an appropriate subscripted variable to store this data.

b.   Define an appropriate DIM statement.

It is possible to dimension several arrays with one DIM statement. For example, the dimension statement

```
10 DIM A(1000), B$(5), A(5,4)
```

defines the array $A(0)$, . . . , $A(1000)$, the string array $B\$(0)$, . . . , $B\$(5)$, and the two-dimensional array $A(I,J)$, $I=0$, . . . , 5; $J=0$, . . . , 4.

We now know how to set aside memory space for the variables of an array. We must next take up the problem of assigning values to these variables. We can use individual LET statements, but with 1000 variables in an array, this can lead to an unmanageable number of statements. There are more convenient methods that make use of loops. The next two examples illustrate two of these methods.

Example 1.   Define an array $A(J)$, $J=1, 2, \ldots, 1000$ and assign the following values to the variables of the array:

$A(1)=2$, $A(2)=4$, $A(3)=6$, $A(4)=8$, . . .

Solution.   We wish to assign each variable a value equal to twice its subscript. That is, we wish to assign $A(J)$ the value $2*J$. To do this we use a loop:

```
10 DIM A(1000)
20 FOR J = 1 TO 1000
30    A(J) = 2*J
40 NEXT J
50 END
```

Note that the program ignores the variable *A(0)*. Like any variable that has not been assigned a value, it has the value zero.

TEST YOUR UNDERSTANDING 2 (answer on page 150)

Write a program that assigns the variables *A(0)*, . . . , *A(30)* the values *A(0)=0*, *A(1)=1*, *A(2)=4*, *A(3)=9*, ...

When the computer is first turned on or reset, all variables (including those in arrays) are cleared. All numeric variables are set equal to 0, and all string variables are set equal to the null string (the string with no characters in it). If you wish to return all variables to this state during the execution of a program, use the **CLEAR** command. For example, when the computer encounters the command

```
570 CLEAR
```

it resets all the variables. The CLEAR command can be convenient if, for example, you wish to use the same array to store two different sets of information at two different stages of the program. After the first use of the array you can then prepare for the second use by executing a CLEAR.

Example 2.   Define an array corresponding to the employee record table above. Input the values given and print the table on the screen.

Solution.   Our program prints the headings of the columns and then asks for the table entries, one row at a time. We will store the entries in the array *B$(I,J)*, where *I* is one of *1, 2, 3, 4, 5* and *J* is one of *1, 2, 3, 4*. We dimension the array as *B$(5,4)*.

```
10  ' ***********************************************
20  ' This program sets up an array to hold four
30  '   pieces of data for each of five employees,
40  '   accepting values from the user and
50  '   displaying them in a table
60  ' ***********************************************
100   DIM B$(5,4):          ' Set up array
110   FOR I=1 TO 5:         ' Input the data
120       INPUT "SS#,Age,Sex,Mar.St.";B$(I,1),
          B$(I,2),B$(I,3),B$(I,4)
130   NEXT I
140   CLS:                  ' Print the table
150   PRINT "Soc. Sec. #", "Age", "Sex","Marital Status"
160   FOR I=1 TO 5
170     PRINT B$(I,1),B$(I,2),B$(I,3),B$(I,4)
180   NEXT I
190   END
```

Note that line 120 is a single program line, and not two. It was typed without using the ENTER key until the end of the second physical line.

TEST YOUR UNDERSTANDING 3 (answer on page 150)
Suppose that your program uses a 9×2 array $A\$(I,J)$, a 9×1 array $B\$(I,J)$, and a 9×5 array $C(I,J)$. Write an appropriate DIM statement.

If you plan to dimension an array, always insert the DIM statement before the variable first appears in your program. Otherwise, the first time BASIC comes across the array, it assumes that the subscripts go from 0 to 10. If it subsequently comes across a DIM statement, it will think you are changing the size of the array in the midst of the program, something which is not allowed. If you try to change the size of an array in the middle of a program, you will get this error message:

```
Duplicate Definition
```

In our discussion above, we have been very casual about ignoring unused subscripts, such as $A(0)$. In some programs, there may be so many large arrays that memory space becomes precious. Sometimes, considerable memory space may be conserved by carefully planning which subscripts will be used and defining only those variables. You may eliminate unused 0 subscripts using the **OPTION BASE** statement. For example, the statement

```
10 OPTION BASE 1
```

begins all arrays with subscript 1. This statement must be used in a program prior to the dimensioning of any arrays.

Deleting Arrays

It is very simple to create an array that occupies a horrendous amount of memory space. For example, consider this seemingly harmless statement:

```
10 DIM A(10,10,10,10)
```

It defines an array with 10,000 entries. BASIC requires four bytes for each entry, so the array takes up 40,000 bytes of RAM! For this reason, you must do some planning so that your arrays do not overflow available memory. One technique for this involves deleting arrays from memory in order to make room for other arrays. You may do this using the **ERASE** statement. For example, to delete the above array, we can use the statement

```
20 ERASE A
```

Once you execute *ERASE,* all the values of array $A(\ )$ are lost and the *DIM* statement dimensioning $A(\ )$ is cancelled. In particular, you may redimension an array after an ERASE statement.

The ERASE statement may be used to delete several arrays at once, as in this statement:

```
30 ERASE B,C,D
```

ANSWERS TO TEST YOUR UNDERSTANDINGS 1, 2, and 3

1: a. `A(I,J), I=1,2,3,4; J=1,2`

 b. `DIM A(4,2)`

2: ```
10 DIM A(30)
20 FOR J=0 TO 30
30   A(J)=J^2
40 NEXT J
50 END
```

3: `DIM A$(9,2),B$(9,1),C(9,5)`

## 7.2  Inputting Data

In Section 7.1, we introduced arrays and discussed several methods for assigning values to the variables of an array. The most flexible method was via the INPUT statement. However, this can be a tedious method for large arrays. Fortunately, BASIC provides us with an alternate method for inputting data.

A given program may need many different numbers and strings. You may store the data needed in one or more **DATA** statements. A typical DATA statement has the form

`10 DATA 3.457, 2.588, 11234, "WINGSPAN"`

Note that this DATA statement consists of four data items, three numeric and one string. The data items are separated by commas. You may include as many data items in a single DATA statement as the line allows. Moreover, you may include any number of DATA statements in a program and they may be placed anywhere in the program, although a common placement is at the end of the program (just before the END statement). Note that we enclosed the string constant *"WINGSPAN"* in quotation marks. Actually this is not necessary. A string constant in a DATA statement does not need quotes, as long as it does not contain a comma or colon, or start with a blank.

The DATA statements may be used to assign values to variables and, in particular, to variables in arrays. Here's how to do this. In conjunction with the DATA statements, you use one or more **READ** statements. For example, suppose that the above DATA statement appears in a program. Further, suppose that you wish to assign these values:

$A = 3.457, B = 2.588, C = 11234, Z\$ = $ *"WINGSPAN"*

This can be accomplished via the READ statement:

`100 READ A,B,C,Z$`

Here is how the READ statement works. On encountering a READ statement, the computer looks for a DATA statement. It then assigns values to the variables
```

in the READ statement by taking the values, in order, from the DATA statement. If there is insufficient data in the first DATA statement, the computer continues to assign values using the data in the next DATA statement. If necessary, the computer proceeds to the third DATA statement, and so forth.

TEST YOUR UNDERSTANDING 1 (answer on page 154)
Assign the following values:

$A(1)=5.1,\ A(2)=4.7,\ A(3)=5.8,\ A(4)=3.2,\ A(5)=7.9,\ A(6)=6.9$

The computer maintains an internal pointer that points to the next DATA item to be used. If the computer encounters a second READ statement, it will start reading where it left off. For example, suppose that instead of the above READ statement, we use the two READ statements

```
100 READ A,B
200 READ C,Z$
```

Upon encountering the first statement, the computer looks for the location of the pointer. Initially, it points to the first item in the first DATA statement. The computer assigns the values $A=3.457$ and $B=2.588$. Moreover, the position of the pointer is advanced to the third item in the DATA statement. Upon encountering the next READ statement, the computer assigns values beginning with the one designated by the pointer, namely $C=11234$ and $Z\$=$ "WINGSPAN".

TEST YOUR UNDERSTANDING 2 (answer on page 154)
What values are assigned to A and $B\$$ by the following program?

```
10 DATA 10,30,"ENGINE","TACH"
20 READ A,B
30 READ C$,B$
40 END
```

The following example illustrates the use of DATA statements in assigning values to an array.

Example 1.   Suppose that the monthly electricity costs of a certain family are as follows:

Jan.	$89.74	Feb.	$95.84	March	$79.42
Apr.	78.93	May	72.11	June	115.94
July	158.92	Aug.	164.38	Sep.	105.98
Oct.	90.44	Nov.	89.15	Dec.	93.97

Write a program calculating the average monthly cost of electricity.

Solution.   Let us unceremoniously dump all of the numbers shown above into DATA statements at the end of the program. Arbitrarily, let's start the DATA statements at line 1000, with END at 2000. This allows us plenty of room. To calculate the average, we must add up the numbers and divide by 12. To do this, let us first create an array $A(J)$, $J = 1, 2, \ldots, 12$ and set $A(J)$ equal to the cost of electricity in the Jth month. We do this via a loop and the READ statement. We then use a loop to add all the $A(J)s$. Finally, we divide by 12 and PRINT the answer. Here is the program.

```
10 ' *************************************************
20 ' This program finds the average of twelve monthly
30 '   costs read into an array from DATA statements
40 ' *************************************************
100 DIM A(12):       ' Set up the array
110 FOR J=1 TO 12:   ' Read in the data
120    READ A(J)
130 NEXT J
140 C=0
150 FOR J=1 TO 12
160    C=C+A(J):     ' C accumulates the sum
170 NEXT J
180 C=C/12:          ' Divide sum by 12 to find avg
190 PRINT "THE AVERAGE MONTHLY COST OF ELECTRICITY
    IS",C
1000 DATA 89.74, 95.84, 79.42, 78.93, 72.11, 115.94
1010 DATA 158.92, 164.38, 105.98, 90.44, 89.15, 93.97
2000 END
```

The following program can be helpful in preparing the payroll of a small business.

Example 2.   A small business has five employees. Here are their names and hourly wages.

Name	Hourly Wage
Joe Polanski	7.75
Susan Greer	8.50
Allan Cole	8.50
Betsy Palm	6.00
Herman Axler	6.00

Write a program that accepts as input hours worked for the current week, and calculates the current gross pay and the amount of Social Security tax to be withheld from their pay. (Assume that the Social Security tax amounts to 7.05 percent of gross pay.)

Solution.   Let us keep the hourly wage rates and names in two arrays, called $A(J)$ and $B\$(J)$, respectively, where $J = 1, 2, 3, 4, 5$. Note that we can't use a single two-dimensional array for this data since the names are string data, and the hourly wage rates are numerical. (Recall that BASIC does not allow us to mix the two kinds of data in an array.) The first part of the program is to assign the values to the variables in the two arrays. Next, the program will, one by one, print out the names of the employees and ask for the number of hours worked during the current week. This data will be stored in the array $C(J)$, $J = 1, 2, 3, 4, 5$. The program then computes the gross wages as $A(J)*C(J)$ (that is, *<wage rate>* times *<number of hours worked>*). This piece of data will be stored in the array $D(J)$, $J = 1, 2, 3, 4, 5$. Next, the program computes the amount of Social Security tax to be withheld as $.0705*D(J)$. This piece of data is stored in the array $E(J)$, $J = 1, 2, 3, 4, 5$. Finally, all the computed data is printed on the screen. Here is the program.

```
10  ' **********************************************
20  ' This program determines the Social Security
30  '    tax due from five employees whose salary
40  '    rates are read into an array and whose
50  '    hours are typed in by the user
60  ' **********************************************
100    DIM A(5),B$(5),C(5),D(5),E(5)
110    FOR J=1 TO 5:          ' Read in the data
120      READ B$(J),A(J)
130    NEXT J
140    FOR J=1 TO 5:          ' Input hours worked
150      PRINT "TYPE CURRENT HOURS OF", B$(J)
160      INPUT C(J)
170      D(J)=A(J)*C(J)
180      E(J)=.0705*D(J)
190    NEXT J
200  'Print in a table the employee names, wages and tax
210    PRINT "EMPLOYEE","GROSS WAGES","SOC.SEC.TAX"
220    FOR J=1 TO 5
230      PRINT B$(J),D(J),E(J)
240    NEXT J
300    DATA JOE POLANSKI, 7.75, SUSAN GREER, 8.50
310    DATA ALLAN COLE, 8.50, BETSY PALM, 6.00
320    DATA HERMAN AXLER, 6.00
400  END
```

In certain applications, you may wish to read the same DATA statements more than once. To do this you must reset the pointer via the **RESTORE** statement. For example, consider the following program:

```
10 DATA 2.3, 5.7, 4.5, 7.3
20 READ A,B
30 RESTORE
40 READ C,D
50 END
```

Line 20 sets *A* equal to *2.3* and *B* equal to *5.7*. The *RESTORE* statement in line 30 moves the pointer back to the first item of data, 2.3. The *READ* statement of line 40 then sets *C* equal to *2.3* and *D* equal to *5.7*. Note that without the

RESTORE in line 30, the *READ* statement in line 40 would set *C* equal to *4.5* and *D* equal to *7.3*.

There are two common errors in using READ and DATA statements. First, you may instruct the program to READ more data than is present in the DATA statements. For example, consider the following program.

```
10 DATA 1,2,3,4
20 FOR J=1 TO 5
30    READ A(J)
40 NEXT J
50 END
```

This program attempts to read five pieces of data, but the DATA statement only has four. In this case, you will receive an error message:

```
Out of data in 30
```

A second common error is attempting to assign a string value to a numeric variable or vice versa. Such an attempt leads to a **Type mismatch** error.

ANSWERS TO TEST YOUR UNDERSTANDINGS 1 and 2

```
1:  10 DATA 5.1,4.7,5.8,3.2,7.9,6.9
    20 FOR J=1 TO 6
    30    READ A(J)
    40 NEXT J
    50 END

2:  A = 10, B$ = "TACH"
```

7.3   Formatting Your Output

In this section, we will discuss the various ways in which you can format output on the screen and on the printer. IBM PC BASIC is quite flexible in the form in which you can cast output. You have control over the size of the letters on the screen, placement of output on the line, degree of accuracy to which calculations are displayed, and so forth. Let us begin by reviewing what we have already learned about printing.

Semicolons in PRINT Statements

The IBM PC BASIC screen may be set for 40- or 80-character lines using the WIDTH statement. This gives 40 or 80 print positions in each line. These are divided into print zones of 14 characters each.[1] To start printing at the beginning of the next print zone, insert a comma between the items to be printed.

In many applications, it is necessary to print more columns than there are print zones. Or, output may look better if the columns are less than a full print zone wide. To avoid any space between consecutive print items, separate them in the PRINT statement by a semicolon. Consider this instruction:

```
10 PRINT "PERSO";"NAL COMPUTER"
```

It results in the output

```
PERSONAL COMPUTER
```

The semicolon suppresses any space between the display of *PERSO* and *NAL COMPUTER*.

In displaying numbers, remember that all positive numbers begin with a blank space, which is in place of the understood plus (+) sign. Negative numbers, however, have a displayed minus (-) sign and do not begin with a blank space. For example, the statement

```
20 PRINT "THE VALUE OF A IS";2.35
```

results in the display

```
THE VALUE OF A IS 2.35
```

The space between the *S* and the *2* comes from the blank, which is considered part of the number 2.35. On the other hand, the statement

```
30 PRINT "THE VALUE OF A IS";-2.35
```

results in the display

```
THE VALUE OF A IS-2.35
```

To obtain a space between the *S* and the -, we must include a space in the string constant:

```
30 PRINT "THE VALUE OF A IS ";-2.35
```

TEST YOUR UNDERSTANDING 1 (answer on page 161)
Write a program that allows you to input two numbers. The program should then display them as an addition problem in the form 5 + 7 = 12.

At the completion of a PRINT statement, BASIC automatically supplies an ENTER so that the cursor moves to the beginning of the next line. You may suppress this ENTER by ending the PRINT statement with a semicolon. For example, the statements

---

[1]For an 80-column width, the last print zone has only 10 characters. For a 40-column width, the last print zone has only 12 characters.

```
40 PRINT "THE VALUE OF A IS";
50 PRINT 2.35
```

results in the display

THE VALUE OF A IS 2.35

TEST YOUR UNDERSTANDING 2 (answer on page 161)
Describe the output from this program.

```
10 A=5:B=3:C=8
20 PRINT "THE VALUE OF A IS",A
30 PRINT "THE VALUE OF B";
40 PRINT " IS";B
50 PRINT "THE VALUE OF C IS";-C
60 END
```

Our discussion so far has been oriented to the display of data on the screen. However, you may also use semicolons in LPRINT statements to control spacing of output on the printer.

Horizontal Tabbing

You may begin a print item in any print position. To do this, use the **TAB** command. The print positions are numbered from 1 to 255, going from left to right. (Note that a line may be up to 255 characters long. On the screen, an oversized line wraps around to the next line. However, the line prints correctly on a printer having a wide enough print line.) For example, the command *TAB(7)* means to move to column 7. TAB is always used in conjunction with a PRINT statement. For example, the PRINT statement

50 PRINT TAB(7) A

prints the value of the variable *A,* beginning in print position 7. It is possible to use more than one TAB per PRINT statement. For example, the statement

100 PRINT TAB(5) A; TAB(15) B

prints the value of *A* beginning in print position 5, and the value of *B* beginning in print position 15. Note the semicolon between the two TAB instructions.

TEST YOUR UNDERSTANDING 3 (answer on page 161)
Write an instruction printing the value of *A* in column 25 and the value of *B* seven columns further to the right.

In some applications, you may wish to to add a certain number of spaces between output items (as opposed to TABbing where the next item appears in a specified column). This may be accomplished using the **SPC** (= space) function, which works very much like TAB. For example, to print the values of A and B with 5 blank spaces between them, we may use the statement

```
110 PRINT A; SPC(5) B
```

Formatting Numbers

IBM PC BASIC has rather extensive provisions for formatting numerical output. Here are some of the things you may specify with regard to printing a number:

- Number of digits of accuracy
- Alignment of columns (one's column, ten's column, hundred's column, and so forth)
- Display and positioning of the initial dollar sign
- Display of commas in large numbers (as in 1,000,000)
- Display and positioning of + and - signs.

All of these formatting options may be requested with the **PRINT USING** statement. Roughly speaking, you tell the computer what you wish your number to look like by specifying a "prototype." For example, suppose you wish to print the value of the variable A with four digits to the left of the decimal point and two digits to the right. This can be done via the instruction

```
10 PRINT USING "####.##"; A
```

Here, each # stands for a digit and the period stands for the decimal point. If, for example, A was equal to 5432.381, this instruction would round the value of A to the specified two decimal places and would print the value of A as

```
5432.38
```

On the other hand, if the value of A is 932.547, then the computer prints the value as

```
932.55
```

In this case, the value is printed with a leading blank space, since the format specified four digits to the left of the decimal point. This sort of printing is especially useful in aligning columns of figures like this:

```
  367.1
 1567.2
29573.3
    2.4
```

The above list of numbers can be printed using this program:

```
10 ' *******************************************
20 ' This program lists four numbers read into
30 '   an array, with decimal points lined up
40 ' *******************************************
50 DATA 367.1, 1567.2, 29573.3, 2.4
60 FOR J=1 TO 4
70    READ A(J)
80    PRINT USING "#####.#";A(J)
90 NEXT J
100 END
```

TEST YOUR UNDERSTANDING 4 (answer on page 161)

Write an instruction that prints the number 456.75387 rounded to two decimal places.

You may use a single PRINT USING statement to print several numbers on the same line. For example, the statement

```
10 PRINT USING "##.##"; A,B,C
```

prints the values of *A*, *B*, and *C* on the same line, all in the format ##.##. Only one space is allowed between each of the numbers. Additional spaces may be added by using extra #s. If you wish to print numbers on one line in two different formats, then you must use two different PRINT USING statements, with the first ending in a semicolon (;) to indicate a continuation on the same line.

If you try to display a number larger than the prototype, the number will be displayed preceded by a percent (%) symbol. For example, consider the statement

```
10 PRINT USING "###"; A
```

If the value of A is 5000, then the display will look like this:

```
%5000
```

TEST YOUR UNDERSTANDING 5 (answer on page 161)

Write a program to calculate and display the numbers 2^J, $J = 1,2,3, \ldots ,15$. The columns of numbers should be properly aligned on the right.

You may have the computer insert a dollar sign on a displayed number. These two statements illustrate the procedure:

```
10 PRINT USING "$####.##"; A
20 PRINT USING "$$####.##";A
```

Suppose that the value of A is 34.78. The results of lines 10 and 20 will then be displayed as

```
$   34.78
 $34.78
```

Note the difference between the displays produced by lines 10 and 20. The single $ produces a dollar sign in the fifth position to the left of the decimal point. This is just to the left of the four digits specified in the prototype #### . ##. However, the $$ in line 20 indicates a ''floating dollar sign.'' The dollar sign is printed in the first position to the left of the number without leaving any space.

Example 1. Here is a list of checks written by a family during the month of March.

$15.32, $387.00, $57.98, $3.47, $15.88

Print the list of checks on the screen with the columns properly aligned and the total displayed below the list of check amounts, in the form of an addition problem.

Solution. We first read the check amounts into an array $A(J)$, $J = 1, 2, 3, 4, 5$. While we read the amounts, we accumulate the total in the variable B. We use a second loop to print the display in the desired format.

```
10  ' ************************************************
20  ' This program displays several monetary amounts
30  '   and their total, aligned by decimal points
40  ' ************************************************
100 DATA 15.32, 387.00, 57.98, 3.47, 15.88
110 FOR J=1 TO 5
120     READ A(J):          ' Read a data item
130     B=B+A(J):           ' Add it to the total
140     PRINT USING "$###.##"; A(J): ' Display the item
150 NEXT J
160 PRINT "_____"
170 PRINT USING "$###.##"; B
180 END
```

Here is what the output will look like:

```
$ 15.32
$387.00
$ 57.98
$  3.47
$ 15.88
_____
$479.65
```

Note that line 160 is used to print the line under the column of figures.

The PRINT USING statement has several other variations. To print commas in large numbers, insert a comma anywhere to the left of the decimal point. For example, consider the statement

```
10 PRINT USING ###,###; A
```

If the value of A is 123456, it will be displayed as

123,456

The PRINT USING statement may also be used to position plus and minus signs in connection with displayed numbers. A plus sign at the beginning or the end of a prototype causes the appropriate sign to be printed in the position indicated. For example, consider the statement

10 PRINT USING "+####.###"; A

Suppose that the value of A is -458.73. It will be displayed as

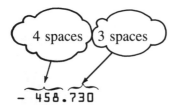

– 458.730

Similarly, consider the statement

10 PRINT USING "+###.##"; A

Suppose that A has the value .05873. Then A will be displayed as

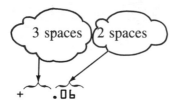

+   .06

Important Note: In the above discussion, we have only mentioned output on the screen. However, all of the features mentioned may be used on a printer via the LPRINT USING instruction. Note, however, that the wider line of the printer allows you to display more data than the screen. In particular, there are more 14-character print fields (just how many depends on which printer you own), and you may TAB to a higher-numbered column than on the screen.

Recall that BASIC uses two different representations for numbers—the usual decimal representation and scientific (or exponential notation). You may use ^ ^ ^ ^ to format numbers into scientific notation. For example, to display a number in scientific notation with two digits to the left of the decimal point and two to the right, use the format string

"##.##^^^^"

In this format, the number 100 is displayed as

`10.00E+01`

Other Variants of PRINT USING

There are several further things you can do with the PRINT USING statement. They are especially useful to accountants and others concerned with preparing financial documents.

If you precede the prototype with **, this causes all unused digit positions in a number to be filled with asterisks. For example, consider the statement

`10 PRINT USING "**####.#";A`

If *A* has the value 34.86, the value is displayed as

`****34.9`

Note that four asterisks are displayed since six digits to the left of the decimal point are specified in the prototype, the asterisks count, but the value of A uses only two. The remaining four are filled with asterisks.

You may combine the action of ** and $. You should experiment with this combination. It is especially useful for printing dollar amounts of the form

`$*******387.98`

Such a format is especially useful in printing amounts on checks to prevent modification.

By using a minus sign immediately after a prototype, you will print the appropriate number with a trailing minus sign if it is negative and with no sign if it is positive. For example, the statement

`10 PRINT USING "####.##-"; A`

with *A* equal to *-57.88* results in the display

`57.88-`

On the other hand, if *A* is equal to *57.88,* the display is

`57.88`

This format for numbers is often used in preparing accounting reports.

ANSWERS TO TEST YOUR UNDERSTANDINGS 1, 2, 3, 4, and 5

```
1:  10 INPUT A,B
    20 PRINT A;" +";B;" =";A+B
    30 END
```

```
2:   THE VALUE OF A IS 5
     THE VALUE OF B IS 3
     THE VALUE OF C IS-8

3:   10 PRINT TAB(25) A;TAB(32) B

4:   10 PRINT USING "###.##"; 456.75387

5:   10 FOR J=1 TO 15
     20   PRINT USING "#####"; 2^J
     30 NEXT J
     40 END
```

7.4   Gambling with Your Computer

One of the most interesting features of your computer is its ability to generate events whose outcomes are "random." For example, you may instruct the computer to "throw a pair of dice" and produce a random pair of integers between 1 and 6. You may instruct the computer to "pick a card at random from a deck of 52 cards." You may also program the computer to choose a two-digit number "at random." And so forth. The source of all such random choices is the BASIC function **RND.** To explain how this function works, let us consider this program:

```
10 ' ******************************************
20 ' This program prints 500 random numbers
30 '    between 0.0000000 and 1.0000000
40 ' ******************************************
50 FOR X=1 TO 500
60   PRINT RND
70 NEXT X
80 END
```

This program consists of a loop that prints 500 numbers, each called RND. Each of these numbers lies between 0.000000 (inclusive) and 1.000000 (exclusive). Each time the program refers to RND (as in line 20 here), the computer makes a "random" choice from among the numbers in the indicated range. This is the number that is printed.

To obtain a better idea of what we are talking about, generate some random numbers using a program like the one above. Unless you have a printer, 500 numbers will be too many for you to look at in one viewing. You should print four random numbers on one line (one per print zone) and limit yourself to 25 displayed lines at one time. Here is a partial printout of such a program:

```
.245121    .305003    .311866    .515163
.984546    .901159    .727313    6.83401E-03
.896609    .660212    .554489    .818675
.583931    .448163    .86774     .0331043
.137119    .226544    .215274    .876763
```

What makes these numbers "random" is that the procedure the computer uses to select them is "unbiased," with all numbers having an equal likelihood of selection. Moreover, if you generate a large collection of random numbers, then numbers between 0 and .1 will comprise approximately 10 percent of those chosen, those between .5 and 1.0 will comprise 50 percent of those chosen, and so forth. In some sense, the random number generator provides a uniform sample of the numbers between 0 and 1.

TEST YOUR UNDERSTANDING 1 (answer on page 169)
Assume that RND is used to generate 1000 numbers. Approximately how many of these numbers would you expect to lie between .6 and .9?

The random number generator is controlled by a so-called "seed" number, which controls the sequence of numbers generated. Once a particular seed number has been chosen, the sequence of random numbers is fixed. This would make computer games of chance rather uninteresting since they would always generate the same sequence of play. This may be prevented by changing the seed number using the **RANDOMIZE** command. A command of the form

```
10 RANDOMIZE
```

causes the computer to print out the display

```
Random Number Seed (-32768 to 32767)?
```

You then respond with a number in the indicated interval. Suppose, for example, you choose 129. The computer will then reseed the random number generator with the seed 129 and generate the sequence of random numbers corresponding to this seed. Another method of choosing a seed number is with a command of this form:

```
20 RANDOMIZE 129
```

This command sets the seed number to 129 without asking you. Later in this section, we will show you how to use the computer's internal clock to provide a seed number. This is a method of generating a seed over which no one has any control.

The function RND generates random numbers lying between 0 and 1. However, in many applications, we will require randomly chosen **integers** lying in a certain range. For example, suppose that we wish to generate random integers chosen from among 1, 2, 3, 4, 5, 6. Let us multiply RND by 6, to obtain 6*RND. This is a random number between 0.00000 and 5.99999. Next, let us add 1 to this number. Then 6*RND + 1 is a random number between 1.00000 and 6.99999. To obtain integers from among 1, 2, 3, 4, 5, 6, we must "chop off" the decimal portion of the number 6*RND + 1. To do this, we use the **INT** function. If X is any number, then $INT(X)$ is the largest integer less than or equal to X. For example,

```
INT(5.23)=5, INT(7.99)=7, INT(100.001)=100
```

Be careful in using INT with negative X. The definition we gave is correct, but unless you think things through, it is easy to make an error. For example,

```
INT(-7.4)=-8
```

since the largest integer less than or equal to -7.4 is equal to -8. (Draw -7.4 and -8 on a number line to see the point!)

Let us get back to our random numbers. To chop off the decimal portion of *6*RND + 1*, we compute *INT(6*RND + 1)*. This last expression is a random number from among 1, 2, 3, 4, 5, 6. Similarly, the expression

```
INT(100*RND+1)
```

may be used to generate random numbers from among the integers 1, 2, 3, . . . , 100.

TEST YOUR UNDERSTANDING 2 (answer on page 169)

Generate random integers from 0 to 1. (This is the computer analogue of flipping a coin: 0 = heads, 1 = tails) Run this program to generate 50 coin tosses. How many heads and how many tails occur?

Example 1.   Write a program that turns the computer into a pair of dice. Your program should report the number rolled on each as well as the total.

Solution.   We will hold the value of die #1 in the variable *X* and the value of die #2 in variable *Y*. The program will compute values for X and Y, and print out the values and the total *X + Y*.

```
10  ' ************************************
20  ' This program simulates the roll of
30  '    two dice, displaying the value of
40  '    each roll and their total
50  ' ************************************
100 RANDOMIZE
110 CLS
120 X=INT(6*RND + 1)
130 Y=INT(6*RND + 1)
140 PRINT "LADIES AND GENTLEMEN, BETS PLEASE!"
150 INPUT "ARE ALL BETS DOWN(Y/N)"; A$
160 IF A$ = "Y" THEN 170 ELSE 140
170 PRINT "THE ROLL IS",X,Y
180 PRINT "THE WINNING TOTAL IS";X+Y
190 INPUT "PLAY AGAIN(Y/N)"; B$
200 IF B$="Y" THEN 110
210 PRINT "THE CASINO IS CLOSING. SORRY!"
220 END
```

Note the use of computer-generated conversation on the screen. Note also, how the program uses lines 120-130 to allow the player to control how many times the game will be played. Finally, note the use of the command RANDOM-IZE in line 100. This will generate a question to allow you to choose a seed number.

TEST YOUR UNDERSTANDING 3 (answer on page 169)
Write a program that flips a "biased coin." Let it report "heads" one-third of the time and "tails" two-thirds of the time.

You may enhance the realism of a gambling program by letting the computer keep track of bets as in the following example.

Example 2.   Write a program that turns the computer into a roulette wheel. Let the computer keep track of bets and winnings for up to five players. For simplicity, assume that the only bets are on single numbers. (In the next example, we will let you remove this restriction!)

Solution.   A roulette wheel has 38 positions: 1-36, 0, and 00. In our program, we will represent these as the numbers 1-38, with 37 corresponding to 0 and 38 corresponding to 00. A spin of the wheel will consist of choosing a random integer between 1 and 38. The program will start by asking the number of players. For a typical spin of the wheel, the program will ask for bets by each player. A bet will consist of a number (1-38) and an amount bet. The wheel will then spin. The program will determine the winners and losers. A payoff for a win is 32 times the amount bet. Each player has an account, stored in an array $A(J)$, $J = 1, 2, 3, 4, 5$. At the end of each spin, the accounts are adjusted and displayed. Just as in Example 1, the program asks if another play is desired. Here is the program.

```
1   ' ************************************************
2   ' This program runs a roulette wheel for up to
3   '   five people, allowing bets on any number
4   ' ************************************************
5     RANDOMIZE
10    INPUT "NUMBER OF PLAYERS";N
20    DIM A(5),B(5),C(5): 'At Most 5 Players
30    FOR J= 1 TO N :    'Initial Purchase of Chips
40      PRINT "PLAYER "; J
50      INPUT "HOW MANY CHIPS"; A(J)
60    NEXT J
100 PRINT "LADIES AND GENTLEMEN! PLACE YOUR
        BETS PLEASE!"
110 FOR J=1 TO N :               'Place Bets
120     PRINT "PLAYER "; J
130     INPUT "NUMBER, AMOUNT"; B(J),C(J):'INPUT BET
140 NEXT J
200 X=INT(38*RND + 1):          'Spin the wheel
220 PRINT "THE WINNER IS NUMBER"; X
300 'Compute winnings and losses
310 FOR J=1 TO N
320   IF X=B(J) THEN 400
```

```
330    A(J)=A(J)-C(J):              'Player J loses
340    PRINT "PLAYER ";J;"LOSES"
350    GOTO 420
400    A(J)=A(J)+32*C(J):           'Player J wins
410    PRINT "PLAYER ";J;"WINS "; 32*C(J); "DOLLARS"
420 NEXT J
430 PRINT "PLAYER BANKROLLS": 'Display game status
440 PRINT
450 PRINT "PLAYER", "CHIPS"
460 FOR J=1 TO N
470    PRINT J,A(J)
480 NEXT J
500 INPUT "DO YOU WISH TO PLAY ANOTHER ROLL (Y/N)";R$
510 CLS
520 IF R$ = "Y" THEN 100:        'Repeat game
530 PRINT "THE CASINO IS CLOSED. SORRY!"
600 END
```

Try a few spins of the wheel. The program is fun as well as instructive. Note that the program allows you to bet more chips than you have. We will leave it to the exercises to add in a test that there are enough chips to cover the bet. You can also build lines of credit into the game! In the next example, we will illustrate how the roulette program may be extended to incorporate the bets even and odd.

Before we proceed to the next example, however, let's discuss one further defect of the program in Example 2. Note that line 5 contains a RANDOMIZE statement. The program will then ask for a random number seed. The person who selects the random number seed has control over the random number sequence and hence over the game. This is most unsatisfactory. However, there is a simple way around this difficulty.

The IBM PC has an internal clock that is set each time you sign on the computer. This clock keeps track of time in hours minutes and seconds. The value of the clock is accessed via the function **TIME$.** We will discuss use of the clock in detail in Chapter 14. For the moment however, let's borrow a fact from that discussion. The current reading of the seconds portion of the clock is equal to

`VAL(RIGHT$(TIME$,2))`

Let's use this number as our random number seed. (It is unlikely that anyone can control the precise second at which the game begins.)

Example 3.   Modify the roulette program of Example 2, so that it allows bets on even and odd. A one-dollar bet on either of these pays one dollar in winnings.

Solution.   Our program will now allow three different bets: on a number and on even or odd. Let us design subroutines, corresponding to each of these bets, which determine whether player J wins or loses. For each subroutine, let X be the number (1-38) which results from spinning the wheel. In the preceding program, a bet by player J was described by two numbers: $B(J)$ equals the number bet and *C(J)* equals the amount bet. Now let us add a third number to describe a bet. Let *D(J)* equal 1 if *J* bets on a number, 2 if *J* bets on even, and 3 if *J* bets on odd. In case *D(J)* is 2 or 3, we will again let *C(J)* equal the amount bet, but *B(J)* will be ignored. The subroutine for determining the winners of bets on numbers can be obtained by making small modifications to the corresponding portion of our previous program, as follows:

```
1000 'Bet=NUMBER
1010 IF B(J)=X THEN 1050
1020 PRINT "PLAYER ";J; " LOSES"
1030 A(J)=A(J)-C(J)
1040 GOTO 1070
1050 PRINT "PLAYER ";J; " WINS"; 32*C(J); "DOLLARS"
1060 A(J)=A(J) + 32*C(J)
1070 RETURN
```

Here is the subroutine corresponding to the bet even. In line 2010, we use the test *INT(X/2) = X/2* to determine whether or not *X* is even. The function *INT* throws away the fraction part of the number *X/2*. For even numbers *X*, then, *INT(X/2)* is the same as *X/2*, whereas for odd *X*, the two are different.

```
2000 'BET=EVEN
2010     IF INT(X/2) = X/2 THEN 2050
2020     PRINT "PLAYER ";J;" LOSES"
2030     A(J)=A(J)-C(J)
2040     GOTO 2070
2050     PRINT "PLAYER " ;J;" WINS ";C(J);" DOLLARS"
2060     A(J)=A(J)+C(J)
2070 RETURN
```

Finally, here is the subroutine corresponding to the bet odd.

```
3000 'Bet=ODD
3010     IF INT(X/2) < X/2 THEN 3050
3020     PRINT "PLAYER ";J;" LOSES"
3030     A(J)=A(J)-C(J)
3040     GOTO 3070
3050     PRINT "PLAYER ";J;" WINS ";C(J);" DOLLARS"
3060     A(J)=A(J)+C(J)
3070 RETURN
```

Now we are ready to assemble the subroutines together with the main portion of the program, which is almost the same as before. The only essential alteration is that we must now determine, for each player, which bet was placed.

```
1 ' *****************************************
2 ' This program runs a roulette wheel for
3 '    up to five people, allowing bets on
4 '    any number, or EVEN or ODD
5 ' *****************************************
10 CLS
20 RANDOMIZE VAL(RIGHT$(TIME$,2))
30 INPUT "NUMBER OF PLAYERS";N
40 DIM A(5),B(5),C(5)
```

```
50 FOR J=1 TO N
60    PRINT "PLAYER ";J
70    INPUT "HOW MANY CHIPS";A(J)
80 NEXT J
90 PRINT "LADIES AND GENTLEMEN! PLACE YOUR
   BETS PLEASE!"
100 FOR J=1 TO N:          'Place bets
110    PRINT "PLAYER" ;J
120    PRINT "BET TYPE:1=NUMBER BET, 2=EVEN, 3=ODD"
130    INPUT "BET TYPE (1,2, OR 3)";D(J)
140    IF D(J)=1 THEN 170
150    INPUT "AMOUNT";C(J)
160    GOTO 180
170    INPUT "NUMBER, AMOUNT BET";B(J),C(J)
180 NEXT J
190 X=INT(38*RND+1):     'Spin Wheel
200 CLS
210 PRINT "THE WINNER IS NUMBER";X
220 FOR J=1 TO N:          'Determine winnings and losses
230    ON D(J) GOSUB 1000,2000,3000
240 NEXT J
250 PRINT "PLAYER BANKROLLS"
260 PRINT "PLAYER", "CHIPS"
270 FOR J=1 TO N
280    PRINT J,A(J)
290 NEXT J
300 INPUT "DO YOU WISH TO PLAY ANOTHER ROLL(Y/N)";R$
310 CLS
320 IF R$="Y" OR R$="y" THEN 90
330 PRINT "THE CASINO IS CLOSED. SORRY!"
340 END
1000 'Bet=NUMBER
1010      IF B(J)=X THEN 1050 ELSE 1020
1020      PRINT "PLAYER ";J; " LOSES"
1030      A(J)=A(J)-C(J)
1040      GOTO 1070
1050      PRINT "PLAYER ";J; " WINS";
                  32*C(J); "DOLLARS"
1060      A(J)=A(J)+32*C(J)
1070 RETURN
2000 'Bet=EVEN
2010      IF INT(X/2)=X/2 THEN 2050
2020      PRINT "PLAYER ";J;" LOSES"
2030      A(J)=A(J)-C(J)
2040      GOTO 2070
2050      PRINT "PLAYER " ;J;" WINS ";C(J);" DOLLARS"
2060      A(J)=A(J)+C(J)
2070 RETURN
3000 'Bet=ODD
3010      IF INT(X/2) < X/2 THEN 3050
3020      PRINT "PLAYER ";J;" LOSES"
3030      A(J)=A(J)-C(J)
3040      GOTO 3070
3050      PRINT "PLAYER ";J;" WINS ";C(J);" DOLLARS"
3060      A(J)=A(J)+C(J)
```

```
3070 RETURN
4000 END
```

Note how the subroutines help to organize our programming. Each subroutine is easy to write and each is a small task, and you will have less to think about than when considering the entire program. It is advisable to break a long program into a number of subroutines. Not only is it easier to write in terms of subroutines, but it is much easier to check the program and to locate errors since subroutines may be individually tested.

You may treat the output of the random number generator as you would any other number. In particular, you may perform arithmetic operations on the random numbers generated. For example, *5*RND* multiplies the output of the random number generator by 5, and *RND + 2* adds 2 to the output of the random number generator. Such arithmetic operations are useful in producing random numbers from intervals other than 0 to 1. For example, to generate random numbers between 2 and 3, we may use *RND + 2*.

Example 4.   Write a program that generates 10 random numbers lying in the interval from 5 to 8.

Solution.   Let us build up the desired function in two steps. We start from the function RND, which generates numbers from 0 to 1. First, we adjust for the length of the desired interval. From 5 to 8 is 3 units, so we multiply RND by 3. The function *3*RND* generates numbers from 0 to 3. Now we adjust for the starting point of the desired interval, namely 5. By adding 5 to *3*RND,* we obtain numbers lying between $0 + 5$ and $3 + 5$, that is between 5 and 8. Thus, *3*RND + 5* generates random numbers between 5 and 8. Here is the program required.

```
10 FOR J=1 TO 10
20   PRINT 3*RND+5
30 NEXT J
40 END
```

Example 5.   Write a function to generate random integers from among 5, 6, 7, 8, . . . , 12.

Solution.   There are eight consecutive integers possible. Let us start with the function *8*RND,* which generates random numbers between 0 and 8. Since we wish our random number to begin with 5, let us add 5 to get *8*RND + 5*. This produces random numbers between 5.00000 and 12.9999. We now use the INT function to chop off the decimal part. This yields the desired function:

```
INT(8*RND+5)
```

ANSWERS TO TEST YOUR UNDERSTANDINGS 1, 2, and 3

1:   about 300

```
2:  10 FOR J=1 TO 50
    20    PRINT INT(2*RND)
    30 NEXT J
    40 END

3:  10 LET X=INT(3*RND)
    20 IF X=0 THEN PRINT "HEADS" ELSE PRINT "TAILS"
    30 END
```

8
Easing Programming Frustrations

8.0 Chapter Objectives

AS YOU HAVE PROBABLY DISCOVERED by now, programming can be a tricky and frustrating business. You must first figure out the instructions to give the computer. Next, you must type the instructions into RAM. Finally, you must run the program. Usually after the first run, you must figure out why the program won't work. This process can be tedious and frustrating, especially in dealing with long or complex programs. We should emphasize that programming frustrations often result from the limitations and inflexibility of the computer to understand exactly what you are saying. In talking with another person, you usually sift out irrelevant information, correct minor errors, and still maintain the flow of communication. With a computer, however, you must clear up all of the imprecisions before the conversation can even begin.

Fortunately, your computer has many features designed to ease the programming burdens, and to help you track down errors and correct them. We will describe these features in this chapter. We will also present some more tips to help you develop programs more quickly and with fewer errors.

In this chapter, we cover:

- Flowcharting.
- Debugging using TRACE.
- Using error messages.
- Debugging strategies.

8.1 Flowcharting

In the last three chapters, our programs were fairly simple. By the end of Chapter 7, however, we saw them becoming more involved. And there are many programs that are much more lengthy and complex. You might be wondering how it is possible to plan and execute such programs. The key idea is to reduce large programs to a sequence of smaller programs that can be written and tested separately.

The old saying "A picture is worth a thousand words" is true for computer programming. In designing a program, especially a long one, it is helpful to draw a picture depicting the instructions of the program and their interrelationships. Such a picture is called a flowchart.

A **flowchart** is a series of boxes connected by arrows. Within each box is a series of one of more computer instructions. The arrows indicate the logical flow of the instructions. Let's illustrate the use of a flowchart to plan a program to convert feet to inches. One foot contains 12 inches, so we convert feet to inches using the formula

number-of-inches = 12 x number-of-feet

This formula is a general one. It may be used to convert any value for number-of-feet into the corresponding number-of-inches. When we create our program to carry out this calculation, we want it to work in the same way. It should ask the user for the number-of-feet. Then it should calculate the number-of-inches and display the value on the screen. Let's call the program *FEET TO INCHES*. Here are the steps the program must follow:

PROGRAM: FEET TO INCHES

    Ask user for the value of number-of-feet;

    Calculate number-of-inches;

    Print number-of-inches;

END PROGRAM.

Note the unusual manner in which we have written out the program. The first line contains the title of the program (*FEET TO INCHES*). The last line indicates the end of the program. The indented lines indicate the procedures to be carried out by the program. The procedures are carried out in the order in which they are listed.

Our program can be represented in a flowchart, as shown in Figure 8-1.

The flowchart indicates the procedures the program carries out. A flowchart is read from the top, starting at the box marked **Start**. Each box in the flowchart indicates a single procedure. Each box has an arrow leaving it. This arrow points to the box containing the next procedure. By following the arrows, you can trace the order in which the various procedures are carried out. The program ends when it reaches the box marked **Stop**.

Flowcharts are used to design most programs, especially large programs involving many procedures with complex interrelationships. They help in the planning and writing of a program, and serve as a handy reference to explain the code long after it is written.

Figure 8-1.

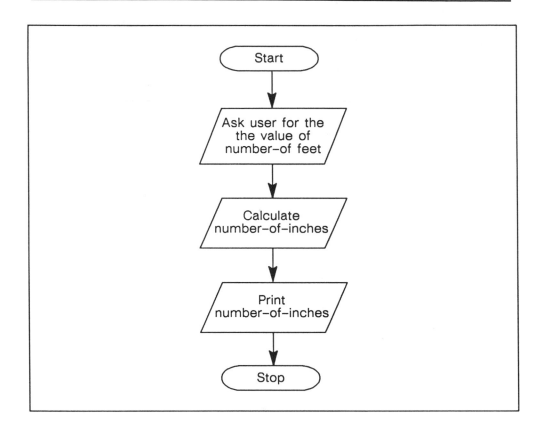

Top-Down Program Design

Some programs involve thousands of procedures and hundreds of thousands of lines of code. The way to write such programs (and all but the most trivial programs) is to break the program plan into a number of smaller segments, called **modules**. Each module can be broken into even smaller segments, called **submodules**. The process of breaking the plan continues until the segments are small enough to be readily programmed. This approach to programming is called **top-down program design**, since it starts from the whole plan (the "top") and breaks it "down" into smaller and smaller segments.

The initial breaking of the plan into modules leads to an initial flowchart called the **main-control** or **macro** flowchart or **hierarchy chart**. This flowchart indicates the over-all logical flow of the program. The creation of submodules breaks each of the boxes in the initial flowchart into a flowchart of its own. Each level of breaking of the plan leads to a new level of flowcharts in the initial flowchart.

As the plan becomes more and more specific, the flowchart also becomes more and more specific. In Figure 8-2, we show the top-down design of a program for entering orders and preparing bills for a telephone sales firm. The figure shows how boxes in the initial flowchart are expanded into whole flowcharts at the next level.

Figure 8-2.

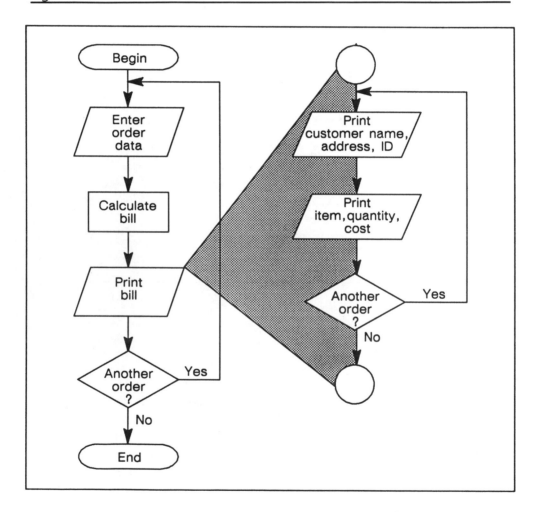

Flowchart Symbols

Flowcharts contain symbols with specific meanings. The symbols are standardized through the American National Standards Institute (ANSI), so they have the same meanings in all flowcharts. Here are the main symbols used in flowcharts.

Terminal. The terminal symbol is used to indicate either a beginning, end, or interruption point of a program.

Processing Function. The processing function symbol indicates a function for numerical or text processing. An example of a numerical processing function is calculating payroll deductions for state and local taxes; a text processing function is deleting all spaces in front of a word or phrase.

Input/Output. The input/output symbol indicates action by an input/output device. These actions include reading the keyboard, printing on the screen, printing on the printer, reading a diskette, writing on a hard disk, and so on.

Decision. The decision symbol indicates that a decision has to be made. A question is asked within the box. The box has two exit arrows. The path taken by the program depends on the answer to the question.

Connector. The connector symbol is used to indicate a connection to another part of the flowchart without drawing a continuous line. For example, if the connector symbol contains the letters A3, it connects to a similarly-labeled connector symbol elsewhere on the flowchart.

Switch. The switch symbol indicates setting of a switch. (A switch is a program variable that can have one of the two values 0 or 1.) Switches are often used to indicate conditions which can be either true or false and whose truth value changes during program execution. For example, a program printing mailing labels might require a switch indicating if there are any labels remaining to be printed. This switch starts out with the value 1 (= true) indicating that there are further labels to be printed. After the last label is printed, the switch is changed to 0 (= false), indicating that there are no further labels to be printed.

Subroutine. The subroutine symbol indicates use of a standard procedure defined by a subroutine. Typically, programmers build standard subroutines for procedures that occur in many different programs. These subroutines are often stored until they are used in programs. A subroutine symbol indicates that the subroutine box in the flowchart is expanded as a set of flowchart boxes that further describe the processing which takes place in the subroutine.

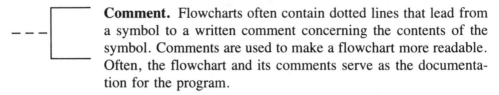 **Comment.** Flowcharts often contain dotted lines that lead from a symbol to a written comment concerning the contents of the symbol. Comments are used to make a flowchart more readable. Often, the flowchart and its comments serve as the documentation for the program.

We will see how the various flowchart symbols are used later in the chapter, where we will discuss some practical examples of program planning.

8.2   Some Flowcharting Examples

The best way to become familiar with flowcharts is to see how they are prepared for a number of typical problems. That's what we will do in this section. The problems we pose are typical (but simple) ones that arise when managing a small business. The problems are arranged roughly in order of increasing difficulty.

Problem 1.   Kreativ Komputers is a company with a single product, a tutorial program in reading for elementary school students. How does the company construct a flowchart for a program that prints bills? The data for the customer's name and address and the number of copies of the program are entered via the keyboard. The price of the program is included within the program and is not given as part of the input.

The program consists of three main procedures:

1. Inputting the customer data and the number of copies (N).
2. Computing the amount owed (A) from the formula $A = N \times P$, where P is the price per program.
3. Printing out the bill.

The flowchart incorporating these three procedures is shown in Figure 8-3.

Each of the boxes in the flowchart must be expanded to give more detail. The first box can be expanded to the flowchart in Figure 8-4(a). This flowchart has the user input the customer data in response to a series of questions.

Similarly, the box calling for printing out the bill can be expanded to the flowchart in Figure 8-4(b). The latter flowchart details exactly what gets printed on the bill.

Problem 2.   Kreativ Komputers expands its product line to include more than 100 different tutorial programs and various computer accessories. How does

Figure 8-3.

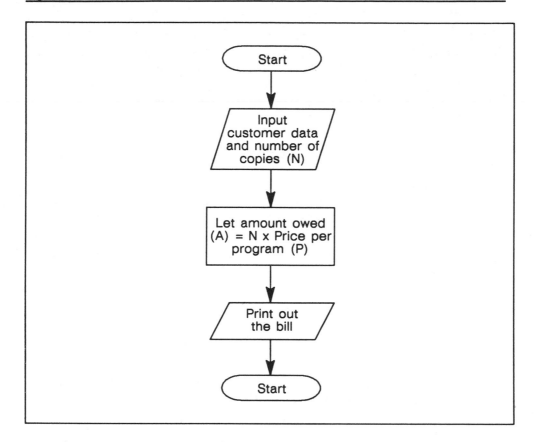

the company construct a flowchart for a program that will let it print out its bills? The prices of the items are stored in a table within the program and are not supplied as part of the input data.

The difference between Problem 1 and Problem 2 is that Problem 2 requires the program to allow for many different items on the bill. This is easily solved by having the program repeatedly ask for an item name and the quantity ordered.

The principal new difficulty is how to tell the computer that there are no more items. There are many ways to do this. Perhaps the simplest is to agree ahead of time that when the user types the character ''@'' in response to the name of an item, there are no more items to be included on the bill. This means that the program used to solve Problem 2 has to make a decision. After the name of an item is given, the program must ask: Is the item name ''@''? If so, then the program prints out the bill. If not, the program computes the billable amount for the named item. The flowchart describing the program is shown in Figure 8-5.

We won't attempt to expand the boxes of this flowchart, since we are mainly interested in demonstrating the use of the decision box at this point.

Problem 3.   The customer list of Kreativ Komputers is contained in a data file on a disk. How does the company construct a flowchart for a program that prints out the customer list on peel-off labels? The labels are on continuous form paper. Six lines of printing are required to space from the top of one label to the top of the next. A customer's name and address take up three lines.

An address label may be printed by first printing the three lines of customer data (1. Name, 2. Street Address, 3. City, State, and Zip Code), followed by three blank lines.

The main problem is to read the list of customers from the data file on the disk. We won't go into detail on how this is done. It is enough to say that the program can start at the beginning of the data file and read the customer data, one customer at a time. The program can also determine whether there is any more customer data to be read. The flowchart uses a decision box to determine whether there is any more data to be read. If so, it reads one customer's address data and prints the corresponding label. Then it repeats the procedure. If there is no more customer data to be read, the program ends.

The flowchart appears in Figure 8-6.

Problem 4.   Kreativ Komputers keeps a data file of all its customers and the year-to-date total of their orders. How does the company construct a flowchart for a program that prints out a list of all customers who have ordered more than $500.00 and less than $1000.00 for the year to date?

This problem is similar to Problem 3, except that not all of the customer data is to be printed out. After reading the customer data from the file, the program must check that the year-to-date total of sales is more than $500.00 (> $500.00) and less than $1000.00 (< $1000.00). If so, the customer data is printed out. If not, the customer data is ignored. Note that two new decisions are required, one to see if the total is more than $500.00 and one to see if the total is less than $1000.00. As in Problem 3, we require a decision to determine when the last customer data has been processed.

The flowchart appears in Figure 8-7.

Problem 5.   Kreativ Komputers wants to include three separate procedures in a single program. The user must be able to select from a menu which of the three procedures is to be run. After the procedure is run, the user must be able to run another procedure (or perhaps the same procedure again).

This problem asks us to construct a menu that allows the user to choose from among three programs. Such menus are commonly used to help a program user choose from a list of options. For simplicity, let's call the procedures Procedure 1, Procedure 2, and Procedure 3, and assume that they have already been

Figure 8-4.

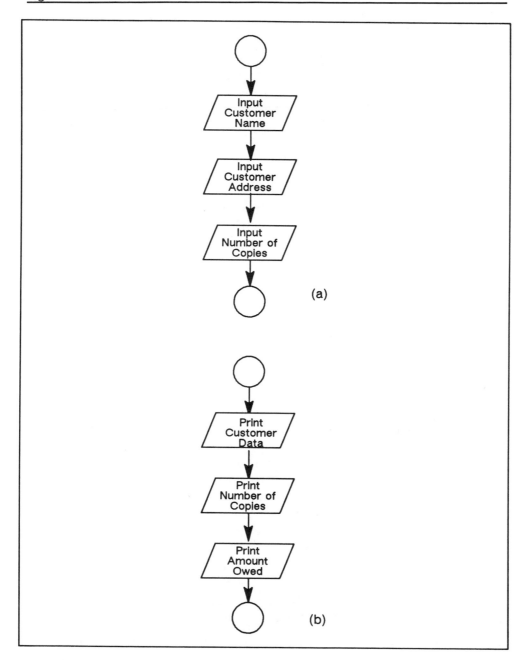

Figure 8-5.

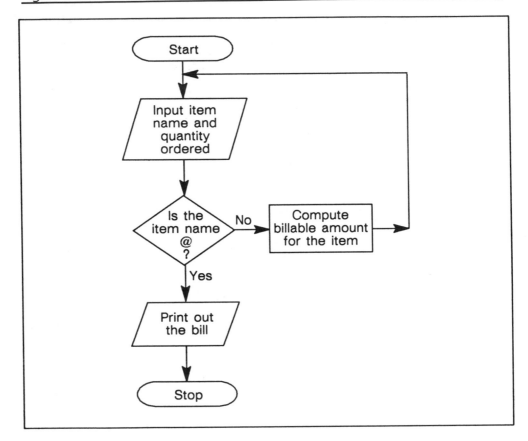

defined. The program begins by displaying a menu that asks the user to type *1* for Procedure 1, *2* for Procedure 2, *3* for Procedure 3, or *4* to end the program. The program inputs the user's response and determines if the response is a *1, 2, 3*, or *4*. If the response is anything else, the program redisplays the menu and asks the user to try again. Checking for a valid response requires several decisions, as shown in the flowchart in Figure 8-8.

Problems 2, 3, 4, and 5 illustrate the use of decisions in flowcharting. Let's now look at flowcharts involving loops.

Problem 6.   Kreativ Komputers must print 50 copies of a sales report. How can the company construct a flowchart for a program that accomplishes this task?

This task involves a simple loop—50 repetitions of the same task. In dealing with such a loop, it is convenient to introduce a **counter**, which keeps track of the current repetition number. (In coding the program from the flowchart, the

Figure 8-6.

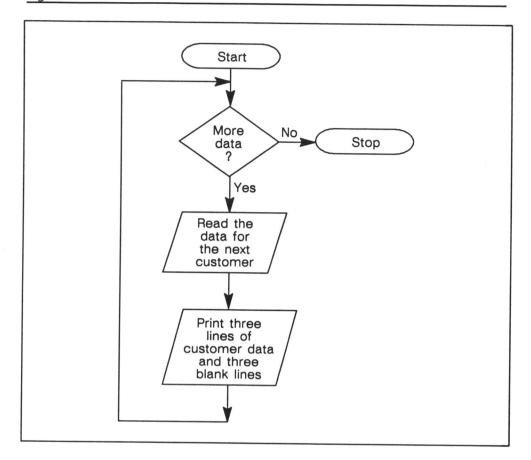

counter is the variable in the FOR ... NEXT loop. In this problem, we'll call the counter I. Initially, I will be set to 1, indicating that the first repetition of the loop is beginning.

The **body of the loop** consists of the program section to be repeated. In this problem, the body of the loop consists of the procedure for printing one copy of the report. After the procedure is carried out, the counter is increased by 1, and I is replaced by $I + 1$ to indicate that the program is ready for the next repetition of the body of the loop. The program must now determine whether I is greater than 50, that is, whether the loop been repeated often enough. If not, the body of the loop is executed again. This process is repeated until the desired number of repetitions have been carried out. The flowchart for this process is shown in Figure 8-9.

Note that the loop consists of a section of the flowchart that cycles back on itself. The program keeps cycling around the loop until the counter I equals 50. The program then leaves the loop and reaches the **end** box.

Figure 8-7.

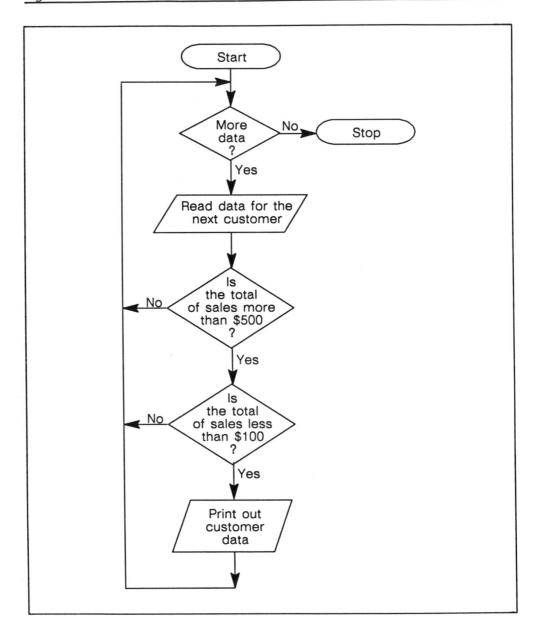

In Problem 6, we use the loop counter *I* to count the number of repetitions of the loop. The variable I can be used for other purposes within the loop, though, as the next Problem illustrates.

Problem 7.   How can Kreativ Komputers construct a flowchart for a program that prints the numbers 1 through 1000?

Let us use a loop to control printing consecutive numbers. Let *I* be the loop counter, starting from 1. Suppose that the *I*th repetition of the loop prints the number *I*. Then the first repetition prints out 1, the second 2, the third 3, and so forth. This simple loop is illustrated in the flowchart in Figure 8-10.

Problem 8.   How can Kreativ Komputers construct a flowchart that calculates the sum of the numbers 1 through 1000?

This problem introduces another new idea—the **accumulator**, which we introduced without comment in our earlier discussion of loops. Solving the problem involves having the program accumulate the sum using the variable *S*. Initially, *S* will be set equal to 0. The sum is computed by adding the numbers from 1 to 1000, to the number *S* one at a time. The program uses a loop with 1000 repetitions. The first repetition of the loop adds 1 to S, the second repetition 2, and so on. In general, the *I*th repetition adds the number *I* to *S*. At the end of the last loop, the accumulator *S* is equal to the desired sum.

The flowchart for this problem is shown in Figure 8-11.

Problem 9.   Kreativ Komputers took out a car loan to buy a truck to deliver its products. The loan charges 1.25 percent interest per month. The beginning balance is $7,000 and the monthly payment is $242.25. How can the company construct a flowchart for a program that prints a chart displaying the balance at the end of each month for the next 12 months?

Let *B* equal the balance at any particular time, *I* the interest for the current month, and *M* the month number. The interest may be calculated using the formula

$$I = .0125 \times B$$

That is, the interest equals 1.25 percent of the current balance. The payment is $242.25. Of this, an amount *I* goes to interest and

$$242.25 - I$$

goes to reduce the balance. The new balance is

$$B - (242.25 - I)$$

That is, after the payment, the value of *B* is replaced by the last quantity. This is shown in the notation

$$B \longrightarrow B - (242.25 - I)$$

Figure 8-8.

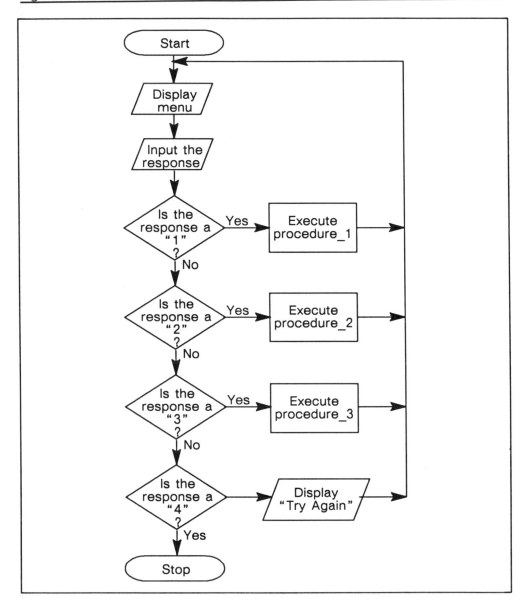

Figure 8-9.

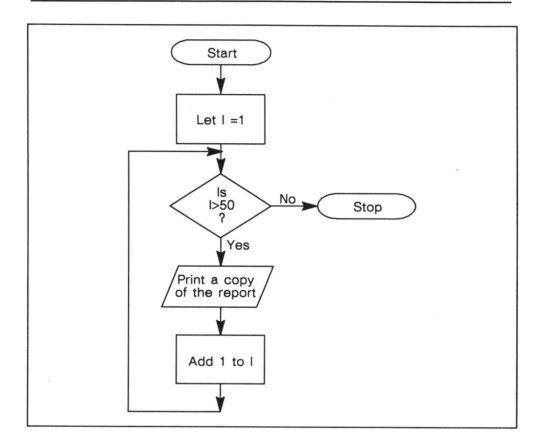

Read this as B is replaced by *B - (242.25 - I)*. This new value of the balance is now printed out. The same set of calculations is now repeated with the new balance. The sequence of calculations is repeated 12 times, corresponding to 12 monthly payments.

A flowchart for this problem is shown in Figure 8-12.

8.3 Errors and Debugging

An error is sometimes called a ''bug'' in computer jargon. The process of finding these errors or ''bugs'' in a program is called **debugging**. This can often be a ticklish task. Manufacturers of commercial software must regularly repair bugs they discover in their own programs! Your IBM Personal Computer is equipped with a number of features to help detect bugs.

Figure 8-10.

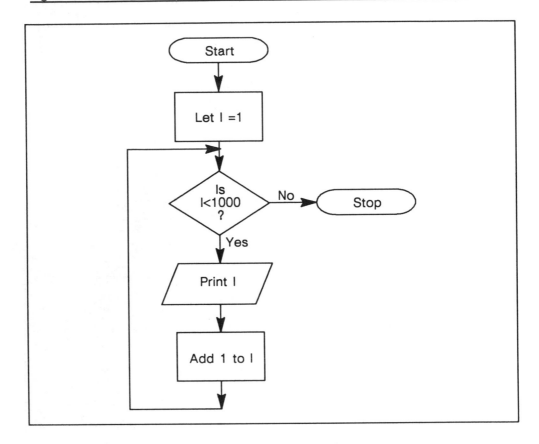

The Trace

Often your first try at running a program results in failure, while giving you no indication as to why the program is not running correctly. For example, your program might just run indefinitely, without giving you a clue as to what it is actually doing. How can you figure out what's wrong? One method is to use the trace feature. Let us illustrate use of the trace, by debugging the following program designed to calculate the sum $1 + 2 + \ldots + 100$. The variable S is to contain the sum. The program uses a loop to add each of the numbers 1, 2, 3, ..., 100 to S, which is initially 0.

```
10   S=0
20   J=0
30   S=S + J
40   IF J=100 THEN 100 ELSE 200
```

Figure 8-11.

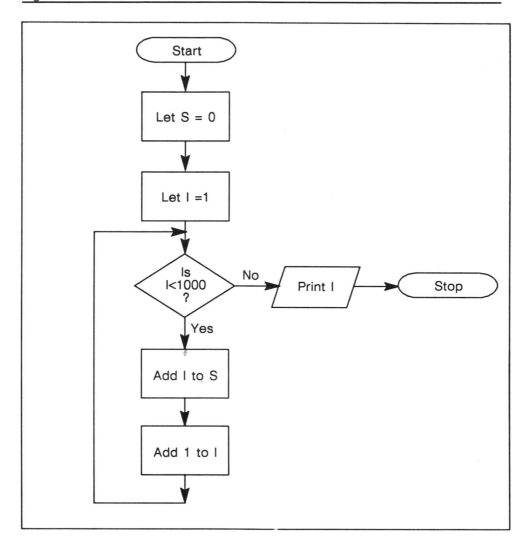

```
100 J=J+1
110 GOTO 20
200 PRINT S
300 END
```

This program has two errors in it. (Can you spot them right off?) All you know initially is that the program is not functioning normally. The program runs, but prints out the answer 0, which we recognize as nonsense. How can we locate the errors? Let's turn on the trace function by typing *TRON* (**TR**ace **ON**) and pressing ENTER. The computer responds with *Ok*. Now type *RUN*. The computer

Figure 8-12.

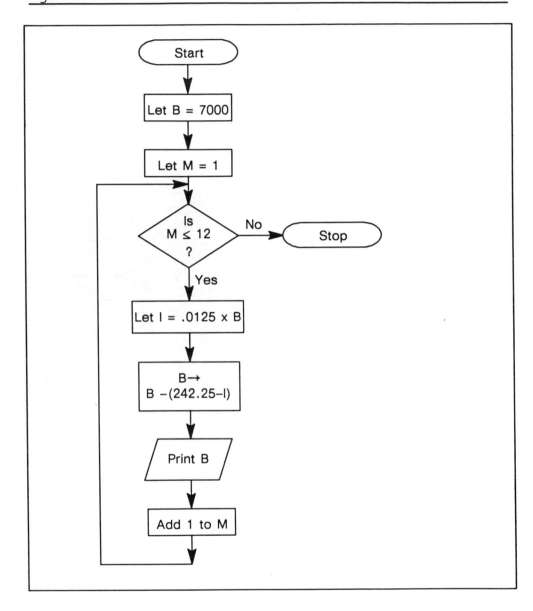

will run our program and print out the line numbers of all executed instructions. Here is what our display looks like:

```
TRON
Ok

RUN
[10] [20] [30]0] [200] 0
[300]
```

The numbers in brackets indicate the line numbers executed. That is, the computer executes, in order, lines 10, 20, 30, 40, 200, and 300. The zero not in brackets is the program output resulting from the execution of line 200. The list of line numbers is not what we were expecting. Our program was designed (or so we thought) to execute line 100 after line 40. No looping is taking place. How did we get to line 200 after line 40? This suggests that we examine line 40. Lo and behold! There is an error. The line numbers 100 and 200 appearing in line 40 have been interchanged (an easy enough mistake to make). Let's correct this error by retyping the line:

```
40 IF J=100 THEN 200 ELSE 100
```

In triumph, we run our program again. Here is the output:

```
[10] [20] [30] [40] [100] [110] [20] [30]
[40] [100] [110] [20] [30] [40] [100] [110]
[20] [30] [40] [100]
Break in 110
```

Actually, the above output goes whizzing by us as the computer races madly on executing the instructions. After about 30 seconds, we sense that something is indeed wrong since it is unlikely that our program could take this long. We stop execution by means of the Ctrl-Break key combination. The last line indicates that we interrupted the computer while it was executing line 110.

Actually, your screen will be filled with output resembling the above. You will notice that the computer is in a loop. Each time it reaches line 110, the loop goes back to line 20. Why doesn't the loop ever end? In order for the loop to terminate, *J* must equal 100. Well, can *J* ever equal 100? Of course not! Every time the computer executes line 20, the value of *J* is reset to 0. Thus, *J* is never equal to 100 and line 40 always sends us back to line 20. We clearly don't want to reset *J* to 0 all the time. After increasing *J* by 1 (line 100), we wish to add the new *J* to *S*. We want to go to 30, not 20. We correct line 110 to read

```
110 GOTO 30
```

We run our program again. There will be a rush of line numbers on the screen followed by the output 5050, which appears to be correct. Our program is now running properly. We turn off the trace by typing *TROFF* (**TR**ace **OFF**) and pressing ENTER. Finally, we run our program once more for good measure. The above sequence of operations is summarized in the following display:

```
[40] [200] 5050
[300]
Ok

TROFF
Ok

RUN
5050
Ok
```

In our example above, we displayed all the line numbers executed. For a long program, this may lead to a huge list of line numbers. You may be selective by using TRON and TROFF within your program. Just use them with line numbers, just like any other BASIC instruction. When BASIC encounters a TRON, it begins to display the line numbers executed. When BASIC encounters a TROFF, it stops displaying line numbers. To debug a program, you may temporarily add TRON and TROFF instructions at selected places. As you locate the bugs, remove the corresponding trace instructions.

Error Messages

In the example above, the program actually ran. A more likely occurrence is that there is a program line (or lines) which the computer is unable to understand due to an error or some other sort of problem. In this case, program execution ends too soon. The computer often can help in this instance since it is designed to recognize many of the most common errors. The computer will print an error message indicating the error type and the line number in which it occurred. The line with the error is automatically displayed, ready for editing. Suppose that the error reads

```
Syntax Error in 530
530   Y=(X+2(X^2-2)
```

We note that there is an open parenthesis "(" without a corresponding close parenthesis ")". This is enough to trigger an error. We modify line 530 to read

```
530   Y=X+2(X^2-2)
```

We RUN the program again and find that there is still a syntax error in line 530! This is the frustrating part since not all errors are easy to spot. However, if you look closely at the expression on the right, you will note that we have omitted the * to indicate the product of *2* and *(X^2-2)*. This is a common mistake, especially for those familiar with the use of algebra. (In algebra, the product is usually indicated without any operation sign.) We correct line 530 again (you may either retype the line or use the line editor).

```
530   Y=X+2*(X^2-2)
```

Now there is no longer a syntax error in line 530!

Section 8.4 contains a list of the most common error messages. There are a number of errors not included in our list, especially those associated with disk BASIC. For a complete list of error messages, the reader is referred to the *IBM Personal Computer BASIC Reference Manual*.

8.4   Common Error Messages

Syntax Error. There is an unclear instruction (misspelled?), mismatched parentheses, incorrect punctuation, illegal character, or illegal variable name in the program.

Undefined line number. The program uses a line number that does not correspond to an instruction. This can easily arise if you delete lines that are mentioned elsewhere. It can also occur when testing a portion of a program that refers to a line not yet written.

Overflow. A number too large for the computer.

Division by zero. Attempting to divide by zero. This may be a hard error to spot. The computer will round to zero any number smaller than the minimum allowed. Use of such a number in subsequent calculations can result in division by zero.

Illegal function call. (For the mathematically-minded.) Attempting to evaluate a function outside of its mathematically defined range. For example, the square root function is defined only for non-negative numbers, the logarithm function only for positive numbers, and the arctangent only for numbers between -1 and 1. Any attempt to evaluate a function at a value outside these respective ranges will result in an illegal function call error.

Missing Operand. Attempting to execute an instruction missing required data.

Subscript Out of Range. Attempting to use an array with one or more subscripts outside the range allowed by the appropriate DIM statement.

String Too Long. Attempting to specify a string containing more than 255 characters.

Out of Memory. Your program will not fit into the computer's memory. This could result from large arrays or too many program steps or a combination of the two.

String Formula Too Complex. Due to the internal processing of your formula, your string formula resulted in a string expression that was too long or complex. This error can be corrected by breaking the string expression into a series of simpler expressions.

Type Mismatch. Attempting to assign a string constant as the value of a numeric variable, or a numeric constant value to a string variable.

Duplicate Definition. Attempting to DIMension an array that has already been dimensioned. Note that once you refer to an array within a program, even if you don't specify the dimensions, the computer will regard it as being dimensioned at 10.

NEXT without FOR. A NEXT statement that does not correspond to a FOR statement.

RETURN without GOSUB. A RETURN statement is encountered while not performing a subroutine.

Out of Data. Attempting to read data that isn't there. This can occur in reading data from DATA statements, or diskettes.

Can't Continue. Attempting to give a CONT command after the program has ENDed, or before the program has been RUN (such as after an EDIT session).

8.5   Further Debugging Hints

Debugging is something between a black art and a science. Tracking down program bugs can be a very tricky business, and to be good at it you must be a good detective. In the preceding section, we listed some of the clues BASIC automatically supplies, namely the error messages. Sometimes, however, these clues are not enough to diagnose a bug. (For example, your program may run without errors. It may just not do what it is supposed to. In this case, no error messages will be triggered.) In such circumstances you must be prepared to supply your own clues. Here are some techniques.

Insert Extra PRINT Statements

You may temporarily insert extra PRINT statements into your program to print out the values of key variables at various points in the program. This technique allows you to keep track of a variable as your program is executed.

Insert STOP Commands

It is possible that your program planning may contain a logical flaw. In this case, it is possible to write a program that runs without error messages, but which does not perform as you expect it to. You may temporarily insert a STOP command to force a halt after a specified portion of the program.

This debugging technique may be used in several ways.

1. When the program encounters a STOP instruction, it halts execution and prints out the line number at which the program was stopped. If the program does stop, you will know that the instructions just before the STOP were executed. On the other hand, suppose that the program continues on its merry way. This tells you that the program is avoiding the instructions immediately preceding the STOP. If you determine the reason for this behavior, then you will likely correct a bug.

2. When the program is halted, the values of the variables are preserved. You may examine them to determine the behavior of your program. (See below for more information.)

3. You may insert several STOP instructions. After each halt, you may note the behavior of the program (line number, values of key variables, and so forth). You may continue execution by typing *CONT* and pressing ENTER. Note that if you change a program line during a halt, then you may not continue execution, but must restart the program by typing RUN and pressing ENTER.

Examine Variables in the Immediate Mode

When BASIC stops executing your program, the current values of the program variables are not destroyed. Rather, they are still in memory and may be examined as an indication of program behavior. This is true even if the program is halted by means of a STOP instruction or by hitting Ctrl-Break.

Suppose that a program is halted and that the BASIC prompt *Ok* is displayed. For example, to determine the current values of the program variables *INVOICE* and *FILENAME$*, type

```
PRINT INVOICE, FILENAME$
```

and press ENTER. Note that there is no line number. This instruction is in immediate mode. BASIC will display the current values of the two variables, just as if the PRINT statement was contained in a program:

```
145.83      ACCTPAY.MAR
```

Warning: As soon as you make any alteration in your program (correct a line, add a line), BASIC resets all the variables. The numeric variables will be reset to zero and the string variables will be set to null. Therefore, if you wish to have an accurate reading of the variable values as they emerge from your program, be sure to request them before making any program changes.

Execute Only a Portion of Your Program

Sometimes it helps to run only a portion of your program. You may start execution at any line using a variation of the RUN command. For example, to begin execution at line 500, type

`RUN 500`

and press ENTER. Note, however, that the RUN command causes all variables to be reset. If some earlier portion of your program sets some variables, then starting the program in the middle may not give an accurate picture of program operation. To get around this problem, you may set variables in immediate mode and start the program using the GOSUB instruction. For example, suppose that the earlier portion of your program set *INVOICE* equal to 145.83 and *FILE-NAME$* equal to *ACCTPAY.MAR*. To accurately run a portion of the program depending on these variable values, first type

`INVOICE=145.83:FILENAME$="ACCTPAY.MAR"`

and press ENTER. (These instructions can be entered on separate lines, each followed by ENTER.) To start the program at line 500, you type

`GOSUB 500`

and press ENTER. Note that it is not sufficient to use the command

`RUN 500`

The RUN command automatically resets the variables.

9

String Manipulation

9.0   Chapter Objectives

IN THIS CHAPTER, WE DISCUSS some of the fine points about strings. In particular, we discuss:

- ASCII codes.

- Control characters.

- Dealing with strings containing quotation marks.

- Operations on strings, including string concatenation, taking the length of a string, forming substrings using LEFT$, RIGHT$, and MID$, translating strings of digits into their numerical equivalents and vice versa, and searching for substrings using INSTR.

- Using ASCII codes to deal with cursor movement.

- Application of everything learned in the chapter to build a game of blackjack.

9.1   ASCII Character Codes

Each keyboard character is assigned a number between 1 and 255. The code number assigned is called the **ASCII code** of the character. For example, the letter "A" has ASCII code 65, while the letter "a" has ASCII code 97. Also included in this correspondence are the punctuation marks and other keyboard characters. As examples, 40 is the ASCII code of the open parenthesis "(" and 62 is the ASCII code of the greater-than symbol ">".

Even the keys corresponding to non-printable characters have ASCII codes. For example, the space bar has ASCII code 32, and the backspace key ASCII code 8. The printable characters have ASCII codes between 32 and 127. Table 9-1 lists all these characters and their corresponding ASCII codes.

We will discuss the ASCII control codes 0-31 in Section 9.3. For now, however, let's call attention to just two:

Table 9-1. ASCII character codes for printable characters.

ASCII value	Character	ASCII value	Character	ASCII value	Character
032	(space)	064	@	096	`
033	!	065	A	097	a
034	"	066	B	098	b
035	#	067	C	099	c
036	$	068	D	100	d
037	%	069	E	101	e
038	&	070	F	102	f
039	'	071	G	103	g
040	(	072	H	104	h
041	)	073	I	105	i
042	*	074	J	106	j
043	+	075	K	107	k
044	,	076	L	108	l
045	-	077	M	109	m
046	.	078	N	110	n
047	/	079	O	111	o
048	0	080	P	112	p
049	1	081	Q	113	q
050	2	082	R	114	r
051	3	083	S	115	s
052	4	084	T	116	t
053	5	085	U	117	u
054	6	086	V	118	v
055	7	087	W	119	w
056	8	088	X	120	x
057	9	089	Y	121	y
058	:	090	Z	122	z
059	;	091	[	123	{
060	<	092	\	124	¦
061	=	093	]	125	}
062	>	094	∧	126	~
063	?	095	—	127	⌂

*Courtesy of International Business Machines Corporation.

ASCII Code	Name	Action
10	Line Feed	Moves cursor down one line
13	Carriage Return	Moves cursor to the leftmost position on the current line

Pushing the ENTER key generates a carriage return and a line feed. That is, ENTER generates the two ASCII codes 13 and 10.

The computer uses ASCII codes to refer to letters and control operations. Any file, whether it is a program or data, may be reduced to a sequence of ASCII codes. Consider the following address:

```
John Jones
2 S. Broadway
```

As a sequence of ASCII codes, it is stored as

```
74,111,104,110,32,74,111,110,101,115,13,10,
50,32,83,46,32,66,114,111,,97,100,119,97,121,13,10
```

Note that the spaces are included (number 32) as are the carriage returns (ASCII code 13) and line feeds (ASCII code 10). The effect of this sequence is to move the cursor to the leftmost position of the next line.

ASCII codes allow us to represent any text generated by the keyboard as a sequence of numbers. This includes all formatting instructions like spaces, carriage returns, upper and lowercase letters, and so forth. Moreover, once a piece of text has been reduced to a sequence of ASCII codes, it also may be faithfully reproduced on the screen or on a printer.

TEST YOUR UNDERSTANDING 1 (answer on page 199)

Write a sequence of ASCII codes to reproduce this ad:

FOR SALE: Beagle puppies. Pedigreed.

8 weeks. $125.

You may refer to characters by their ASCII codes by using the function **CHR$**. For example, *CHR$(74)* is the character corresponding to ASCII code 74 (uppercase J); CHR$(32) is the character corresponding to ASCII code 32 (space). The PRINT and LPRINT instructions may be used in connection with CHR$. For example, the instruction

```
10 PRINT CHR$(74)
```

displays an uppercase J in the first position of the first print field.

TEST YOUR UNDERSTANDING 2 (answer on page 199)
Write a program to print the ad of Test Your Understanding 1 from its ASCII codes.

To obtain the ASCII code of a character, use the command **ASC**. For example, the command

```
20 PRINT ASC("B")
```

prints the ASCII code of the character "B", namely 66. In place of "B", you may use any string. The computer will return the ASCII code of the first character of the string. For example, the instruction

```
30 PRINT ASC(A$)
```

prints the ASCII code of the first character of the string *A$*.

TEST YOUR UNDERSTANDING 3 (answer on page 199)
Determine the ASCII codes of the characters *$, g, X,* and + without looking at the chart.

ASCII codes have many uses in writing even the most simple programs. For example, suppose that you wish to print out a quotation mark on the screen. To do so, you must create a string consisting of a quotation mark. The usual way to define a string is to enclose it in quotation marks. However, if you attempt to do that in this case, you arrive at " " ". Unfortunately, here is how BASIC looks at that string. The first quotation mark tells BASIC that a string is about to begin. The second quotation mark tells BASIC that the string just ended. The third quotation mark is ignored! For example, the command

```
PRINT """
```

prints nothing on the screen!

The ASCII codes provide a way out of this dilemma. The ASCII code of " is 34, and *CHR$(34)* is a string consisting of a single quotation mark. So we may print " on the screen with the statement

```
PRINT CHR$(34);
```

In a similar fashion, ASCII codes may be used to include carriage returns and line feeds within a string. Note that you cannot type a string that includes carriage returns or line feeds from the keyboard. Hitting ENTER is a signal for BASIC to accept the line just typed. However, it will not include the carriage return and line feed as part of the string. This must be done using ASCII codes. (More about how this is done in Section 9.2.)

ANSWERS TO TEST YOUR UNDERSTANDINGS 1, 2, and 3

```
1:   70,79,82,32,83,65,76,69,58,32,66,101,97,103,108,101,32,
     112,117,112,112,105,101,115,46,32,80,101,100,105,103,114,
     101,13,100,46,13,10,56,32,119,101,101,107,115,46,32,36,49,
     50,53,46,13
```

```
2:   10 DATA 70,79,.........(insert data from 1)
     11 DATA ........
     12 DATA ........
     20 FOR J=1 TO 54
     30    READ A
     40    PRINT CHR$(A);
     50 NEXT J
     60 END
```

```
3:   10 DATA $,g,X,+
     20 FOR J=1 TO 4
     30    READ A$
     40    B=ASC(A$)
     50    PRINT A$, B
     60 NEXT J
     70 END
```

9.2   Operations on Strings

In earlier chapters, our strings contained only printable characters. Let us now extend that definition to allow characters corresponding to any ASCII code. So, for example, a string may now include line feeds, carriage returns, and any of the other control characters we soon will define. The control characters in a string are treated just like any of the other characters.

Concatenation

BASIC lets you perform a number of different operations on strings. The most fundamental operation is **string addition** (or, in computer jargon, **string concatenation**). Suppose that $A\$$ and $B\$$ are strings, with $A\$ = $ ''*word*'' and $B\$ = $ ''*processor*''. Then the sum of $A\$$ and $B\$$, denoted $A\$ + B\$$, is the string obtained by adjoining $A\$$ and $B\$$, namely

''*wordprocessor*''

Note that no space is left between the two strings. To include a space, suppose that $C\$ = $ '' ''. $C\$$ is the string consisting of a single space. Thus $A\$ + C\$ + B\$$ is the string

''*word processor*''

TEST YOUR UNDERSTANDING 1 (answer on page 204)
If *A$* = ''*4*'' and *B$* = ''*7*'', what is *A$* + *B$*?

TEST YOUR UNDERSTANDING 2 (answer on page 204)
Set *A$* equal to the string

  He said, ''No''. <carriage return>

The Length of a String

You may compute the length of a string by using the **LEN** function. For example,

```
LEN("BOUGHT")
```

is equal to six, since the string ''*BOUGHT*'' has six letters. Similarly, if *A$* is equal to the string

```
"Family Income"
```

then *LEN(A$)* is equal to 13. (The space between the words counts!) Note that carriage returns, line feeds, and other control characters count in the length.

Here is an application of the LEN instruction.

Example 1.   Write a program that inputs the string A$ and then centers it on a line of the display. (Assume an 80-character line.)

Solution.   A line is 80 characters long, with the spaces numbered from 1 to 80. The string *A$* takes up *LEN(A$)* of these spaces, so there are *80-LEN(A$)* spaces to be distributed on either side of *A$*. The line should begin with half of the *80-LEN(A$)* spaces, or with *(80-LEN(A$))/2* spaces. So we should tab to column *(80-LEN(A$))/2 + 1*. Here is our program.

```
10 ' *****************************
20 ' This program centers a string
30 ' given by the user
40 ' *****************************
50 INPUT "String to be centered";A$
60 CLS
70 PRINT TAB((80-LEN(A$))/2+1);A$
80 END
```

TEST YOUR UNDERSTANDING 3 (answer on page 204)
Use the program of Example 1 to center the string ''The IBM Personal Computer''.

Substrings

It is possible to dissect strings using the three commands *LEFT$*, *RIGHT$*, and *MID$*. These commands allow you to construct a string consisting of a specified number of characters taken from the left, right, or middle of a designated string. Consider the command

```
10 A$=LEFT$("LOVE",2)
```

The string *A$* consists of the two leftmost characters of the string *"LOVE"*. That is, *A$* = *"LO"*. Similarly, the commands

```
20 B$="tennis"
30 C$=RIGHT$(B$,3)
```

set *C$* equal to the string consisting of the three rightmost letters of the string *B$*, namely *C$* = *"nis"*. Similarly, if *A$* = *"Republican"*, then the command

```
40 D$=MID$(A$,5,3)
```

sets *D$* equal to the string consisting of the three characters starting with the fifth character of *A$*, which is *D$* = *"bli"*.

TEST YOUR UNDERSTANDING 4 (answer on page 204)
Determine the string constant

```
RIGHT$(LEFT$("computer",4),3)
```

Example 2. Write a program that accepts as input a seven-digit telephone number and prints on the screen the first three and the last four digits separated by a hyphen.

Solution. We input the seven digits of the telephone number as a string. We then use RIGHT$ and LEFT$ to extract the desired strings from this string.

```
10  '********************************
20  'This program accepts a seven-digit
30  'telephone number and reformats it
40  'so that the first three digits and
50  'the last four are separated by a
60  'hyphen.
70  '********************************
100 INPUT "TELEPHONE NUMBER";T$
110 PRINT LEFT$(T$,3);
120 PRINT "-";
130 PRINT RIGHT$(T$,4)
140 END
```

Example 3. Write a program that accepts as input a name consisting of a first name followed by a last name separated by a space. The program should determine the last name and display it on the screen.

Solution.   Our program searches for the first space and then extracts the leftmost portion of the string, starting from the character after the space.

```
10  '***************************************
20  'This program determines the last name
30  'from a first name-last name combination,
35  'where the two names are separated by
40  'a space.
50  '***************************************
100 INPUT "NAME(FIRST LAST);NME$
110 S=INSTR(NME$,' '): 'Search for space between names
120 LAST$ = RIGHT$(NME$,S+1)
130 PRINT LAST$
140 END
```

Strings Representing Numbers

In manipulating strings, it is important to recognize the difference between numerical data and string data. The number *14* is denoted by *14*; the string consisting of the two characters *14* is denoted *"14"*. The first is a numerical constant and the second a string constant. We can perform arithmetic using the numerical constants. However, we cannot perform any of the character manipulation supplied by the instructions RIGHT$, MID$ and LEFT$. Such manipulation may only be performed on strings. How may we perform character manipulation on numerical constants? BASIC provides a simple method. We first convert the numerical constants to string constants by using *STR$*. For example, the number 14 may be converted into the string

```
" 14"
```

using the command

```
10 A$=STR$(14)
```

As a result of this command, *A$* has the value *" 14"*. Note the blank in front of the *14*. This occurs because BASIC automatically leaves a space for the sign of a number. If the number is positive, then the sign prints out as a space. If the number is negative, then the sign prints out as a minus $(-)$.

As another example, suppose that the variable B has the value *1.457*. *STR$(B)* is then equal to the string

```
" 1.457"
```

To convert strings consisting of numbers into numerical constants, use **VAL**. Consider this command:

```
20 B=VAL("3.78")
```

This sets *B* equal to *3.78*. You may even use VAL for strings consisting of a number followed by other characters. VAL picks off the initial number portion and throws away the part of the string beginning with the first non-numerical character. For example,

```
VAL("12.5 inches")
```

is equal to *12.5*.

TEST YOUR UNDERSTANDING 5 (answer on page 204)

Suppose that *A$* equals *"5 percent"* and *B$* equals *"758.45 dollars"*. Write a program that starts from *A$* and *B$* and computes five percent of $758.45.

The INSTR Statement

In some applications, it is necessary to search a string for a particular pattern. Here are some examples of such searches:

- Find the location of the first *"A"* in the string *A$*.
- Find the location of the first period in the string *B$*.
- Find the location of the first *"1"* in *A$* occurring after the eighth character.
- Does the sequence of characters *"ABS"* occur anywhere in the string *A$*?

All such searches are greatly simplified using the **INSTR** (= INSTRing) function. This function may be used in either of two formats. The simplest is

```
10 P=INSTR(A$,B$)
```

In response to this statement, *P* is set equal to the location of the first occurrence of *B$* in *A$*. For example, suppose that

```
A$="This is a test of the INSTR statement."
B$="te"
```

In this case, the first occurrence of *B$* in *A$* is at the beginning of the word *"test"*. The location of the initial *t* is the eleventh character. So *INSTR(A$,B$)* has the value *11*.

If *B$* does not occur in *A$*, then INSTR has the value zero. Therefore, to determine whether the string *"ABS"* occurs in *A$*, we can use the program

```
10 P=INSTR(A$,"ABS")
20 IF P=0 THEN PRINT "ABS DOES NOT OCCUR"
30 IF P>0 THEN PRINT "ABS OCCURS"
```

The second format of the INSTR statement allows you to begin the search for *B$* beginning with a designated location *m*. In this format the statement has the form

```
P=INSTR(m,A$,B$)
```

For example, if we wish the search for *B$* to begin with the eighth character of *A$*, we can use the instruction

```
P=INSTR(8,A$,B$)
```

ANSWERS TO TEST YOUR UNDERSTANDINGS 1, 2, 3, 4, and 5

1: `"47"`

2: `A$ =`
   `"He said, "+CHR$(34)+"No"+CHR$(34)+"."+CHR$(13)+CHR$(10)`

3: Type *RUN* and press ENTER. When prompted, type in the given string.

4: `"omp"`

5:
```
10 A$="5 percent":B$="758.45 dollars"
20 A=VAL(A$):B=VAL(B$)
30 PRINT A$," of ",B$," is"
40 PRINT A*B*.01
50 END
```

9.3   Control Characters

Table 9-2 contains a list of the control characters corresponding to ASCII codes 0-31. Some comments on the functions of the various codes are in order.

- Code 000 (null) is exactly what its name suggests. It is a character that does nothing. It often is used in communications, where a message will be started with a string of nulls.

- Codes 001-006 are graphics characters. You use them for games.

- Code 7 (beep) beeps the speaker of the computer.

- Code 8 (backspace) backspaces the cursor one space.

- Code 9 (tab) moves the cursor to the next tab stop. BASIC automatically places tab stops every five characters across the line.

- Code 10 (line feed) advances the cursor one line down.

- Code 11 (home) positions the cursor at the upper left corner of the screen.

- Code 12 (form feed) advances the paper on the printer to the top of the next page.

- Code 13 (carriage return) returns the cursor to the leftmost position on the current line.

- Codes 14-27 are further graphics characters for use in displays.
- Code 28 (cursor right) moves the cursor to the right one space.
- Code 29 (cursor left) moves the cursor to the left one space.
- Code 30 (cursor up) moves the cursor up one space.
- Code 31 (cursor down) moves the cursor down one space.

To use the ASCII control codes, you PRINT them as if they were printable characters. For example, to move the cursor one space up, use the statement

```
PRINT CHR$(30);
```

Note that the statement ends with a semicolon (;). This prevents BASIC from issuing a carriage return and line feed following the PRINT statement. Otherwise, they would ruin the cursor positioning accomplished by control character 30.

More on the Cursor

The ASCII codes controlling cursor motion allow you to position the cursor relative to its current position. You may move the cursor to a specific position on the screen using the **LOCATE** statement. The format of this statement is

```
LOCATE row,column
```

For example, to position the cursor in column 5 of row 20, use the statement

```
LOCATE 20,5
```

We can determine the column in which the cursor is currently located by using the BASIC function **POS(0)**. For example, if the cursor currently is located in column 37, then POS(0) is equal to 37. The variable **CSRLIN** always equals the number of the line in which the cursor is currently located. For example, if the cursor currently is located in line 5, then CSRLIN is equal to 5. You may use POS(0) and CSRLIN exactly as you would any other variables in BASIC.

TEST YOUR UNDERSTANDING 1 (answer on page 205)
Write a program to move the cursor two spaces to the right and two spaces down.

ANSWER TO TEST YOUR UNDERSTANDING 1
```
1:  10 PRINT CHR$(28);CHR$(28);CHR$(31);CHR$(31);
    20 END
```

Table 9-2. ASCII codes for control characters.

ASCII value	Character	Control character
000	(null)	NUL
001	☺	SOH
002	●	STX
003	♥	ETX
004	♦	EOT
005	♣	ENQ
006	♠	ACK
007	(beep)	BEL
008	▫	BS
009	(tab)	HT
010	(line feed)	LF
011	(home)	VT
012	(form feed)	FF
013	(carriage return)	CR
014	♫	SO
015	☼	SI
016	►	DLE
017	◄	DC1
018	↕	DC2
019	‼	DC3
020	¶	DC4
021	§	NAK
022	▬	SYN
023	↨	ETB
024	↑	CAN
025	↓	EM
026	→	SUB
027	←	ESC
028	(cursor right)	FS
029	(cursor left)	GS
030	(cursor up)	RS
031	(cursor down)	US

*Courtesy of International Business Machines Corporation.

9.4   A Friendly Game of Blackjack

In this section, we present a version of the popular card game Blackjack. In this game, the player (we will allow only one at a time) vies with the dealer. The player makes a bet. The player and dealer are then dealt two cards each. The dealer's first card is face down and the others are face up. The object is to get a hand that totals as closely as possible to 21 without going over. Numbered cards have their usual values; jacks, queens, and kings all have value 10; and aces have a value of either 1 or 11 at the player's (or dealer's) discretion. The player goes first, deciding, one card at a time, whether to be hit (given another card) or to stand (decline further cards). If the player's total goes over 21, the player **busts** and loses the amount bet. If the player hits 21 exactly, he automatically wins the amount bet.

If the player stops before busting or achieving 21, the dealer plays. First he turns over his first card. As long as the dealer's total is less than 16, he must draw a card. The dealer continues until he either busts, gets 21, or gets at least 16. If the dealer busts, the player wins. Otherwise, the player with the highest total wins. In case of ties, the dealer wins.

Our program to implement this game employs most of what we have learned about string manipulation. The deck of cards is represented as a string:

"AHADACAS2H2D2C2S......"

Here AH stands for the ace of hearts, 2D for the two of diamonds, and so forth. Picking a card then involves choosing a random odd position in the string. The card chosen is then determined by extracting the two-character substring that stands for the character. (See lines 6000 on in the listing below.)

The program uses the various graphics characters in the IBM PC's character set (see Chapter 12) to draw the cards on the screen (See lines 5000 on in the listing below). These are characters with ASCII codes from 0 to 31 and from 128 to 255. In this program we use characters to form rectangles (ASCII codes 187, 188, 200, 201, 205) and the characters for the various card suits (ASCII codes 3, 4, 5, and 6). (IBM wisely chose to include these in its character set.)

Here is the listing of the program. It is highly structured and liberally commented so that it is more or less self-explanatory.

```
1000 '*******************************************
1010 'This program plays the traditional game of black-
1020 'jack. You play against the dealer( the computer).
1030 ' Program designed by Jonathan Goldstein.
1040 '*******************************************
1050 GOSUB 2030: 'Initialize program
1060 LOCATE 23,1
1070 INPUT "HOW MANY CHIPS($1 DOLLAR PER CHIP)";MONEY
1080 WHILE GAMEEND=FALSE
1090     CLS
```

```
1100        GOSUB 3000: 'Initialization
1110        GOSUB 4000: 'Place bet
1120        LOCATE 10,20: PRINT "DEALER'S HAND"
1130        LOCATE 20,20: PRINT "PLAYER'S HAND"
1140        GOSUB 4040: 'Deal initial cards
1150        GOSUB 4100: 'Test for blackjack
1160        WHILE BUST=FALSE AND BLACKJACK = FALSE AND
            HIT=TRUE
1170            LOCATE 10,1
1180            INPUT "HIT(H) OR STAND(S)",HIT$
1190            LOCATE 10,1:PRINT SPACE$(80);
1200            IF HIT$="S" OR HIT$="s" THEN
                HIT=FALSE:GOTO 1220
1210            CARD=PLAYER:GOSUB 6000: 'Deal player's
                card
1220            GOSUB 4100: 'Test for blackjack or
                bust
1230        WEND
1240        IF BLACKJACK = TRUE OR BUST = TRUE THEN 1380
1250        GOSUB 7000: 'Turn over dealer's 1st card
1260        WHILE TOTAL(DEALER) < 16  AND BLACKJACK=FALSE
1270            CARD=DEALER:GOSUB 6000: 'Deal dealer's
                card
1280            GOSUB 4100: 'Test for blackjack or
                bust
1290        WEND
1300    'Announce results
1310        IF BLACKJACK = TRUE OR BUST = TRUE THEN 1380
1320        FOR J=1 TO 2
1330            IF TOTAL(J) <= 11 AND ACE(J) = TRUE
                THEN TOTAL(J)=TOTAL(J)+10
1340        NEXT J
1350        LOCATE 10,1:PRINT SPACE$(80)
1360        IF TOTAL(DEALER) >= TOTAL(PLAYER) THEN PRINT
            "Dealer Wins!" :WINNER=DEALER
1370        IF TOTAL(DEALER) < TOTAL(PLAYER) THEN PRINT
            "Player Wins!" :WINNER=PLAYER
1380        BEEP:BEEP:BEEP:BEEP:BEEP:BEEP
1390        IF WINNER = PLAYER THEN MONEY = MONEY+BET
            ELSE MONEY = MONEY-BET
1400        PRINT "PLAYER BALANCE $";MONEY
1410        FOR J=1 TO 10000:NEXT J
1420        CLS: INPUT "PLAY AGAIN(Y/N)";RESPONSE$
1430        IF RESPONSE$ <> "Y" AND RESPONSE$ <> "y" THEN
            GAMEEND=TRUE
1440 WEND
1450 END
2000 '***************************************************
2010 '                   Subroutines
2020 '***************************************************
2030 'Initialization of program
2040    TRUE=1:FALSE=0
2050    GAMEEND = FALSE
2060    CLS:SCREEN 0:WIDTH 80:RANDOMIZE TIMER:KEY OFF
2070    FULLDECK$="2S2H2C2D3S3H3C3D4S4H4C4D5S5H5C5D6S
```

```
         6H6C6D7S7H7C7D8S8H8C8D9S9H9C9D0S0H0C0DJSJHJCJD
         QSQHQCQDKSKHKCKDASAHACAD"
2080     TOP$=CHR$(201)+CHR$(205)+CHR$(205)+CHR$(205)+
         CHR$(205)+CHR$(205)+CHR$(205)+CHR$(205)+
         CHR$(205)+CHR$(187)
2090     SIDE$= CHR$(186)+"           "+CHR$(186)
2100     BOTTOM$=CHR$(200)+CHR$(205)+CHR$(205)+
         CHR$(205)+CHR$(205)+CHR$(205)+CHR$(205)+
         CHR$(205)+CHR$(205)+CHR$(188)
3000 'Initialization of hand
3010     REMAININGCARDS=52
3020     REMAININGDECK$ = FULLDECK$
3030     PLAYER=0:DEALER=1
3040     PLAYERCARDS = 0:DEALERCARDS=0
3050     ACE(PLAYER)=FALSE:ACE(DEALER)=FALSE
3060     BLACKJACK=FALSE
3070     BUST=FALSE
3080     HIT = TRUE
3090     TOTAL(DEALER)=0:TOTAL(PLAYER)=0
3100     FOR J=1 TO 10
3110             DEALER$(J)=""
3120             PLAYER$(J)=""
3130     NEXT J
3140 RETURN
4000 'Place bet
4010     CLS: LOCATE 23,1:PRINT
         "PLAYER BALANCE: $";MONEY
4020     LOCATE 21,1:INPUT "Enter bet:",BET
4030 RETURN
4040 'Deal Initial Cards
4050  CARD=DEALER:CLS: GOSUB 6000:
         "Deal 1st card for Dealer
4060  CARD=PLAYER:GOSUB 6000: "Deal 1st card for Player
4070  CARD=DEALER:GOSUB 6000: "Deal 2nd card for Dealer
4080  CARD=PLAYER:GOSUB 6000: 'Deal 2nd card for Player
4090  RETURN
4100 'Test for blackjack or bust
4110     TOTAL(CARD)=0:ACE=FALSE:BLACKJACK=FALSE
4120     IF CARD=DEALER THEN NUMCARDS=DEALERCARDS
         ELSE NUMCARDS=PLAYERCARDS
4130     FOR J=1 TO NUMCARDS : 'Compute total of hand
4140             IF CARD=DEALER THEN CARD$=DEALER$(J)
                 ELSE CARD$ = PLAYER$(J)
4150             A$=LEFT$(CARD$,1)
4160             IF A$="0" OR A$="J" OR A$="Q" OR A$="K"
                 THEN COUNT=10 ELSE IF A$= "A" THEN
                 COUNT = 1 ELSE COUNT = VAL(A$)
4170             IF A$="A" THEN ACE(CARD)=TRUE
4180             TOTAL(CARD) = TOTAL(CARD)+COUNT
4190     NEXT J
4200     IF TOTAL(CARD)<=21 THEN GOTO 4260
4210 '   Bust
4220     BUST=TRUE
4230     LOCATE 10,1:PRINT SPACE$(80)
4240     IF CARD = PLAYER THEN PRINT "Player Busted!"
```

```
             ELSE PRINT "Dealer Busted!"
4250         WINNER=1-CARD
4260   '     Blackjack
4270         IF (TOTAL(CARD)=21) OR (TOTAL(CARD)=11 AND
             ACE(CARD)=TRUE) THEN BLACKJACK=TRUE
4280         IF BLACKJACK = FALSE THEN 4320
4290         LOCATE 10,1:PRINT SPACE$(80)
4300         IF CARD=PLAYER THEN PRINT "Blackjack.
             Player wins!" ELSE PRINT "Blackjack.
             Dealer Wins"
4310         WINNER=CARD
4320   RETURN
5000   'Display current card
5010         IF CARD=PLAYER THEN XLOC=11*PLAYERCARDS-10
             ELSE XLOC = 11*DEALERCARDS-10
5020         IF CARD=PLAYER THEN YLOC=14 ELSE YLOC=1
5030         LOCATE YLOC,XLOC
5040         PRINT TOP$
5050         FOR J=1 TO 5
5060              LOCATE YLOC+J,XLOC:PRINT SIDE$
5070         NEXT J
5080         LOCATE YLOC+6,XLOC:PRINT BOTTOM$
5090         A$=RIGHT$(C$,1)
5100         B$=LEFT$(C$,1)
5110         IF B$="0" THEN B$="10"
5120         IF A$="H" THEN A$=CHR$(3)
5130         IF A$="D" THEN A$=CHR$(4)
5140         IF A$="C" THEN A$=CHR$(5)
5150         IF A$="S" THEN A$=CHR$(6)
5160         BA$=B$+A$
5170         LOCATE YLOC+3,XLOC+4
5180         IF CARD=PLAYER OR DEALERCARDS>=2 THEN PRINT BA$
5190   RETURN
6000   'Deal card to the hand specified by CARD
6010       'If deck is empty start new deck
6020              IF REMAININGCARDS>0 THEN 6050
6030              REMAININGCARDS=52
6040              REMAININGDECK$=FULLDECK$
6050       'Select card and adjust deck
6060              POSITION=(INT(REMAININGCARDS*
                  RND(1))+1)*2-1
6070              C$ = MID$(REMAININGDECK$,POSITION,2)
6080              FIRSTHALF$=LEFT$(REMAININGDECK$,
6090              SECONDHALF$=RIGHT$(REMAININGDECK$,
                          2*REMAININGCARDS-
                          POSITION-1
6100              REMAININGDECK$=FIRSTHALF$+SECONDHALF$
6110              REMAININGCARDS=REMAININGCARDS-1
6120       'Assign card to dealer or player
6130              IF CARD = DEALER THEN 6170
6140              PLAYERCARDS=PLAYERCARDS+1
6150              PLAYER$(PLAYERCARDS)=C$
6160              GOTO 6190
6170              DEALERCARDS=DEALERCARDS+1
6180              DEALER$(DEALERCARDS)=C$
```

```
6190     'Display card
6200             GOSUB 5000
6210 RETURN
7000 'Turn over dealer's first card
7010    C$=DEALER$(1)
7020    A$=RIGHT$(C$,1)
7030    B$=LEFT$(C$,1)
7040    IF B$="0" THEN B$="10"
7050    IF A$="H" THEN A$=CHR$(3)
7060    IF A$="D" THEN A$=CHR$(4)
7070    IF A$="C" THEN A$=CHR$(5)
7080    IF A$="S" THEN A$=CHR$(6)
7090    BA$=B$+A$
7100    LOCATE 4,5
7110    PRINT BA$
7120 RETURN
```

10

Variable Types and Functions

10.0   Chapter Objectives

IN THIS CHAPTER, WE DISCUSS the various types of numbers used by
BASIC, including:

- Single-precision constants and variables.

- Double-precision constants and variables.

- Integer constants and variables

In addition, we survey the various types of built-in and user-defined functions
that BASIC incorporates.

10.1   Types of Numeric Constants

Up to this point, we have used the computer to perform arithmetic without giving
much thought to the level of accuracy of the numbers involved. However, when
doing scientific programming, it is absolutely essential to know the number of
decimal places of accuracy of the computations. Let's begin this chapter by
discussing the form in which BASIC stores and uses numbers.

Actually, BASIC recognizes three different types of numeric constants: integer, single-precision, and double-precision.

An **integer constant** is an ordinary integer (positive or negative) in the range
from -32768 to +32767. (32768 is 2 raised to the fifteenth power. This number
is significant to the internal workings of the computer.) Here are some examples
of integer numeric constants:

7, 58, 3712, -15, -598

Integer constants may be stored very efficiently in RAM. Moreover, arithmetic with integer constants takes the least time. Therefore, in order to realize these
efficiencies, BASIC handles integer constants in a special way.

A **single-precision constant** is a number with seven or fewer digits that is not an integer. Some examples of single-precision constants are

5.135, -63.5785, 1234567, -1.467654E12

Note that a single-precision constant may be expressed in "scientific" or "floating-point" notation, as in the final example shown here. In such an expression, however, you are limited to seven or fewer digits. In IBM PC BASIC, single-precision constants must lie within these ranges:

$-1x10^{38}$ and $-1x10^{-38}$ and $1x10^{-38}$ and $1x10^{38}$

This limitation seldom is much of a limitation in practice. After all, 1×10^{-38} equals

.00000000000000000000000000000000000001

(37 zeros followed by a 1), which is about as small a number as you are ever likely to encounter! Similarly, 1×10^{38} equals

100,000,000,000,000,000,000,000,000,000,000,000,000

(a 1 followed by 38 zeros), which is large enough for most practical calculations.

A **double-precision constant** is a number containing more than seven digits. Here are some examples of double-precision numbers:

2.0000000000, 3578930497594, -3946.635475495

Scientific notation also may be used to represent double-precision numbers. Use the letter *D* to precede the exponent. For example, the number

2.7575757575D-4

equals the double-precision constant

.00027575757575

The number

1.3145926535D15

equals the double-precision constant

1,314,159,265,350,000

A double-precision constant may have up to 17 digits. Double-precision constants are subject to the same range limitations as single-precision constants.

Single-precision constants occupy more RAM than integer constants. Moreover, arithmetic with single-precision constants proceeds slower than integer arithmetic. Similarly, double-precision constants occupy even more memory, and arithmetic proceeds even slower than with single-precision constants.

BASIC recognizes each of the three types of numerical constants and uses only as much arithmetic power as necessary.

Here are the rules for determining the type of a numerical constant:

1. Any integer in the range -32768 and 32767 is an integer constant.

2. Any number with seven or fewer digits that is not an integer constant is a single-precision constant. Any number in scientific notation using *E* before the exponent is assumed to be a single-precision constant. If a number has more than seven digits in scientific notation but uses an *E*, it is interpreted as a double-precision constant. For example, the number

    1.23456789E + 15

    is interpreted as the double-precision constant

    1.23456789D + 15

3. A number with more than seven digits is interpreted as a double-precision constant. If more than 17 digits are specified, then the number is truncated after the seventeenth digit and written in scientific notation. For example, the number

    123456789123456789
    is interpreted as the double-precision constant
    1.2345678912345678D + 17

The type of a numeric constant may be specified by means of a **type declaration tag**. For instance, a numeric constant followed by % is interpreted as an integer constant. For example, 1% is interpreted as the integer constant 1. A % sign in a number containing a decimal will be ignored. For example, the number

1.85%

is interpreted as the single-precision constant

1.85

If the constant containing a % is too large to be an integer constant (that is, not in the range -32768 to + 32767), an overflow error will occur. A numeric constant followed by ! is interpreted as a single-precision constant and truncated accordingly. For example, the constant

1.23456789!

is interpreted as

1.234567

The constant

123456789!

is truncated to seven significant digits and written in scientific notation as:

1.234567E8

A # serves as a type declaration tag to indicate a double-precision constant. For example, the constant

1.2#

is interpreted as the 17-digit double-precision constant

1.2000000000000000

In scientific notation, the letter D serves as a type declaration tag.

TEST YOUR UNDERSTANDING 1 (answers on page 217)

Write out the decimal form of the following numbers:

   a.   -7.5%

   b.   4.58923450183649E + 12

   c.   270D-2

   d.   12.55#

   e.   -1.62!

A type declaration tag supersedes rules 1-3 above in determining the type of a numeric constant.

Let's discuss the way BASIC performs arithmetic with the various constant types. The variable type resulting from an arithmetic operation is determined by the variable types of the data entering into the operation. For example, the sum of two integer constants will be an integer constant, provided that the answer is within the range of an integer constant. If not, the sum will be a single-precision constant. Arithmetic operations among single-precision constants will always yield single-precision constants. Arithmetic constants among double-precision constants yield a double-precision result. Here are some examples of arithmetic:

5% + 7%

The computer adds the two integer constants 5 and 7 to obtain the integer constant 12.

4.21! + 5.2!

The computer adds the two single-precision constants *4.21* and 5.2 to obtain the single-precision result *9.41*.

3/2

Here the two constants 3 and 2 are integers. However, since the result, 1.5, is not an integer, it is assumed to be a single-precision type.

The result of

1!/3!

is the single-precision constant *.3333334*. Similarly, the result of the double-precision calculation

1#/3#

is the double-precision constant *.33333333333333333*.

TEST YOUR UNDERSTANDING 2 (answers on page 217)

What result will the computer obtain for the following problems?

a. 2!/5! + 1!/3!

b. .4% + .3333333333333333333%

c. .4# + .33333333333333333333#

d. .4! + .33333333333333333333!

It is important to realize that if a number does not have an exact decimal representation (such as 1/3 = .333 . . .), or if the number has a decimal representation that has too many digits for the constant type being used, the computer will then be working with an approximation of the number rather than the number itself. The built-in errors caused by the approximations of the computer are called **round-off errors**. Consider the problem of calculating

1/3 + 1/3 + 1/3

As we have seen above, *1/3* is stored as the single-precision constant *.3333334*. The computer will form the sum as

.3333334 + .3333334 + .3333334 = 1.0000002

The sum has a round-off error of *.0000002.*

BASIC displays up to seven digits for a single-precision constant. Due to round-off error, however, the answer to any single arithmetic operation is guaranteed accurate to only six places. Double-precision constants are displayed rounded off to 16 digits. For a single arithmetic operation, the computer's design guarantees that a double-precision answer will be accurate to 16 digits. If you perform many such operations, it is possible that cumulative round-off error will make the sixteenth or earlier digits inaccurate.

ANSWERS TO TEST YOUR UNDERSTANDINGS 1 and 2

1: a. -7.5   b. 4,589,235,000,000   c. 2.7000000000000000
    d. 12.550000000000000   e. -1.620000

2: a. .7333333   b. 0   c. .73333333333333333
    d. .7333333

10.2   Variable Types in BASIC

In the previous section we introduced the various types of numerical constants: integer, single-precision, and double-precision. There is a parallel set of types for variables.

A **variable of integer type** takes on values that are integer type constants. An integer type variable is indicated by the symbol % after the variable name. For example, here are some variables of integer type:

A%, BB%, A1%

In setting the value of an integer type variable, the computer rounds any fractional parts to obtain an integer. For example, the instruction

`10 A% = 2.54`

sets the value of *A* equal to the integer constant *3*. Integer type variables are useful when keeping track of integer quantities, such as line numbers in a program.

A **variable of single-precision** type is one whose value is a single-precision constant. A single-precision type variable is indicated by the symbol ! after the variable name. Here are some examples of single-precision variables:

K!, W7!, ZX!

In setting the value of a single-precision variable, all digits beyond the seventh are rounded. For example, the instruction

`20 A! = 1.23456789`

sets *A!* equal to *1.234568*.

If a variable is used without a type designator, the computer assumes that it is a single-precision variable. All of the variables we have used until now have been single-precision variables. These are, by far, the most commonly used variables.

A **double-precision variable** is a variable whose value is a double-precision constant. Such variables are useful in computations where great numerical accuracy is required. A double-precision variable is indicated by the tag # after the variable name. Here are some examples of double-precision variables:

B#, C1#, EE#

In setting the values of double-precision variables, all digits after the seventeenth digit are rounded.

Note that the variables A%, A!, A#, and A$ are four distinct variables. You could, if you wish, use all of them in a single program. (But it would probably be very confusing and may produce errors if you did.)

TEST YOUR UNDERSTANDING 1 (answers on page 219)

What values are assigned to each of these variables?

a.   A# = 1#

b.   B% = 5.22%

c.   CC! = 1387.5699

Using the type declaration tags %, !, and # is a nuisance since they must be included whenever the variable is used. There is a way around this tedium. The instructions **DEFINT**, **DEFSNG**, and **DEFDBL** may be used to define the types of variables for an entire program, so that type declaration tags need not be used. Consider the instruction

```
100 DEFINT A
```

It specifies that every variable beginning with the letter A(such as A, AB, or A1) should be considered as a variable of integer type. Here are two variations of this instruction:

```
200 DEFINT A,B,C
300 DEFINT A-G
```

Line 200 defines any variables beginning with A, B, or C to be of integer type. Line 300 defines any variables beginning with any of the letters A through G to be of integer type. The DEFINT instruction is usually used at the beginning of a program, so that the resulting definition is in effect throughout the program.

The instruction DEFSNG works exactly like DEFINT and is used to define certain variables to be single-precision. The instructions DEFDBL and DEFSTR work the same way for double-precision and string variables, respectively.

Note that type declaration tags override the DEF instructions. For example, suppose that the variable A was defined to be single-precision using a DEFSNG instruction at the beginning of the program. It is legal to use A# as a double-precision variable, since the type declaration tag #will override the single-precision definition.

WARNING: Here is a mistake that is easy to make. Consider this program:

```
10 LET A# = 1.7
20 PRINT A#
30 END
```

This program seems harmless enough. We set the double-precision variable A# to the value 1.7 and then display the result. You probably expect to see the display

1.700000000000000

If you actually try it, the display will read

1.700000047683716

What went wrong? Well, it has to do with the way the internal logic of the computer works and the way in which numbers are represented in binary notation. Without going into details, let us merely observe that the computer interprets *1.7* as a *single-precision constant*. When this single-precision constant is converted into a double-precision constant (an operation that makes use of the binary representation of *1.7*), the result coincides in its first 16 digits with the number given above. Does this mean that we must worry about such craziness? Of course not! What we really should have done in the first place is to write

```
10 A# = 1.7#
```

The display is then *1.7*, exactly as expected.

ANSWERS TO TEST YOUR UNDERSTANDING 1
1: a. 1.0000000000000000   b. 5   c. 1387.570

10.3   Mathematical Functions in BASIC

In performing scientific computations, it is often necessary to use a wide variety of mathematical functions, including the natural logarithm and the exponential and trigonometric functions. BASIC has a wide range of these functions "built-in." In this section we describe these functions and their use.

All mathematical functions in BASIC work in a similar fashion. Each function is identified by a sequence of letters (**SIN** for sine, **LOG** for natural logarithm, and so forth). To evaluate a function at a number X, we write X in parentheses after the function name. For example, the natural logarithm of X is written *LOG(X)*. The program uses the current value of the variable X and calculates the natural logarithm of that value. For example, if X is currently 2, then the computer will calculate *LOG(2)*.

Instead of the variable X, we may use any type of variable: integer, single-precision, or double-precision. We also may use numerical constants of any type. For example, *SIN(.435678889658595)* asks for the sine of a double-precision numerical constant. Note, however, that BASIC returns only a single-precision result accurate to six digits. For example, the above value of the sine function will be computed as

SIN(.435678889658595) = .422026

To obtain double-precision values for the various built-in functions, you must request BASIC using the /D option. That is, when you type BASICA to start BASIC, use a command line of the form:

BASICA /D

BASIC lets you calculate a function of any expression. Consider the expression $X^2 + Y^2 - 3*X$. It is perfectly acceptable to call for calculations such as

SIN(X^2 + Y^2 - 3*X)

The computer will first evaluate the expression $X^2 + Y^2 - 3*X$ using the current values of the variables X and Y. For example, if $X = 1$ and $Y = 4$, then $X^2 + Y^2 - 3*X = 1^2 + 4^2 - 3*1 = 14$. The above sine function will be calculated as *SIN(14) = .9906074*.

Trigonometric Functions

BASIC has the following trigonometric functions available:

SIN(X) = the sine of the angle X

COS(X) = the cosine of the angle X

TAN(X) = the tangent of the angle X

Here the angle X is expressed in terms of radian measure. In this measurement system, *360* degrees equal two times *pi* radians. Or one degree equals *.017453* radians, and one radian equals *57.29578* degrees. If you want to calculate trigonometric functions with the angle *X* expressed in degrees, use these functions:

SIN(.017453*X)

COS(.017453*X)

TAN(.017453*X)

The three other trigonometric functions, *SEC(X)* (secant), *CSC(X)* (cosecant), and *COT(X)* (cotangent), may be computed from the formulas

SEC(X) = 1/COS(X)

CSC(X) = 1/SIN(X)

COT(X) = SIN(X)/COS(X)

Here, as above, the angle X is in radians. To compute these trigonometric functions with the angle in degrees, replace X by with

.017453*X

BASIC only has one of the inverse trigonometric functions, namely the arctangent, denoted **ATN(X)**. This function returns the angle whose tangent is X. The angle returned is expressed in radians. To compute the arctangent with the angle expressed in degrees, use the function

57.29578*ATN(X)

TEST YOUR UNDERSTANDING 1 (answer on page 224)
Write a program that calculates *sin 45°*, *cos 45°*, and *tan 45°*.

Logarithmic and Exponential Functions

BASIC allows you to compute e^x using the exponential function

EXP(X)

Furthermore, you may compute the natural logarithm of X via the function

LOG(X)

You may calculate logarithms to base b using the formula

$LOG_b(X) = LOG(X)/LOG(b)$

Example 1.   Prepare a table of values of the natural logarithm function for values $X = .01, .02, .03, \ldots, 100.00$. Output the table on the printer.

Solution.   Here is the desired program. Note that our table has two columns with a heading over each column.

```
10 LPRINT "X", "LOG(X)"
20 FOR J=.01 TO 100.00 STEP .01
30   LPRINT J, LOG(J)
40 NEXT J
50 END
```

TEST YOUR UNDERSTANDING 2 (answer on page 224)
Write a program that evaluates the function $f(x) = (sin\ x) / (log\ x + e^x$ for $x = .45\ and\ x = .7$.

Example 2.   Carbon dating is a technique for calculating the age of ancient artifacts by measuring the amount of radioactive carbon-14 remaining in the artifact, as compared with the amount present if the artifact were manufactured today. If *r* denotes the proportion of carbon-14 remaining, then the age *A* of the object is calculated from the formula

A = -(1/.00012)*LOG(r)

Suppose that a papyrus scroll contains 47 percent of the carbon-14 of a piece of papyrus just manufactured. Calculate the age of the scroll.

Solution.   Here *r* = *.47* so we use the above formula.

```
10 R = .47
20 A = -(1/.00012)*LOG(R)
30 PRINT "THE AGE OF THE PAPYRUS IS", A, "YEARS"
40 END
```

Powers

BASIC has a square root function, denoted **SQR(X)**. As with all the functions considered so far, this function accepts any type of input and outputs a single-precision constant (unless double-precision values are requested when you start BASIC). For example, the instruction

```
10 Y = SQR(2.00000000000000000)
```

sets *Y* equal to *1.414214*.

Actually, the exponentiation procedure we learned in Chapter 5 works equally well for fractional and decimal exponents, and, therefore, provides an alternate method for extracting square roots. Here is how to use it. Taking the square root of a number corresponds to raising the number to the *1/2* power. We may calculate the square root of *X* as

X^(1/2)

Note that the square root function, SQR(X), operates with greater speed so it is preferred. The alternate method is more flexible, however. For instance, we may extract the cube root of *X* as

X^(1/3)

or we may raise *X* to the *5.389* power, as follows:

X^5.389

Greatest Integer, Absolute Value, and Related Functions

Here are several extremely helpful functions. The greatest integer less than or equal to *X* is denoted **INT(X)**. For example, the largest integer less than or equal to *5.46789* is *5*, so

INT(5.46789) = 5

Similarly, the largest integer less than or equal to *-3.4* is *-4* (on the number line, *-4* is the first integer to the left of *-3.4*). Therefore:

INT(-3.4) = -4

Note that for positive numbers, the INT function throws away the decimal part. For negative numbers, however, INT works a little differently. To throw away the decimal part of a number (positive or negative), we use the function **FIX(X)**. For example:

FIX(5.46789) = 5

FIX(-3.4) = -3

The absolute value of X is denoted **ABS(X)**. Recall that the absolute value of X is X itself if X is positive or *0*, and is *-X* if X is negative. Thus:

ABS(9.23) = 9.23

ABS(0) = 0

ABS(-4.1) = 4.1

Just as the absolute value of X ''removes the sign'' of X, the function **SGN(X)** throws away the number and leaves only the sign. For example:

SGN(3.4) = +1

SGN(-5.62) = -1

Conversion Functions

BASIC includes functions for converting a number from one type to another. For example, to convert X to integer type, use the function **CINT(X)**. This function rounds the decimal part of X. Note that the resulting constant must be in the integer range of -32768 to 32767 or an error will result.

To convert X to single-precision, use the function **CSNG(X)**. If X is of integer type, then CSNG(X) causes the appropriate number of zeros to be appended to the right of the decimal point to convert X to a single-precision number. If X is double-precision, then X is rounded to seven digits.

To convert X to double-precision, use the function **CDBL(X)**. This function appends the appropriate number of zeros to X to convert it to a double-precision number.

ANSWERS TO TEST YOUR UNDERSTANDINGS 1 and 2

```
1:  10 A = .017453
    20 PRINT SIN(45*A), COS(45*A), TAN(45*A)
    30 END
2:  10 DATA .45,.7
    20 FOR J=1 TO 2
    30    READ A
    40    PRINT SIN(A)/(LOG(A)+EXP(A))
    50 NEXT J
    60 END
```

10.4   Defining Your Own Functions

In mathematics, functions are usually defined by specifying one or more formulas. For instance, here are formulas to define the functions $f(x)$, $g(x)$, and $h(x)$:

$$f(x) = (x^2-1)^{1/2}$$

$$g(x) = 3x^2 - 5x - 15$$

$$h(x) = 1/(x-1)$$

Note that each function is named by a letter, namely f, g, and h, respectively. BASIC allows you to define functions like these and to use them by name throughout your program. To define a function, we use the **DEF FN** instruction. This instruction is used before the first use of the function in the program. For example, to define the function $f(x)$ above, we use the instruction:

```
10 DEF FNF(X) = (X^2 - 1)^(1/2)
```

To define the function $g(x)$ above, we use the instruction:

```
20 DEF FNG(X) = 3*X^2 - 5*X - 15
```

Note that in each case, we use a letter (F or G) to identify the function. Suppose that we wish to calculate the value of the function G for $X = 12.5$. Once the function has been defined, this calculation may be described to the computer as *FNF(12.5)*. Such calculations may be used throughout the program and save the effort of retyping the formula for the function in each instance.

You may use any valid variable name as a function name. For example, you may define a function *INTEREST* by the statement:

```
10 DEF FNINTEREST(X) = ...
```

Moreover, in defining a function, you may use other functions. For example, if *FNF(X)* and *FNG(X)* are as defined above, then we may define their product by the instruction

```
30 DEF FNC(X) = FNF(X)*FNG(X)
```

All of the functions above are functions of a single variable. However, BASIC allows functions of several variables as well. They are defined using the same procedure as above. To define the function

$$A(X,Y,Z) = X^2 + Y^2 + Z^2$$

use the instruction

```
40 DEF FNA(X,Y,Z) = X^2 + Y^2 + Z^2
```

You may even let one of the variables be a string variable. Consider this function:

```
50 DEF FNB(A$) = LEN(A$)
```

This function computes the length of the string $A\$$.

Finally, functions may produce a string as a function value. The name for such a function must end in $\$$. Consider this function:

```
60 DEF FND$(A$,J) = LEFT(A$,J)
```

This function of the two variables $A\$$ and J computes the string consisting of the J leftmost characters of the string $A\$$. For example, suppose that $A\$$ = ''computer'' and $J = 3$. Then:

```
FND$(A$,J) = "com"
```

11

Your Computer as a File Cabinet

11.0   Chapter Objectives

IN THIS CHAPTER, WE INTRODUCE THE BASIC techniques for dealing with files on diskette or hard disk. In this chapter, we:

- Define sequential files.

- Study the BASIC statements for OPENing, CLOSEing, WRITEing, and reading sequential files.

- Study the way BASIC writes sequential files on diskette or hard disk.

- Study the BASIC statements for dealing with random access files.

- Give a short introduction to the subject of sorting.

- Survey the BASIC commands for manipulating files.

11.1   What Are Files?

A **file** is a collection of information stored on a mass storage device (diskette, cassette, or hard disk). There are two common types of files: program files and data files.

Program Files.   When a program is stored on diskette, it is stored as a *program file*. You already have created some program files by saving BASIC programs on diskette. In addition to the programs you create, your DOS diskette contains program files that are necessary to run your computer, such as DOS and the BASIC language.

Data Files.   Computer programs used in business and industry usually refer to files of information that are kept in mass storage. For example, a personnel department will keep a file of data on each employee: name, age, address, social security number, date employed, position, salary, and so forth. A warehouse will maintain an inventory for each product with the following information: product name, supplier, current inventory, units sold in the last reporting period, date of the last shipment, size of the last shipment, and units sold in the last 12 months. These files are called *data files*.

In this chapter, we discuss the procedures for handling files in general and data files in particular.

Consider the following example. Suppose that a teacher stores grades in a data file. For each student in the class, there are four exam grades. A typical entry in the data file contains the following data items:

student name, exam grade #1, exam grade #2,

exam grade #3, exam grade #4

In a data file, the data items are organized in sequence. So the beginning of the above data file might look like this:

```
"John Smith", 98, 87, 93, 76, "Mary Young",
99, 78, 87, 91, "Sally Ronson", 48, 63, 72,
80, ...
```

The data file consists of a sequence of string constants (the names) and numeric constants (the grades), with the various data items arranged in a particular pattern (name followed by four grades). This particular arrangement is designed so the file may be read and understood. For instance, if we read the data items above, we know in advance that the data items are in groups of five with the first one a name and the next four the corresponding grades.

In this chapter, we will learn to create data files containing information such as the data files—sequential and random access. For each type of file we will learn to perform the following operations:

1. Create a data file.
2. Write data items to a file.
3. Read data items from a file.
4. Alter data items in a file.
5. Search a file for particular data items.

11.2 Sequential Files

A **sequential file** is a data file in which the data items are accessed in order. That is, the data items are written in consecutive order into the file, and are read in the order in which they were written. You may add data items only to the end of a sequential file. If you wish to add a data item somewhere in the middle of the file, it is necessary to rewrite the entire file. Similarly, if you wish to read a data item at the end of a sequential file, it is necessary to read all the data items in order and to ignore those that you don't want.

OPENing and CLOSEing Sequential Files

Before you perform any operations on a sequential file, you must first open the file. You should think of the file as being contained in a file cabinet drawer (the diskette). In order to read the file, you must first open the file drawer. This is accomplished using the BASIC instruction **OPEN**. When OPENing a file, you must specify the file and indicate whether you will be reading from the file or writing into the file. For example, to OPEN the file *B:PAYROLL* for input (for reading the file), we use a statement of the form

```
10 OPEN "B:PAYROLL" FOR INPUT AS #1
```

The *#1* is a reference number we assign to the file when opening it. As long as the file remains open, you refer to it by its reference number rather than the more cumbersome file specification *B:PAYROLL*. The reference number is quite arbitrary. You may assign any positive integer you wish. Just make sure that you don't assign two files that are to be open simultaneously to the same reference number. (If you try this, BASIC will give you an error message.)

Here is an instruction for opening the file *"GAMES"* on cassette for input:

```
10 OPEN "CAS1:GAMES" FOR INPUT AS #1
```

Here is an alternate form of the instruction for opening a file for input:

```
10 OPEN "I",#1,"B:PAYROLL"
```

Here the letter *"I"* stands for *"Input"*.

To OPEN the file *B:GRADES.AUG* for output (that is, to write in the file), we use an instruction of the form

```
20 OPEN "B:GRADES.AUG" FOR OUTPUT AS #2
```

Here is an alternate way to write the same instruction:

```
20 OPEN "O",#2,"B:GRADES.AUG"
```

The letter *"O"* stands for "Output."

BASIC initially allows you to work with three open diskette files at a time. Only one cassette file may be open at a time. This number may be increased by giving the appropriate command when you start BASIC. For example, to allow use of as many as five files at once, start BASIC with the command

```
BASICA /F:5
```

The "switch" */F:5* is what tells BASIC to set aside memory for simultaneous manipulation of up to five files.

In maintaining any filing system, it is necessary to be neat and organized. The same is true of computer files. A sequential file may be opened for input or for output, but not both simultaneously. As long as the file remains open, it accepts instructions (input or output) of the same sort designated when it was opened. To change operations, it is necessary to first close the file. For example, to close the file *B:PAYROLL* from line 10 above, we use the instruction

```
40 CLOSE #1
```

After giving this instruction, we may reopen the file for output using an instruction similar to that given in line 20 above. It is possible to close several files at a time. For example, the statement

```
50 CLOSE #5,#6
```

closes the files with reference numbers 5 and 6. We may close all currently open files with the instruction

```
50 CLOSE
```

In an OPEN or CLOSE statement, the # is optional. Thus, it is perfectly acceptable to use

```
50 OPEN 1,2
50 CLOSE 5,6
```

Good programming practice dictates that all files be closed after use. In any case, the BASIC commands NEW, RUN, and SYSTEM automatically close any files that might have been left open by a preceding program.

WRITEing Data Items Into a Sequential File

Suppose that we wish to create a sequential file called *INVOICE.001*, which contains the following data items:

```
DJ SALES   50357 4  $358.79   4/5/81
```

That is, we want to write into the file the string constant *DJ SALES* followed by the two numeric constants *50357* and *4*, followed by the two string constants *$358.79* and *4/5/81*. Here is a program that does exactly that:

```
10 ' This program writes five data items to a file
100 OPEN "B:INVOICE.001" FOR OUTPUT AS #1
110 WRITE#1, "DJ SALES", 50357!,4,"$358.79", "4/5/81"
120 CLOSE #1
130 END
```

The *#1* portion of line 110 refers to the identification number given to the file in the OPEN instruction in line 100, namely 1. In a **WRITE#** statement, a comma must follow the file number.

Note that the **WRITE** instruction works very much like a PRINT statement, except that the data items are "printed" in the file instead of on the screen.

While a file is open, you may execute any number of WRITE instructions to insert data. Moreover, you may WRITE data items that are values of variables, as in the statement

```
200 WRITE #1, A, A$
```

This instruction will write current values of A and A$ into the file.

Example 1.   Write a program to create a file whose data items are the numbers 1, 1^2, 2, 2^2, 3, 3^2, ..., 100, 100^2.

Solution.   Let's call the file *SQUARES* and store it on the diskette in drive A:.

```
10 ' *********************************************
20 ' This program makes a file of all the integers
30 '    from 1 to 100 and their squares
40 ' *********************************************
50 OPEN "A:SQUARES" FOR OUTPUT AS #1
60 FOR J=1 TO 100
70    WRITE#1, J,J^2
80 NEXT J
90 CLOSE #1
100 END
```

Example 2.   Create a data file consisting of names, addresses, and telephone numbers from your personal telephone directory. Assume that you will type the addresses into the computer and will tell the computer when the last address has been typed.

Solution.   We use INPUT statements to enter the various data. Let *NME$* denote the name of the current person, *ADDRESS$* the street address, *CITY$* the city , *STATE$* the state, *ZIPCODE$* the zip code, and *TELEPHONE$* the telephone number. For each entry, there is an INPUT statement corresponding to each of these variables. The program then writes the data to the diskette. Here is the program.

```
10 ' ************************************
20 ' This program creates a file holding
30 '    entries from a telephone directory
40 '    which are entered by the user
50 ' ************************************
100 OPEN "TELEPHON" FOR OUTPUT AS #1
110 INPUT "NAME"; NME$
120 INPUT "STREET ADDRESS"; ADDRESS$
130 INPUT "CITY"; CITY$
140 INPUT "STATE"; STATE$
150 INPUT "ZIP CODE"; ZIP$
160 INPUT "TELEPHONE"; PHONE$
170 WRITE#1, NME$,ADDRESS$,CITY$,STATE$,ZIP$,PHONE$
200 ' Check whether there is more data
210 INPUT "ANOTHER ENTRY (Y/N)"; G$
220 IF G$="Y" THEN 110
230 CLOSE #1
240 END
```

Note the unusual spelling of *NAME (NME)*. We are forced into this queer spelling since NAME is a BASIC reserved word. You should use the above program to set up a computerized telephone directory of your own. It is very instructive. Moreover, when coupled with the search program given below, it will allow you to look up addresses and phone numbers using your computer.

TEST YOUR UNDERSTANDING 1

Use the above program to enter the following addresses into the file:

```
John Jones
1 South Main St. Apt. 308
Phila. Pa. 19107
527-1211

Mary Bell
2510 9th St.
Phila. Pa. 19138
937-4896
```

Reading Data Items

To read items from a data file, it is first necessary to open the file for **INPUT** (that is, for INPUT from the diskette.) Consider the telephone file in Example 2. We may open it for input, via the instruction

```
300 OPEN "TELEPHON" FOR INPUT AS #2
```

Once the file is open, it may read via the instruction

```
400 INPUT #2, NME$,ADDRESS$,CITY$,STATE$,ZIP$,PHONE$
```

This instruction reads six data items from the file (corresponding to one tele-phone-address entry), assigns *NME$* the value of the first data item, *ADDRESS$* the second, and so forth.

In order to read a file, it is necessary to know the precise format of the data in the file. For example, the form of the above INPUT statement was dictated by the fact that each telephone-address entry was entered into the file as six consec-utive string constants. The file INPUT statement works like any other INPUT statement: faced with a list of variables separated by commas, it assigns values to the indicated variables in the order in which the data items are presented. How-ever, if you attempt to assign a string constant to a numeric variable or vice versa, BASIC reports an error.

As long as a file is open for INPUT, you may continue to INPUT from it, using as many INPUT statements as you like. These may, in turn, be intermin-gled with statements that have nothing to do with the file you are reading. Each

INPUT statement begins reading the file where the preceding INPUT statement left off.

Here's how to determine if you have read all data items in a file. BASIC maintains the functions *EOF(1), EOF(2),...,* one for each open file. These functions may be used like logical variables. That is, they assume the possible values true or false. You may test for the end of the file using an IF...THEN statement. For example, consider the statement

```
100 IF EOF(1) THEN 2000 ELSE 10
```

This statement causes BASIC to determine if you are currently at the end of file #1. If so, the program will go to line 2000. Otherwise, the program will go to line 10. Note that you are not at the end of the file until after you read the last data item.

If you attempt to read past the end of a file, BASIC will report an **Input Past End** error. Therefore, before reading a file, it is a good idea to determine whether you are currently at the end of the file.

Example 3.   A data file, called NUMBERS, consists of numerical entries. Write a program to determine the number of entries in the file.

Solution.   Let us keep a count of the current number we are reading in the variable *COUNT*. Our procedure will be to read a number, increase the count, then test for the end of the file.

```
10 ' ******************************
20 ' This program counts the number
30 ' of entries in a sequential file
40 ' ******************************
100 COUNT = 0:              ' Initialize COUNT
110 OPEN "NUMBERS" FOR INPUT AS #1
120 IF EOF(1) THEN 200:   ' Out of data?
130 INPUT #1,A            ' Read an item
140 COUNT=COUNT+1         ' Increment COUNT
150 GOTO 120
200 PRINT "THE NUMBER OF NUMBERS IN THE FILE IS",COUNT
210 CLOSE
220 END
```

Example 4.   Write a program that searches for a particular entry of the telephone directory file created in Example 2.

Solution.   We will *INPUT* the name corresponding to the desired entry. The program then reads the file entries until a match of names occurs. Here is the program.

```
10 ' **********************************
20 ' This program searches a file of
30 ' telephone listings for the entry
40 ' of a name given by the user
50 ' **********************************
100 OPEN "TELEPHON" FOR INPUT AS #1
110 INPUT "NAME TO SEARCH FOR"; Z$
```

```
120 INPUT #1, A$,B$,C$,D$,E$,F$
130 IF A$ = Z$ THEN 200:    'Matching item?
140 IF EOF(1)  THEN 300:    'Out of data?
150 GOTO 120:    'On to the next item
200 CLS:          'Print the entry
210 PRINT A$
220 PRINT B$
230 PRINT C$,D$,E$
240 PRINT F$
250 GOTO 400
300 CLS:          'No match
310 PRINT "THE NAME IS NOT ON FILE"
400 CLOSE 1
410 END
```

TEST YOUR UNDERSTANDING 2

Use the above program to locate Mary Bell's number in the telephone file created in Test Your Understanding 1.

Example 5.   (Mailing List Application) Suppose that you have created your computerized telephone directory, using the program in Example 2. Assume that the completed file is called TELEPHON and it is on the diskette in drive A:. Write a program that reads the file and prints out the names and addresses onto mailing labels.

Solution.   Let's assume that your mailing labels are of the "peel-off" variety, which can be printed continuously on your printer. Further, let's assume that the labels are six printer lines high, so that each label has room for five lines of print with one line space between labels. (These are actual dimensions of labels you can buy.) We will print the name on line 1, the address on line 2, the city, state, and zip codes all on line 3, with the city and state separated by a comma.

```
10  ' **************************************
20  ' This program prints a mailing label
30  '    for each entry in a directory
40  '    of telephone book listings
50  ' **************************************
100 OPEN "TELEPHON" FOR INPUT AS #1
110 IF EOF(1) THEN 1000
120 INPUT #1, A$, B$, C$, D$, E$, F$
130 LPRINT A$              :'PRINT NAME
140 LPRINT B$              :'PRINT ADDRESS
150 LPRINT C$;             :'PRINT CITY
160 LPRINT ",";            :'PRINT COMMA
170 LPRINT TAB(10) D$;     :'PRINT STATE
180 LPRINT TAB(20) E$      :'PRINT ZIP CODE
190 LPRINT:LPRINT:LPRINT   :'NEXT LABEL
200 GOTO 110
1000 CLOSE 1
1010 END
```

Adding to a Data File

Here is an important fact about writing data files: writing a file destroys any previous contents of the file. (In contrast, you may read a file any number of times without destroying its contents.) Consider the file *TELEPHON* created in Example 2 above. Suppose we write a program that opens the file for output and writes what we suppose are additional entries in our telephone directory. After this write operation, the file *TELEPHON* will contain only the added entries. All of the original entries will have been lost! How, then, may we add items to a file that already exists? Easy. IBM PC BASIC has a special instruction to do this. Rather than OPEN the file for *OUTPUT*, we OPEN the file for **APPEND**, using the instruction

```
500 OPEN "TELEPHON" FOR APPEND AS #1
```

The computer locates the current end of the file. Any additional entries to the file will be written beginning at that point. However, the previous entries in the file will be unchanged.

Example 6.   Write a program that adds entries to the file *TELEPHON*. The additions should be typed via INPUT statements. The program may assume that the file is on the diskette in drive *A:*.

Solution.   To add items to the file, we first *OPEN* the file for *APPEND*. We then ask for the new entry via an *INPUT* statement and write the new entry into *TELEPHON*. Here is the program.

```
10  ' *******************************
20  ' This program adds entries to a
30  '    file of telephone listings
40  ' *******************************
100 OPEN "TELEPHON" FOR APPEND AS #1
110 PRINT "TYPE ENTRY:NAME,STREET ADDRESS,CITY, STATE,"
120 PRINT "ZIP CODE, TELEPHONE NO."
130 INPUT A$,B$,C$,D$,E$,F$
140 WRITE#1, A$, B$, C$, D$, E$, F$
150 INPUT "ANOTHER ENTRY  (Y/N)"; Z$
160 IF Z$ <> "Y" THEN 200
170 CLS
180 GOTO 110     :'Add another entry
200 CLOSE 1
210 END
```

TEST YOUR UNDERSTANDING 3

Use the above program to add your name, address, and telephone number to the telephone directory created in Test Your Understanding 1.

11.3 More About Sequential Files

When you **WRITE** a data item to a sequential file, BASIC automatically includes certain ''punctuation'' that allows the data to be read:

1. Strings are surrounded by quotation marks.

2. Data items are separated by commas.

3. The last data item in the WRITE# statement is followed by a carriage return (*CHR$(13)*). In what follows, we denote this character by *<CR>*.

4. Positive numbers are inserted in the file without a leading blank.

For example, suppose that *A$ = ''JOHN'', B$ = ''SMITH'', C = 1234*, and *D = -14*. Consider the following WRITE# statement:

```
10 WRITE#1, A$,B$,C,D
```

Here is how this statement WRITEs the data into file #1:

```
"JOHN","SMITH",1234,-14<CR>
```

When the above data is read by an *INPUT#* statement, the quotation marks, commas, and ENTER enable BASIC to separate the various data items from one another. For this reason, the punctuation marks are called **delimiters**. In using the WRITE# statement, you need not worry about delimiters. However, in other sequential file statements, you are not so lucky.

Consider, for instance, the **PRINT#** statement. This statement may be used to PRINT data to a file exactly as if the data were being printed on the screen. All of the usual features of PRINT, such as TAB, SPC, and semicolons, are active. However, the PRINT# statement does not include any delimiters. Consider the above variables *A$, B$, C*, and *D*. The statement

```
20 PRINT#1, A$;B$;C;D
```

writes the following image to file #1:

```
JOHNSMITH 1234-14<CR>
```

Note that:

1. The space before the positive number *1234* is included in the file.

2. There are no separations between the data items.

3. There are no quotation marks around the strings.

In order to correctly read the individual data items, you must supply delimiters in your PRINT# statement. Here's how. First, put commas as strings in PRINT#:

```
20 PRINT#1, A$;",";B$;",";C;",";D
```

Here's how the image in the file will now look:

`JOHN,SMITH, 1234,-14<CR>`

The individual data items now may be read.

This is not quite the end of the story, however! Notice that the strings still do not have quotation marks around them. In this example, no harm will be done. To understand why, let's discuss the operation of the INPUT# statement.

INPUT recognizes as delimiters both commas and ENTER. When faced with a stream of data in a file, here is what INPUT# does:

1. INPUT# scans the characters and peels off characters until it finds a delimiter. This indicates the end of the current data item. (The delimiter is not included as part of the data item.)

2. If a numeric data item has been requested, INPUT# checks that the data item is a number (no illegal characters such as *A*, *$*, or *;*). If illegal characters are detected, a **Type Mismatch** error occurs.

3. If a string data item has been requested, INPUT# checks to see whether the data item is surrounded by quotation marks. If so, it removes them.

Understanding the above sequence can prevent embarrassing errors. One such error can occur if you wish to include a comma within a data item. For example, suppose that *A$ = "SMITH,JOHN"*, *B$ = "CARPENTER"*. The PRINT# statement

`30 PRINT#1, A$;",";B$`

writes the following image to the file:

`SMITH,JOHN,CARPENTER<CR>`

A subsequent INPUT# statement

`40 INPUT#1, A$,B$`

results in *A$ = "SMITH" and B$ = "JOHN"*. To get around this problem, you must explicitly include quotation marks around strings that include a comma. A string that consists of a quotation mark is just *CHR$(34)*. (34 is the ASCII code for a quotation mark.) To include the quotation marks around the string *A$ = "Smith,John"*, you may use the statement

`50 PRINT#1, CHR$(34);A$;CHR$(34);",";B$`

The file image is now

`"SMITH,JOHN",CARPENTER<CR>`

Quotation marks must enclose strings containing commas, semicolons, beginning or ending blanks, or ENTER.

As you can see, the PRINT# statement is much less convenient than WRITE#. In most cases, it is much simpler to use WRITE#. However,

PRINT# has its advantages. With a PRINT#, you may include the **USING** option to format your data. For example, to write the value of the variable *A* to the file in the format *##.#*, use the statement

```
60 PRINT#1, USING "##.#";A
```

The INPUT# statement reads a single data item at a time. However, in some applications you may wish to read an entire line from a file. That is, you wish to read data until you encounter an ENTER. This may be done with the **LINE INPUT#** statement. For example, suppose that the following data is contained in file #1:

```
SMITH,JOHN,CARPENTER<CR>
```

The statement

```
70 LINE INPUT#1, A$
```

sets *A$ = "SMITH,JOHN,CARPENTER"*. Note the following curious twist, however. If you saved your string data with quotation marks around it, those quotation marks are included as part of the string read by LINE INPUT#. If you plan to read data lines via a LINE INPUT# statement, it is usually wise to save the data using PRINT# so that no extraneous quotation marks are generated.

File Buffers

You may have noticed that the drive light does not always turn on when you are writing to a file. For example, try this experiment: OPEN a data file and write a single numerical data item to the file, but don't CLOSE the file. The disk drive does nothing. However, if you run this program a second time, the drive light will go on. This may seem strange. However, it has to do with the way BASIC writes (and reads) diskette files.

Diskette drives are very slow when compared with the speed at which BASIC executes non-diskette operations. In order to speed up diskette operations, BASIC writes to the diskette using **file buffers**. A file buffer (or "buffer" for short) is an area of RAM where BASIC temporarily stores data to be written to a file. There is one buffer corresponding to each open file. BASIC reserves the space for a buffer as part of the OPEN operation. When you use any file writing operation, BASIC writes the corresponding information into the file's buffer. When the buffer is full, BASIC writes the data to the file.

The **CLOSE** operation forces all buffers (full or not) to be written to their corresponding files. When you don't close a file (as in our above experiment), the buffer may be sitting with some data that has not yet been written to diskette. In this case, a RUN or END command will also cause the buffers to be written to diskette. Also, as soon as you modify the program in RAM, the buffers will be written to diskette. In our experiment, it was the RUN statement that caused the drive lights to go on, to write the final results of the previous run.

11.4   Random Access Files

The files considered so far in this chapter are all examples of **sequential files**. That is, the files are all written sequentially, from beginning to end. These files are very easy to create, but are cumbersome in many applications, since they must be read sequentially. In order to read a piece of data from the end of the file, it is necessary to read all data items from the beginning of the file. **Random access files** do not suffer from this difficulty. Using a random access file, it is possible to access the precise piece of data you want. Of course, there is a price to be paid for this convenience. (No free lunches!) You must work a little harder to learn how to use random access files.

A random access file is divided into segments of fixed length called **records**. (See Figure 11-1.) The length of a record is measured in terms of bytes. For a string constant, each character, including spaces and punctuation marks, counts as a single byte. For example, the record consisting of the string

`ACCOUNTING-5`

is of length 12.

To store a data item in a random access file, all data must be converted into string form. This applies to numeric constants and values of numeric variables. (See below for the special instructions for performing this conversion.) A number (more precisely, a single-precision number) is converted into a string of length 4, no matter how many digits this number has. A record may contain the four data items: *ACCOUNTING, 5000, .235*, and *7886*. These pieces of data are stored in order, with no separations between them. The length of this particular record is 22 bytes (10 for ACCOUNTING and four each for the numerical data items). (See Figure 11-2.)

To write data to a random access file, it is necessary to first open it. To open a file named *DEPTS* as a random access file with a record length of *22*, use the instruction

Figure 11-1. **A random access file.**

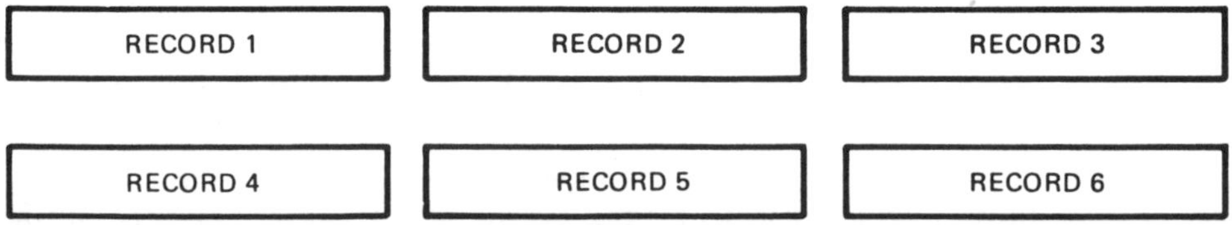

RECORD 1	RECORD 2	RECORD 3

RECORD 4	RECORD 5	RECORD 6

```
10 OPEN "DEPTS" AS #1 LEN=22
```

Next, we must describe the structure of the records of the file. For example, suppose that each record of file #1 is to start with a 10-character string followed by three numbers (converted to string form). Further, suppose that the string represents a department name, the first number the current department income, the second number the department's efficiency rating, and the third number the current department's overhead. We indicate this situation with the instruction

```
20 FIELD #1, 10 AS DEPT$, 4 AS INCOME$, 4
   AS EFFICIENCY$, 4 AS OVERHEAD$
```

This instruction identifies the file with the number used when the file was opened. Each section of the record is called a **field**. Each field is identified by a string variable and the number of bytes reserved for that variable.

Figure 11-2. **A typical record.**

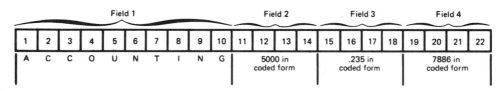

Writing to a Random Access File

To write a record to a random access file, it is first necessary to assemble the data corresponding to the various fields. This is done using the **LSET** and **RSET** instructions. For example, to set the *DEPT$* field to the string ''ACCOUNT-ING'', we use the instruction

```
30 LSET DEPT$="ACCOUNTING"
```

To set the *DEPT$* field to the value of the string variable *N$*, we use

```
40 LSET DEPT$=N$
```

If *N$* contains fewer than 10 characters, the rightmost portion of the field is filled with blanks. This is called **left justification**. If *N$* contains more than 10 characters, the field is filled with the leftmost 10 characters.

The instruction RSET works exactly the same as LSET, except that the unused spaces appear on the left side of the field. (The strings are **right justified**.)

To convert numbers to strings for inclusion in random access files, we use the **MKS$** (or **MKI$** or **MKD$**) function. For example, to include *.753* in the *EFFICIENCY$* field, we first replace it by the string *MKS$(.753)*. To include the value of the variable INC in the *INCOME$* field, we first replace it by

MKS$(INC). After the conversion, we use the *LSET* (or *RSET*) commands to insert the string in the field. In the case of the two examples cited, the sequence is carried out by the respective instructions:

```
50 LSET EFFICIENCY$=MKS$(.753)
60 LSET INCOME$=MKS$(INC)
```

Once the fields of a particular record have been set (using LSET or RSET), you may write the record to the file using the **PUT** instruction. Records are numbered within the file, starting from one. The significant feature of a random access file is that you may record or retrieve information from any particular record. For example, to write the current data into record 38 of file #1, we use the instruction

```
80 PUT #1, 38
```

TEST YOUR UNDERSTANDING 1 (answer on page 244)

Write a program to create a file containing the following records:

ACCOUNTING	5000	.235	7886
ENGINEERING	3500	.872	2200
MAINTENANCE	4338	.381	5130
ADVERTISING	10832	.951	12500

Reading a Random Access File

To read a random access file, you must first open it using an instruction of the form

```
90 OPEN "DEPTS" AS #1 LEN=23
```

Note: This is the same as the instruction for opening a random access file for writing. Random access files differ from sequential files in this respect. By opening a random access file you prepare it for both reading and writing. Before closing the file, you may read some records and write others.

The next step in reading a random access file is to define the record structure using a **FIELD** statement, such as

```
100 FIELD #1, 10 AS DEPT$, 4 AS INCOME$, 4 AS
       EFFICIENCY$, 4 AS OVERHEAD$
```

This is the same instruction we used for writing to the file. Until the FIELD instruction is overridden by another, it applies to all reading and writing for file #1.

To perform the actual reading operation, we use the *GET* statement. For example, to read record *4* of the file, we use the statement

```
110 GET #1, 4
```

The variables *DEPT$, INCOME$, EFFICIENCY$,* and *OVERHEAD$* are now set equal to the appropriate values specified in record *4* of file *#1*. We can, for example, print the value of *DEPT$* using the statement

```
120 PRINT DEPT$
```

If we wish to use the value of *EFFICIENCY$* (in a numerical calculation or in a PRINT statement, for instance), it is necessary first to convert it back into numerical form. This is accomplished using the CVS function. The statement

```
130 PRINT CVS(EFFICIENCY$)
```

prints out the current value of *EFFICIENCY$*; the statement

```
140 LET N=100*CVS(EFFICIENCY$)
```

sets the value of *N* equal to 100 times the numerical value of *EFFICIENCY$*.

It is important to note that field variables such as *DEPT$* and *EFFICIENCY$* contain the values assigned in the most recent GET statement. In order to manipulate data from more than one GET statement, it is essential to assign the values from one GET statement to some other variables before issuing the next GET statement.

TEST YOUR UNDERSTANDING 2 (answer on page 244)

Consider the random access file of Test Your Understanding 1. Write a program to read record 3 of that file and print the corresponding four pieces of data on the screen.

Random access files use no delimiters to separate data items within the file. Rather, the data items are sandwiched together, using the number of characters specified for each field. In order to peel those data items back apart, you must divide the file into records of the correct length and each record into fields of the proper numbers of bytes.

In our discussion above, we used the instructions **MKS$** and **CVS** to convert numerical data to string format and back to numerical format. These functions apply to single-precision numbers. In addition to single-precision numbers, there are double-precision numbers (up to 17 digits) and integers (whole numbers between -32768 and +32767). To convert a double-precision number to a string, we use the function **MKD$**; to convert back to numerical form, **CVD**. To convert an integer to a string, use the function **MKI$**; to convert back to numerical form, use **CVI**.

In either numerical form or string form an integer is represented by two bytes, a single-precision number by four bytes and a double-precision number by eight bytes. In particular, this means that MKI\$ produces a 2-byte string, MKS\$ a 4-byte string, and MKD\$ an 8-byte string.

BASIC provides several functions that help you keep track of random access files. The **LOF** (=Length Of File) function gives the actual number of bytes in the file. For example, suppose that file #2 contains 140 bytes. Then

```
LOF(#2)
```

is equal to 140. The LOF function may be used to determine the number of records currently in the file, according to the formula

<number of records> = LOF(<file number>)/ <record length>

Note that random access files cannot have any ''holes.'' That is, if you write record 150, BASIC sets aside space for records 1 through 149, even if you write nothing in these records.

The **LOC** (LOCation) function gives the number of the last record read or written to the file. For example, if the last record written or read to file #1 was record 48, then LOC(#1) is equal to 58.

Here is an example that illustrates most of the procedures for using random access files.

Example 1.   Write a program to create an address/telephone directory using a random access file. The program should allow for updating the directory and for directory search corresponding to a given name.

Solution.   The program first opens the random access file *TELEPHON*, used to store the various directory entries. Note that the record length is set equal to 128. This allows us to use *LOF* to calculate the number of records in the file using either BASIC 2.0 or later. The program then displays a menu allowing you to choose from among the various options: Add an entry to the directory, Search the directory, Exit from the program. After an option is completed, the program redisplays the menu allowing you to make another choice. The code corresponding to the three options begins at program lines 1000, 2000, and 3000, respectively. Here is the program.

```
10   '*****************************************
20   ' This program incorporates all of the
30   ' routines needed to create and manage
40   ' a telephone directory file using
50   ' random access file techniques.
60   '*****************************************
1000 'Main Program
1010 'Open File For Random Access
1020 OPEN "TELEPHON" AS #1 LEN=128
1030 FIELD#1, 20 AS NME$, 20 AS ADDRESS$,
          20  AS CITY$, 20 AS STATE$, 5 AS ZIPCODE$,
          20 AS TELEPHONE$, 23 AS BLANK$
1040 LSET BLANK$=""
1050 'Option Menu
```

```
1060 CLS:PRINT "OPTIONS"
1070 PRINT "1. MAKE ENTRY IN DIRECTORY"
1080 PRINT "2. SEARCH DIRECTORY"
1090 PRINT "3. EXIT PROGRAM"
1100 INPUT "CHOOSE OPTION (1/2/3)";OPT
1110 ON OPT GOSUB 2000,3010,4010
1120 GOTO 1060
2000 'Add to file
2010 CLS
2020 INPUT "NAME";N$
2030 LSET NME$=N$
2040 INPUT "ADDRESS";N$
2050 LSET ADDRESS$=N$
2060 INPUT "CITY";N$
2070 LSET CITY$=N$
2080 INPUT "STATE";N$
2090 LSET STATE$=N$
2100 INPUT "ZIPCODE";N$
2110 LSET ZIPCODE$=N$
2120 INPUT "TELEPHONE NUMBER";N$
2130 LSET TELEPHONE$ = N$
2140 PUT #1
3000 RETURN
3010 'Search for a name
3020 NREC=LOF(1)/128
3030 INPUT "NAME TO SEARCH FOR";N$
3040 R=1
3050 GET #1, R
3060 GOSUB 5000: IF M$=N$ THEN 3100
3070 R=R+1
3080 IF R>NREC THEN PRINT "NAME IS NOT ON FILE":
         GOTO 4000
3090 GOTO 3050
3100 PRINT NME$
3110 PRINT ADDRESS$
3120 PRINT CITY$
3130 PRINT STATE$
3140 PRINT ZIPCODE$
3150 PRINT TELEPHONE$
4000 RETURN
4010 'Exit from program
4020 CLOSE
4030       END
5000 'Strip trailing blanks
5010 M$=NME$
5020 IF RIGHT$(M$,1) <> CHR$(32) THEN 5050
5030 M$ = LEFT$(M$,LEN(M$)-1)
5040 GOTO 5020
5050 RETURN
```

Note that line 3020 computes the number of records using the LOF function. In searching the file for a given name *N$*, the records are read one by one and the first field is compared with *N$*. Note, however, that the first field is always 20 characters long. If the corresponding name has less than 20 characters, the field contains one or more trailing blanks. In comparing the first field with *N$*, it is necessary first to remove these blanks. This is done in the subroutine beginning in line 5000.

Setting the Random File Buffer Size

When BASIC is started, it sets aside a portion of RAM to aid in reading and writing random access files. This piece of RAM is called a **random file buffer**. Its size places a limit on the record size of your random access files. You may specify any record size you wish (see below). However, if you don't specify the size of the random access buffer, BASIC will allow only 128 bytes.

Suppose, for example, that you wish to use random access files with record lengths as large as 200 bytes. You may arrange for this by starting BASIC as follows:

1.   Obtain the DOS prompt *A>*.

2.   Type
     ```
     BASIC /S:200 <ENTER>
     ```

3.   BASIC then displays the *Ok* prompt and you may program as usual.

If you attempt to use a FIELD statement requiring more bytes than are contained in the random access buffer, a **Field Overflow** error will result.

ANSWERS TO TEST YOUR UNDERSTANDINGS 1 and 2

```
1:  10 OPEN "DEPTS" AS #1, LEN=23
    20 FIELD #1, 11 AS DEPT$, 4 AS INCOME$, 4 AS
       EFFICIENCY$, 4 AS OVERHEAD$
    30 FOR J=1 TO 4
    40    READ A$,B,C,D
    50    LSET DEPT$=A$
    60    LSET INCOME$=MKS$(B)
    70    LSET EFFICIENCY$=MKS$(C)
    80    SET OVERHEAD$=MKS$(D)
    90    PUT #1,J
   100 NEXT J
   110 DATA "ACCOUNTING",5000,.235,7886
   120 DATA "ENGINEERING",3500,.872,2200
   130 DATA "MAINTENANCE",4338,.381,5130
   140 DATA "ADVERTISING",10832,.951,12500
   150 CLOSE #1
   160 END

2:  10 OPEN "DEPTS" AS #1, LEN=23
    20 FIELD #1, 10 AS DEPT$, 4 AS INCOME$, 4 AS
       EFFICIENCY$,4 AS OVERHEAD$
    30 GET #1, 3
    40 PRINT "DEPARTMENT","INCOME","EFFICIENCY","OVERHEAD"
```

```
50 PRINT DEPT$,CVS(INCOME$),CVS(EFFICIENCY$),
   CVS(OVERHEAD$)
60 CLOSE #1
70 END
```

11.5   An Application of Random Access Files

In this section, we work out a detailed example illustrating the application of random access files. We will design and build a "list manager" program, which allows you to manipulate a list. A program of this sort is sometimes called a **database management program**.

Our program will manipulate typical lists. A typical list is structured into a series of entries, with each entry divided into a series of data items. We have allowed each entry of our list to contain as many as five string items and five numerical items. The string items are listed first. A typical list entry has the form

```
ITEM #1  (STRING)
ITEM #2  (STRING)
ITEM #3  (STRING)
ITEM #4  (STRING)
ITEM #5  (STRING)
ITEM #6  (NUMBER)
ITEM #7  (NUMBER)
ITEM #8  (NUMBER)
ITEM #9  (NUMBER)
ITEM #10 (NUMBER)
```

It is not necessary to use all 10 items. The entries of a particular list might consist of three strings followed by two numbers, for example. The program asks for the structure of the list entries (number of strings and number of numbers). The program then assumes that all entries of the list contain the specified numbers of data items of each type.

The list manager allows you to perform the following activities:

1. Give a name to a list and create a corresponding random access file to contain the list.

2. Give titles to the various items (*"NAME"*, *"ADDRESS"*, *"SALARY"*, *"TELEPHONE #"*). An item title may be up to 12 characters long.

3. Enter list items. The program displays the various item names and allows you to type in the various items for the list entry. You may repeat the entry operation as many times as you wish, thereby compiling lists of any length.

4. Change list entries. You may change a list entry by re-entering its data items.

5. Display list entries. You may display a single list entry or an entire set of consecutive list entries.

6. Search the list. You may search the list for entries in which a particular item (say ZIPCODE) has a particular value (say 20001). The program will inform you of a match and give the entry number. It will then ask you if you wish to see the corresponding list entry. If so, it will display the entry for you. After you are done examining the entry, you press ENTER, and the program will continue to search for further matches.

The following program is highly structured (major tasks correspond to subroutines) and the listing is reasonably self-explanatory. However, you should note the following:

1. The titles of the list are stored in record 1.

2. The actual list entries are stored beginning in record 2. The entry number (list entry 5) is always one less than the corresponding record (record 6).

3. There are two menus. The main menu allows you to choose among the following activities:

```
Specify Titles
Specify List Entry
Search and Display
Exit
```

The second menu is displayed if you choose the *Search and Display* option on the main menu. The various options in this second menu are:

```
Display Single List Entry
Display Consecutive List Entries
Search
```

4. Entry items are numbered from 1 to 10, with the strings 1 to 5 and the numbers 6 to 10. This numbering holds even if some items are not used. That is, the first numerical item is always 6.

Here is a listing of the program.

```
10 '**************
20 ' List Manager
30 '**************
100 'Main Program
110 GOSUB 4200:    'Obtain file name and open file
120 GOSUB 1010:    'Display Main Menu
130 ON REPLY GOSUB 2000,3000,4100,4140
140 GOTO 120
1000 'Display main menu
1010      CLS
1020      PRINT "THE LIST MANAGER"
1030      PRINT:PRINT
1040      PRINT "PROGRAM ACTIVITIES"
1050      PRINT
```

```
1060        PRINT "1. ASSIGN DATA ITEM TITLES"
1070        PRINT "2. SPECIFY LIST ENTRY"
1080        PRINT "3. SEARCH AND DISPLAY LIST"
1090        PRINT "4. EXIT FROM LIST MANAGER"
1100        PRINT
1110        INPUT   "DESIRED ACTIVITY(1-4)";REPLY
1120 RETURN
2000 'Assign Data Item Titles
2010    CLS
2020    IF LOF(1)=1 THEN 2050:       'New File ?
2030    GOSUB 4400:                  'Get old titles
2040    FOR ITEMNUMBER=1 TO 10
2050            PRINT "DATA ITEM #";ITEMNUMBER;
                     TAB(20) "CURRENT DEF'N: ";
2060            PRINT A$(ITEMNUMBER)
2070            INPUT "NEW DEF'N: ";TITLE$(ITEMNUMBER)
2080            LSET A$(ITEMNUMBER)=TITLE$(ITEMNUMBER)
2090    NEXT ITEMNUMBER
2100    PUT #1,1:       'Record new titles
2110    RETURN
3000 'Specify list entry
3010    CLS
3020    INPUT "LIST ENTRY NUMBER (0=NEW ENTRY)";
                ENTRYNUMBER
3030    IF ENTRYNUMBER=0 THEN ENTRYNUMBER=LOC(1)+1
                ELSE ENTRYNUMBER=ENTRYNUMBER+1
3040    GOSUB 4400:                 'Obtain titles
3050    PRINT "LIST ENTRY #";ENTRYNUMBER-1;
                TAB(20) "SPECIFY ENTRY ITEMS"
3060    FOR ITEMNUMBER=1 TO STRINGFIELDS
3070            PRINT "Data Item Title: ";
                     TITLE$(ITEMNUMBER)
3080            INPUT "ENTRY (STRING)";ENTRY$
3090            LSET A$(ITEMNUMBER)=ENTRY$
3100    NEXT ITEMNUMBER
3110    FOR ITEMNUMBER=6 TO 5+NUMERICFIELDS
3120            IF TITLE$(ITEMNUMBER)="" THEN 3160
3130            PRINT "Data Item Title:";
                     TITLE$(ITEMNUMBER)
3140            INPUT "ENTRY (NUMBER)";ENTRY
3150            LSET A$(ITEMNUMBER)=MKS$(ENTRY)
3160    NEXT ITEMNUMBER
3170    PUT #1,ENTRYNUMBER
3180    RETURN
4000 'Various Subroutines
4100 'Search and Display List
4110    GOSUB 4700:       'Search and Display Menu
4120    ON REPLY GOSUB 4800,4900,5100
4130    RETURN
4140 'Exit
4150    CLS
4160    CLOSE #1
4170    END
4180 RETURN
4200 'Obtain filename and open file
4210    CLS
```

```
4220      CLOSE
4230      PRINT "THE LIST MANAGER"
4240      INPUT "NAME OF FILE";FILENAME$
4250      INPUT "NUMBER OF STRING FIELDS
                (1-5)";STRINGFIELDS
4260      INPUT "NUMBER OF NUMERIC FIELDS
                (1-5)";NUMERICFIELDS
4270      OPEN FILENAME$ AS #1
4280      FIELD 1, 12 AS A$(1), 12 AS A$(2), 12 AS A$(3),
          12 AS A$(4), 12 AS A$(5), 12 AS A$(6),
          12 AS A$(7), 12 AS A$(8), 12 AS A$(9),
          12 AS A$(10)
4290      GOSUB 4400:                 'Read Old titles
4300    RETURN
4400  'Read old titles
4410      GET #1,1
4420      FOR J=1 TO 10
4430           TITLE$(J)=A$(J)
4440      NEXT J
4450    RETURN
4500  'Display entry
4510      CLS
4520      PRINT:                      'Advance to 2nd line
4530      GOSUB 4400:                 'Read titles
4540      IF DISPLAYENTRY > LOF(1)/128 THEN 4680:
                          'Non-existent record
4550      GET #1, DISPLAYENTRY
4560      FOR ITEMNUMBER=1 TO STRINGFIELDS
4570           ENTRY$(ITEMNUMBER)=A$(ITEMNUMBER)
4580           PRINT TITLE$(ITEMNUMBER);
                          TAB(21) ENTRY$(ITEMNUMBER)
4590      NEXT ITEMNUMBER
4600      FOR ITEMNUMBER=6 TO 5+NUMERICFIELDS
4610           IF A$(ITEMNUMBER)="" THEN 4620
                                    ELSE 4640
4620           PRINT TITLE$(ITEMNUMBER)
4630           GOTO 4660
4640           ENTRY(ITEMNUMBER)=CVS(A$(ITEMNUMBER))
4650           PRINT TITLE$(ITEMNUMBER);
                          TAB(21) ENTRY(ITEMNUMBER)
4660      NEXT ITEMNUMBER
4670      LOCATE 1,1
4680    RETURN
4700  'Display and Search Menu
4710      CLS
4720      PRINT "DISPLAY AND SEARCH MENU"
4730      PRINT : PRINT
4740      PRINT "1. DISPLAY ENTRY WITH GIVEN NUMBER"
4750      PRINT "2. DISPLAY CONSECUTIVE ENTRIES"
4760      PRINT "3. SEARCH"
4770      PRINT
4780      INPUT "ACTIVITY(1-3)";REPLY
4790    RETURN
4800  'Display entry with given number
4810      CLS
4820      PRINT:                      'Advance to 2nd line
```

```
4830      INPUT "Number of entry to display";DISPLAYENTRY
4840      DISPLAYENTRY=DISPLAYENTRY+1
4850      IF DISPLAYENTRY > LOF(1)/128 THEN 4890
4860      GOSUB 4500
4870      INPUT "TO CONTINUE, HIT ENTER KEY";REPLY$
4880      IF REPLY$="" THEN 4790 ELSE 4670
4890    RETURN
4900  'Display consecutive entries
4910      CLS
4920      PRINT:                        'Advance to 2nd line
4930      INPUT "NUMBER OF FIRST ENTRY TO
                 DISPLAY";DISPLAYENTRY
4940      DISPLAYENTRY=DISPLAYENTRY+1
4950      IF DISPLAYENTRY > LOF(1)/128 THEN 5020
4960      GOSUB 4500
4970      LOCATE 1,1
4980      INPUT "DISPLAY NEXT ENTRY=0,RETURN TO MAIN
          MENU=1";REPLY
4990      IF REPLY=1 THEN 5020
5000      DISPLAYENTRY=DISPLAYENTRY+1
5010      GOTO 4950
5020  RETURN
5100  'Search
5110      CLS
5120      INPUT "ITEM NUMBER TO SCAN";ITM
5130      PRINT "LOOK FOR ITEM NUMBER";ITM;" EQUAL TO";
5140      IF ITM<6 THEN INPUT MATCHSTRING$
5150      IF ITM>5 THEN INPUT MATCHNUMBER
5160      L=LEN(MATCHSTRING$): 'L=length of the match
                                string
5170      MATCHSTRING$=MATCHSTRING$+SPACE$(12-L):
                                'Add blanks
5180      LNGTH=LOF(1)/128
5190      FOR J=2 TO LNGTH
5200            GET #1, J
5210            IF ITM > 5 THEN A=CVS(A$(ITM))
                      ELSE A$=A$(ITM)
5220            IF ITM < 6 AND A$=MATCHSTRING$
                      THEN GOSUB 5300
5230            IF ITM > 5 AND A=MATCHNUMBER
                      THEN GOSUB 5300
5240      NEXT J
5250    RETURN
5300  'Response to a match
5310      CLS
5320      LOCATE 1,1
5330      PRINT "MATCH IN ENTRY";J-1
5340      INPUT "Do You Wish to Display Entry
          (1=Yes,0=No)";REPLY
5350      IF REPLY=1 THEN 5360 ELSE 5400
5360      DISPLAYENTRY=J
5370      GOSUB 4500
5380      INPUT "TO CONTINUE, HIT ENTER KEY";REPLY$
5390      IF REPLY$="" THEN 5400 ELSE 5380
5400    RETURN
```

Note that the fields of the file records are all 12 characters wide. This is to accommodate the titles in record 1. Since we do not specify a record length, BASIC assumes that the records are 128 characters long. We are using 120 (12 characters per field x 10 fields) of these characters. If you wish, you may redesign this program to accommodate more data items and longer string items and titles. However, if you use more than 128 characters per record, it is necessary to initialize BASIC to allow for a sufficiently large random access file buffer.

11.6   Sorting Techniques

In the preceding sections, we have discussed the mechanisms to create, read, and write data files. In this section, we discuss the organization of data within such files.

If a data file is to be of much use, we must be able to easily access its data. At first this might seem like a simple requirement. After all, we can always search through a data file, examining records until we find the one we want. Unfortunately, this is just not always possible. Until now, we have been working with rather short data files. However, many applications require dealing with data files containing thousands or even tens of thousands of records. When a data file is large, even the great speed of the computer is insufficient to guarantee a speedy search. Indeed, if we are required to search through an entire file for a piece of data, we might be required to wait for hours! For this reason (as well as others), we usually organize the contents of a file in some way, so that access to its data is improved. Here are some examples of common file organizations:

1. A file of data on customers may be arranged in alphabetical order, according to the customer name.

2. A mailing list may be arranged according to zip code.

3. An inventory list might be arranged according to part number.

4. A credit card company most likely arranges its customer account files according to their credit card number.

In each example, the records in the data file are arranged in a certain order, based on the value of a particular field in the record (name field, zip code field, part number field, card number field). In maintaining such files, it is essential to be able to arrange the records in the desired order. The process of arranging a set of data items is called **sorting**. Actually, sorting is an extremely important topic to computer programmers and has been the subject of many research papers and books. In this section, we will give an introduction to sorting by describing one of the more elementary sorting techniques—the **bubble sort**.

Let's begin by stating our problem in simple terms. Let's suppose that we wish to arrange the records of a file according to a particular field, say field 1.

PROBLEM.   Arrange the records so that the values in field 1 are in ascending order.

For the sake of our initial discussion, let's suppose that the field values are numbers. (Later, we will deal with fields containing strings.)

Let's set up arrays $A()$ and $B()$ as follows: Read the various values of field 1 into the array A().

$A(1)$ = the value of field 1 for record 1,

$A(2)$ = the value of field 1 for record 2,

$A(3)$ = the value of field 1 for record 3,

and so forth. We wish to rearrange the records according to certain rules. Because the actual records may be quite long, we will deal only with the contents of field 1. In order to keep track of the record to which a particular field value belongs, we will use the array $B()$. That is,

$B(1)$ = the record number for the field value A(1),

$B(2)$ = the record number for the field value A(2),

$B(3)$ = the record number for the field value A(3),

and so forth. Assume that we initially read the values into array $A()$ according to increasing record number. Then we initially have

$B(1)=1,\ B(2)=2,\ B(3)=3,\ ...$

The Bubble Sort Procedure

The **bubble sort** procedure allows you to arrange a set of numbers in increasing order. It involves repeatedly executing a simple reordering process that involves reordering consecutive items. Each repetition of the process is called a **pass**. Let's illustrate the procedure to arrange the following list of numbers in increasing order:

90, 38, 15, 48 , 80, 1

Pass 1.   Start from the right end of the list. Compare the adjacent numbers. If they are out of order, switch them. Otherwise leave them alone. Continue this procedure with each pair of adjacent numbers, proceeding from right to left. Here are the results:

90, 38, 15, 48, 1, 80 (1 < 80 so the pair 80,1 is reversed)

90, 38, 15, 1, 48, 80 (1 < 48 so the pair 48,1 is reversed)

90, 38, 1, 15, 48, 80 (1 < 15 so the pair 15,1 is reversed)

90, 1, 38, 15, 48, 80 (1 < 38 so the pair 38,1 is reversed)

1, 90, 38, 15, 48, 80 (1 < 90 so the pair 90,1 is reversed)

This is the end of Pass 1. Note that the number 1 has assumed its correct place in the list.

Pass 2.   Apply the procedure of Pass 1 to the rightmost five numbers of the current list.

1, 90, 38, 15, 48, 80 (48 < 80 so no exchange)

1, 90, 38, 15, 48, 80

1, 90, 15, 38, 48, 80

1, 15, 90, 38, 48, 80

Note that the number 15 has now been moved to its proper position on the list.

Pass 3.   Apply the procedure of Pass 1 to the rightmost four numbers of the current list.

1, 15, 90, 38, 48, 80

1, 15, 90, 38, 48, 80

1, 15, 38, 90, 48, 80

Pass 4.   Apply the procedure of Pass 1 to the rightmost three numbers of the current list.

1, 15, 38, 90, 48, 80

1, 15, 38, 48, 90, 80

Pass 5.   Apply the procedure of Pass 1 to the rightmost two numbers of the current list.

1, 15, 38, 48, 80, 90

The list is now in order.

Note the following characteristic of the bubble sort procedure. At each step, the smallest remaining number is moved to its proper position in the list. Suppose that we view the original list as written vertically:

90

38

15

48

1

80

Then at each step, the least number in the remaining list moves to its proper level in the list. Think of each number as a bubble under water, whose buoyancy is determined by the value of the number. Then at each step, a bubble moves up as far as it can toward the surface. This is the reason for the name **bubble sort**.

We have carried out the manipulations in the above example in excruciating detail to aid us in writing a correct program to implement the bubble sort procedure. Let's suppose that the items to be ordered are stored in the array *A()* of size *N*. Here is a program that carries out the bubble sort procedure.

```
1000 'Bubble Sort Subroutine
1010 FOR I=2 TO N
1020   FOR J=N TO I STEP -1
1030     IF A(J-1) > A(J) THEN SWAP A(J-1), A(J)
1040   NEXT J
1050 NEXT I
1060 RETURN
```

Note that we have written this program as a subroutine to be included in a larger program. Note that the DIM statement for the array *A()* as well as the number *N* of numbers to be sorted must be set in the larger program. You may test this program with the sequence of numbers *100, 99, 98, 97, 96, ..., 1* by inserting the lines of code:

```
10 ' ****************************************
20 ' This program incorporates a subroutine
30 ' to bubble sort 100 numbers.
40 ' ****************************************
100 DIM A(100)
110 N=100
120 FOR J=1 TO N
130   A(J)=101-J
140 NEXT J
150 GOSUB 1000
160 FOR J=1 TO 100
170   PRINT J, A(J)
180 NEXT J
190 END
1000 'Bubble Sort Subroutine
1010 FOR I=2 TO N
1020   FOR J=N TO I STEP -1
1030     IF A(J-1) > A(J) THEN SWAP A(J-1), A(J)
1040   NEXT J
1050 NEXT I
1060 RETURN
```

We may use this routine to infer some interesting characteristics of sort routines. Here is a set of run times for various values of *N*, using the sequence *N, N-1, N-2, ..., 1*. (This is the worst case since interchanges are required at each step.)

Value of Run Time for Bubble Sort

N = 100 67 seconds

N = 50 17 seconds

N = 20 4 seconds

N = 10 1 second

First note that, with only 100 items to be sorted, the run time is already substantial. Second, note the way that the run time increases as the number of items increases. It appears that if the number of items is doubled then the run time increases by a factor of four. Similarly, multiplying the number of items by three increases the run time by nine. Generally, in this worst-case scenario, multiplying the number of items by k multiplies the run time by k^2. On average, the run times are not this bad. However, we have chosen a particularly bad case to illustrate the manner in which sorting times quickly become unmanageable.

One of the principal problems with our bubble sort procedure is the fact that it is written in interpretive BASIC. In order to do any serious sorting, it is necessary to compile the program into machine language. This may be done using the **BASIC compiler**.

Let's return to our original problem, namely that of sorting the records of a file. Let's use the bubble sort procedure to sort the array $A()$. However, at each interchange, we will interchange the corresponding elements of the array $B()$. At the end of the subroutine, the array $A()$ will be in ascending order and $B(J)$ will equal the number of the record from which $A(J)$ was taken. Here is the program.

```
1000 'Bubble Sort Subroutine for File Records
1010 FOR I=2 TO N
1020    FOR J=N TO I STEP -1
1030       IF A(J-1) > A(J) THEN
                SWAP A(J-1), A(J):
                SWAP B(J-1),B(J)
1040    NEXT J
1050 NEXT I
1060 RETURN
```

The array $B()$ may be stored in a file and used to read out the records of the file according to the increasing order of the particular field.

The bubble sort procedure performs particularly poorly for data that is almost in order and is sorted into the correct order by one of the early passes. The procedure as stated above has no way of knowing that that data is already in order and that no further sorting is necessary. Let's now improve the bubble sort algorithm by building a test into each pass to determine whether any further sorting is necessary.

Our test is based on the value of a variable *SORTFLAG*. Initially, we set *SORTFLAG* equal to zero. During each pass, we set *SORTFLAG* equal to 1 when an interchange takes place. At the end of the pass, we examine the value of *SORTFLAG*. If *SORTFLAG* is 0, then no interchange took place and the algorithm is terminated. Otherwise, *SORTFLAG* is set equal to 0, and the algorithm goes on to the next pass. Here is the code for the modified bubble sort routine.

```
200 'Modified Bubble Sort Subroutine
210 SORTFLAG=0
220 FOR I=2 TO N
230   FOR J=N TO I STEP -1
240     IF A(J-1) > A(J) THEN SWAP A(J-1), A(J):
                              SORTFLAG=1
250   NEXT J
260   IF SORTFLAG=0 THEN I=N ELSE SORTFLAG=0
270 NEXT I
280 RETURN
```

Note the logic in line 260. If *SORTFLAG* is equal to 0, then the loop variable *I* is set equal to *N*. In this case, the *NEXT I* in line 270 causes the *I* loop to terminate. Otherwise, *SORTFLAG* is set equal to 0 and the next value of *I* is considered.

TEST YOUR UNDERSTANDING 1

Compare the times required by both the original and modified bubble sort routines in sorting the following list of numbers into ascending order:

5, 4, 3, 2, 1, 6, 7, 8, 9, ..., 98, 99, 100

Order Relations Among Strings

We arrange single characters in order by their respective ASCII codes. We say that a character *A$* is less than the character *B$* provided that *A$* comes before *B$* in the ASCII table. If *A$* is less than *B$*, we write

A$ < B$

For example, the following are valid inequalities among characters:

"A" < "B" ("A" has ASCII code 65, "B" has ASCII code 66)

"a" < "b" ("a" has ASCII code 97, "b" has ASCII code 98)

Note that arranging alphabetic characters in ascending order amounts to arranging them in alphabetic order. However, the following comparisons are valid and are not usually considered in alphabetic arrangements:

"A" < "a"

"0" < "a" ("0" has ASCII code 48)

"" > "#" ("*" has ASCII code 42, "#" has ASCII code 35)*

" " < "0" (" " has ASCII code 32)

Strings having more than a single letter are compared as follows: First compare first letters. If they are the same, compare second letters. If the first two letters are the same, compare third letters. And so forth. For example, consider the two strings *"Smith"* and *"SMITH"*. Their first letters are the same, so we compare their second letters *"m"* and *"M"*, respectively. According to their ASCII codes *"M"* comes before *"m"*, so:

"SMITH" < *"Smith"*

If the compared strings consist of only uppercase or only lowercase letters, then this comparison procedure arranges the strings in the usual alphabetic order. However, the procedure may be used to compare any strings. For example:

*"**#"* < *"**0"*

Here is a bit of useful notation for strings. The notation

A\$ >= B\$

means that either

A\$ > B\$ or A\$ = B\$

Simply, this means that *A\$* either succeeds *B\$* in alphabetical order, or *A\$* and *B\$* are the same. The notation *A\$ <= B\$* has a similar meaning.

Using the above string order relation, we may design a modified bubble sort procedure for sorting a string array *A\$()* into increasing order. Here is the subroutine.

```
300 'Modified Bubble Sort Subroutine for Strings
310 SORTFLAG=0
320 FOR I=2 TO N
330    FOR J=N TO I STEP -1
340       IF A$(J-1) > A$(J) THEN SWAP A$(J-1), A$(J):
                                  SORTFLAG=1
350    NEXT J
360    IF SORTFLAG=0 THEN I=N ELSE SORTFLAG=0
370 NEXT I
380 RETURN
```

When this routine is used to sort an array consisting only of uppercase or only of lowercase letters, it sorts the array into alphabetical order. Here is an example of this procedure.

Example 1.   Write a program to alphabetize the following list of words: *egg, celery, ball, bag, glove, coat, pants, suit, clover, weed, grass, cow,* and *chicken.*

Solution.   We set us a string array *A\$(J)*, which contains these 13 words and apply the bubble sort subroutine.

```
10 ' *********************************
20 ' This program alphabetizes a list
30 ' of words provided as data.
40 ' *********************************
100 DIM A$(13)
```

```
110 N = 13
120 DATA egg,celery,ball,bag,glove,coat
130 DATA pants, suit, clover, weed, grass
140 DATA cow, chicken
150 'Set up array A$
160 FOR J=1 TO N
170    READ A$(J)
180 NEXT J
190 'Sort array A$()
200 GOSUB 300
210 'Print Sorted Array
220 FOR J=1 TO N
230   PRINT A$(J)
240 NEXT J
250 END
300 'Modified Bubble Sort Subroutine for Strings
310 SORTFLAG=0
320 FOR I=2 TO N
330   FOR J=N TO I STEP -1
340     IF A$(J-1) > A$(J) THEN SWAP A$(J-1), A$(J):
        SORTFLAG=1
350   NEXT J
360   IF SORTFLAG=0 THEN I=N ELSE SORTFLAG=0
370 NEXT I
380 RETURN
```

This program can be modified to make a program alphabetizing any collection of strings. We will leave the details to the exercises.

In this section, we have only scratched the surface of the subject of sorting. For an extensive treatment, see *Algorithms + Data Structures = Programs* by Niklaus Wirth, Prentice-Hall, Inc. Englewood Cliffs, New Jersey, 1976.

11.7   BASIC File Commands

BASIC has a number of useful commands that you may use to perform various manipulations on files.

The Directory

You may request, from within BASIC, a directory of the files on a given diskette or in a given directory of a hard disk. This may be done using the **FILES** command. For example, to list all the files in the current directory, type

```
FILES <ENTER>
```

This command is similar to the DOS command DIR, except that this command is used within BASIC.

The FILES command is very versatile. You use it to provide a listing of all files matching a given file spec. For example, to list all files having an extension *.BAS* on drive *B:*, use the command

```
FILES "B:*.BAS"
```

Similarly, to list all files on drive *B:*, use the command

```
FILES "B:*.*"
```

or

```
FILES "B:"
```

TEST YOUR UNDERSTANDING 1 (answer on page 261)

Write a command that lists all files on the current drive with a three-letter extension that begins with the letter *B*.

Erasing Files

You may erase files using the command **KILL.** The format of this command is

```
KILL <file specification>
```

For example, to erase the file *EXAMPLE.TXT*, use the command

```
KILL "EXAMPLE.TXT"
```

To erase all files on the diskette in drive *B:*, use the command

```
KILL "B:*.*"
```

This last form of the KILL command is very dangerous. You might be erasing some files you don't really want to erase. Use this form of the KILL command with some care.

Note that the KILL command may be used to erase program files as well as data files.

In order to KILL a file, you must include any filename extension in the old filename. Be careful here. If the old file is a BASIC program and if you saved it without specifying an extension, BASIC automatically added the extension BAS. In order to specify the filename for the KILL command, you must include the extension BAS.

TEST YOUR UNDERSTANDING 2 (answers on page 261)

Write BASIC commands to erase the following files:

a. The BASIC program named *"COLORS"*

b.   The BASIC program *"INVOICE.001"*

Renaming a File

You may rename a file by using the **NAME** command. For example, to change the name of *ROULETTE* to *GAME*, we use the command

```
NAME "ROULETTE" AS "GAME"
```

Note that the old name always comes **first**, followed by the new name. An error occurs if either *ROULETTE* doesn't exist or if there is already a file on the diskette with the name GAME.

To rename a program file, you must include any filename extension in the old filename. Be careful here. If the old file is a BASIC program, and if you saved it without specifying an extension, BASIC automatically added the extension BAS. To specify the filename for the NAME command, you must include the extension BAS.

Saving Programs

As we learned in Chapter 5, you may save the current program on diskette, using the SAVE command. Let's take this opportunity to point out a few additional features of this command. BASIC allows a program to be saved in any of three alternate formats—**compressed format, ASCII format**, and **protected format**.

Compressed Format.   This is the format we have used to save programs until now. In this format, the various words of BASIC (LET, PRINT, IF, THEN, etc.) are reduced to a numerical shorthand, which allows the program to be stored in reduced space. The compressed format is also called **tokenized**.

ASCII Format.   In ASCII format, the program is stored letter for letter as you typed it. This requires more diskette space. However, it allows the program to be MERGEd and CHAIN MERGEd. (See below.) Also, a program file must be saved in ASCII format if it is to be used as a source code file for the BASIC compiler.

To save a program in ASCII format, use the command

```
SAVE <filespec>,A
```

For example, to save the program *TAXES* on the diskette in drive *B:* in ASCII format, we use the command

```
SAVE "B:TAXES",A
```

Protected Format.   Once a program has been saved in protected format, also known as **binary format**, it may not be listed. This provides a mild degree of protection against snoopers. To save *TAXES* on drive *B:* in binary format, we use the command

```
SAVE "B:TAXES",P
```

BASIC provides no way to translate a program from binary back into a listable format, so use this format with some care.

Merging Programs

BASIC has the ability to merge the program currently in RAM with another program on a diskette. This is especially useful in inserting standard subroutines into a program and is accomplished using the **MERGE** command. For example, to merge the current program with the program *PAYROLL* we use the command

```
MERGE PAYROLL
```

Suppose the program currently in RAM contains lines 10, 20, 30, and 100, and *PAYROLL* contains lines 40, 50, 60, 70, 80, 90, and 100. The merged program would contain the lines 10, 20, 30, 40, 50, 60, 70, 80, 90, and 100. Line 100 would be taken from *PAYROLL*. (The lines of *PAYROLL* would replace those of the current program in case of duplicate line numbers.) To use the MERGE feature, the program from diskette must have been SAVEd in ASCII format. In the case of the above example, the command that SAVEd *PAYROLL* must be of the form

```
SAVE "PAYROLL", A
```

In case *PAYROLL* was not SAVEd using such a command, it is first necessary to *LOAD "PAYROLL"* and resave it using the above command. (Watch out! If you type in a program, say *OX* as an example, to merge with *PAYROLL*, remember to save it before giving the MERGE command. If you don't, you will lose *OX*.)

TEST YOUR UNDERSTANDING 3 (answers on page 261)

a.   SAVE the following program in ASCII format under the name *GHOST*.

```
10 PRINT 5+7
100 END
```

b.   Type in the program

```
30 PRINT 7+9
40 PRINT 7-9
```

c.   MERGE the programs of a. and b.

ANSWERS TO TEST YOUR UNDERSTANDINGS 1, 2, and 3

1:   `FILES "*.B??"`

2:   a. `KILL "COLORS.BAS"`
     b. `KILL "INVOICE.001"`

3:   a. Type in the program, then give the command
        `SAVE "GHOST",A`

   b. Type NEW followed by the given program.
   c. Type MERGE ''GHOST'' .

12

An Introduction to
Graphics and Sound

12.0   Chapter Objectives

BASIC ON THE IBM FAMILY OF personal computers is capable of quite sophisticated graphics and sound. This chapter is an introduction to these capabilities and includes:

- Line graphics in text mode.
- Setting colors and graphics modes.
- Relative and absolute coordinates in graphics mode.
- Drawing lines, rectangles, and circles.
- Drawing bar charts and pie charts.
- Painting regions of the screen.
- The Graphics Macro Language.
- Saving and recalling graphics images.
- Setting user-defined coordinates in graphics mode.
- Writing programs to produce sound and music.

12.1   Graphics in Text Mode

When you first start BASIC, the screen is in **text mode**, in which the video display can display only characters from the standard IBM character set. (More about that below.) In text mode, the display contains 25 rows of either 40 or 80 characters each. You may change from 80-character to 40-character width using the WIDTH statement. The various character positions divide the screen into small rectangles. Figure 12-1 shows the subdivision of the screen corresponding to an 80-character line width.

The rectangles into which we have divided the screen are arranged in rows and columns. The rows are numbered from 1 to 25, with row 1 at the top of the screen and row 25 at the bottom. The columns are numbered from 1 to 80, with column 1 at the extreme left and column 80 at the extreme right. Each rectangle on the

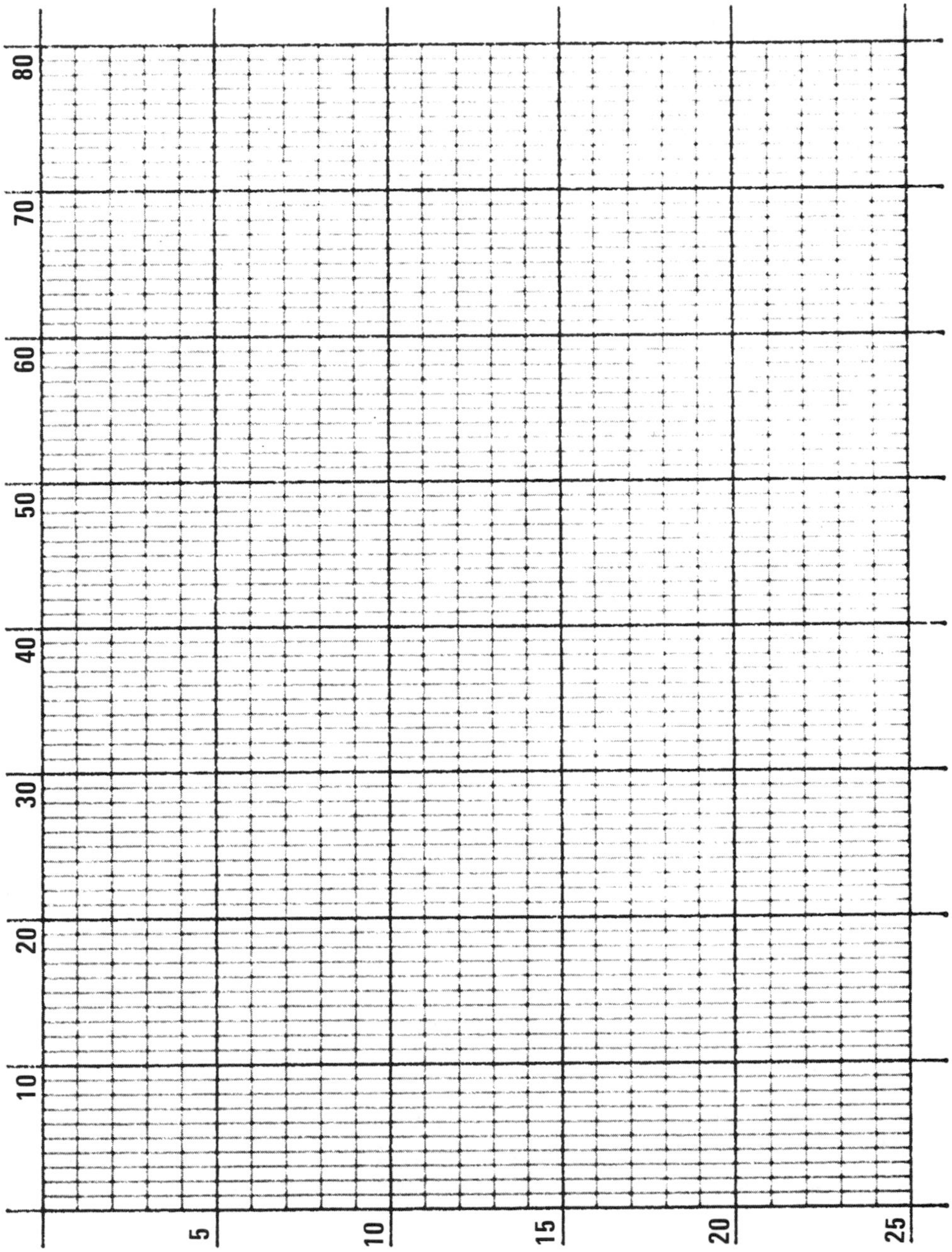

Figure 12-1. **Screen layout for text mode (80-character width).**

screen is identified by a pair of numbers, indicating the row and column. For example, the rectangle in the 12th row and 16th column is shown in Figure 12-2.

We may print characters on the screen using the PRINT and PRINT USING instructions. For graphics purposes, it is important to be able to precisely position characters on the screen. This may be done using the **LOCATE** instruction.

Remember that printing always occurs at the current cursor location. To locate the cursor at row *x* and column *y*, we use the instruction

```
100 LOCATE x,y
```

Example 1.   Write a set of BASIC instructions to print the words *IBM Personal Computer* beginning at row 20, column *10*.

Solution.

```
10 LOCATE 20,10
20 PRINT "IBM Personal Computer"
```

Until now, we have printed only characters such as those found on a typewriter keyboard (letters, numbers, and punctuation marks). Actually, the IBM PC has a very extensive set of characters, including a collection of graphics characters, as shown in Figure 12-3. Note that each character (including graphics characters) is identified by an ASCII code. In Chapter 9, we introduced the characters corresponding to ASCII codes 0-127. In Figure 12-3, we list the characters corresponding to ASCII codes 128-255. For example, the character with ASCII code 179 is a vertical line (∣). To place this character at the current cursor position, we use the instruction

```
30 PRINT CHR$(179);
```

Note the semicolon that prevents the PRINT statement from sending an unwanted carriage return and line feed. (In most printing involving graphics, you will want to use the semicolon.)

You may insert a graphics character into a program line by holding down the Alt key and entering the character number on the numeric keypad (the calculator-like set of numbers on the right side of the keyboard). This has the advantage that in a PRINT statement, you can see the character to be printed. For example, the above statement line appears on the screen as

```
30 PRINT (∣) ;
```

where the symbol is entered from the keyboard by holding down Alt and typing *179*. In what follows, we will use the CHR$ notation to make clear the code numbers of the various characters. In your own work, however, use the Alt key to indicate graphics characters.

TEST YOUR UNDERSTANDING 1 (answer on page 270)

Write a set of instructions to print graphics character 179 in row 18, column 22.

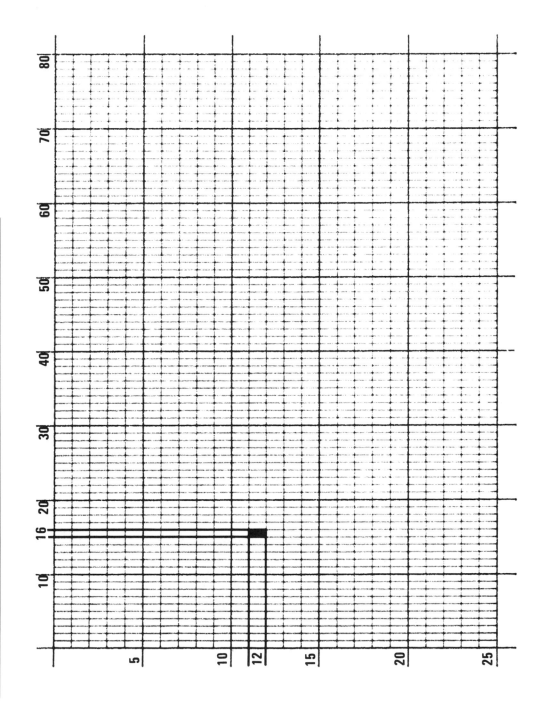

Figure 12-2.

Figure 12-3.   **IBM graphics and special characters.**

ASCII value	Character	ASCII value	Character	ASCII value	Character	ASCII value	Character
128	Ç	166	ª	204	╠	242	≥
129	ü	167	º	205	═	243	≤
130	é	168	¿	206	╬	244	⌠
131	â	169	⌐	207	╧	245	⌡
132	ä	170	¬	208	╨	246	÷
133	à	171	½	209	╤	247	≈
134	å	172	¼	210	╥	248	°
135	ç	173	¡	211	╙	249	•
136	ê	174	«	212	╘	250	·
137	ë	175	»	213	╒	251	√
138	è	176	░	214	╓	252	ⁿ
139	ï	177	▒	215	╫	253	²
140	î	178	▓	216	╪	254	■
141	ì	179	│	217	┘	255	(blank 'FF')
142	Ä	180	┤	218	┌		
143	Å	181	╡	219	█		
144	É	182	╢	220	▄		
145	æ	183	╖	221	▌		
146	Æ	184	╕	222	▐		
147	ô	185	╣	223	▀		
148	ö	186	║	224	α		
149	ò	187	╗	225	β		
150	û	188	╝	226	Γ		
151	ù	189	╜	227	π		
152	ÿ	190	╛	228	Σ		
153	Ö	191	┐	229	σ		
154	Ü	192	└	230	µ		
155	¢	193	┴	231	τ		
156	£	194	┬	232	Φ		
157	¥	195	├	233	Θ		
158	Pts	196	─	234	Ω		
159	ƒ	197	┼	235	δ		
160	á	198	╞	236	∞		
161	í	199	╟	237	Ø		
162	ó	200	╚	238	∈		
163	ú	201	╔	239	∩		
164	ñ	202	╩	240	≡		
165	Ñ	203	╦	241	±		

Courtesy of International Business Machines Corporation.

TEST YOUR UNDERSTANDING 2 (answer on page 270)
Write a program to display all 128 graphics characters on the screen.

We may use the graphics characters to build up various images on the screen, as the next example shows.

Example 2. Write a program that draws a horizontal line across row 10 of the screen. (Assume that you have a 80-column screen.)

Solution. Just in case the screen contains some unrelated characters, begin by clearing the screen using the CLS instruction. Then print character *196* (a horizontal line) across row 10 of the screen. Here is the program.

```
10 ' **********************************
20 ' This program prints a horizontal
30 ' line across row 10 of the screen.
40 ' **********************************
50 CLS
60 LOCATE 10,1
70 FOR J=1 TO 80
80    PRINT CHR$(196);
90 NEXT J
100 END
```

Note that the semicolon in the PRINT statement causes the characters to be printed in consecutive positions. Lines 30-60 may be abbreviated using the STRING$ function. The function value *STRING$(80,196)* equals a string consisting of 80 copies of character 196. So lines 30-60 can be written more simply as

```
30 PRINT STRING$(80,196);
```

Example 3. Write a program that draws a vertical line in column 25 from row 5 to row 15. The program should blink the line 50 times.

Figure 12-4.

Solution. The blinking effect may be achieved by repeatedly clearing the screen. Here is our program.

```
10 ' **************************************
20 ' This program draws a vertical line
30 ' in column 25 from row 5 to row 15,
40 ' blinking 50 times before stopping.
50 ' **************************************
100 CLS
110 FOR K=1 TO 50:'K CONTROLS BLINKING
120    FOR J=5 TO 15
130          LOCATE J,25
140          PRINT CHR$(179);
150    NEXT J
160    CLS
170 NEXT K
180 END
```

TEST YOUR UNDERSTANDING 3 (answer on page 270)
Write a program to draw a vertical line from row 2 to row 20 in column 8.

Example 4. Draw a pair of x- and y-axes as shown in Figure 12-4. Label the vertical axis with the word *Profit* and the horizontal axis with the word *Month*. (Assume that you have a 40-column screen.)

Solution. The program must draw two lines and print two words. The only real problem is to determine the positioning. The word *Profit* has six letters. Let's start the vertical line in the position corresponding to the seventh character column. We'll run the vertical line from the top of the screen (row 1) to within two character rows from the bottom. On the next-to-last row, we will place the word *Month*. The layout of the screen is shown in Figure 12-5. Here is our program to generate the display.

```
10 ' **********************************
20 ' This program draws a pair of axes
30 ' labeled "Profit" and "Month".
40 ' **********************************
100    CLS
110 'Print Labels
120    LOCATE 1,1
130    PRINT "Profit"
140    LOCATE 23,75
150    PRINT  "Month"
160 'Print the vertical axis
170    FOR J=1 TO 22
180          LOCATE J,7: PRINT CHR$(179);
190    NEXT J
200 'Print the corner
210    LOCATE 22,7: PRINT CHR$(192);
220 'Print the horizontal axis
```

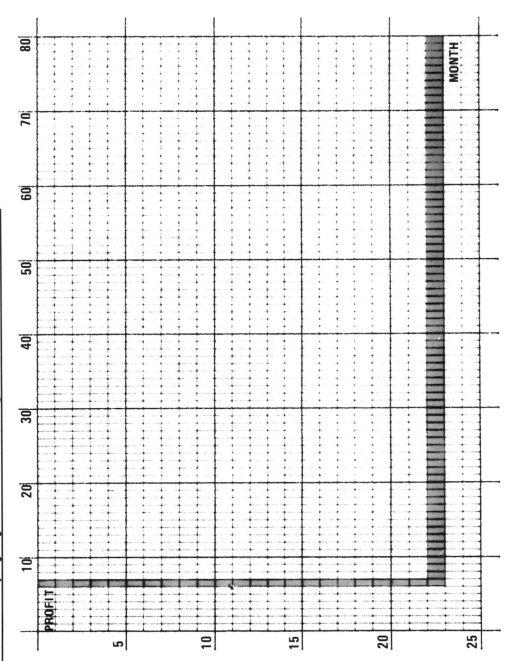

Figure 12-5. Display layout for chart of Figure 12-4.

```
230   FOR J=8  TO 80
240       LOCATE 22,J: PRINT CHR$(196);
250   NEXT J
260 GOTO 260    :'Pause until user hits Ctrl-BREAK
270 END
```

Note the infinite loop in line 100. This loop will keep the display on the screen indefinitely while the computer spins its wheels. To stop the program, press Ctrl-Break. To see the reason for the infinite loop, try running the program after deleting line 100. Note how the *Ok* interferes with the graphics. The infinite loop prevents the BASIC prompt from appearing on the screen.

ANSWERS TO TEST YOUR UNDERSTANDINGS 1, 2, and 3

```
1:   10 LOCATE 18,22
     20 PRINT CHR$(179)

2:   10 FOR J=128 TO 255
     20    PRINT CHR$(J); " "; :'One space between characters
     30 NEXT J
     40 END

3:   10 CLS
     20 FOR J=2 TO 20
     30    LOCATE J,8: PRINT CHR$(179);
     40 NEXT J
     50 END
```

12.2   Colors and Graphics Modes

There are three screen modes in IBM PC BASIC, as listed below:

Screen Mode	Description
0	text
1	medium resolution, 4 colors
2	high resolution, 2 colors

So far, we have discussed only text mode. For the rest of this chapter, let's focus on the two graphics modes.

Medium-Resolution Graphics.   In this mode, the screen is divided into 200 rows of 320 rectangles each. You may display 16 or 4 colors, depending on the mode.

High-Resolution Graphics.   In this mode, the screen is divided into 200 rows of 640 rectangles each. You may display up to four colors simultaneously, or you may disable color and use only ''black and white.''

You may select between the various display modes by using the **SCREEN** command. This command has the form

`SCREEN <mode>`

For example, to choose high-resolution, 2-color mode, give the command

`SCREEN 2`

You may use the SCREEN command to switch from one display mode to another, either within a program or by using a keyboard command. Note, however, that the SCREEN command automatically clears the screen. When BASIC is started, the display is automatically in text mode (SCREEN 0).

Pixels

Each of the small screen rectangles (more properly, dots) is called a **pixel** (= "picture element"). You may color each pixel on an individual basis.

Graphics Coordinates.   Each pixel is specified by a pair of coordinates *(x,y)*, where *x* is the column number and *y* is the row number. Note the following important facts:

1. **Rows and columns are numbered beginning with 0** (not 1 as in text mode). In the medium-resolution graphics mode, the rows are numbered from 0 to 199 and the columns from 0 to 319. In high-resolution graphics mode, the rows are numbered from 0 to 199 and the columns from 0 to 639.

2. Coordinates in graphics mode are specified with the column (*x*-coordinate) first. **This is the opposite of the coordinates in the text mode.** (for example, the LOCATE statement requires the row first.)

Relative Coordinates in Graphics Mode.   In graphics mode, the cursor is not visible. Instead, the computer keeps track of the **last point referenced**. This is the point whose coordinates were most recently used in a graphics statement. You may specify the position of new points by giving coordinates relative to the last point referenced. Such coordinates are called **relative coordinates**. Relative coordinates always are preceded by the word *STEP*. For example, suppose that the last point referenced is (100,75). Then here is a point specified by relative coordinates

`STEP (20,30)`

This is the point that is 20 units to the right and 30 units up from the last referenced point. This is the point with coordinates (120,105).

Similarly, consider the point specified by the relative coordinates:

`STEP (-10,-40)`

Figure 12-6. **Coordinates in graphics mode.**

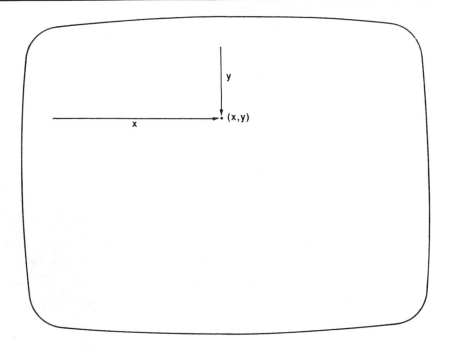

This is the point that is 10 units to the left and 40 units down from the point (120,105); that is, the point (90,35).

TEST YOUR UNDERSTANDING 1 (answers on page 275)

Suppose that the last referenced point is (50,80). Determine the coordinates of the following points.

    a.   **STEP (50,50)**

    b.   **STEP (-20,10)**

    c.   **STEP (10,-40)**

    d.   **STEP (-20,-50)**

Figure 12-7. **Relative graphics coordinates.**

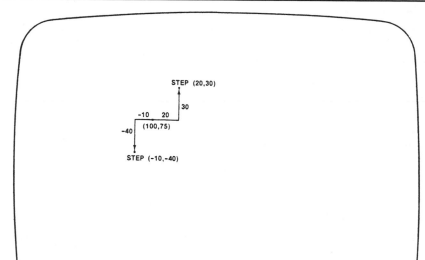

Colors

To use color in your display, you must first enable color with the **SCREEN** statement

SCREEN 1,0 (means low-resolution graphics, color ON)

You may disable color with the statement

SCREEN 1,1 (means low-resolution graphics, color OFF)

Once color has been enabled, you may choose both background and foreground colors. A pixel is considered part of the **background** (at a particular moment) unless its color has been explicitly set by a graphics statement. When you execute CLS, all pixels are set equal to the background color. A non-background pixel is said to belong to the foreground.

Here are the possible screen colors, numbered 0-15.

0 - black	8 - gray
1 - blue	9 - light blue
2 - green	10- light green
3 - cyan	11- light cyan
4 - red	12- light red

5 - magenta   13- light magenta
6 - brown   14- yellow
7 - white   15- high-intensity white

Foreground colors may be selected from one of two palettes:

Palette 0	**Palette 1**
0 - background	0 - background
1 - green	1 - cyan
2 - red	2 - magenta
3 - brown	3 - white

Choosing Colors

Background and foreground colors are set using the **COLOR** statement like this:

```
100 COLOR 12,0
```

This statement sets the background color as light red (color 12) and the palette of the foreground color as 0. These choices remain in effect until they are changed with another COLOR statement.

TEST YOUR UNDERSTANDING 2 (answer on page 275)
Write BASIC statements that select the medium-resolution graphics, set the background color to high-intensity white, and the foreground palette to 1.

Illuminating Pixels.   The **PSET** statement is used to illuminate a pixel. For example, the statement

```
200 PSET (100,150),1
```

will illuminate the pixel at (100,150) in color 1 of the currently chosen palette. Similarly, to turn off this pixel use the statement

```
300 PRESET (100,150)
```

Actually, this last instruction turns on pixel (100,150) in the background color. This is equivalent to turning it off. In using the **PSET** and **PRESET** statements, you may specify the pixel in **relative form**. For example, the statement

```
400 PSET STEP (100,-150), 2
```

turns on the pixel that is 100 blocks to the right and 150 blocks up from the current cursor position, using color 2.

ANSWERS TO TEST YOUR UNDERSTANDINGS 1 and 2

1:   a. (100,130)   b. (30,90)   c. (60,40)   d. (30,30)

2:   10   SCREEN 1 : COLOR 15,1

12.3   Lines, Rectangles, and Circles

Straight Lines

You may use the PSET and PRESET statements to design color graphics displays. However, BASIC has a rich repertoire of instructions that greatly simplify the task. Consider the task of drawing straight lines. This may be accomplished using the **LINE** statement. For example, to draw a line connecting the pixels (20,50) and (80,199), use the statement

```
10 LINE (20,50)-(80,199)
```

Example 1.   Draw a triangle in medium-resolution mode with corners at the three points *(150,20)*, *(50,100)*, and *(250,130)*. (See Figure 12-8.)

Figure 12-8. **A triangle.**

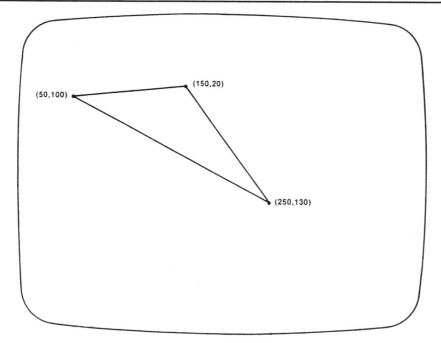

Solution.   We must draw three lines: from (150,20) to (50,100); from (50,100) to (250,130); and from (250,130) to (150,20). Here is the program.

```
10 SCREEN 2
20 LINE (150,20)-(50,100)
30 LINE (50,100)-(250,130)
40 LINE (250,130)-(150,20)
50 END
```

Drawing Lines Using Relative Coordinates

To draw a line from the last referenced point to *(100,90)*, use the statement

```
20 LINE -(100,90)
```

To draw a line from the last referenced point to the point *80* units to the right and *100* units above, use the statement

```
30 LINE -STEP(80,-100)
```

Example 2.   Let's reconsider the triangle of Example 1. The point *(150,80)* is inside the triangle. Draw lines connecting this point to each of the corners of the triangle. (See Figure 12-9).

Figure 12-9.   **More triangles.**

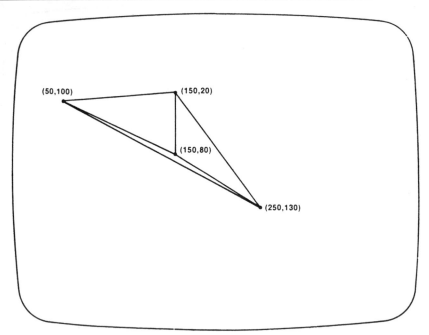

Solution.   The point *(150,80)* needs to go with three line statements. We use the shorthand form to draw lines from this point to the three corners of the triangle. To make *(150,80)* the last referenced point, we first PSET it.

```
10 SCREEN 2
20 LINE (150,20)-(50,100)
30 LINE -(250,130)
40 LINE -(150,20)
50 PSET (150,80)
60 LINE -(150,20)
70 PSET (150,80)
80 LINE -(50,100)
90 PSET (150,80)
100 LINE -(250,130)
110 END
```

Using Colors with LINE

You also may specify the color of a line. For example, if you wish to draw the line in statement 10 in color 1 of the current palette, use the statement

```
40 LINE (20,50)-(80,199),1
```

This line is drawn in Figure 12-10.

Note that there are lines the computer cannot draw perfectly. Lines on a diagonal are displayed as a series of visible "steps." This is as close as the computer can get to a straight line within the limited resolution provided by the graphics modes. The higher the resolution (that is, the more pixels on the screen), the better your straight lines will look.

TEST YOUR UNDERSTANDING 1 (answers on page 286)
a.   Draw a line connecting (0,100) to (50,75) in color 2.
b.   Draw the triangle with vertices (0,0), (50,50), and (100,30).

Rectangles

The LINE statement has several very sophisticated variations. To draw a rectangle you need to specify a pair of opposite corners in a LINE statement and add the code *B* (for Box) at the end of the statement. For example, to draw a rectangle, two of whose corners are at *(50,100)* and *(90,175)*, use the statement

```
50 LINE (50,100)-(90,175),1,B
```

This statement draws the desired rectangle with the sides in color 1 of the current palette (see Figure 12-11A.) The inside of the rectangle will be in the background color. You may paint the inside of the rectangle in the same color as

Figure 12-10.

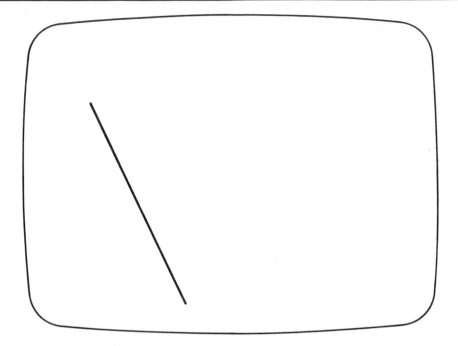

the sides by changing the *B* to *BF* (*B=Box, BF=Box Filled*). (See Figure 12-11B.) These instructions greatly simplify drawing complex line displays.

TEST YOUR UNDERSTANDING 2 (answers on page 286)

a. Draw a rectangle with corners at (10,10), (10,100), (50,100), (50,10).

b. Draw the rectangle of a. and color it and its interior with color 2.

Mixing Text and Graphics

You may include text with your graphics. Use either PRINT or PRINT USING exactly as if you were in text mode. You may use LOCATE to position the cursor at a particular (text) line and column. Note the following, however:

1. In medium-resolution graphics mode, you may use only a 40-character line width. This corresponds to the "large" characters. In high-resolution graphics, you may use only an 80-character line width. This corresponds to "small" characters.

2. Text will print in color 3 of the current palette.

In planning text displays to go with your graphics, note that all letters (regardless of line width) are 8 pixels wide and 8 pixels high. For example, the character at the top left corner of the screen occupies pixels *(x,y)*, where *x* and *y* both range between 0 and 7.

Example 3. Write a command to erase text line 1 of the screen in medium-resolution mode.

Solution. Our scheme for erasing a line is to draw a rectangle over the line, with color equal to the background color (color 0). The first text line of the screen occupies pixel *(x,y)*, where *x* ranges from 0 to 319 (*x* equals the column number) and *y* ranges from 0 to 7 (*y* equals the row number). Here is the desired statement:

```
LINE (0,0)-(319,7),0,BF
```

Circles

BASICA has the facility for drawing circles and circular arcs. To draw a circle, you must specify the center and the radius, and, optionally, the color. For example, here is the command to draw a circle at center *(100,100)* and radius *50*:

```
CIRCLE (100,100),50
```

Since no color has been specified, the circle will be drawn in color 3 (see Figure 12-12).

To draw the same circle in color *1*, we use the statement

```
CIRCLE (100,100),50,1
```

Note that the circles on the screen are not smooth, but have a "ragged" appearance. This is due to the limited resolution of the screen. If you use high-resolution mode, you will notice that the appearance of your circles improves greatly.

Circular arcs are somewhat more complicated to draw since their description is based on the radian system of angle measurement. Let's take a few moments to describe radian measurement.

Recall the number *pi* from high school geometry. *Pi* is a number, denoted by the Greek letter π, that is approximately equal to 3.1415926. . . (the decimal expansion goes on forever). Ordinarily, angles are measured in degrees, with 360 degrees equaling one complete revolution. In radian measurement, there are *2*pi* radians in a revolution. That is:

2*pi radians=360 degrees

1 radian=360/(2*pi) degrees

Figure 12-11A. **The B option.**

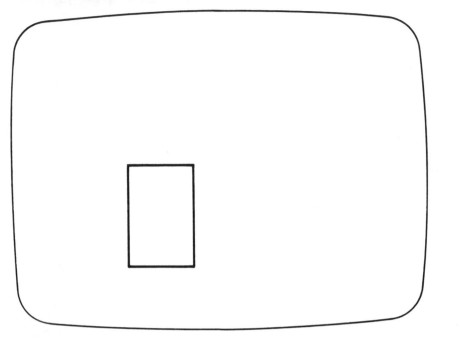

Figure 12-11B. **The BF option.**

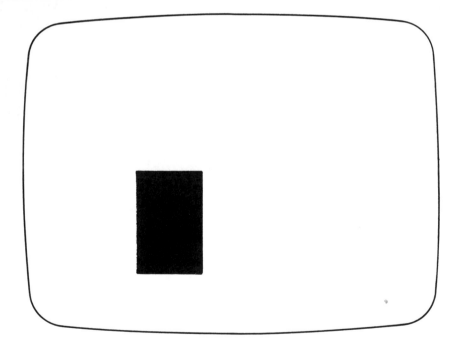

Figure 12-12.

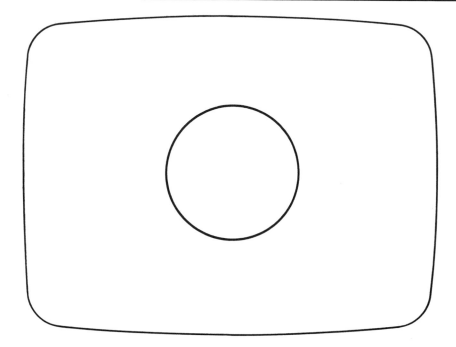

If you use the value of *pi* and carry out the arithmetic, you find that 1 radian is approximately 57 degrees. When describing angles to the computer, you must always use radians.

To draw a circular arc, you use the following variation of the **CIRCLE** statement:

```
CIRCLE (xcenter,ycenter),radius,color,
       startangle, endangle
```

where *startangle* and *endangle* are measured in radians. For example, to draw a circular arc for the above circle, corresponding to an angle of *1.5* radians, beginning at angle *.1* radians, use the command

```
CIRCLE (100,100),50,1,.1,1.5
```

The resulting arc is pictured in Figure 12-13.

Note that Figure 12-13 does not include the sides of the sector. To include a side on a circular arc, put a minus sign on the corresponding angle. (We can't use -0, however. See below.) For example, to include both side in Figure 12-13, use the statement

```
CIRCLE (100,100),50,1,-.1,-1.5
```

The resulting arc will look like the one in Figure 12-14.

Figure 12-13.

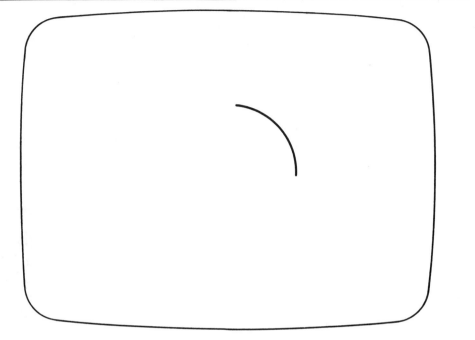

Figure 12-14.

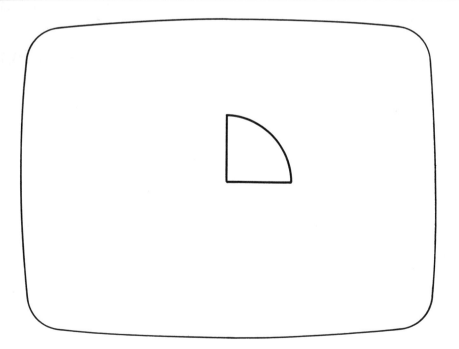

TEST YOUR UNDERSTANDING 3 (answers on page 286)

a. Draw a circular arc with radius 60, center (125,75), and going from a starting angle of .25 radians to an ending angle of .75 radians.

b. Draw the same circular arc as in a., but with sides included.

If you have an angle 0 and wish to include a side, just note that the angle 0 and the angle $2*pi$ are the same. Just replace 0 by $2*pi = 6.28. . .$, and put a minus sign on this new angle!

Aspect Ratio.   The CIRCLE statement has an added complication we haven't yet mentioned, namely the aspect ratio. Usually, when you plot circles on graph paper, you use the same scale on the x-axis as on the y-axis. If, for example, a unit on the x-axis is larger than a unit on the y-axis, your circle appears as an ellipse, stretched out in the x-direction.

Similarly, if the unit on the y-axis is larger than the unit on the x-axis, the circle appears as an ellipse stretched out in the y-direction. So, like it or not, the geometry of circles is intimately bound up with that of ellipses. For this reason, the CIRCLE statement may also be used to draw ellipses.

Consider the following example in high-resolution graphics mode:

```
CIRCLE (300,100),100,,,,.5
```

This statement plots an ellipse with center (300,100). The extra commas are placeholders for the unspecified color, beginning angle, and ending angle. The x-radius is 100. The number .5 is called the **aspect ratio**. It tells us that the y-radius is .5 times the x-radius, or 50.

Similarly, consider the statement

```
CIRCLE (300,100),100,,,,1.5
```

Here the aspect ratio is 1.5, which is larger than 1. In this case, BASIC assumes that the radius 100 is the y-radius. The x-radius is 1.5 times the y-radius, or 45. The corresponding ellipse is shown in Figure 12-16.

What is the aspect ratio for a circle? Well, that's a tricky question. On first glimpse, you probably guessed that the aspect ratio is 1. And indeed it is if you are looking for a mathematical circle. However, if you draw a circle with an aspect ratio of 1, you will get an ellipse. The reason is that the scales on the x- and y-axes are different. Let's consider high-resolution graphics mode. The screen is 640 × 200 pixels. The ratio of width to height is 200/640, or 5/16. To achieve a circle, you would expect to have to multiply the x-radius by 5/16 to get the proper y-radius; that is, an aspect ratio of 5/16. Well, not quite! TV screens are not square. The ratio of width to height is 4/3. In order to achieve an ellipse that is visually a circle, we must multiply by 5/16 *and* by 4/3. In other words, the aspect ratio is

$$(5/16) * (4/3) = 5/12$$

Figure 12-15.   **The ellipse CIRCLE (300,100),100,,,,,.5.**

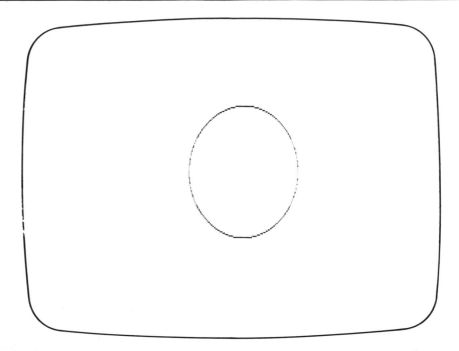

Strange, but true. In medium-resolution mode, the aspect ratio giving a visual circle is 5/6. If you use the CIRCLE statement without any aspect ratio, BASIC assumes an aspect ratio of 5/6 in medium-resolution mode and 5/12 in high-resolution mode. With these aspect ratios, circles look like circles. However, the y-radius is quite different from the x-radius!

You can get even finer grained control over circles and ellipses if you apply some mathematics. Suppose that an ellipse (or circle) has its center at the point with coordinates $(x0,y0)$. Suppose that the horizontal half-axis has length A and the vertical half-axis has length B. Then a typical point (x,y) on the ellipse takes the form

$$x = x0 + A*cos(t)$$

$$y = y0 + B*sin(t)$$

where t is an angle between 0 and $2*pi$ radians. The geometric meaning of the angle t is shown in Figure 12-17. The above equations are called the **parametric equations for the ellipse**. They are very useful in drawing graphics.

For example, here is a program that draws an ellipse with center (320,100) (the center of the screen in high-resolution mode) by plotting dots in a ''sweep'' fashion (see Figure 12-18). This graph may be used to simulate the motion of a planet around the sun.

Figure 12-16. **The ellipse** *CIRCLE (300,100),100,,,,,1.5.*

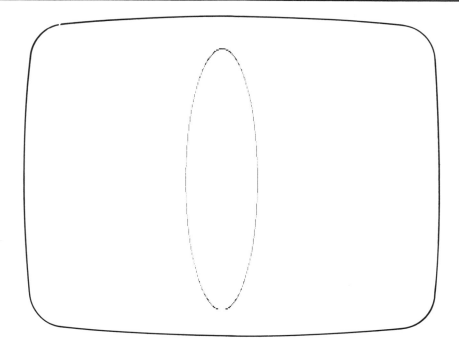

Figure 12-17. **An ellipse in parametric form.**

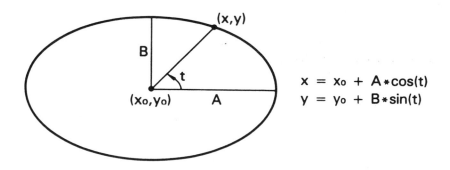

$$x = x_0 + A*\cos(t)$$
$$y = y_0 + B*\sin(t)$$

```
1  '*******************************************
2  ' This program depicts the orbit of a
3  ' planet as it travels about the sun
4  ' in an elliptical path.
5  '*******************************************
10 SCREEN 2:CLS:KEY OFF
20 FOR T=0 TO 6.28 STEP .05
30   X=320+200*COS(T):Y=100+30*SIN(T)
```

```
40    PSET (X,Y)
50    FOR K=1 TO 25:NEXT K
60 NEXT T
70 END
```

Note that line 50 provides a delay between plotting of consecutive dots.

ANSWERS TO TEST YOUR UNDERSTANDINGS 1, 2, and 3

1: a. `10 LINE (0,100)-(50,75),2`
    b. `10 LINE (0,0)-(50,50)`
       `20 LINE (50,50)-(100,30)`
       `30 LINE (100,30)-(0,0)`

2: a. `10 LINE (10,10)-(50,100),,B`
    b. `10 LINE (10,10)-(50,100),2,BF`

3: a. `10 CIRCLE (125,75),60,,.25,.75`
    b. `10 CIRCLE (125,75),60,,-.25,-.75`

Figure 12-18. **Simulating a planetary orbit.**

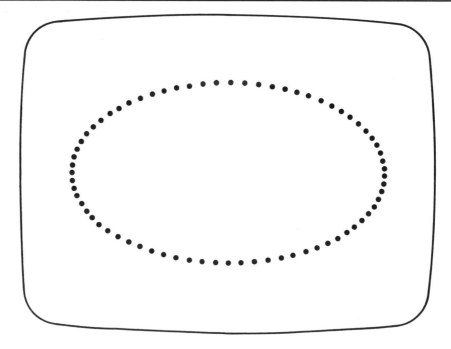

12.4   Computer Art

The graphics statements of IBM PC BASIC may be used to draw interesting computer art on the screen. As a taste of what can be done, the program below draws random polygons on the screen. The program is written in high-resolution graphics mode, so that the screen has dimensions 640 x 200. The program first chooses the number $N\%$ of sides of the polygon. The polygon may have up to six sides. Next, the program picks out $N\% + 1$ random points (it takes $N\% + 1$ points to draw a polygon of N sides). The points are stored in the arrays $X\%(J\%)$ and $Y\%(J\%)$, where $J\% = 0, 1, 2, \ldots, N\%$. To generate only closed polygons, we define the point $(X\%(N\% + 1), Y\%(N\% + 1))$ to be the initial point $(X\%(0), Y\%(0))$. The program then draws lines between consecutive points. Figure 12-19, shows a typical polygon.

The program then erases the polygon and repeats the entire procedure to draw a different polygon. The program draws 50 polygons.

```
10  '**********************************************
11  ' This program draws a number of randomly
12  ' shaped polygons. After each polygon is
13  ' drawn, it is erased, giving a flickering
14  ' effect.
15  ' **********************************************
20  SCREEN 2:CLS:KEY OFF
30  RANDOMIZE VAL(RIGHT$(TIME$,2))
40  FOR M%=1 TO 50
50    C%=1:GOSUB 90:            'Draw random polygon
60    C%=0:GOSUB 190:           'Erase polygon
70  NEXT M%
80  END
90  'Draw random polygon
100 'Determine number of sides
110 N%=INT(5*RND(1) + 1):       'N=# sides <= 6
120 'Compute coordinates of vertices
130 FOR J%=0 TO N%
140   X%(J%)=INT(640*RND(1))
150   Y%(J%)=INT(200*RND(1))
160 NEXT J%
170 X%(N%+1)=X%(0):Y%(N%+1)=Y%(0)
180 'Draw sides
190 FOR J%=1 TO N%+1
200   LINE (X%(J%-1),Y%(J%-1))-(X%(J%),Y%(J%)),C%
210 NEXT J%
220 RETURN
```

Here is a second program that draws a regular polygon (one with equal sides and angles) and then draws inscribed replicas of the original polygon, each of smaller size, until the interior of the original polygon is filled with the inscribed replicas. (See Figure 12-20.)

Figure 12-19. **A typical polygon.**

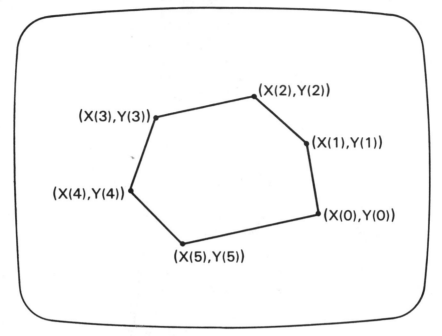

Figure 12-20. **Inscribed polygons.**

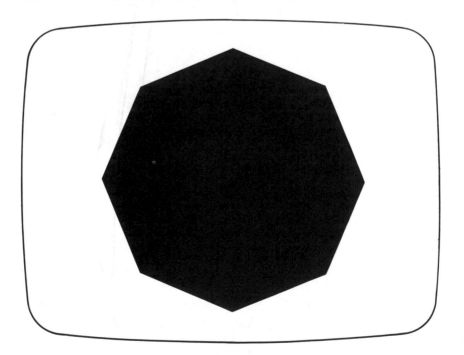

Here are the mathematics necessary to draw a regular polygon. Suppose that you wish to draw a regular polygon having N sides and inscribed in a circle of radius R and centered at the point *(X0,Y0)*. (See Figure 12-21.) The vertices are then the points *(X(J),Y(J))* *(J=0,1,2,. . .,N)*, where

$$X(J) = X0 + R*COS(2*PI*J/N)$$
$$Y(J) = Y0 + R*(5/12)*SIN(2*PI*J/N)$$

Figure 12-21. **An inscribed polygon.**

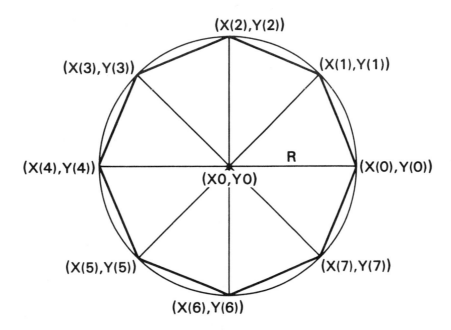

The factor 5/12 corrects for the aspect ratio, so that the circle in which the polygons is inscribed will appear visually as a circle. For our program, the user chooses the value of *N* (up to 20). The center of the polygon is the center of the screen (320,100) in high-resolution. Use an initial value of 100 for the radius *R*. Then draw polygons corresponding to the same value of *N*, but with successively smaller values of *R*. Shrinking the radius circle in which the polygon is inscribed gives the illusion that the polygon is growing inward. Here is the program.

```
10 '*******************************************
20 ' This program draws a sequence of
30 ' inscribed polygons which grow in-
40 ' ward.
50 '*******************************************
100 DIM X%(21),Y%(21)
110 INPUT "NUMBER OF SIDES";N%
```

```
120 IF N%>20 THEN 110
130 SCREEN 2:CLS:KEY OFF
140 PI=3.14159
150 FOR R%=100 TO 0 STEP -4
160   GOSUB 190
170 NEXT R%
180 END
185 'Calculate vertices
190   FOR J%=0 TO N%
200    X%(J%)=320+R%*COS(2*PI*J%/N%)
210    Y%(J%)=100+R%*(5/12)*SIN(2*PI*J%/N%)
220   NEXT J%
230   X%(N%+1)=X%(0):Y%(N%+1)=Y%(0)
235 'Draw polygon
240   FOR J%=0 TO N%
250     LINE (X%(J%),Y%(J%))-(X%(J%+1),Y%(J%+1))
260   NEXT J%
270 RETURN
```

12.5   Drawing Bar Charts

In this section, we'll apply what we have just learned about drawing lines and rectangles to draw the bar chart shown in Figure 12-22.

Figure 12-22.   **A bar chart.**

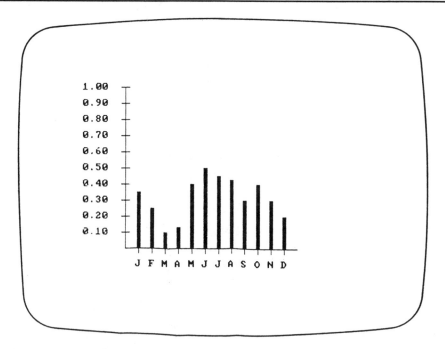

In setting up any graphics display, some planning is necessary to make the display look "pretty." The main goal in this section is to illustrate the planning procedure.

This display is not too complicated, so let's stick to medium-resolution graphics.

Note that there are 10 bars to be displayed. Also, we must put a tick mark under each bar and a letter lined up centered on the tick mark. Each letter is eight pixels wide. So we can approximate the centering of the letters on the tick marks by placing the tick marks in one of the columns 4, 12, 20, 28, ... (The corresponding letters occupy columns 0-7, 8-15, 16-23, 24-31, ...)

Similarly, to center the labels on the vertical axis on the tick marks there, choose the rows for the tick marks from among 4, 12, 20, ...

Let's place the vertical axis beginning in row four. This allows us to place the top tick mark in the proper row. There are at most 195 screen rows in which to place the rest of the vertical axis. We must divide the vertical axis into 10 equal parts. This suggests that each vertical part is 16 rows high. This causes the vertical axis to be 160 rows high and ends in row 164. We need to leave room for four characters (= 32 columns) to the right of the vertical axis as well as the tick marks. And let's not push the labels too far to the left. Finally, the vertical axis must be in one of the columns 4, 12, 20, 28, ... One possibility is to put the vertical axis in column 52. It turns out that this gives a reasonable looking display.

The horizontal axis begins at the point (52,164). The horizontal axis is divided into 13 equal parts. Let's make each part two characters (= 32 columns) wide. This means that the right endpoint of the horizontal axis is (52 + 13*16,164).

Here is the section of the program to draw the two axes:

```
100 'Draw axes
110 LINE (52,164)-(52+16*13,164)
120 LINE (52,164)-(52,4)
```

Next, let's draw the tick marks and print the labels. For the vertical axis, we use a PRINT USING statement to format the labels to contain one digit to the right of the decimal point. For the horizontal axis, we read the labels into a string array A$(). That is, A$(1) = "J", A$(2) = "F",. . . . To print the labels on the horizontal axis, we then print the various string array entries. Here is the program segment that draws the tick marks and labels the axes:

```
200 'Draw tick marks
210 FOR J=1 TO 10
220   LINE (47,164-16*J)-(57,164-16*J)
221   LOCATE 21-2*J,1
222   PRINT USING "#.##";J/10;
230 NEXT J
240 FOR J=1 TO 12
250   LINE (52+16*J,164)-(52+16*J,169)
260   LOCATE 23,(52+16*J)/8
270   PRINT A$(J);
```

```
280 NEXT J
```

Note the positioning of the labels. The labels on the vertical axis are in rows 1, 3, 5, 7, . . ., 19. However, the first label in is row 19, the tenth in row one. To achieve the correct positioning, we locate the cursor in row *21-2*J*. When *J* is 1, the label is put in row 21-2*1 = 19, and when *J* is 10, the label is put in row 21-2*10 = 1. (The labels start from row 21 and back up two rows at a time.)

Similarly, the position of the *J*th horizontal label is gotten by dividing the column position, namely *52 + 16*J* by 8 (since a character occupies eight columns). Note that this division always leaves a remainder of four. The LOCATE statement drops any fractional part, so the character is positioned at the character position, which starts just to the right of the tick mark. This is how the positioning was set up.

Now we have drawn everything but the bars. We store the height of the *J*th bar in the variable *BAR(J)*. The scale on the vertical axis is from 0 to 1 and the axis is 160 rows high. The height of the *J*th bar is *BAR(J)*160*. The *J*th bar runs from row 164 to row 164-BAR(J)*160. Let's make the bar extend for five columns, two on either side of the tick mark. This means that the *J*th bar starts in column

```
52+16*J - 2 = 50+16*J
```

Similarly, the *J*th bar ends in column

```
52+16*J + 2 = 54+16*J
```

Here are the instructions to draw the bars:

```
300 'Draw bars
310 FOR J=1 TO 12
320   LINE (50+16*J,164)-(54+16*J,164-BAR(J)*160),,BF
330 NEXT J
```

Finally, we assemble the various pieces into a single program.

```
1 '*******************************
2 ' This program draws a bar chart
3 ' corresponding to fixed data.
4 '*******************************
10 DIM A$(12),BAR(12)
20 CLS:SCREEN 1
30 KEY OFF
40 FOR J=1 TO 12
50   READ A$(J)
60 NEXT J
70 FOR J=1 TO 12
80   READ BAR(J)
90 NEXT J
100 'Draw axes
110 LINE (52,164)-(52+16*13,164)
120 LINE (52,164)-(52,4)
200 'Draw tick marks
210 FOR J=1 TO 10
220   LINE (47,164-16*J)-(57,164-16*J)
```

```
221   LOCATE 21-2*J,1
222   PRINT USING "#.##";J/10;
230 NEXT J
240 FOR J=1 TO 12
250   LINE (52+16*J,164)-(52+16*J,169)
260   LOCATE 23,(52+16*J)/8
270   PRINT A$(J);
280 NEXT J
300 'Draw bars
310 FOR J=1 TO 12
320   LINE (50+16*J,164)-(54+16*J,164-BAR(J)*160),,BF
330 NEXT J
1000 DATA J,F,M,A,M,J,J,A,S,O,N,D
1010 DATA .35,.25,.10,.13,.40,.50,.45,.425,
          .30,.40,.30,.20
2000 GOTO 2000
```

12.6   Drawing Pie Charts

As an application of the CIRCLE command, let's draw the pie chart shown in
Figure 12-23.

To draw this pie chart, let's begin by creating an array to contain the various
data and to list the data as shown on the left. We put the category names (Food,
Clothing, and so forth) in an array $B\$(\ )$. The numerical quantities are put in an
array $A(\ )$. The first part of our program then consists of reading the data from
DATA statements and setting up the two arrays. Also, we perform screen intial-
ization by choosing SCREEN 2 (high-resolution graphics mode), and turning the
function key display off. Here is the section of the program that accomplishes all
these tasks.

```
100 'Program initialization
110   DIM A(7), B$(7),ANGLE(7)
120   DATA food, .20, rent, .18, clothing,
          .10, taxes, .20
130   DATA entertainment, .10, car, .15,
          savings, .07
140   FOR J=1 TO 7
150       READ B$(J), A(J)
160   NEXT J
170   SCREEN 2: 'high resolution
180   KEY OFF:  'turn off function keys
```

Our next step is to create the left portion of the display. This requires some
care and planning. Let's skip the top four lines and begin the display in the fifth
line. We set up the numbers in our DATA statements as decimals rather than
percentages since the computation of angles that follows is more conveniently
carried out in terms of decimals. However, to display percentages, we multiply
each number $A(J)$ by 100. To get a formatted display, we use the PRINT USING
statement. Let's put the category description in print zone 1 and the percentage in

Figure 12-23.

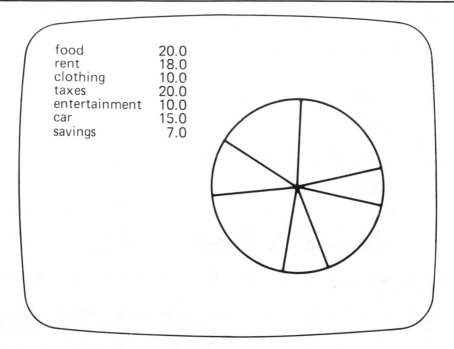

food	20.0
rent	18.0
clothing	10.0
taxes	20.0
entertainment	10.0
car	15.0
savings	7.0

print zone 2. Here are the instructions corresponding to this section of the program. Pay particular attention to the PRINT statements in lines 240 and 250.

```
200 'Display listed data
210   CLS
220   PRINT:PRINT:PRINT:PRINT
230   FOR J=1 TO 7
240        PRINT B$(J),;: 'print and move to
                              2nd print field
250        PRINT USING "##"; 100*A(J);"%"
260   NEXT J
```

Finally, we come to the section of the program in which we draw the pie. The *J*th data item corresponds to the proportion *A(J)* of the total pie. In angular measure, this corresponds to *A(J)*(2*PI)* (recall that *2*PI* radians corresponds to the entire pie). The first slice of the pie begins at angle *ANGLE(0)*, which we set at 0; it ends at *ANGLE(1)=A(1)*(2*PI)*. The second slice begins where the first slice ends; namely, at *ANGLE(1)*. It ends at *ANGLE(1)+A(2)*(2*PI)*. And so forth. Here is the section of the program that draws the various pie slices.

```
300 'Draw Pie
310   ANGLE(0)=0
320   PI=3.14159
330   FOR J=1 TO 7
```

```
340         T=A(J)*(2*PI):     'T=angle for current
                                 data item
350         ANGLE(J)=ANGLE(J-1)+T
360         CIRCLE (450,100),100,,-ANGLE(J),ANGLE(J-1)
370     NEXT J
```

Note that in line 360, we did not specify a color. Nevertheless, we left space for the color parameter by inserting an extra comma. (The space for the color is an imaginary one between the two commas.) If BASIC calls for a parameter in a certain place, you may usually omit the parameter as long as you leave a place for it. If you don't, BASIC can't understand your statement.

You might wonder how we chose the center of the circle at (450,100) and the radius of 100. Well, it was mostly trial and error. We played around with various circle sizes and placements and chose one that looked good! In graphics work, do not be afraid to let your eye be your guide.

For convenience, we now assemble the entire program into one piece.

```
10  ' *****************************************
20  ' This program draws a simple pie graph
30  ' for the data given in the program.
40  ' *****************************************
100 'Program intialization
110   DIM A(7), B$(7),ANGLE(7)
120   DATA food, .20, rent, .18, clothing, .10,
            taxes, .20, entertainment
130   DATA .10, car, .15, savings, .07
140   FOR J=1 TO 7
150     READ B$(J), A(J)
160   NEXT J
170   SCREEN 2:              'high resolution
180   KEY OFF:               'turn off function keys
200 'Display listed data
210   CLS
220   PRINT:PRINT:PRINT:PRINT
230   FOR J=1 TO 7
240     PRINT B$(J),:'print and move to 2nd print field
250     PRINT USING "##.#"; 100*A(J)
260   NEXT J
300 'Draw Pie
310   ANGLE(0)=0
320   PI=3.14159
330   FOR J=1 TO 7
340     T=A(J)*(2*PI):     't=angle for current data item
350     ANGLE(J)=ANGLE(J-1)+T
360     CIRCLE (450,100),100,,-ANGLE(J),-ANGLE(J-1)
370   NEXT J
400 END
```

This program is subject to a number of enhancements, some of which will be suggested in the exercises.

12.7 Painting Regions of the Screen

Using the graphics commands of BASIC, it is possible to draw a tremendous variety of shapes. For example, Figure 12-24 shows a triangle you may draw using several LINE statements. Figure 12-25 shows a circle drawn using the CIRCLE statement. Underneath each shape is a statement to draw the shape. The boundary lines of each shape are specified in the graphics statements used to draw it. The triangle is drawn in color 2. No color is indicated in the case of the circle, so it is drawn in color 3.

The **PAINT** statement allows you to color the "inside" of a region, just as if the region were in a coloring book and you used a crayon to color it. For example, we may use the PAINT command to paint the interiors of the triangle of Figure 12-24 and the circle of Figure 12-25.

The format of the PAINT command is

```
PAINT (x;y),color,boundary
```

Here *(x,y)* is a point of the region to be painted, *color* is the color paint to use, and *boundary* is the color of the boundary. PAINT starts from the point *(x,y)* and begins to paint in all directions. Whenever it encounters the boundary color, it stops PAINTing in that direction.

For example, consider the triangle in Figure 12-24. The point (75, 75) lies inside the triangle. And the triangle itself is drawn in color 2. Suppose that we wish to color the interior of the triangle in color 3. The appropriate PAINT statement is

```
PAINT (75,75),3,2
```

TEST YOUR UNDERSTANDING 1

Write a statement to color the interior of the circle of Figure 12-25 in color 1.

PAINT is a very straightforward statement to understand. The main difficulty, however, is in specifying a point within the region. Or, to put it more precisely, if we are given a region, how do we specify a point within it? Well, that's a mathematical question. I just happen to be a mathematician so I can't resist explaining a little mathematics at this point!

Let's begin by considering the case of the rectangle $(x1,y1)-(x2,y2)$. The center of the rectangle is at the point $((x1+x2)/2, (y1+y2)/2)$; that is, to obtain the coordinates of the center of the rectangle, we average the values of the coordinates of the opposite corners. See Figure 12-27.

Another way of getting the same answer is to average the values of the coordinates of all four corners: $(x1,y1)$, $(x1,y2)$, $(x2,y2)$, $(x2,y1)$. Now there are four

Figure 12-24.   **A triangle.**

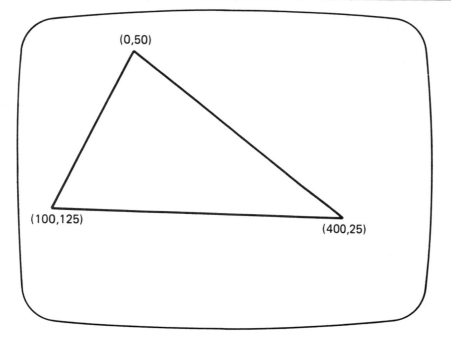

Figure 12-25.   **A circle.**

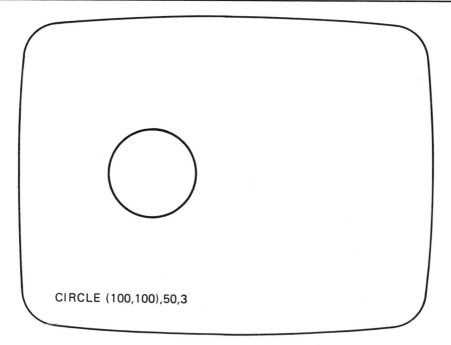

Figure 12-26.   **PAINTing the interior of the triangle.**

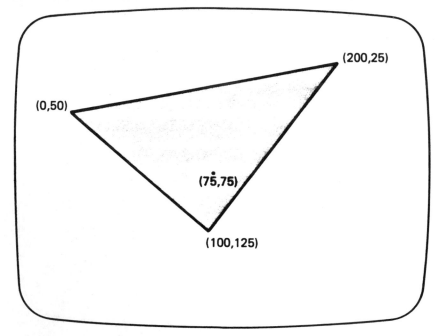

Figure 12-27.   **The center of a rectangle.**

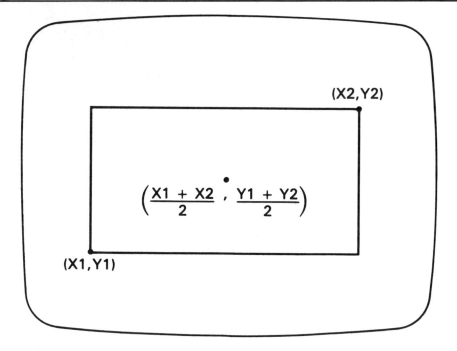

x-coordinates to add up, but we must divide by four. We obtain *(2*x1 + 2*x2)/4 = (x1 + x2)/s* and do the same for the *y*-coordinate.

Let's now consider a triangle with vertices *(x1,y1), (x2,y2), (x3,y3)*. Suppose that you average the coordinates to obtain

(*(x1 + 2 + x3)/3, (y1 + y2 + y3)/3*)

This point is called the *centroid* of the triangle and is always inside the triangle.

Well, what works for 3- and 4-sided figures works in a more general setting. For many figures bounded by straight lines, you may compute a point within the figure simply by averaging the coordinates of the vertices. For which figures does this apply? The simplest such figures are the so-called **convex bodies**. We say that a figure is **convex** if, whenever you connect two points within the figure by a line, all points of the line are inside the figure. (See Figure 12-28.)

Figure 12-28. **Convex and non-convex figures.**

A Convex Figure   A Non-Convex Figure

A convex figure bounded by line segments is a type of polygon. Suppose that the vertices of such a polygon are *(x1,y1), (x2,y2), ... , (xn,yn)*. Then the point

($(x_1 + \ldots + x_n)/n$, $(y_1 + \ldots + y_n)/n$)

obtained by averaging the *x*- and *y*-coordinates is called the **centroid** of the polygon. And the centroid is always inside the polygon.

So if you wish to PAINT a convex polygon, just compute the centroid. This will give you the point to use in the PAINT statement!

12.8 The Graphics Macro Language

Using the various statements of PC BASIC, you may draw some very complex screen images. However, the programs can become rather complex. Many drawings consist only of straight lines, in various positions on the screen. Such drawings may be concisely described and drawn using the Graphics Macro Language, as implemented in the **DRAW** statement.

To understand the DRAW command, it helps to think of an imaginary pen you may use to draw on the screen. The motion of the pen is controlled by a graphics language used by DRAW. The format of the DRAW command is

`DRAW <string>`

Here *<string>* is a sequence of commands from the graphics language.

In giving commands, you will refer to points on the screen. The action of many of the commands will depend on the **last point referenced**. This is the point most recently referred to in a graphics command associated with DRAW. The CLS and RUN statements both set the last point referenced to the center of the screen. (This is (160,100) in medium-resolution graphics and (320,100) in high-resolution graphics.)

The graphics commands associated with DRAW are indicated by single letters. The most fundamental is the *M* command, which has the format

`DRAW "M x,y"`

Figure 12-29. **An angle.**

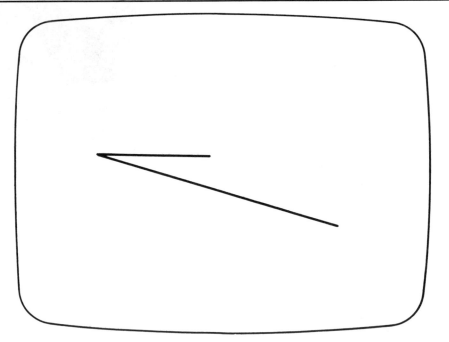

which draws a straight line from the last point referenced to the point with coordinates *(x,y)*. After the statement is executed, the point *(x,y)* becomes the last point referenced.

Here are two variations on the M command:

1. If *M* is preceded by *N*, then the last point referenced is not changed. For example, here is a DRAW command to draw an angle as shown in Figure 12-29 (the vertex of the angle is at (360,100) and the computer is assumed to be in SCREEN 2):

   ```
   DRAW "M 500,100 NM 200,50"
   ```

2. If *M* is preceded by *B*, then the last referenced point is changed, but no drawing takes place. The *BM* command is used to relocate the pen. For example, here is a command to draw the angle of Figure 12-30, with the vertex located at *(300,110)*:

   ```
   DRAW "BM 300,110 M 500,100 NM 200,50"
   ```

TEST YOUR UNDERSTANDING 1 (answer on page 306)
Use the DRAW command to draw the triangle of Figure 12-24.

Using Relative Coordinates.   In our discussion above, all of our coordinates were **absolute**; that is, we specified the actual coordinates. However, you also may use this form of the *M* command:

   M +r,+s

It will draw a line from the last referenced point to the point that is *r* units to the right and *s* units down. (Down is in the direction of increasing *y*-coordinates!) In a similar fashion, we may use the commands

   M -r,+s

   M -r,-s

   M +r,-s

Specifying Coordinates Using Variables.   The coordinates in an M command may be specified by variables *<variable1>* and *<variable2>*, respectively. Here is the form of the command:

   M = <variable1>;, = <variable2>;

Note the semicolons and the comma. You need these. For example, to draw a line from the last referenced point to the point specified by the values of the variables A and B, use the command

   M =A;, =B;

Figure 12-30. **Another angle.**

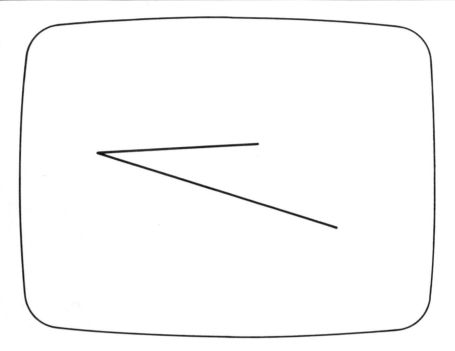

By preceding = signs with a + sign, we may use variables to specify a relative coordinate position. For example, to draw the line to the point that is *A* units to the right and *B* units down, use the command

$$M + = A;, + = B;$$

Note that the signs of *A* and *B* give the actual direction of motion. For example, if *A* is negative, then the motion will be *ABS(A)* units to the left.

Figure 12-31 is an example of the sophisticated pictures you can compose using DRAW. Here is a program to create this display.

```
10 ' This program draws the pattern in Figure 12-31
20 SCREEN 1:CLS:KEY OFF
30 FOR R=0 TO 6.3 STEP .1
40    A=160+70*COS(R):B=100+70*SIN(R)
50    DRAW "NM =A;,=B;"
60 NEXT R
70 END
```

TEST YOUR UNDERSTANDING 2 (answer on page 306)
Use the random number generator to generate 50 pairs of random points. Use DRAW to draw a line associated with each pair.

Figure 12-31. **A complex display.**

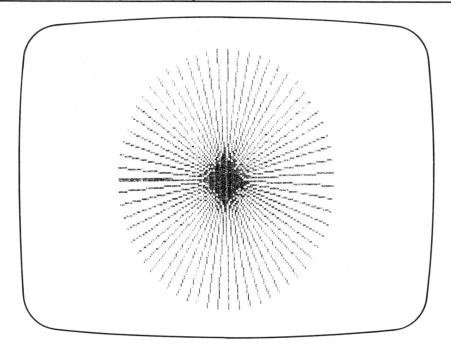

More About Relative Motions.   In most drawing, coordinates are given in relative rather than absolute form. To shorten the lengths of the strings involved in describing such motions, DRAW includes the following commands:

U n   - Move n units up
D n   - Move n units down
L n   - Move n units left
R n   - Move n units right
E n   - Move n units northeast (n units to the right, n units up)
F n   - Move n units southeast (n units to the right, n units down)
G n   - Move n units southwest (n units to the left, n units down)
H n   - Move n units northwest (n units to the left, n units up)

The effect of these commands is shown in Figure 12-32.

You may use the *N* and *B* options with the commands *U-G*. For example, the command

```
DRAW "NU 50"
```

draws a line from the last referenced point upward for 50 units. However, the last referenced point is not updated. Similarly, the command

```
DRAW "BU 50"
```

Figure 12-32. **The relative motion commands *U-G*.**

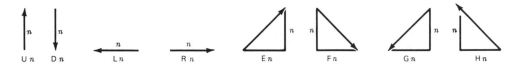

updates the last referenced point to the point 50 units up from the current point. However, no line is drawn.

You also may use variables in connection with the commands *U-G*. For example, consider the command

```
DRAW "U =A;"
```

It draws a line from the last referenced point *A* units upward. (If the value of *A* is negative, then the motion will be downward.)

Color.   You may specify color within DRAW by using the command

```
C n
```

Here *n* is 0, 1, 2 or 3 and refers to a color in the current palette.

Here is a program to draw the sailboat of Figure 12-33.

```
10 ' This program draws a sailboat
20 SCREEN 1,0: CLS: KEY OFF
30 COLOR 7,0
40 DRAW "C1 L60 E60 D80 C2 L60 F20 R40 E20 L20"
50 END
```

The background is white, the sail green, and the boat red.

Angle.   You may rotate a figure through an angle that is a multiple of 90 degrees. Just precede the DRAW string (describing the figure in unrotated form) with the command

```
A n
```

Here

$n=0$: no rotation

$n=1$: 90-degree rotation clockwise

$n=2$: 180-degree rotation clockwise

$n=3$: 270-degree rotation clockwise

For example, here is a program that illustrates the sailboat of Figure 12-33 rotated through the various possible angles. (See Figure 12-34.)

Figure 12-33.   **A sailboat.**

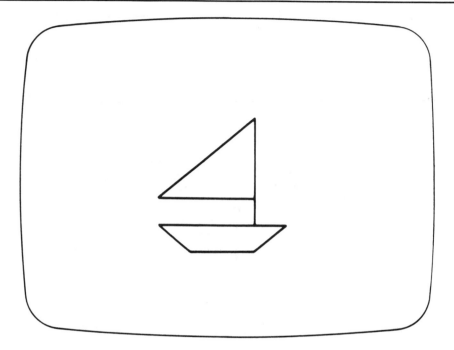

```
10 ' This program draws a rotated sailboat
20 CLS: SCREEN 1: KEY OFF: PSET (160,100)
30 INPUT "ANGLE (0-3)";N
40 DRAW "A=N; BU40 L30 E30 D40 L30 F10 R20 E10 L10"
50 END
```

You may rotate a figure through any angle, clockwise or counterclockwise, using the command *TA n*. Here *n* is an angle between -360 and 360 degrees. Positive angles are counterclockwise and negative angles are clockwise. For example, to turn a figure counterclockwise through a *30* degree angle, use the command

```
TA 30
```

Scale.   You may automatically scale figures (make them larger or smaller) using the command

```
S n
```

All line lengths are multiplied by *n/4*. Here *n* is an integer in the range 1 to 255.

TEST YOUR UNDERSTANDING 3 (answer on page 306)

Write a command to draw the sailboat of Figure 12-33, but at half scale.

Figure 12-34. **Rotated sailboats.**

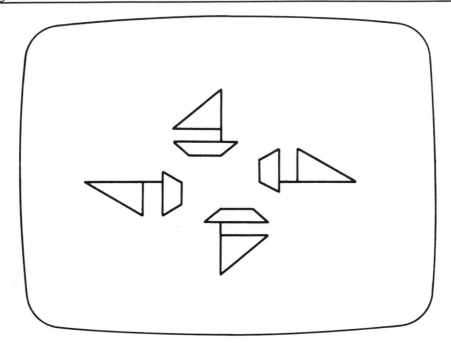

Substrings. You may define a string, *A$*, outside a draw statement and then use it in the form

```
DRAW A$
```

Often, you will wish to use one string several times within a single picture. (This is convenient, for example, if you wish to draw the same figure in several parts of the screen.) You may incorporate a string *A$* within a larger string by preceding it with the letter *X*. For example, here is a statement that draws *A$*, moves up 50 units, and draws *A$* again:

```
DRAW "XA$; BU50; XA$"
```

Note that *X* commands are separated from adjacent commands with semicolons.

ANSWERS TO TEST YOUR UNDERSTANDINGS 1, 2, and 3

```
1:  DRAW "BM 0,50 M 100,125 M 400,25 M 0,50"

2:  10 DIM X(50),Y(50),XX(50),YY(50)
    20 CLS: SCREEN 2: KEY OFF
    30 FOR J=1 TO 50
    40     X(J)=INT(RND*620)): XX(J)=INT(RND*620))
    50     Y(J)=INT(RND*200)): YY(J)=INT(RND*200))
    60     DRAW "BM =X(J); =Y(J); M =XX(J);=YY(J);"
```

```
70 NEXT J
80 END
```
3:   DRAW "S2 C1 L60 E60 D80 C2 L60 F20 R40 E20 L20"

12.9   Saving and Recalling Graphics Images

IBM PC BASIC contains commands that allow you to save and recall the contents of any rectangle on the screen. This is extremely convenient in many graphics applications, particularly animation.

Let's begin this discussion with a description of the image to be saved. The image must consist of a rectangular portion of the screen. The rectangle in question may start and end anywhere, and may contain text characters, portions of text characters, or a graphics image. You specify the rectangle by giving the coordinates of two opposite vertices: either the upper-left and lower-right, or the lower-left and upper-right. Thus a rectangle is specified in the same way as in using the LINE statement to draw a rectangle. Here are some specifications of rectangles:

(0,0)-(100,100)

(3,8)-(30,80)

In specifying rectangles, remember to indicate the coordinates in terms of the current graphics mode (either medium- or high-resolution). In either graphics mode, text characters occupy 8×8 rectangles. For example, the character in the upper-left corner of the screen occupies the rectangle (0,0)-(7,7). (Lines of text are always eight pixels high.)

TEST YOUR UNDERSTANDING 1 (answer on page 310)
Specify the rectangle consisting of the second text line of the screen. (Assume that you are in the medium-resolution graphics mode.)

The GET statement allows you to store the contents of a rectangle in an array. You may use any array as long as it is big enough. Suppose that the rectangle is x pixels long and y pixels high. Then the size of the array must be at least

$4 + (2*x+7)*y/32$

in medium-resolution and

$4 + (x+7)*y/32$

in high-resolution. (Recall that the size of the array is specified in a DIM statement.) For example, suppose that the array is 10 pixels wide and 50 pixels high and is in medium-resolution. The array required to store the rectangle must contain at least

$4 + (2*10+7)*50/32$ or 46

elements. We can use an array $A()$ defined by the statement

```
DIM A(46)
```

Once a sufficiently large array has been dimensioned, you may store in it the contents of the rectangle using the GET statement, which has the form

```
GET (x1,y1)-(x2,y2), arrayname
```

For example, to store the rectangle (0,0)-(9,49) (this rectangle is 10 by 50) in the array $A()$, use the statement

```
GET (0,0)-(9,49), A
```

To summarize, to store the contents of a rectangle in an array, you must:

1. Use a DIM statement to define a rectangle of sufficient size.

2. Execute a GET statement.

You may redisplay the rectangle at any point on the screen by using the **PUT** statement. For example, to redisplay the rectangle stored in A, use the statement

```
PUT (100,125), A
```

This particular statement redisplays the rectangle in A, with the upper-left corner of the rectangle at the point (100,125).

To see GET and PUT in action, examine the following program.

```
1  '*******************************************
2  ' This program prints a letter A in the
3  ' 1,1 position. It copies the letter to
4  ' an array and redisplays it at graphics
5  ' location 100,100.
6  '*******************************************
10 SCREEN 1
20 DIM LETTER(9)
30 LOCATE 1,1
40 PRINT "A"
50 GET (0,0)-(7,7),LETTER
60 CLS
70 PUT (100,100),LETTER
80 END
```

Line 10 puts BASIC in medium-resolution graphics mode. We are out to store an 8 x 8 array, so we use the above formulas to calculate the required array size, which works out to 9. In lines 30-40, we print a letter A, and in line 50, we store the image in the array *LETTER*. We then clear the screen. Line 70 recovers the image from the array and places it with its upper-left corner at the point (100,100).

Don't erase the screen yet. Type

```
PUT (100,100),LETTER <ENTER>
```

Note that the letter *A* at (100,100) disappears. If you type the same line again, the *A* reappears. Use this feature to create the illusion of motion across the screen. Suppose that you wish to create the illusion that the letter *A* is moving across the screen. Merely display it and erase it from consecutive screen positions. The screen creates the displays faster than the eye can view them. What you see is a continuous motion of the letter across the screen. Here is a program to create this animation.

```
1  '*****************************************
2  ' This program demonstrates the principles
3  ' of animation by making the letter A
4  ' appear to move across the screen.
5  '*****************************************
10 SCREEN 1
20 DIM LETTER(9)
30 LOCATE 1,1
40 PRINT "A"
50 GET (0,0)-(7,7),LETTER
60 CLS
70 FOR XPOSITION = 0 TO 311
80   PUT (XPOSITION,0),LETTER
90   PUT (XPOSITION,0),LETTER
100 NEXT XPOSITION
110 END
```

Note that the *XPOSITION* runs from 0 to 311. Although the screen is 319 pixels wide, the variable *XPOSITION* specifies the upper-left corner of the rectangle, which is 8 × 8. Therefore, 311 is the largest possible value of the variable.

Animation is the backbone of all the arcade games that have become so popular in recent years. We will apply the above principles of animation in designing several computer games later in the book.

Saving a Screen Image on Diskette

Storing large graphics images (such as the entire screen) takes a great deal of memory. To store the entire screen takes more than 16,000 bytes. Compare this with the fact that BASIC can use a maximum of 65,536 bytes. Because graphic images tend to use such large amounts of memory, it is often necessary to save the screen image on diskette. Here is a program for saving the current screen image on diskette under the filename SCREEN.

```
10 DEF SEG = &HB800
20 BSAVE "SCREEN",0,&H4000
```

To recall the stored image to the screen, use the program

```
10 DEF SEG = &HB800
20 BLOAD "SCREEN",0
```

ANSWER TO TEST YOUR UNDERSTANDING 1
1:   (0,8)-(319,15)

12.10   VIEW and WINDOW

In this section, we discuss the VIEW and WINDOW statements—two very powerful graphics enhancements provided in BASIC 2.00 and later.

The **WINDOW** statement allows you to define your own coordinate system on the screen. For example, consider the statement

```
WINDOW (-2,0)-(2,100)
```

It causes the screen coordinates to be redefined, as shown in Figure 12-35. Note that the lower-left corner becomes the point (-2,0) and the upper-right corner becomes the point (2,100). The x-coordinates of the screen run from -2 on the left to 2 on the right. The y-coordinates run from 0 at the bottom to 100 on the top. The point in the middle of the screen is (0,50).

After using a WINDOW command, all graphics commands work with the new coordinates. For example, suppose that we execute the above WINDOW statement. The statement

```
PSET (0,50)
```

turns on the pixel at the center of the screen.

TEST YOUR UNDERSTANDING 1 (answers on page 315)
Assume that the screen coordinates are defined by the WINDOW command of Figure 12-35. Describe the location of these points:

   a.   (1,75)   b.   (-1,100)   c.   (2,10)

The WINDOW statement does not disturb the contents of the screen, so you may use several different coordinate systems within a single program. Moreover, the placement of text is still governed by the usual text coordinate system (lines 1-25, columns 1-40 or 80), so you can mix text and graphics determined by a WINDOW command.

The WINDOW statement automatically reorders the values of the extreme x- and y-coordinates so that the lesser x-coordinate is on the left, the greater on the right, the lesser y-coordinate is at the bottom, and the greater is on the top. For example, the following WINDOW statements are all equivalent:

Figure 12-35. **Cartesian coordinates (-2,0)-(2,100).**

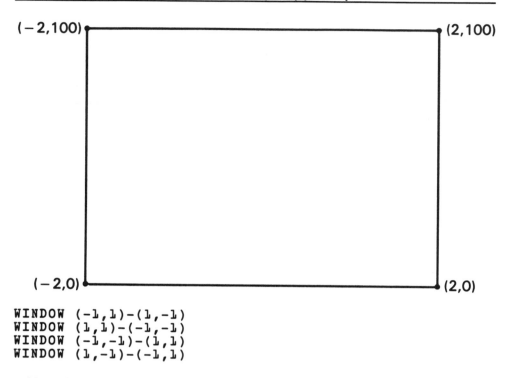

$(-2,100)$ ——————————————— $(2,100)$

$(-2,0)$ ——————————————— $(2,0)$

```
WINDOW (-1,1)-(1,-1)
WINDOW (1,1)-(-1,-1)
WINDOW (-1,-1)-(1,1)
WINDOW (1,-1)-(-1,1)
```

Note that the above statements turn the screen into a portion of a Cartesian coordinate system, of the same type used in graphing points and equations in algebra. Note also that increasing values of the y-coordinate correspond to moving up the screen. This is the exact opposite of the normal graphics coordinates, in which the pixel rows are numbered from 0 (top of screen) to 199 (bottom of screen). A coordinate system in which increasing values of the y-coordinate correspond to moving **down** the screen are called **screen coordinates**. You may use the WINDOW statement to create a set of screen coordinates using the SCREEN option. For example, the statement

```
WINDOW SCREEN (-2,0)-(2,100)
```

creates a coordinate system as shown in Figure 12-36. Note that y-coordinate 0 is now at the top of the screen.

Example 1.   Use the WINDOW command to draw an expanding family of rectangles beginning at the center of the screen.

Solution.   Let's use a single line statement, namely

```
LINE (-.1,-.1)-(.1,.1),,B
```

Figure 12-36.   **Screen coordinates (-2,0)-(2,100).**

to draw a rectangle with center (0,0). But let's use a sequence of WINDOW commands to redefine the coordinate system so that the radius .1 corresponds to successively larger distances on the screen. That is, we will let the Jth coordinate system be generated by the statement

```
WINDOW (-1/J,-1/J)-(1/J,1/J)
```

for $J=1, 2, \ldots ,10$. For the first coordinate system, the screen corresponds to (-1,-1)-(1,1). So the distance .1 seems small. (It corresponds to only .05 of the way across the screen). On the other hand, for $J=10$, the coordinate system corresponds to (-.1,-.1)-(.1,.1), so .1 is halfway across the screen. Here is our program.

```
1 '****************************************
2 ' This program draws a sequence of
3 ' rectangles with one nested inside
4 ' the next.
5 '****************************************
10 SCREEN 2:KEY OFF
20 CLS
30 FOR J=1 TO 10
40    WINDOW (-1/J,-1/J)-(1/J,1/J)
50    LINE (-.1,-.1)-(.1,.1),,B
60 NEXT J
70 END
```

The output of the program is shown in Figure 12-37.

The WINDOW statement ignores points corresponding to positions off the screen. This procedure is known as **clipping**.

RUN, SCREEN, and WINDOW with no parameters disable any previous WINDOW command.

VIEW

The **VIEW** statement allows you to restrict screen activity to a portion of the screen. For example, to restrict all screen activity to the rectangle *(20,10)-(100,200)*, use the statement

```
VIEW SCREEN (20,10)-(100,200)
```

This statement turns the rectangle (20,10)-(100,200) in a **viewport**. While a viewport is in effect, you may not plot any points outside the viewport. For example, if a CIRCLE statement refers to a circle that lies partially outside a viewport, then only the portion within the viewport is drawn.

If you execute CLS while a viewport is in effect, you will erase **only** the inside of the viewport.

Figure 12-37. **Expanding rectangles.**

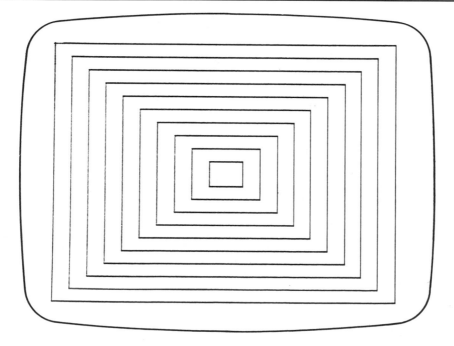

Note that the viewport applies only to graphics commands. Text commands may apply to any position on the screen, even though a viewport is in effect. For example, you may use LOCATE and PRINT as if the viewport were not present.

The full form of the VIEW statement is

```
VIEW [SCREEN] (x1,y1)-(x2,y2),[color],[boundary]
```

The *[color]* option allows you to fill in the viewport with a particular color. The *[boundary]* option allows you to put a rectangular boundary around the viewport. The value of *[boundary]* determines the color of the bounding rectangle.

For example, the statement

```
VIEW SCREEN (10,20)-(200,100),3,2
```

defines a viewport colored in color *3* with a boundary in color *2*, and the statement

```
VIEW SCREEN (10,20)-(200,100),,2
```

defines a viewport with a boundary in color *2*. The interior of the viewport is the background color.

You may omit the SCREEN parameter to obtain plotting relative to the viewport. For example, consider the statement

```
VIEW (10,20)-(200,100)
```

It defines the same viewport as above. However, the point *(x,y)* in a graphics statement is interpreted to mean *(x + 10,y + 20)*. In other words, the upper-left corner of the viewport is considered as the corner of the screen. The same clipping rule as for **VIEW SCREEN** applies: If a point (as computed relative to the viewport) lies outside the viewport, then it is not plotted.

You may disable a viewport using the statement

```
VIEW
```

Similarly, using RUN or SCREEN will cancel a viewport.

You may combine VIEW and WINDOW. For example, consider the statements

```
10 VIEW (80,16)-(559,167),,3
20 WINDOW (0,0)-(20,100)
```

They define a viewport in the rectangle *(80,16)-(558,167)* and then redefine the coordinates **within the viewport** as the Cartesian coordinates *(0,0)-(20,100)*, so *(0,0)* corresponds to the lower-left corner of the viewport and *(20,100)* to the upper-right corner.

On the other hand, consider the statements

```
10 VIEW SCREEN (80,16)-(559,167),,3
20 WINDOW (0,0)-(20,100)
```

Now the WINDOW command refers to the entire screen. *(0,0)* corresponds to the lower-left corner of the screen and *(20,100)* to the upper-right corner of the screen. The viewport serves as a mask to clip off all points that (in the coordinates specified by WINDOW) land outside the viewport.

As we'll see in the next section, viewports are ideal for generating business graphics. We'll use a combination of VIEW and WINDOW to create a custom coordinate system on which to draw a bar graph.

ANSWERS TO TEST YOUR UNDERSTANDING 1

1:

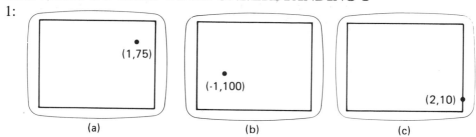

(a)   (b)   (c)

12.11   Sound and Music

The IBM PCs have a small speaker located within the system unit. You may use this speaker to introduce sound and music into your programs. There are three sound commands—**BEEP, SOUND,** and **PLAY**. Let's survey the capabilities of each of these commands.

BEEP

The **BEEP** command is the simplest of the sound commands. It allows you to sound the speaker for 1/4 second. This command gives you no control over the pitch or the duration of the sound.

Here is an example of BEEP in a subroutine that responds to a mistake in input.

```
100 PRINT "YOU MADE A MISTAKE, TRY AGAIN!"
110 BEEP
120 RETURN
```

You also may use a BEEP statement within other statements, as in

```
10 IF X=100 THEN BEEP
```

Professional programs employ sophisticated input routines that subject user input to a number of tests to determine if the input is acceptable. (Is the length correct? Does the input employ any illegal characters?) Here is a simple subroutine of this type. The main program assigns a value to the variable **LENGTH,** which gives the maximum length of an input string. The subroutine illuminates a box, beginning at location (1,1) (top left corner of the screen) to indicate the maximum field size for the input. The routine then allows you to input characters and to display them in the appropriate position in the illuminated field. For each character displayed, part of the illumination disappears. Moreover, using the backspace key restores one character space of illumination. If you attempt to input characters beyond the illuminated field, the routine beeps the speaker.

```
5000 ' **********************************************
5010 ' This subroutine has the user input a string
5020 '   of fixed length into an illuminated box,
5030 '   beeping when the user attempts to input
5040 '   a value that is not legal.
5050 ' **********************************************
5060 'LENGTH is the maximum number of characters
        in input string
5070 'COUNT is the current cursor position in the
        input field
5100 ' Initialize, displaying the box
5110  COUNT=1
5120  CLS
5130  LOCATE 1,1
5140  PRINT ""
5150  LOCATE 1,1
5160  FOR I=1 TO LENGTH
5170        LOCATE 1,I:PRINT CHR$(219);
5180  NEXT I
5190  LOCATE 1,1
5195 ' Scan the keyboard for a character
5200  A$=INKEY$
5210  IF A$="" THEN 5200    :'Wait for key to be struck
5220  IF A$=CHR$(8) THEN GOTO 5300   :'Backspace
5230  IF A$= CHR$(13) THEN 5340      :'Return
5240  IF COUNT=LENGTH+1 THEN 5280    :'Check length
5250  LOCATE 1,COUNT:PRINT A$;       :'Print character
5260  COUNT=COUNT+1
5270  GOTO 5200
5280  BEEP            :'Error
5290  GOTO 5190
5300  COUNT=COUNT-1        :'Remove character from end
5310  IF COUNT=0 THEN BEEP:COUNT=COUNT+1
5320  LOCATE 1,COUNT:PRINT CHR$(219);
5330  GOTO 5190
5340 RETURN
```

SOUND

The second speaker command is called **SOUND**. This handy little command enables you to access any frequency between 37 and 32767 Hertz (cycles per second, also abbreviated Hz). The duration of the sound is measured in clock ticks, and there are 18.2 clock ticks per second. A numeric expression in the range 0 to 65535 (that's slightly over one hour) is used. To produce a sound at 500 Hz and make it last for 40 ticks of the clock, use this statement:

```
SOUND 500, 40
```

Here is an elementary graphics program that has been enhanced by the SOUND command. It draws fixed triangles and random circles and blinks them in a manner suitable for illuminating a rock concert. SOUND provides some audio accompaniment.

```
10  ' ************************************************
20  ' This program creates a sound and light show
30  ' with random sounds and randomly-placed shapes.
40  ' ************************************************
100 KEY OFF
110 'Turns the key line off
120 SCREEN 1
130 'Switches from text mode to graphics mode
140 FOR I=1 TO 100
150    CIRCLE (RND*250, RND*200), 30
160    'Draws a circle with random coordinates
       and a diameter of 30
170    SOUND RND*1000+37,2
180    'Creates a random sound from 37 to 1037 Hz
       with a duration of 2 clock ticks
190    CLS
200    DRAW "E15; F15; L30"
210    'Draws a triangle
220    SOUND RND*1000+37,2
230    CLS
240 NEXT I
250 END
```

Music on the PC

Next on the level of sound sophistication is the PLAY command. It enables you to turn your IBM PC into a piano and play musical compositions as simple or as complex as you like. (There is even an arrangement of Beethoven's *Moonlight Sonata* for the PC!)

A few musical facts will help you a great deal in your programming:

1. Just like a piano, the PC uses seven octaves, numbered 0 to 6. Each octave starts with C and goes to B.

2. Octave 3 starts with middle C.

3. The tempo of a song is the speed at which it is played. On the PC, tempo is measured by the number of quarter notes per second. The tempo may range from 32 to 255.

4. The PC allows you to style your notes as normal, legato, or staccato. Normal means that notes are held down for 7/8 of their defined length.

Legato means that each note will play for the full time period that you set it to play, while staccato means that each note is held for only 3/4 of the time specified. Legato notes sound ''smooth,'' whereas staccato notes are ''crisp.''

PLAY

The **PLAY** command allows you to show your creative musical genius, even if you can't play a comb. It uses a language that allows you to write music in the form of strings. Once the music has been transcribed, the PLAY statement allows you to play it on the speaker.

To use the PLAY command:

1. Code the desired musical notes as a string.

2. Use the PLAY command in the form

    ```
    PLAY <string>
    ```

For example, consider this program. Why not type it in and listen to the results:

```
10 A$="03L4EDCDEE"
20 PLAY "XA$; E2DDD2EGG2; T255XA$; EEDDEDP2C1"
30 END
```

The program probably makes the music look quite mysterious. However, the musical language is quite simple. Here is a summary.

NOTES.   Notes are indicated by the letters A to G with an optional #, +, or -. The # or + after a letter indicates a sharp, while - indicates a flat.

For example, the note ''A sharp'' is written *A#*; ''G flat'' is written *G-*.

LENGTH.   *L* defines the LENGTH of a note. *L1* is a whole note, *L2* is a half note, *L4* is a quarter note, . . . , *L64* is a 64th note. The *L* command defines the length of all subsequent notes until another *L* command is given. For example, to play the string of notes CDEFG in quarter notes, use this string:

```
L4 CDEFG
```

If you wish to define the length of a single note, omit the L and put the number indicating the length after the note. For example, *C4* indicates C is held for a quarter note. Subsequent notes are held for an amount defined by the most recent L command.

As in musical notation, a dot after a note indicates that the note is to be held for one-and-one-half times its usual length.

REST.   *P1* is a whole note rest, *P2* a half note, and so forth.

OCTAVE. Initially, all notes are taken from octave 4 (the octave above the one beginning with middle C). The octave is changed by giving the *O* command. For example, to change to octave 2, the command would be *O2*. After you give an octave command, all notes are taken from the indicated octave unless you change the octave or temporarily overrule the octave (see below). Another method of specifying the octave is by using the symbols > and <. The symbol > means to go up one octave, and the symbol < means to go down one octave.

TEST YOUR UNDERSTANDING 1 (answer on page 320)
Write a string that plays an ascending C major scale in eighth notes, pauses for a half-note, and then plays the same scale descending.

TEST YOUR UNDERSTANDING 2 (answer on page 320)
Write a string that plays the scale of Test Your Understanding 1 in octave 5.

TEMPO. Tempo is the speed at which a composition is played. Tempo is measured in terms of quarter beats per second. Unless you specify otherwise, the tempo is set at 120. You may set the tempo using the *T* command. For example, to set the tempo to 80, use the command *T80*. The tempo remains unchanged until you give another *T* command. The tempo may range from 32 to 255.

TEST YOUR UNDERSTANDING 3 (answer on page 320)
Write a string that plays the scale of Test Your Understanding 1 at a tempo of 80, and at a tempo of 150.

STYLE. You may select the style of notes from among: normal, legato, or staccato. The respective commands are *MN, ML,* and *MS.* The style chosen remains in effect until it is canceled by another style selection.

TEST YOUR UNDERSTANDING 4 (answer on page 320)
Write a string that plays the scale of Test Your Understanding 1 with legato style and then with staccato style.

Ordinarily, the PLAY command causes BASIC to stop while the specified notes are played. However, you also may use the PLAY command in **background mode**. In this mode, while the speaker plays the notes, BASIC continues executing the program, beginning with the statements immediately after the PLAY statement. The background mode may be started with the command *MB*. You may return to normal mode (also called **foreground mode**) with the command *MF*. If you do not explicitly state the mode, BASIC assumes the background mode.

In coding music, you may wish to use the same string a number of times. This occurs, for example, in the case of a refrain. The *X* command allows you to repeat a string without retyping it. Just store the desired string in a string variable, say *A$*. Whenever the string is required, type

`XA$;`

ANSWERS TO TEST YOUR UNDERSTANDINGS 1, 2, 3, and 4

1: `A$="CDEFGAB O5 C P2 C O4 BAGFEDC"`

2: `A$="O5 CDEFGAB O6 C P2 C O5 BAGFEDC"`

3: `A$="T80 CDEFGAB O5 C P2 C O4 BAGFEDC"`
   `A$="T150 CDEFGAB O5 C P2 C O4 BAGFEDC"`

4: `A$="ML CDEFGAB O5 C P2 C O4 BAGFEDC"`
   `A$="MS CDEFGAB O5 C P2 C O4 BAGFEDC"`

13

Some Additional Programming Tools

13.0   Chapter Objectives

IN THIS CHAPTER WE LEARN ABOUT five additional programming tools:

- The **INKEY$** variable will give us additional control over input.
- We will learn to control the function keys and use them to trap events.
- We will learn about the concept of extended ASCII codes, which supply us with the codes corresponding to various additional keys, such as the function keys and cursor motion keys.
- We will learn to respond to errors without stopping the program.
- Finally, we will learn to run several programs in sequence using the **CHAIN** statement.

13.1   The INKEY$ Function

Many programs depend on input from the operator. We have learned to provide such input using the INPUT and LINE INPUT statements. When the program encounters either of these statements, it pauses and waits for input. The program will not proceed unless valid input is provided. The **INKEY$** function provides an alternative method of reading the keyboard.

The Keyboard Buffer

When a key is pressed, BASIC interrupts what it is doing and places the corresponding ASCII code in a reserved section of memory called the **keyboard buffer**. The keyboard buffer has space to record a number of keystrokes. The process of recording information in the keyboard buffer usually proceeds so that you don't even realize that the keyboard buffer is there. For instance, in typing program lines, BASIC is constantly reading the keyboard buffer and displaying the corresponding characters on the screen. In a similar fashion, an INPUT statement reads the keyboard buffer and displays the corresponding characters on the screen. A carriage return (generated by ENTER) tells the INPUT statement to stop reading the buffer.

As characters are read from the buffer, the space they occupy is released. If the buffer is full and you attempt to type a character, you will hear a beep on the speaker. This is to inform you that, until the buffer is read, further typed characters will be lost.

Note that you may type on the keyboard while a program is running. Even though BASIC is busy executing a program, it pauses to place your typed characters in the keyboard buffer, and then return to execution. When the buffer is next read, it will read the characters in the order they were typed. In this way, you may "type ahead" of required program input.

Clearing the Buffer.   In certain applications, you may wish to prevent the user from typing ahead. One way to do this is to empty the buffer prior to requesting input. You may empty the buffer using the statement line

```
DEF SEG = 0:POKE 1050,PEEK(1052):DEF SEG
```

(We will discuss the *DEF SEG, PEEK,* and *POKE* statements later in the book. For now just accept this sequence of statements as something that works to clear the keyboard buffer.)

Actually, there are **two** keyboard buffers in BASIC. When accepting program lines or commands in command mode, BASIC stores partial program lines in the **BASIC line buffer**. This buffer stores lines until they are complete (which you indicate by pressing ENTER). The keyboard buffer, on the other hand, accepts keyboard entries only while BASIC is in the execute mode.

The INKEY$ Variable

The INKEY$ function allows you to read one character from the keyboard buffer. When the program reaches INKEY$, it reads the "oldest" character in the keyboard buffer and returns it as a string. This procedure counts as reading the character, so that the character is removed from the buffer. If there is no character in the keyboard buffer, INKEY$ equals the empty string.

INKEY$ has many uses. For example, suppose that you wish your program to pause until some key is pressed. Here is a statement that accomplishes this task:

```
100 IF INKEY$ = "" THEN 100
```

The program continually tests the keyboard buffer. If there is no character to be read, the test is repeated, and so on until some key has been pressed.

Caution: We have explained the operation of INKEY$ in terms of the keyboard buffer so that you can understand the following trap. If the keyboard buffer is not empty, a reference to INKEY$ removes a character. If you use INKEY$ a second time, you will be referring to the keyboard buffer anew and the value of the first INKEY$ will be lost. Moral: If you wish to use the value of INKEY$ again, store the value in a string variable, as in the statement

```
10 A$ = INKEY$
```

13.2 The Function Keys and Event Trapping

The function keys are the 10 keys labeled F1 through F10 on the left side of the PC keyboard.

The Function Keys as User-Defined Keys

Each function key may be assigned a string constant containing as many as 15 characters. When a function key is depressed, the corresponding string is input to BASIC. In this way, you may reduce typing standard inputs to single keystrokes. This tends to eliminate errors in typing. For example, suppose that an input statement asked for a response of *HIGH, LOW,* or *AVERAGE.* You can define function keys F1, F2, and F3 to be, respectively, the strings

F1: *HIGH <carriage return>*

F2: *LOW <carriage return>*

F3: *AVERAGE <carriage return>*

Pressing F1, for example, is then equivalent to responding to the INPUT statement with the string *HIGH <carriage return>.*

Setting Function Keys.   You may assign strings to the function keys in either command or execution mode. To assign *<string>* to the function key *n,* use the statement

```
KEY n, <string>
```

Suppose that you wish to assign key F1 the string

```
LIST <carriage return>
```

This may be done using the statement

```
10 KEY 1, "LIST"+CHR$(13)
```

Subsequently, whenever you press key F1, the desired string will be input to BASIC. In particular, if you happen to be in the immediate mode, inputting the string will cause the current program to be listed. In effect, you have customized the F1 key to a special application. In a similar fashion, you may customize other keys with commands or keystroke sequences which come up often in your work.

If you assign a null string to a function key (using a command of the form *KEY _,''''*), you will disable the function key.

Note that function key strings may contain any characters with ASCII codes from 0 to 128, so that control characters may be included within the function key string assignments.

To display the current function key string assignments, use the command

KEY LIST

The current string assignments will be displayed on the usual text area of the screen (lines 1-24).

In writing or running a program, it is often convenient to have a reminder of the various key string assignments on the screen at all times. This may be accomplished by giving the command

KEY ON

The first six characters of each function key string will then be displayed in line 25 of the screen. (In case of a line width of 40, only the first five function key strings are displayed.) To turn off the function key display in line 25, use the command

KEY OFF

TEST YOUR UNDERSTANDING 1 (answers on page 328)

  a.   Write commands to assign the following strings to function keys 1-3.

> **F1** - *''ADDITION''*
> **F2** - *''SUBTRACTION''*
> **F3** - *''MULTIPLICATION''*

Disable all other function keys.

  b.   Display the function key assignments in line 25.

Event Trapping

We have described how to input data using INPUT, LINE INPUT, and INKEY$. All of these input methods have the following feature in common: the program decides when to ask for the input. You may use the function keys for a very different form of input.

Suppose you want the program to watch function key F1. The instant F1 is pressed, you wish the program to go to the subroutine in line 1000. This may be accomplished by first turning on event trapping for key F1 via the statement

```
10 KEY(1) ON
```

This tells the program to examine F1 after every program statement is executed. Next, we tell the program that whenever F1 is pushed, go to the subroutine starting in line 1000. We tell the program this in the statement

```
20 ON KEY(1) GOSUB 1000
```

The program will inspect the keyboard buffer at the end of each program statement. When it detects that F1 has been pushed, it will *GOSUB 1000*.

You may use event trapping to implement a menu, as illustrated in the following example.

Example 1. Write a program to test addition, subtraction, and multiplication of two-digit numbers. Let the user select the operation via function keys F1 through F3. Let function key F4 cause the program to end.

Solution. We create four subroutines, corresponding to addition, subtraction, multiplication and *END*. These four subroutines begin in lines 1000, 2000, 3000, and 4000, respectively. What is of most interest to us, however, are lines 10-210. We first clear the screen and define the strings associated with function keys F1 to F4 to be, respectively, *ADD, SUBTR, MULT,* and *EXIT*. We then disable the rest of the function keys. In lines 140-170, we set up the event trapping lines for function keys F1-F4. In lines 180-200, we turn the event trapping on.

In line 210, we select the two numbers to use in our arithmetic. In line 220 we set up an infinite loop that continuously goes from 220 to 210 and back to 220. Note that this infinite loop accesses different random numbers in each repetition. Thus, the problem you get depends on how long you take to press one of the function keys. Therefore, it is really unnecessary to use the RANDOMIZE command to guarantee non-repeatability. The program keeps executing the loop until one of the function keys F1-F4 is pressed. Then it goes to the appropriate subroutine. Notice that the strings attached to F1-F4 are displayed in line 25 of the screen. This is accomplished in line 130. Here is the program.

```
1  ' **********************************************
2  ' This program tests addition, subtraction,
3  '   and multiplication of two-digit numbers.
4  ' **********************************************
10 'Initialize function keys
20    CLS
30    KEY 1, "ADD"
40    KEY 2, "SUBTR"
50    KEY 3, "MULT"
60    KEY 4, "END"
70    KEY 5, ""
80    KEY 6, ""
90    KEY 7, ""
100   KEY 8, ""
110   KEY 9, ""
```

```
120    KEY 10,""
130    KEY ON
140    ON KEY(1) GOSUB 1000
150    ON KEY(2) GOSUB 2000
160    ON KEY(3) GOSUB 3000
170    ON KEY(4) GOSUB 4000
180    FOR J=1 TO 4
190          KEY(J) ON
200    NEXT J
210    X=INT(100*RND):Y=INT(100*RND)
220    GOTO 210
1000   'Addition
1010   CLS
1020   PRINT "ADDITION"
1030   PRINT "PROBLEM"
1040   PRINT X;"+";Y;" EQUALS?"
1050   INPUT ANSWER
1060   IF ANSWER=X+Y THEN 1070 ELSE 1090
1070   PRINT "CORRECT"
1080   GOTO 1100
1090   PRINT "INCORRECT. THE CORRECT ANSWER IS";X+Y
1100   RETURN
2000   'Subtraction
2010   CLS
2020   PRINT "SUBTRACTION"
2030   PRINT "PROBLEM"
2040   PRINT X;"-";Y;" EQUALS?"
2050   INPUT ANSWER
2060   IF ANSWER=X-Y THEN 2070 ELSE 2090
2070   PRINT "CORRECT"
2080   GOTO 2100
2090   PRINT "INCORRECT. THE CORRECT ANSWER IS";X-Y
2100   RETURN
3000   'Multiplication
3010   CLS
3020   PRINT "MULTIPLICATION"
3030   PRINT "PROBLEM"
3040   PRINT X;"*";Y;" EQUALS?"
3050   INPUT ANSWER
3060   IF ANSWER=X*Y THEN 3070 ELSE 3090
3070   PRINT "CORRECT"
3080   GOTO 3100
3090   PRINT "INCORRECT. THE CORRECT ANSWER IS";X*Y
3100   RETURN
4000   'Exit
4010   CLS
4020   KEY OFF
4030   FOR J=1 TO 4
4040          KEY(J) OFF
4050   NEXT J
4060   END
```

There may be certain sections in the program where you want to disallow trapping of function key *n*. This may be done using either of these statements:

```
KEY(n) STOP
KEY(n) OFF
```

You may resume trapping of function key *n* using the statement

```
KEY(n) ON
```

If function key *n* is pressed while a STOP is in effect, the event is remembered. When trapping is turned on, the program immediately jumps to the appropriate subroutine. If you use a *KEY(n) OFF* statement, then function keys are not remembered.

In addition to the function keys, you may trap the cursor motion keys. (These are the four keys on the numeric keypad with arrows pointing in the four possible directions of cursor motion.) The commands for trapping these keys are

```
ON KEY(n) GOSUB
KEY(n) ON
KEY(n) OFF
KEY(n) STOP
```

where *n = 11* corresponds to cursor up, *n = 12* to cursor left, *n = 13* to cursor right, and *n = 14* to cursor down.

Be Wary of the Function Keys

The function keys and their associated BASIC statements are one of the significant features of the PC. However, it is easy to misuse them. I like the function keys so much that I use them to control menu choices in practically all my programs. In such an application, you want the program to respond to a function key by going to a subroutine. At first glance, you might be tempted to implement such a scheme like we did in the above example, using the **ON KEY ... GOSUB** statement.

However, in building serious programs, this approach has serious defects. For one thing, if you compile your program (as you will almost surely want to do for serious applications programs), any event trapping statements cause extra code to be generated. And the extra code is quite burdensome. The only way the compiler can check for event trapping is to put a check after each statement in the program. This can easily add several thousand bytes to your program. But that's not the whole story.

All those tests for event trapping will slow your program considerably. This is not to say that event trapping with the function keys is not a valuable feature. It surely is. However, before you use it, you should ask yourself: Do I really want the program to test for a function key after each instruction? If you are just implementing choices from a menu, the answer should be no!

ANSWERS TO TEST YOUR UNDERSTANDING 1

```
1:   a. 10 DATA ADDITION,SUBTRACTION,MULTIPLICATION
        20 FOR J=1 TO 3
        30   READ A$(J)
        40 NEXT J
        50 FOR J=1 TO 10
        60   KEY J,A$(J)
        70 NEXT J
```

   b. `KEY ON`

13.3   Extended ASCII Codes

The IBM PC keyboard allows for many more key combinations than the standard set of ASCII codes allows. For this reason, the IBM uses **extended ASCII codes** in addition to the standard ones. An extended ASCII code consists of two numbers: a zero followed by one of the numbers 0-255. Here are some examples of extended ASCII codes:

```
0   15
0   71
0   131
```

The extended ASCII codes are generated from the keyboard as follows:

Second Number of Extended ASCII Code	Key(s) Generating Code
15	Shift tab (art)
16-24	Alt-Q,W,E,R,T,Y,U,I,O,P
30-38	Alt-A,S,D,F,G,H,J,K,L
44-50	Alt-Z,X,C,V,B,N,M
59-68	Function Keys F1-F10 (when disabled as soft keys)
71	Home
72	Cursor Up
73	Pg Up
75	Cursor Left
77	Cursor Right
79	End
80	Cursor Down
81	Pg Down
82	Ins
83	Del
84-93	Shift-F1-F10
94-103	Ctrl-F1-F10

Second Number of Extended ASCII Code	Key(s) Generating Code
104-113	Alt-F1-F10
114	Ctrl-PrtSc
115	Ctrl-Space
116	Ctrl-Backspace
117	Ctrl-End
118	Ctrl-PgDn
119	Ctrl-Home
120-131	Alt-1,2,3,4,5,6,7,8,9,0,-,=
132	Ctrl-PgUp

Any ASCII codes that don't appear in the above list may not be generated from the keyboard.

Here is how the extended ASCII codes work. Suppose, for example, that you push the Home key. BASIC inserts its extended ASCII code into the keyboard buffer. The keyboard buffer then contains the two numbers 0 and 71. As an experiment, run this program:

```
10 C$=INKEY$
20 IF C$="" THEN 20
30 PRINT LEN(C$)
40 PRINT ASC(LEFT$(C$,1))
50 PRINT ASC(RIGHT$(C$,1))
```

In response to the INPUT statement, hit the Home key. The program prints out the three numbers *2,0,* and *71*. That is, in response to an extended ASCII code, INKEY$ returns the two-character string *CHR$(0)+CHR$(71)*. The first character, *CHR$(0)*, indicates an extended ASCII code. The second character, *CHR$(71)*, indicates the key pushed, according to the above table.

Using the extended ASCII codes, you may keep track of input from all the keyboard keys.

TEST YOUR UNDERSTANDING 1 (answer on page 331)
Suppose that you press the keys Alt-A followed by End. What will be the contents of the keyboard buffer?

TEST YOUR UNDERSTANDING 2 (answer on page 331)
Write a program that reads a single key from the keyboard buffer. The program should allow you to read a key with an extended ASCII code.

Here is an important note about the function keys: If a function key is enabled, then pressing it causes its associated string to be placed in the keyboard buffer.

However, no extended ASCII code will be generated. On the other hand, if a function key is disabled, pressing it will generate the corresponding extended ASCII code. For example, if F1 has the associated string *"HELP" + CHR$(13)*, then pressing F1 puts a string of five ASCII codes in the keyboard buffer, namely the ASCII codes corresponding to the four letters *HELP* and ASCII code 13. On the other hand, if F1 is disabled, pressing F1 causes the ASCII codes 0 and 59 (the extended code for F1) to be entered into the keyboard buffer.

I prefer to use my function keys by avoiding ON KEY … GOSUB. To do this, I first disable all the function keys as soft keys. I then use a custom input routine that passes on all keyboard characters to an analysis routine. If the key pressed was a function key, the analysis routine passes the extended ASCII code in the variable *E$*. By inspecting *E$*, I can then direct the program to the appropriate subroutine. In this way, all inputs to my program are treated alike. And the savings in memory and run speed are usually considerable.

As an example, consider the following program, which is the command structure we will use to write the bar chart program in Chapter 18. There we will fill in the details of the subroutines in lines 1000-25000.

```
10 KEY OFF
20 MENU$="1 DEF 2 DATA 3 DRAW 4 SAVE 5 RCLL 6 FILE
            7 EXIT"
30 FOR J%=1 TO 10:KEY J%,"":NEXT J%
100 'Main Menu Choice-Bar Chart Program
110 'E$ is returned by the input routine, =the second
120 'character of extended ASCII code
130 LOCATE 25,1
140 PRINT MENU$;
150 C=ASC(E$)
160 IF C=59 THEN 1000
170 IF C=60 THEN 2000
180 IF C=61 THEN 3000
190 IF C=62 THEN 4000
200 IF C=63 THEN 5000
210 IF C=64 THEN 6000
220 IF C=65 THEN 7000 ELSE 25000
1000 'Define bar chart parameters
1999 RETURN
2000 'Input bar chart data
2999 RETURN
3000 'Draw bar chart
3999 RETURN
4000 'Save bar chart
4999 RETURN
5000 'Recall bar chart
5999 RETURN
6000 'Read data file
6999 RETURN
7000 'Exit
7999 RETURN
25000 'Input routine
25999 RETURN
```

Note the following aspects of this program:

1. Line 30 disables the function keys as soft keys so that pressing the function keys returns an extended ASCII code.

2. Lines 130-140 simulate the usual function key display that was turned off in line 10.

3. Lines 150-220 send the program to the appropriate routine selected by the user. Note that these lines use GOTO rather than GOSUB. Each of the routines accepts its own input from the keyboard buffer by repeatedly calling on the input routine. Whenever a function key is spotted, the routine sends the program back to the above control routine.

4. Line 25000 indicates the beginning of the INPUT routine that we will write in Chapter 17.

ANSWERS TO TEST YOUR UNDERSTANDINGS 1 and 2

```
1:  CHR$(0)+CHR$(30)+CHR$(0)+CHR$(79)

2:  10 C$=INKEY$
    20 IF C$="" THEN PRINT "NO CHARACTER IN BUFFER"
    30 IF ASC(LEFT$(C$,1))<>0 THEN 100 ELSE
       C$=RIGHT$(C$,1)
    40 PRINT "EXTENDED CODE: 0,";
    100 PRINT ASC(C$)
    200 END
```

13.4   Error Trapping

At the moment, our programs have only a single way to respond to an error: the program stops and an error message is displayed. Sometimes the program is stopped with good cause, since a logical error prevents BASIC from making any sense of the program. However, there are other instances in which the error is rather innocent: the printer is not turned on, the wrong data diskette is in the drive, or the user provides an incorrect response to a prompt. In each of these situations, it is desirable for the program to report the error to the user and wait for further instructions. Let's learn how to make the program take such action.

Ordinarily, the response to an error is to halt the program. However, an alternative is provided by the

```
ON ERROR GOTO <line number>
```

statement. If your program contains such a statement, BASIC will go to the indicated line number as soon as an error occurs. For example, suppose your program contains the statement

```
ON ERROR GOTO 5000
```

Whenever an error occurs, the program will go to line 5000. Beginning in line 5000, you can program an **error-trapping routine**, which can:

1. Analyze the error.

2. Notify the user of the error.

3. Resume the program and/or wait for further instructions from the user.

The ON ERROR GOTO statement is called an **error-trapping statement.** It may occur anywhere in the program. After you type RUN, BASIC scans your program for the presence of an error-trapping statement. If BASIC finds an error-trapping line, it sets up code to send your program to the desired program line, should an error occur. In order to minimize BASIC's time to search for an error-trapping statement, you should place an error-trapping statement at the beginning of the program.

To see how an error-trapping routine is constructed, let's consider a particular example. Suppose that your program involves reading a data file, which must be on the diskette in the current drive. The program user may place the wrong diskette in the drive or may not insert any diskette at all. Let's write an error-trapping routine to respond to these two types of errors.

Let's begin our error-trapping routine in line 5000. We begin our program with the error-trapping line

```
10 ON ERROR GOTO 5000
```

When an error occurs, BASIC makes a note of the line number in the variable **ERL** (error line) and the error number in **ERR.** It then goes to line 5000. The values of the variables ERL and ERR are at our disposal, just like the values of any other variables.

In our particular example, there are two types of errors to look out for: **File Not Found** (error number 53) and **Disk Not Ready** (error number 71). The first error occurs when the file requested by the program is not on the indicated disk. The second error occurs when either the diskette drive door is open or no diskette is in the drive. The error numbers were obtained from either the list of errors on the summary card at the back of the book or in Appendix A of IBM's *BASIC Reference Manual*. In the case of each error, the error-trapping routine should notify the user and wait for the situation to be corrected. Here is the routine.

```
5000 'Error trapping routine
5010 IF ERR=53 PRINT "File Not Found"
5020 IF ERR=71 PRINT "Disk Not Ready"
5030 IF ERR<>53 AND ERR<>71 THEN
```

```
      PRINT "Unrecoverable Error"
5040  IF ERR<>53 AND ERR<>71 THEN END
5050  PRINT "CORRECT DISKETTE. PRESS ANY KEY WHEN READY."
5060  IF INKEY$="" THEN 5060
5070  RESUME
```

Several comments are in order. Notice that the error-trapping routine only allows recovery in the case of errors 53 and 71. If the error is any other type, line 5040 causes the program to END. Line 5050 tells the operator to correct the situation. In line 5060, the program waits until the operator signals that the situation has been corrected. The RESUME in line 5070 clears the error condition and causes the program to resume execution with the line that caused the error.

Note that we analyzed our errors using ERR. We might just as well have used the line number ERL to choose our response to the error.

The RESUME statement has several useful variations:

- *RESUME NEXT* causes the program to resume with the line immediately after the line which caused the error.
- *RESUME <line number>* causes the program to resume with the indicated line number.

In designing and testing an error-trapping routine, it is helpful to be able to generate errors of a particular type. This may be done using the ERROR statement. For example, to generate an error 50 (field overflow) in line 75, just replace line 75 with

```
75 ERROR 50
```

When the program reaches line 75, it will simulate error 50. The program will then jump to the error-trapping routine to be tested.

13.5 CHAINing Programs

The **CHAIN** instruction allows you to call a BASIC program from within an operating program. For example, the statement

```
2000 CHAIN "SQUARES"
```

causes the program to load and execute the program *SQUARES*. The current program is lost, as well as the values of all its variables. BASIC begins execution of *SQUARES* with its first line.

You may begin execution of *SQUARES* at line 300 by using the statement

```
2000 CHAIN "SQUARES",300
```

You may carry all of the variables of the current program over into *SQUARES* and begin with the first statement of *SQUARES* by using the statement

```
2000 CHAIN "SQUARES",,ALL
```

To carry forward all of the variables of the current program and to begin SQUARES at line 300, use the statement

```
2000 CHAIN "SQUARES",300,ALL
```

A CHAIN statement is useful if a particular program is too large for memory. You may break the program into subprograms and use CHAIN statements to link them together into a single program. In the interest of saving memory, you may wish to carry over only some of the variables of the current program. You may do this with the **COMMON** statement. For example, to pass the variables *A, B,* and *C$* to *SQUARES,* include the following statement in the chaining program:

```
10 COMMON A,B,C$
```

If, in addition, you wish to pass the values of the array *SALARY(),* the COMMON statement should be of the form

```
10 COMMON A,B,C$,SALARY()
```

You may include as many COMMON statements as you wish. However, a variable may appear in only one of them. COMMON may appear anywhere in a program, but it is a good idea to place it at the beginning.

Be careful in using the CHAIN statement. It has the following significant effects:

1. There is no way to pass user-defined functions to the chained program.

2. Any variable types that have been defined by the statements DEFINT, DEFSNG, or DEFDBL will not be preserved.

3. Any error-trapping line number will not be preserved.

4. All files are closed.

The CHAIN statement completely eliminates the current program. You may keep a portion (or all) of the current program by using the CHAIN MERGE statement. For example, the statement

```
CHAIN MERGE "SQUARES",300
```

merges the program *SQUARES* with the current program and resumes execution at line 300. If the line number had not been specified, execution would have resumed at the first line of the new, merged program. The lines of *SQUARES* will be interweaved with the lines of the current program. If a line number in *SQUARES* duplicates a line number in the current program, then the line in the current program will be deleted in favor of the corresponding line in *SQUARES*.

The program to be MERGEd must have been stored in ASCII format. (This is the format created by the command SAVE,A.) Otherwise, BASIC will report a **Bad File Mode** error.

In some applications, you may wish to delete a section of the current program before MERGEing. For example, the statement

```
CHAIN MERGE "SQUARES",300,DELETE 300-1000
```

will first delete lines 300-1000 of the current program, merge *SQUARES* with the current program, and resume execution at line 300 of the resulting program.

CHAIN MERGE leaves files currently open and preserves variables, variable types, and user-defined functions.

An Interesting Application of CHAIN MERGE

Let's now describe an interesting, if unexpected, application of the CHAIN MERGE statement. In many applications, it is necessary to input a function from the keyboard. For example, in a program that displays graphics of functions, it is most convenient to have the user input the formula for the function directly from the keyboard. The problem is how to get this formula into a DEF FN statement while the program is running? The answer: use CHAIN MERGE. Here's how:

1. Input the formula for the function (say, $X^2 + 2*SIN(X)$) using an INPUT statement, which stores the formula in a string *FORMULA$*.

2. Use string manipulations to create a program line, with an appropriate line number, which provides a DEF FN statement for the function.

3. Store the statement line in a file.

4. CHAIN MERGE the contents of the file into the program.

Here is illustrative code for how these steps are carried out.

```
10 INPUT "TYPE FUNCTION FORMULA";FORMULA$
20 DEFINITIONS$ = "100 DEF FNA " + FORMULA$
30 OPEN "FUNCTION" FOR OUTPUT AS #1
40 PRINT #1, DEFINITION$
50 CLOSE #1
60 CHAIN MERGE "FUNCTION",100
```

14

Computer Games

14.0 Chapter Objectives

In the last few years computer games have captured the imaginations of millions of people. In this chapter, we will build several computer games that utilize both the random number generator and the graphics capabilities of the IBM Personal Computer. Actually, as we shall shortly see, these games utilize most of what we have learned and provide a good test of our programming prowess.

Several of the games require that we keep track of time. So we begin this chapter with a discussion of BASIC's mechanisms for timing.

14.1 Telling Time With Your Computer

In many games, we need a clock to time moves. We will start by learning to tell time with the computer.

The IBM Personal Computer Disk Operating System has a built-in clock (a **real-time clock** in computer jargon) which allows your programs to take into account the time of day (in hours, minutes, and seconds) and the date (day, month, and year). You can use this feature for many purposes, such as timing a segment of a program (see Example 1).

Reading the Real-Time Clock

The IBM PC real-time clock keeps track of six pieces of information in the following order:

Month (1-12)

Day (1-31)

Year (00-99)

Hours (00-23)

Minutes (00-59)

Seconds (00-59)

The date is displayed in the following format:

2-15-84

The time is displayed in the following format:

14:38:27

The above displays correspond to February 15, 1984, at 27 seconds after 2:38 PM. Note that the hours are counted using a 24-hour clock, with 0 hours corresponding to midnight. Hours 0-11 correspond to AM, and hours 12-23 correspond to PM. Also note that the year must be in the range 1980-2099.

The clock is programmed to account for the number of days in a month (28, 30, or 31), but it does not recognize leap years.

In BASIC, time is identified using the variable **TIME$**. To display the current time on the screen, use the command

```
10 PRINT TIME$
```

If it is currently 5:10 PM, the computer displays the time in the format

17:10:07

The *:07* denotes 7 seconds past the minute.

BASIC identifies the date using the variable **DATE$**. To display the current date of the screen, use the command

```
20 PRINT DATE$
```

If it is currently Dec. 12, 1984, the computer displays

```
12-12-1984
```

TEST YOUR UNDERSTANDING 1 (answer on page 340)

Display the current time and date.

Setting the Clock

You have an opportunity to set the clock when starting the Disk Operating System. Recall that the initial DOS display asks you for the date. If you accurately answer this question, the computer will keep the correct date as long as it is operating continuously. Note, however, that the computer loses track of this data as soon as it is turned off. You may also use TIME$ and DATE$ to set the time and date as follows. Suppose that the time is *12:03:17* and the date is *10/31/1984*. You type the commands

```
TIME$ = "12:03:17"
DATE$ = "10-31-1984"
```

These commands may be typed whenever the computer is not executing a program and are typed without a line number. These commands may also be used within a BASIC program (with a line number, of course). For example, to reset the time to *00:00:00* within a program, use the statement

```
10 TIME$ = "00:00:00"
```

In setting the date there are two acceptable variations. First, you may replace some or all of the dashes in the date by slashes. All of the following are acceptable forms of the date:

10/31/1984 10-31-1984

10/31-1984 10-31/1984

Second, you may input the year as two digits. For example, you can input 1984 as 84. The computer will automatically supply the missing 19.

TEST YOUR UNDERSTANDING 2 (answer on page 340)
Write instructions to set the time to 2 PM and the date to Jan. 1, 1985.

TEST YOUR UNDERSTANDING 3
Set the clock with today's date and time. Check yourself by printing out the value of the clock.

TEST YOUR UNDERSTANDING 4 (answer on page 340)
Write a program that continually displays the correct time on the screen.

Calculating Elapsed Time

The real-time clock may be used to measure elapsed time. You can ask the computer to count 10 seconds or three days. In such measurements, it is convenient to have the components (that is, the hours, minutes, seconds, and so on) of the time and date available individually. Let's discuss a method for determining these numbers.

Begin with the string TIME$. Suppose that TIME$ is now equal to

"10:07:32"

To isolate the seconds (the 32), we must chop off the initial portion of the string, namely *10:07:*. We may do this using the statement RIGHT$. The statement

```
RIGHT$(TIME$,2)
```

forms a string out of the rightmost two digits of the string TIME$. This is the string *32*. In most applications, we will require the *32* as a number rather than as a string. To convert a string consisting of digits into the corresponding numeric constant, we may use the VAL function. That is, to obtain the *SECONDS* portion of the time as a numeric constant, we use the statement

```
10 SECONDS = VAL(RIGHT$(TIME$,2))
```

In a similar fashion, we may calculate the *HOURS* portion of the time by extracting the left two characters of the time and converting the resulting string into a numeric constant. The statement to accomplish this is

```
20 HOURS = VAL(LEFT$(TIME$,2))
```

Finally, to calculate the *MINUTES* portion of the time, we must extract from TIME$ a string of two characters in length beginning with the fourth character. For this purpose, we use the MID$ statement as follows:

```
30 MINUTES = VAL(MID$(TIME$,4,2))
```

To calculate the *MONTH, DAY*, and *YEAR* portions of the date as numeric constants, we use the statements

```
40 MONTH = VAL(LEFT(DATE$,2))
50 DAY = VAL(MID$(DATE$,4,2))
60 YEAR = VAL(RIGHT$(DATE$,4))
```

The **ON TIMER** statement is even more convenient for calculating elapsed time. Consider the following two statements:

```
10 ON TIMER(10) GOSUB 200
20 TIMER ON
```

The first statement tells the computer that whenever the timer is turned on, BASIC should count 10 seconds and then go to line 200. The time may be turned on anywhere in the program using a statement like the one on line 20.

Example 1. In Example 7 of Section 6.2, we developed a program to test mastery in the addition of two-digit numbers. Redesign this program to allow 15 seconds to answer the question.

Solution. Let us use the real-time clock. After a particular problem has been given, we will start the seconds portion of the clock at 0 and perform a loop that continually tests the seconds portion of the clock for the value 15. When this value is encountered, the program prints out *"TIME'S UP. WHAT IS YOUR ANSWER?"* Here is the program. Lines 50 and 60 contain the loop.

```
1 ' ***********************
2 '          ARITH3
3 ' This program provides a
4 ' timed test of addition of
5 ' 2-digit numbers.
```

```
6  ' *************************
10 FOR J=1 TO 10:'LOOP TO GIVE 10 PROBLEMS
20    INPUT "TYPE TWO 2-DIGIT NUMBERS"; A,B
30    PRINT "WHAT IS THEIR SUM?"
40    ON TIMER(15) GOSUB 100
50    TIMER ON
60    GOTO 60: ' Wait 15 seconds
100   INPUT "TIME'S UP! WHAT IS YOUR ANSWER";C
120   IF A+B=C THEN 200
130   PRINT "SORRY. THE CORRECT ANSWER IS",A+B
140   RETURN 500: 'Go to next proble"
200   PRINT "YOUR ANSWER IS CORRECT! CONGRATULATIONS"
210   R=R+1:      'Increase score by 1
220   RETURN 500: 'GO TO THE NEXT PROBLEM
500 NEXT J
600 PRINT "YOUR SCORE IS",R,"CORRECT OUT OF 10"
700 PRINT "TO TRY AGAIN, TYPE RUN"
800 END
```

TEST YOUR UNDERSTANDING 5 (answer on page 340)

Modify the above program so that it allows you to take as much time as you like
to solve a problem, but keeps track of elapsed time (in seconds) and prints out
the number of seconds used.

ANSWERS TO TEST YOUR UNDERSTANDINGS 1, 2, 4, and 5

```
1:  10 PRINT TIME$ : PRINT DATE$
    20 END
    RUN

2:  TIME$ = "14:00:00"
    DATE$ = "1/1/85"

4:  10 CLS
    20 PRINT TIME$
    30 FOR J=1 TO 500
    40 NEXT J: 'DELAY
    50 GOTO 10
    60 END
```

Note: this program is an infinite loop and needs to be terminated by pressing
the key combination Ctrl-Break.

5:   Delete lines 40-100. Change the RETURNs in lines 140 and 200 to
     GOTOs. Add these lines:

```
40 TIME$ = "00:00:00"
100 INPUT "WHAT IS YOUR ANSWER";C
110 MINUTES = VAL(MID$(TIME$,4,2))
111 SECONDS = VAL(RIGHT$(TIME$,2))
112 PRINT "YOU TOOK",60*MINUTES+SECONDS, "SECONDS"
```

14.2 Blind Target Shoot (Text Mode)

The object of this game is to shoot down a target on the screen by moving your cursor to hit the target. The catch is that you only have a two-second look at your target! The program begins by asking if your are ready. If so, you press any key. The computer then randomly chooses a spot to place the target. It lights up the spot for two seconds. The cursor is then moved to the upper left position of the screen (the so-called "home" position). You must then move the cursor to the target, based on your brief glimpse of it. You have five seconds to hit the target. (See Figure 14-1.)

Figure 14-1. **Blind target shoot.**

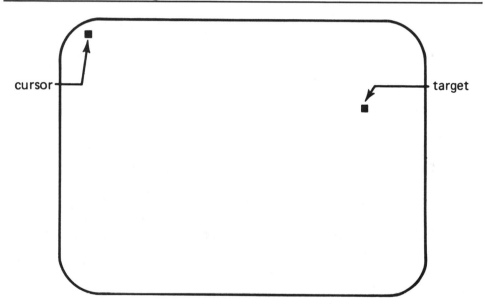

Your score is based on your distance from the target, as measured in terms of the moves it takes to get to the target from your final position. Here is the list of possible scores:

Distance From Target	Score
0	100
1 or 2	90
3 to 5	70
6 to 10	50

11 to 15	30
16 to 20	10
over 20	0

You move the cursor using the cursor motion keys on the numeric keypad. We will use event trapping to interrupt the program while the program is running.

Here is a sample session with the game. The underlined lines are those you type.

```
RUN


BLIND TARGET SHOOT

TO BEGIN GAME, PRESS ANY KEY
```

Press any key. The screen clears. The target is displayed. See Figure 14-2.

The screen is cleared and the cursor is moved to the home position. See Figure 14-3A. The cursor is then moved to the remembered position of the target. See Figure 14-3B. Time runs out. See Figure 14-3C.

The score is calculated. See Figure 14-4.

Here is a listing of our program.

```
10 ' *****************
20 ' ** TARGET SHOOT **
30 ' *****************
100 'Title Screen
110     CLS
120     KEY OFF
130     WIDTH 40
140     RANDOMIZE VAL(RIGHT$(TIME$,2))
150     PRINT "BLIND TARGET SHOOT"
160     PRINT "TO BEGIN GAME, PRESS ANY KEY"
170     IF INKEY$="" THEN 170
180     CLS
190 'Initialization
200     TIME$ = "0:0:0":          'Reset Clock
210     LOCATE ,,0:               'Turn off cursor
```

Figure 14-2.

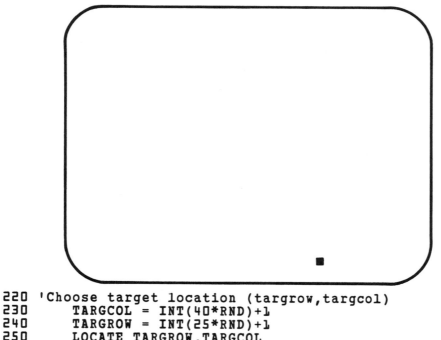

```
220 'Choose target location (targrow,targcol)
230     TARGCOL = INT(40*RND)+1
240     TARGROW = INT(25*RND)+1
250     LOCATE TARGROW,TARGCOL
260     PRINT CHR$(219):          'Display target
270 'Look at target
280     SECONDS = VAL(RIGHT$(TIME$,2))
290     IF SECONDS = 2 THEN 300 ELSE 280
300     'TWO SECONDS ELAPSED
310     LOCATE TARGROW,TARGCOL
320     PRINT " ";:              'Blank out target
330     LOCATE ,,1,1,13
340     PRINT CHR$(11)
350     TIME$ = "0:0:0"
360     X=1:Y=1:
370 'Turn on cursor key trapping
380     ON KEY(11) GOSUB 480
```

Figure 14-3A.   Figure 14-3B.   Figure 14-3C.

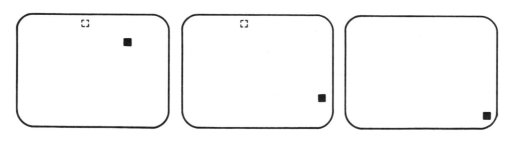

Figure 14-4.

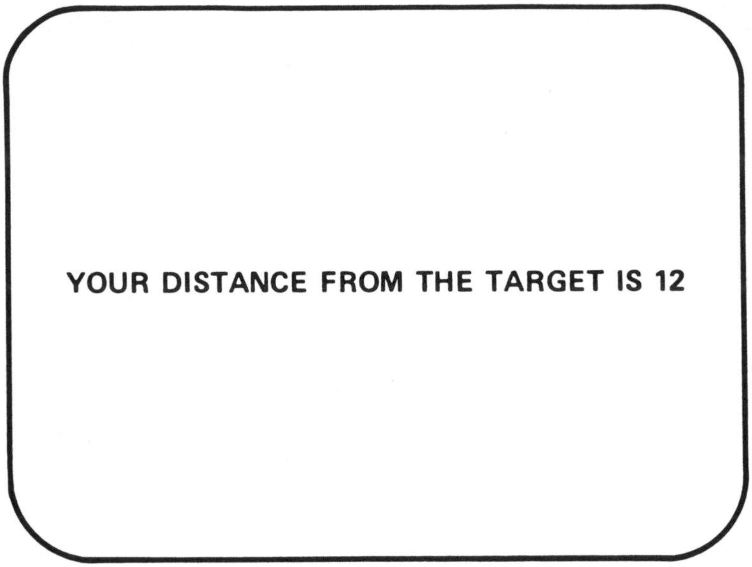

YOUR DISTANCE FROM THE TARGET IS 12

```
390      ON KEY(12) GOSUB 520
400      ON KEY(13) GOSUB 560
410      ON KEY(14) GOSUB 600
420      KEY(11) ON
430      KEY(12) ON
440      KEY(13) ON
450      KEY(14) ON
460      SECONDS = VAL(RIGHT$(TIME$,2))
470      IF SECONDS = 5 THEN 700 ELSE 370
480 'Cursor Up
490      GOSUB 640
500      PRINT CHR$(30);
510  RETURN
520 'Cursor Left
530      GOSUB 640
540      PRINT CHR$(29);
550  RETURN
560 'Cursor Right
570      GOSUB 640
580      PRINT CHR$(28);
590  RETURN
600 'Cursor Down
610      GOSUB 640
620      PRINT CHR$(31);
630  RETURN
640 'Turn off cursor motion trapping
650      KEY(11) OFF
660      KEY(12) OFF
670      KEY(13) OFF
680      KEY(14) OFF
690  RETURN
700 'Compute score
```

```
710    D = ABS(POS(0)-TARGCOL)+ABS(CSRLIN-TARGROW)
720    CLS
730    PRINT "YOUR DISTANCE FROM THE TARGET IS";D
740    IF D=0 THEN PRINT "CONGRATULATIONS"
750    IF D=0 THEN PRINT "YOU HIT THE TARGET!"
760    SC = 100
770    IF D>0 THEN SC=SC-10
780    IF D>2 THEN SC = SC-20
790    IF D>5 THEN SC = SC-20
800    IF D>10 THEN SC=SC-20
810    IF D>15 THEN SC = SC-20
820    IF D>20 THEN SC = SC-10
830    PRINT "YOUR SCORE IS",SC
840    INPUT "DO YOU WISH TO PLAY AGAIN(Y/N)";B$
850    IF B$ = "Y" OR B$="y" THEN 180 ELSE 860
860    END
```

14.3   Shooting Gallery

In this section, we develop a game called Shooting Gallery, that simulates the shooting galleries of carnivals. The player has a gun that he or she may fire at a moving target. (See Figure 14-5.) The program keeps track of the hits. The game shows 20 moving targets during one play.

The design of this game incorporates most of what we know. Let's begin by enabling event trapping of the cursor motion keys up, down, right, and left. The right and left motions will tell the program that we wish to move the gun to the right or left. The cursor up key will fire the gun. Lines 10-80 in the program below turn on the appropriate trapping.

This program will be in the medium-resolution graphics mode. The gun will initially be in the center of the last text row of the screen. The first position of the bullet after being fired will be in row 185. We will keep track of the horizontal position of the gun in the variable *GUNPOSITION* and the vertical and horizontal positions of the bullet in the variables *BULLETROW* and *BULLETCOL*, respectively. Line 90 initializes *GUNPOSITION* and *BULLETROW*.

For the gun, we will use the small house-shaped figure (ASCII character 127). The bullet will be a vertical arrow (ASCII character 24) and the target will be a happy face (ASCII character 2). All of these figures are to be animated, so it is necessary to get all of them in appropriate arrays *A%*, *B%*, and *C%*. This is done in lines 100-210. Using % means that the arrays will contain integers. Limiting the type of number that the arrays can contain will speed up program execution. (This is a concern since animations tend to run slowly in BASIC.)

Line 220 places the gun in its initial position. The main program is contained in lines 230-330. There is an outer loop for 20 targets and an inner loop each step of

Figure 14-5. **The game of Shooting Gallery.**

which moves the target two columns across the screen and the bullet (if any have been fired) eight rows up the screen. If you fire the gun (cursor up key), the program is interrupted and the gun firing routine is called. This displays the bullet in its initial position. All subsequent motion of the bullet is controlled by the main loop. The bullet disappears when it reaches the row of the target. The target disappears when it hits the right edge of the screen. If the bullet and the target are at the same place at the same time, both disappear and you are credited with a hit.

The BEEP command is used to sound the speaker when you score a hit. Also, note the use of the function ABS in line 670. *ABS(X)* is just *X* with its sign removed. For example, *ABS(+5) = 5*, whereas *ABS(-5) = 5*.

```
1  ' **********************
2  ' ** SHOOTING GALLERY **
3  ' **********************
10 ' Initialization
20      KEY OFF
30      ON KEY(11) GOSUB 590
40      ON KEY(12) GOSUB 530
50      ON KEY(13) GOSUB 470
60      KEY(11) ON
70      KEY(12) ON
80      KEY(13) ON
90      GUNPOSITION=160:BULLETROW=185
100     DIM A%(100),B%(100),C%(100)
110     SCREEN 1,0
```

```
120        CLS
130        PRINT CHR$(2)
140        GET (0,0)-(7,7),A%
150        CLS
160        PRINT CHR$(127)
170        GET (0,0)-(7,7),B%
180        CLS
190        PRINT CHR$(24)
200        GET (0,0)-(7,7),C%
210        CLS
220        PUT (GUNPOSITION,185),B%
230 'Main program loop
240        FOR TARGET=1 TO 20
250                PUT (0,8),A%
260                FOR COLUMN=2 TO 312 STEP 2
270                        GOSUB 340:          'Move target
280                        GOSUB 380:          'Move bullet
290                NEXT COLUMN
300                IF COLUMN=316 THEN 320
310                PUT (312,8),A%
320        NEXT TARGET
330        END
340 'Move target
350        PUT (COLUMN-2,8),A%
360        PUT (COLUMN,8),A%
370 RETURN
380 'Move bullet
390        IF BFLAG=0 THEN 460
400        PUT (BULLETCOL,BULLETROW),C%
410        BULLETROW=BULLETROW-8
420        IF BULLETROW<10 THEN GOSUB 670 ELSE 450
430        BFLAG=0
440        GOTO 460
450        PUT (BULLETCOL,BULLETROW),C%
460 RETURN
470 'Move gun 8 steps to right
480        PUT (GUNPOSITION,185),B%
490        GUNPOSITION=GUNPOSITION+8
500        IF GUNPOSITION>311 THEN GUNPOSITION=311
510        PUT (GUNPOSITION,185),B%
520 RETURN
530 'Move gun 8 steps to left
540        PUT (GUNPOSITION,185),B%
550        GUNPOSITION=GUNPOSITION-8
560        IF GUNPOSITION<0 THEN GUNPOSITION=0
570        PUT (GUNPOSITION,185),B%
580 RETURN
590 'Shoot gun
600        IF BFLAG=1 THEN 650
610        BFLAG=1
620        BULLETCOL=GUNPOSITION
630        BULLETROW=177
640        PUT (BULLETCOL,BULLETROW),C%
650 RETURN
660 'Determine if target is hit
670        IF ABS(BULLETCOL-COLUMN)<7 THEN GOSUB 690
```

```
680 RETURN
690 'Erase target and bullet
700     PUT (COLUMN,8),A%
710     BEEP
720     SCORE=SCORE+1
730     LOCATE 1,1
740     PRINT "SCORE";SCORE;" hits";
750     COLUMN=314
760 RETURN
```

14.4   Tic Tac Toe (Graphics Mode)

In this section, we present a program for the traditional game of tic tac toe. We won't attempt to let the computer execute a strategy. Rather, we will let it be fairly stupid and choose its moves randomly. We will also use the random number generator to ''flip'' for the first move. Throughout the program, you will be *O* and the computer will be *X*. Here is a sample game.

Figure 14-6.

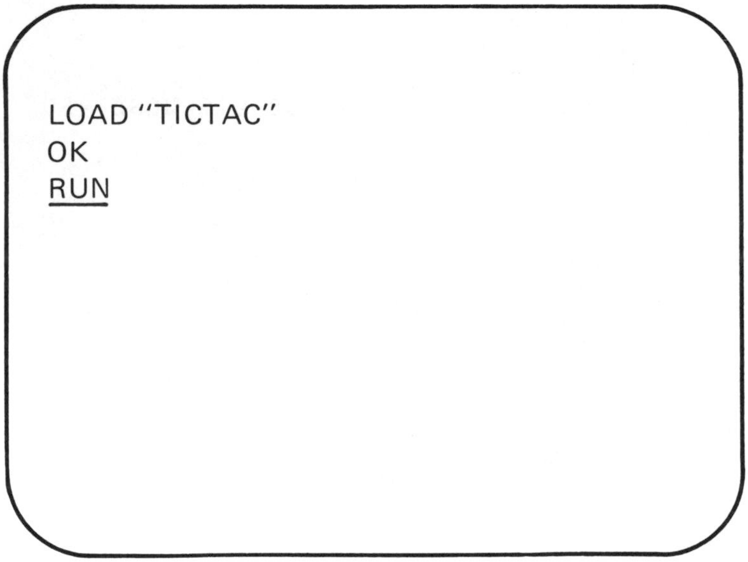

```
LOAD "TICTAC"
OK
RUN
```

Figure 14-7.

```
TIC TAC TOE
YOU WILL BE O;THE COMPUTER WILL BE X
THE POSITIONS OF THE BOARD ARE NUMBERED
AS FOLLOWS:

        1            2            3
        4            5            6
        7            8            9

THE COMPUTER WILL TOSS FOR FIRST.
YOU GO FIRST.
WHEN READY TO BEGIN TYPE 'R'
R
```

TEST YOUR UNDERSTANDING 1 (answer on page 353)
How can the computer toss to see who goes first?

The computer now draws a tic tac toe board. See Figure 14-8.

The computer now displays your move and makes a move of its own. See Figure 14-9.

The computer now makes its move and so on until someone wins or a tie game results.

Here are the variables used in the program.

- $Z = 0$ if it's your move and $Z = 1$ if it is the computer's.
- $A\$(J)$ $(J=1, 2, \ldots, 9)$ contains either O, X, or the empty string, indicating the current status of position J.
- $S =$ the position of the current move.
- $M =$ the number of moves played (including the current one).

We used a video display worksheet to lay out the board, and to determine the coordinates for the lines and the Xs and Os.

Here is a listing of our program.

```
10 ' ******************************************
20 '             TIC TAC TOE
30 ' This program plays the traditional game
40 ' of tic tac toe against an opponent,
50 ' drawing a board on the screen, and
```

Figure 14-8.

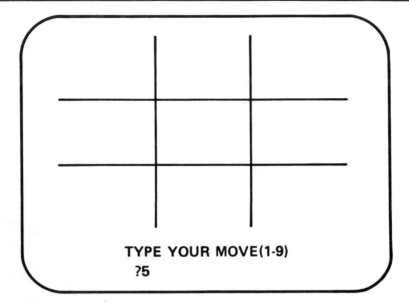

Figure 14-9.

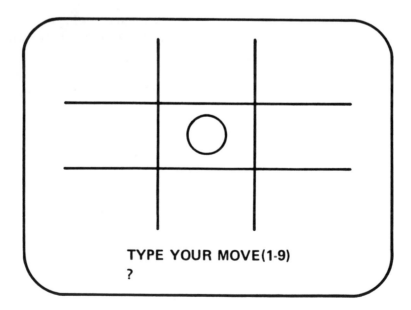

```
60  ' determining when there is a winner.
70  ' ****************************************
1000 'Initialization
1010     CLEAR:KEY OFF
1020     SCREEN 1
1030     RANDOMIZE VAL(RIGHT$(TIME$,2))
1040     DIM A$(9)
1050     DIM B$(9)
1060     CLS
1070     PRINT "TIC TAC TOE"
1080     PRINT "YOU WILL BE O; THE COMPUTER WILL BE X"
1090     PRINT "THE POSITIONS ON THE BOARD ARE
                   NUMBERED"
1100     PRINT "AS FOLLOWS"
1110     PRINT "1";TAB(8) "2";TAB(16) "3"
1120     PRINT "4";TAB(8) "5";TAB(16) "6"
1130     PRINT "7";TAB(8) "8";TAB(16) "9"
1140     PRINT "THE COMPUTER WILL TOSS FOR FIRST"
1150     FOR J=1 TO 2000:NEXT J
1160     IF RND(1) > .5 THEN 1170 ELSE 1210
1170     PRINT "YOU GO FIRST"
1180     FOR J=1 TO 2000:NEXT J
1190     Z=0:                        'Player goes first
1200     GOTO 1240
1210     PRINT "I'LL GO FIRST"
1220     FOR J=1 TO 2000:NEXT J
1230     Z=1:                        'Computer goes first
1240     PRINT "WHEN READY TO BEGIN, PRESS ANY KEY"
1250     IF INKEY$="" THEN 1250
1260     CLS
2000 'Main program
2010     GOSUB 3000:                 'Draw game board
2020     FOR M=1 TO 9:                   'M=move #
2030             IF Z=0 THEN GOSUB 5000
2040             IF Z=1 THEN GOSUB 6000
2050             Z=1-Z
2060             IF WIN=1 THEN 2100
2070     NEXT M
2080             PRINT "THE GAME IS TIED"
2090             FOR J=1 TO 2000:NEXT J
2100     CLS
2110     LOCATE 1,1
2120     INPUT "ANOTHER GAME(Y/N)';R$
2130     IF R$="Y" OR R$="y" THEN 1010 ELSE END
3000 'Draw TIC TAC TOE Board
3010     CLS
3020     LINE (103,8)-(103,191)
3030     LINE (206,8)-(206,191)
3040     LINE (8,70)-(311,70)
3050     LINE (8,132)-(311,132)
3060     RETURN
4000 ' Display current game status
4010     LOCATE 5,7: PRINT A$(1);
4020     LOCATE 5,20: PRINT A$(2);
4030     LOCATE 5,33: PRINT A$(3);
```

```
4040        LOCATE 14,7: PRINT A$(4);
4050        LOCATE 14,20: PRINT A$(5);
4060        LOCATE 14,33: PRINT A$(6);
4070        LOCATE 21,7: PRINT A$(7);
4080        LOCATE 21,20: PRINT A$(8);
4090        LOCATE 21,33:PRINT A$(9);
4100 RETURN
5000 'Player's Move
5010            LOCATE 1,1
5020            INPUT "TYPE YOUR MOVE(1-9)";S
5030            IF S<1 OR S>9 THEN 5050
5040            IF A$(S) = "" THEN 5100
5050            LOCATE 1,1
5060            LINE (0,0)-(319,7),0,BF:'Blank out
                                          first row
5070            PRINT "ILLEGAL MOVE"
5080            FOR J=1 TO 2000:NEXT J
5090            GOTO 5000
5100            A$(S) = "O"
5110            GOSUB 7000:        'Is game over?
5120            LINE (0,0)-(319,7),0,BF:'Blank out
                                          first row
5130            GOSUB 4000:        'Display move
5140 RETURN
6000 'Computer's Move
6010    LOCATE 1,1
6020    PRINT "Here's my move!";
6030    GOTO 8000:    'Is there a winning move?
6040    'If not, choose random move
6050    S = INT(9*RND+1)
6060    IF A$(S) = "" THEN 6070 ELSE 6050
6070    A$(S) = "X"
6080    FOR J=1 TO 2000:NEXT J: 'Delay
6090    GOSUB 7000:                'Is game over?
6100    GOSUB 4000:                'Display move
6110 RETURN
7000 'Is the game over?
7010    IF Z = 0 THEN C$ = "O" ELSE C$ = "X"
7020    IF A$(1) = A$(2) THEN 7030 ELSE 7050
7030    IF A$(2) = A$(3) THEN 7040 ELSE 7050
7040    IF A$(3) = C$ THEN 7260
7050    IF A$(1) = A$(4) THEN 7060 ELSE 7080
7060    IF A$(4) = A$(7) THEN 7070 ELSE 7080
7070    IF A$(7) = C$ THEN 7260
7080    IF A$(1) = A$(5) THEN 7090 ELSE 7110
7090    IF A$(5) = A$(9) THEN 7100 ELSE 7110
7100    IF A$(9) = C$ THEN 7260
7110    IF A$(2) = A$(5) THEN 7120 ELSE 7140
7120    IF A$(5) = A$(8) THEN 7130 ELSE 7140
7130    IF A$(8) = C$ THEN 7260
7140    IF A$(3) = A$(6) THEN 7150 ELSE 7170
7150    IF A$(6) = A$(9) THEN 7160 ELSE 7170
7160    IF A$(9) = C$ THEN 7260
7170    IF A$(4) = A$(5) THEN 7180 ELSE 7200
7180    IF A$(5) = A$(6) THEN 7190 ELSE 7200
```

```
7190      IF A$(6) = C$ THEN 7260
7200      IF A$(7) = A$(8) THEN 7210 ELSE 7230
7210      IF A$(8) = A$(9) THEN 7220 ELSE 7230
7220      IF A$(9) = C$ THEN 7260
7230      IF A$(3) = A$(5) THEN 7240 ELSE 7320
7240      IF A$(5) = A$(7) THEN 7250 ELSE 7320
7250      IF A$(7) = C$ THEN 7260 ELSE 7320
7260      GOSUB 4000
7270      LOCATE 1,1
7280      PRINT SPACE$(80);
7290      LOCATE 1,1
7300      PRINT C$ , "WINS THIS ROUND":WIN=1
7310      FOR J=1 TO 2000:NEXT J
7320 RETURN
8000 'Look for a winning move
8010      COUNT = 0
8020      FOR I=1 TO 9
8030              IF A$(I) = "X" THEN B(I) = 1
8040              IF A$(I) = "" THEN B(I) = 0
8050              IF A$(I) = "O" THEN B(I) = -1
8060      NEXT I
8070      COUNT = COUNT+1
8080      IF COUNT = 9 THEN 8180
8090      READ I,J,K
8100      S = B(I)+B(J)+B(K)
8110      IF S =  2 THEN 8120 ELSE 8070
8120      IF B(J) = 0 THEN A$(J) = "X" ELSE 8140
8130      GOTO 8310
8140      IF B(K) = 0 THEN A$(K) = "X" ELSE 8160
8150      GOTO 8310
8160      IF B(I) = 0 THEN A$(I) = "X" ELSE 8070
8170      GOTO 8310
8180      RESTORE
8190      COUNT = 0
8200      COUNT = COUNT + 1
8210      IF COUNT = 9 THEN 8320
8220      READ I,J,K
8230      S = B(I)+B(J)+B(K)
8240      IF S=-2 THEN 8250 ELSE 8200
8250      IF B(J) = 0 THEN A$(J) = "X" ELSE 8270
8260      GOTO 8310
8270      IF B(K) = 0 THEN A$(K) = "X" ELSE 8290
8280      GOTO 8310
8290      A$(I) = "X"
8300      GOTO 8310
8310      RESTORE : GOTO 6080
8320      RESTORE:GOTO 6040
8330      DATA 1,2,3,4,5,6,7,8,9,1,4,7,2,
                5,8,3,6,9,1,5,9,3,5,7
```

ANSWER TO TEST YOUR UNDERSTANDING 1

1: See lines 1140-1240 of the tic tac toe program.

15

Memory Management

15.0   Chapter Objectives

IN THIS CHAPTER, WE WILL explore the memory of the IBM PC. We will describe the way in which numbers and text are stored and the way the memory is organized. Our discussions include:

- The properties of the binary and hexadecimal number systems.
- Bits, bytes, and memory addressing.
- How BASIC's various data types are stored in memory.
- Logical operations on bytes and their applications, in particular to graphics.
- Some useful memory locations.

Actually, as we have seen, binary and hexadecimal arithmetic arises throughout the book. So let's begin with a discussion of these important number systems.

15.1   Binary and Hexadecimal Numbers

Decimal Representation of Numbers.   In grade school, we learned to perform arithmetic using the decimal number system. In this system, numbers are written as strings of digits chosen from among the 10 numbers 0, 1, 2, 3, 4, 5, 6, 7, 8, 9. Here are some examples of these familiar numbers:

14312, -928372, 29831029831902938290

Such strings of digits are interpreted according to a system of place value. We proceed from right to left. The digit in the extreme right position represents the number of 1s, the next digit the number of 10s, the next digit the number of 100s, the next digit the number of 1000s, and so forth. For example, the number 1935 stands for

1	1000s	1*1000 =	1000
9	100s	9* 100 =	900
3	10s	3* 10 =	30
5	1s	5* 1 =	5
			1935

The values of the various digit positions, that is, the numbers 1, 10, 100, 1000, . . .are all powers of 10:

$1 = 10^0$, $10 = 10^1$, $100 = 10^2$, $1000 = 10^3$, ...

Another way of expressing the number 1935 is

$1*10^3 + 9*10^2 + 3*10^1 + 5*10^0$

Note that we have arranged the digits in their usual order, which corresponds to decreasing powers of 10.

Binary Representation of Numbers. In the binary number system, numbers are represented by strings formed from the two digits 0 and 1. Here are some examples of binary numbers:

10, 01110000111, 100100100100

Just as the decimal number system is based on powers of 10, the binary number system is based on powers of two, that is, on the numbers

$2^0 = 1$, $2^1 = 2$, $2^2 = 4$, $2^3 = 8$, $2^4 = 16$,...

We interpret a binary number by examining the digits from right to left. The rightmost digit of a binary number corresponds to the number of 1s, the next digit to the number of 2s, the next digit to the number of 4s, and so forth. For example, the binary number 1101 stands for

1	8s	=	8
1	4s	=	4
0	2s	=	0
1	1s (rightmost digit)	=	1
1101		=	13

That is, the binary number 1101 corresponds to the decimal number 13.

TEST YOUR UNDERSTANDING 1 (answer on page 361)
What decimal number corresponds to the binary number 10101010?

The above calculation for converting a binary number into its decimal equivalent may be tedious. However, we may let the computer do the work for us. Here is a simple program that performs the conversion.

```
10 '*****************************************
20 'This program converts the number given
30 'in the string N$ to the decimal number
40 'D.
50 '*****************************************
```

```
100 'Convert binary to decimal
110 INPUT "NUMBER TO CONVERT";N$
120 E=0:'E=current power of 2
130 D=0:'D=decimal equivalent
140 L=LEN(N$)
150 IF L=0 THEN 210
160 IF RIGHT$(N$,1) = "1" THEN D=D+2^E:GOTO 180
170 IF RIGHT$(N$,1) <> "0" THEN 230
180 E=E+1
190 N$=LEFT$(N$,L-1)
200 GOTO 140
210 PRINT "Decimal Equivalent=";D
220 GOTO 240
230 PRINT "Input Not In Proper Format"
240 END
```

Converting from Decimal to Binary.   As we have seen, every binary number has a decimal equivalent. The reverse is also true: every decimal number has a binary equivalent. For example, consider the decimal number 61. Let's divide it by 2 to obtain a quotient 30 and remainder 1. Write these results in the form

$$61 = 30*2 + 1$$

There is a 2 present now. But the quotient 30 does not yet involve a 2. So we divide the 30 by 2 to obtain the quotient 15 and remainder 0. Write this result in the form

$$30 = 15*2 + 0$$

If we insert this expression for 30 into the expression for 61, we obtain the result

$$61 = (15*2+0)*2 + 1$$
$$= 15*2^2 + 0*2 + 1$$

This is now closer to a representation of 61 by powers of 2. But the 15 does not yet involve 2. So let's now repeat the above procedure using the number 15 instead of 30. First we divide by 2 to obtain a quotient of 7 and a remainder of 1. Next, we write the equation

$$15 = 7*2 + 1$$

and we substitute this equation into our preceding expression for 61:

$$61 = (7*2 + 1)*2^2 + 0*2 + 1$$
$$= 7*2^3 + 1*2^2 + 0*2 + 1$$

This is a better representation of 61. To improve it, we repeat the procedure using the number 7:

$$7 = 3*2 + 1$$
$$61 = (3*2+1)*2^3 + 1*2^2 + 0*2 + 1$$
$$= 3*2^4 + 1*2^3 + 1*2^2 + 0*2 + 1$$

Repeat the procedure using the number 3:

$$3 = 1*2 + 1$$
$$61 = (1*2+1)*2^4 + 1*2^3 + 1*2^2 + 0*2 + 1$$
$$= 1*2^5 + 1*2^4 + 1*2^3 + 1*2^2 + 0*2 + 1$$

This last representation of 61 consists only of powers of 2. From this representation, we may read off the binary representation of 61, as the 1 or 0 coefficients of the powers of 2, read from left to right. The representation is

$$61 \ (decimal) = 111101 \ (binary)$$

If you don't believe the computation, just proceed in reverse and convert 111101 to its corresponding decimal number. You will obtain 61 as the result.

The above procedure may be programmed for the computer. However, it is necessary to perform division to obtain an integer quotient and remainder. If you use the operation / to perform the division, you will obtain a decimal answer and no remainder. For example, the result of 61/2 is 30.5 (rather than the desired quotient 30 and remainder 1). To obtain the desired information, it is simplest to use the BASIC operations \ and *mod*.

Recall that the operation \ is called **integer division** and may be used to calculate the quotient of one integer by another. (Recall that an integer is a whole number in the range -32768 to 32767.) Integer division yields only the integer part of the quotient. For example,

$$3\backslash 2 = 1$$
$$16\backslash 2 = 8$$
$$72\backslash 7 = 10$$

The operation *mod* allows you to compute the remainder that results from an integer division. For example, *5 mod 2* yields the remainder of the integer division $5\backslash 2$. That is, *5 mod 2* equals 1.

TEST YOUR UNDERSTANDING 2 (answer on page 361)
What is the value of $(7\backslash 3 + 1)*(18\backslash 5 - 1)$?

TEST YOUR UNDERSTANDING 3 (answers on page 361)
What is the value of

a. 17 mod 7\5

b. 5^2 mod 25\2^2

Using the operations \ and *mod*, we may easily convert a decimal number to its binary equivalent. We repeatedly perform integer division by 2. The remainders of the division provide the digits of the binary number, proceeding from right to left. Here is a program to perform the calculations.

```
10 '************************************
20 'This program converts the decimal
30 'number N to its binary equivalent.
40 '************************************
100 'Main Program
110 INPUT "NUMBER TO CONVERT";N
120 A$ = ""
130 REMAINDER = N MOD 2
140 A$ = RIGHT$(STR$(REMAINDER),1)+A$
150 N=N\2
160 IF N=0 THEN 170 ELSE 130
170 PRINT "The Binary Equivalent Is "; A$
180 END
```

A binary digit (0 or 1) is called a **bit**. The number 1011 is 4 bits long, whereas the number 10010011 is 8 bits long.

TEST YOUR UNDERSTANDING 4 (answers on page 361)

a. List all possible 2-bit numbers.

b. List all possible 3-bit numbers.

In carrying out Test Your Understanding 4, you should have found that there are four *2*-bit numbers and eight *3*-bit numbers. There are 16 possible *4*-bit numbers:

0000, 0001, 0010, 0011, 0100, 0101, 0110, 0111

1000, 1001, 1010, 1011, 1100, 1101, 1110, 1111

It can be proven (in a mathematics text) that the number of possible *N*-bit numbers is equal to 2^N. This fact generalizes the particular cases *(N=2,3,4)* observed above.

As we shall see, *8*-bit and *16*-bit binary numbers play a special role in the internal workings of the IBM PC. The number of *8*-bit binary numbers is $2^8=256$. They represent the numbers *0* through *255*. Similarly, the number of 16-bit binary numbers is $2^16 = 65536$. They represent the numbers 0 through *65535*.

The IBM PC (and all other digital computers) use the binary number system for their operation. It may appear as if the computer uses decimal numbers. However, all data must be converted into binary form if the computer is to process it. And this applies to text data and program statements as well as numerical data. Each type of information is translated into binary according to its own translation scheme. (More about this later.) Computer operations are performed only on binary numbers. When output is required, the computer translates from binary to either numeric or text format.

Hexadecimal Representation of Numbers.   The hexadecimal number system is closely connected with the binary number system and is much easier to work with in many applications. There are 16 possible hexadecimal digits:

0,1,2,3,4,5,6,7,8,9,A,B,C,D,E,F

The digits 0-9 have their usual numerical values, and A,B,C,D,E,F have the respective values

10	11	12	13	14	15
A	B	C	D	E	F

A typical hexadecimal number is a string of hexadecimal digits, such as

A1EFF78A

The rightmost digit indicates the number of 1s, the next digit the number of 16s, the next digit the number of 256s ($256 = 16^2$), and so forth. For example, the above hexadecimal number corresponds to

$$10*16^7 + 1*16^6 + 14*16^5 + 15*16^4 + 15*16^3 + 7*16^2$$
$$+ 8*16 + 10*1$$

The real advantage of hexadecimal is that it offers a shorthand way of writing numbers in binary. The 16 hexadecimal digits correspond to the following 4-digit binary numbers:

Hexadecimal	Binary	Decimal
0	0000	0
1	0001	1
2	0010	2
3	0011	3
4	0100	4
5	0101	5
6	0110	6
7	0111	7
8	1000	8
9	1001	9
A	1010	10
B	1011	11

Hexadecimal	Binary	Decimal
C	1100	12
D	1101	13
E	1110	14
F	1111	15

A binary number may be blocked off in groups of four digits and translated into hexadecimal according to the above table. For example, consider the 25-digit binary number

1111100111001010111100111

To convert it into hexadecimal, first we block it off into groups of four digits, proceeding from right to left:

1 1111 0011 1001 0101 1110 0111

We complete the leftmost group by adding three zeros on the left:

0001 1111 0011 1001 0101 1110 0111

Finally, we translate each 4-digit group into a hexadecimal digit:

0001	*1111*	*0011*	*1001*	*0101*	*1110*	*0111*
1	*F*	*3*	*9*	*5*	*E*	*7*

So the hexadecimal equivalent of the binary number is *1F395E7*. It is clearly simpler to work with the hexadecimal form rather than the binary form of the number.

Hexadecimal Numbers in BASIC

Hexadecimal numbers may be used in IBM PC BASIC on a par with decimal numbers. That is, wherever you can use a decimal number, you may use a hexadecimal number and vice versa. In BASIC, a hexadecimal number is indicated with the prefix *&H*. For example, the hexadecimal number *1A2F* is denoted *&H1A2F*.

It is possible to write a simple program for converting decimal to hexadecimal. However, BASIC has a built-in function that saves us the bother. This function, **HEX\$**, returns a string that is the hexadecimal representation of a given decimal number. For example, we have

```
HEX$(10) equals "A"
HEX$(30) equals "1E"
```

Note that HEX$ returns a string, which may not be used in calculations. On the other hand, &H1E is a number. As far as BASIC is concerned, &H1E is just another name for 30.

ANSWERS TO TEST YOUR UNDERSTANDINGS 1, 2, 3, and 4

1: 170

2: 6

3: a. 0   b. 1

4: a. 00, 01, 10, 11
    b. 000, 001, 010, 011, 100, 101, 110, 111

15.2 Bits, Bytes, and Memory

Our first application of the binary and hexadecimal number systems will be to describe the contents and the addressing scheme used in PC memory. At the same time, we will explore the contents of RAM and describe the various data present in RAM while you are using BASIC.

RAM is broken into a series of 8-bit binary numbers called **bytes**. The size of your RAM is measured in units of 1024 bytes. One 1024-byte unit is called 1K. So a system with 32K of RAM contains 32 x 1024 or 32768 bytes. A system with 64K contains 64 x 1024 or 65536 bytes. Your IBM PC can be expanded to contain as much as 640K. An AT unit can be expanded to contain as much as 3072K.

You should think of RAM as divided into a large number of cubbyholes with each cubbyhole containing a single byte. The cubbyholes of RAM are called **memory locations**. The contents of each memory location may be described by two hexadecimal digits (= 8 bits). For example, here are the contents of four memory locations:

7E 0F FF 81

The memory locations of a computer are numbered, usually beginning with 0. The number asociated with each memory location is called its **address**. For example, in a simple computer system (not the PC) with 4K of RAM, the memory locations have addresses from 0 to 4095 (decimal). At a particular moment, the contents of addresses 3001-3004 might be as follows:

Address   3001   3002   3003   3004

Contents   1A   B0   E8   F1

The computer makes use of addresses in its internal calculations. For this reason, addresses are usually expressed in hexadecimal. Be careful not to confuse an address (a memory location number) with its contents (the data stored in that address).

We observed in the preceding section that 16-bit binary numbers correspond to the decimal numbers 0 through 65535. On the other hand, 64K = 65536. Thus, we see that the 16-bit binary numbers provide exactly enough addresses to handle a 64K memory. To address more memory than 64K requires binary numbers longer than 16 bits. Actually, the IBM PC is designed to economically handle 16-bit numbers, so rather than use addresses consisting of, say 24 or 32 bits, it uses pairs of 16-bit numbers. A typical address on the PC has the form

(segment, offset)

where **segment** and **offset** are 16-bit numbers having the following meanings.

Bytes are numbered beginning with 0. The byte corresponding to a particular address pair (segment, offset) is byte number

16*segment + offset

For example, consider the address pair *(00FF,1F58)*. The segment portion, *00FF*, equals *255* in decimal. The offset portion, *1F58*, equals *8024* in decimal. So the particular address pair corresponds to byte number *16*255 + 8024 = 12104*.

Suppose that we hold the segment portion of an address pair fixed and allow the offset portion to vary. The corresponding address pair runs over a set of 64K consecutive memory locations. Such a section of memory is called a **64K segment**. In programming the 8088 chip (in machine language), such 64K segments play an important role.

The following notation is used to denote an address:

segment:offset

For example, the address in the above example is

00FF:1F58

TEST YOUR UNDERSTANDING 1 (answer on page 367)
The maximum address theoretically possible is *FFFF:000F*. To what byte number does this correspond?

If your computations are correct, you just found that the PC can address more than one million bytes of RAM. Actually, not all these addresses represent RAM locations. Certain addresses refer to ROM that contains portions of BASIC and DOS. Other addresses are reserved for future expansion of the system's capabilities. Here is a diagram of memory organization when BASIC is in use. (A diagram of this sort is called a **memory map**.)

The memory map requires a bit of explanation. The memory locations beginning at *0000:0000* are reserved by DOS. The precise amount of memory required depends on the version of DOS. When BASIC is loaded into RAM, one of the internal registers of the 8088 processor is loaded with the segment address corresponding to the beginning of the BASIC interpreter program. The register con-

```
Memory Location    Contents
0000:0000          DOS
--------------------------------------
DS:0000            BASIC
                   (approximately 17K)
--------------------------------------
DS:xxxx            Current Program
--------------------------------------
DS:yyyy            Variables
--------------------------------------
                   Arrays
--------------------------------------
                   String Space
--------------------------------------
                   BASIC Stack
--------------------------------------
                   Top of Memory
                        or
                   DS:FFFF
--------------------------------------
                   Unused by BASIC
--------------------------------------
A000:0000          System Use
--------------------------------------
F400:0000          ROM
--------------------------------------
```

taining this information is called the Data Segment register and its contents are denoted *DS* on the memory map.

The offsets *xxxx* and *yyyy* give the beginning of the current program and the beginning of the program variables, respectively. Their precise values depend on the version of BASIC. However, they may be obtained from certain memory locations. (See Section 15.5.) Note that BASIC is allowed only one 64K segment. A corollary of this fact is that a BASIC program must lie within that segment, regardless of the amount of memory present in your machine. (This only applies to interpreted BASIC. Compiled programs may be longer than 64K. In fact, they may take advantage of as much memory as you own!)

The BASIC segment of memory ends at either *DS:FFFF* or at the *Top of Memory*. If there is less than 64K that may be allocated to BASIC, then the Top of Memory is set equal to the highest location in your RAM.

You may artificially limit the space occupied by BASIC. For example, you may wish to do this to make room for machine language subroutines or communications buffers. To limit the size of BASIC's segment, call up BASIC's segment, call up BASIC with a command of the form

`BASIC /M: numberofbytes`

Here *numberofbytes* is equal to the desired number of bytes in BASIC's segment. For example, to limit BASIC to 32K, use the command

`BASIC /M:32767`

If you do not limit the size of BASIC, DOS automatically reserves all available memory up to a maximum of 64K.

The memory locations beginning at *A000:0000* are reserved for system functions such as storing the contents of the screen. (Later, we'll show you how to write on the screen by making direct access to the screen memory.)

The locations beginning at *F000:0000* correspond to ROM. In these locations is stored large portions of both DOS and BASIC. Moreover, these locations contain the master program, called the BIOS, which controls the input and output operations between the various system components. This program is the one responsible for reading and interpreting the keyboard input, displaying characters on the screen, reading and writing on diskette, and so forth.

Snooping Into Memory

It's both fun and instructive to snoop around in your computer's memory. The simplest way to do this is to use the program **DEBUG**, which is on your DOS diskette. Let's snoop around within the BASIC interpreter. To use DEBUG, obtain the DOS prompt *A>*, insert your DOS diskette into the current drive, and type

```
DEBUG BASIC <ENTER>
```

After a few seconds, you will see the DEBUG prompt

```
-
```

Type *D* followed by any address. For example, to display the contents of memory beginning at location *0D00:0000*, type

```
D 0D00:0000 <ENTER>
```

The DEBUG program will display the contents of 80 consecutive memory locations beginning with *0D00:0000*. The display will consist of lines of the form

```
0D00:0000 33 1E 4F 4A A1 09 01 00 00 00 00 00 00 FF FF
```

The address at the beginning of the line corresponds to the first entry following.

DEBUG is a powerful program. It allows you to snoop anywhere in memory. For example, we may display the beginning of BASIC by typing

```
DS:0000
```

The DEBUG program will then display 80 consecutive bytes of memory beginning with the address *DS:0000*. The memory contents are displayed in hexadecimal form. When the desired information has been displayed, DEBUG will redisplay its prompt. To see another section of memory, just give another D command followed by the beginning address. If you omit the address, the program will display the 80 bytes that follow those most recently displayed.

TEST YOUR UNDERSTANDING 2

Use the DEBUG program to display

a.   The first 800 bytes of the BASIC interpreter

b.   The contents of memory location *0000:0076*

You say you don't understand what you see? Well, that's because you are looking at a program in machine language. This is the form in which the computer reads and executes programs. We'll have more to say about the meaning of these hexadecimal numbers later.

Addresses Within a BASIC Program

In most BASIC programs you are shielded from dealing directly with specific memory locations. You can name variables, create loops, make decisions, and BASIC automatically keeps track of all the various goings-on in memory. However, in some applications, it is necessary to access a memory location directly. And BASIC has statements that allow you to do this.

At any given moment, there is a current segment number, which is understood as the segment portion of any needed addresses. You specify this segment number by using the **DEF SEG** statement. The format of this statement is

```
DEF SEG = <segment number>
```

This statement defines the segment required for the addresses in the PEEK, POKE, CALL, BLOAD, BSAVE, VARPTR, and USR instructions. (All will be discussed subsequently.) Once you specify a segment number via a DEF SEG instruction, the segment number remains the same until you change it by another DEF SEG instruction.

When BASIC is initialized, the segment number is set equal to the beginning address of the BASIC interpreter (*DS* in the above memory map.) Unless you change this segment number via a DEF SEG instruction, all addresses in BASIC are assumed to have the beginning of the BASIC interpreter as their segment number. After giving a DEF SEG instruction, you may return the segment number to its initial setting with the instruction

```
DEF SEG
```

(The segment number is omitted.)

To read the contents of a memory location, you may use the **PEEK** statement. It has the format

```
x = PEEK(offset)
```

This statement assigns the contents of *:offset* to the numerical variable *x*, where ** is the number assigned by the most recent DEF SEG instruction. The contents of a memory location are given as an integer between 0 and 255. For example, the instruction

```
CONTENTS = PEEK(35873)
```

assigns the contents of memory location *:35873* to the numerical variable contents.

TEST YOUR UNDERSTANDING 3

Use the PEEK instruction to determine the contents of the first four memory locations in which the BASIC interpreter is stored. Compare your results with the information determined in Test Your Understanding 2(a). (Remember that the results of the preceding Test Your Understanding were provided in hexadecimal, whereas PEEK gives its results in decimal.)

You may store a number in a memory location using the **POKE** instruction, which has the format

```
POKE offset, contents
```

For example, consider the instruction

```
POKE 5000, 217
```

It stores the number *217* in location *:5000*. The contents assigned to a memory location must be an integer between 0 and 255.

The PEEK and POKE instructions give you untold power. However, you must use them with care. Be sure not to POKE into a memory location that contains part of the BASIC interpreter, DOS, or any other "non-user" area of memory. You may cause your program to crash!

The various dots of light that comprise the screen display at any given moment are stored, in coded form, in a section of memory. The monochrome display interface uses 4K of memory beginning at *&HB000:0000*, whereas the color/graphics interface uses 16K beginning at *&HB800:0000* and proceeding for 16K bytes. You may write in these memory locations and see what you write. Here is a program that accomplishes this in the case of the color/graphics interface, in medium-resolution graphics mode. The program requests a memory offset. It then stores 255 in the corresponding memory location. Visually, this corresponds to four dots in a row. The position of the dots corresponds to the memory offset selected.

```
1  '*******************************************
2  'This program pokes a bit pattern directly
3  'into screen memory.
4  '*******************************************
10 KEY OFF
20 SCREEN 1
30 DEF SEG = &HB800
```

```
40 LOCATE 1,1
50 INPUT OFFSET
60 CLS
70 POKE OFFSET,255
80 INPUT "Again (Y or N)";A$
90 IF A$="Y" OR A$="y" THEN 40
100 END
```

In many graphics applications, it is most efficient to manipulate displays by writing into or reading directly from the screen memory.

If you consult the memory map provided above, you can see the relative positions of your variables, strings and arrays within the memory. You may locate the exact position of any one of these program elements using the **VARPTR** instruction. For example, suppose that your program uses the variable *ALPHA*. The instruction

```
X = VARPTR(ALPHA)
```

sets X equal to the offset of the first byte of memory that is used to store *ALPHA*. The assumed segment is always the beginning of the BASIC interpreter. This assumed segment is not affected by DEF SEG instructions. We will discuss at a later time the precise way in which variables are stored. At that time, we will use the VARPTR instruction to snoop on some variables in action.

ANSWER TO TEST YOUR UNDERSTANDING 1
1:   1,048,575

15.3   How Data Is Stored in Memory

In the previous section, we discussed the memory of the PC and how the various memory locations are identified by addresses. Let's now turn to the actual contents of the memory locations and discuss how BASIC stores various sorts of data in RAM. We should begin by saying that all locations of RAM and ROM contain binary numbers. What we are really after, however, is the way in which various kinds of data (integers, single-precision numbers, double-precision numbers, strings) are represented as binary numbers.

Positive and Negative Integers

An **integer** is a whole number in the range -32768 to 32767. An integer is stored in RAM as a *16*-bit binary number. Let's spend a moment discussing the layout of such storage.

The bits of a binary number are numbered as in the diagram below:

bit number	15 14 13 12 11 10 9 8 7 6 5 4 3 2 1 0
bit	1 0 1 0 1 1 0 1 1 0 1 0 0 1 1 1

Bit 0 is called the **least-significant** and bit 15 the **most-significant**.

A *16*-bit binary number is called a **word**. Storage of a word requires two (8-bit) bytes. Now here is the confusing part. The two bytes are stored in consecutive memory locations, with the least-significant bits in the first byte and the most-significant bits in the second byte. This may seem perfectly natural, but results in the following confusion. Consider the following *16*-bit number in hexadecimal form: *1A3F*. (Recall that each hexadecimal digit corresponds to four bits.) The most-significant eight bits correspond to *1A* and the least-significant to 3F. Therefore, this *16*-bit number is stored in memory as

3F 1A

And, indeed, if you use DEBUG to look at memory, you will see the bytes displayed in this order. Before you interpret a 16-bit number from RAM, remember to reverse the order of the bytes!

TEST YOUR UNDERSTANDING 1 (answer on page 372)
Here are two consecutive bytes in memory:

A3 1F

To what decimal number does this correspond?

In our discussion so far, we have avoided any mention of negative numbers in binary and hexadecimal. Let's fill in that gap. BASIC uses only the 15 least-significant bits (bits 0 through 14) to represent a positive number. The most-significant bit (bit 15) is always 0 for a positive number. (See Figure 15-1.) This coding method allows representation of $2^{16} = 32,768$ binary numbers, corresponding to the decimal numbers 0 through 32,767.

The most-significant bit (bit 15) is used to indicate the sign of the number. Perhaps the most obvious way of indicating the sign would be to have bit 15 = 0 to mean a positive number and bit 15 = 1 to mean a negative number. **However, this is not what is done**. Instead, negative numbers are indicated using the so-called **two's-complement**.

To form the **two's-complement of a binary number**, proceed as follows:

1. Change every 0 bit to a 1 and vice versa.

2. Add 1 to the resulting number.

For example, to form the two's-complement of 0110, we first reverse each bit to obtain

1001

Then, we add 1 to this last number. We can do this by converting to decimal, performing the addition, and then reconverting to binary. However, it is easy to add directly in binary. Just add corresponding places from right to left, just as if you were adding decimal numbers, and follow these rules:

0 + 0 = 0

0 + 1 = 1

1 + 1 = 0 and carry the 1 to the next place

For example, we have

$$
\begin{array}{r}
1001 \\
+ \quad 1 \\
\hline
1010
\end{array}
$$

Thus, the two's-complement of 0110 is 1010.

Here is the connection between two's-complements and negative numbers: a negative number *-n* is represented in binary by the two's-complement of *n*, considered as a 16-bit number. For example, the binary number *0110* equals the positive decimal number *6*. The binary representation of *-6* is obtained as follows. First, consider *0110* as the *16*-bit number

0000 0000 0000 0110

Figure 15-1. **A positive 16-bit number.**

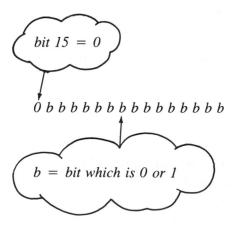

Now form the two's-complement:

1111 1111 1111 1001
*   +   1*

1111 1111 1111 1010

So *-6* is represented by the binary number *1111111111111010*.

Here is an easy way to recognize a negative integer directly from its binary representation. A negative always has its high-order bit equal to 1. Moreover, you may recover the original number by taking the two's-complement a second time. For example, the two's-complement of *1111111111111010* is

0000 0000 0000 0101
*   +   1*

0000 0000 0000 0110

So we retrieve our original number 0110.

TEST YOUR UNDERSTANDING 2 (answer on page 372)
Determine the number represented by the binary number

1111 1111 1001 1100

TEST YOUR UNDERSTANDING 3 (answers on page 372)
Determine the binary representation of

a. *32767*

b. *-32767*

The two's-complement of an integer *n* may be calculated in decimal notation using a very simple procedure:

[two's complement of n] = 65536 - n

For example, the two's-complement of *6* is equal to *65530*. And it is easy to check that *65530* in binary is equal to

1111111111110101

TEST YOUR UNDERSTANDING 4 (answers on page 372)
a. Store the number *-15* in memory location *30000*.

b. Use a PEEK instruction to display the contents of memory location *30000*. What are the contents? Can you explain the results?

The two's-complement procedure may seem to be an obscure way of representing negative numbers. However, it is designed to aid in performing arithmetic among binary numbers with the greatest possible speed.

ASCII Characters

The IBM PC has 255 displayable characters. Each of these characters is given an ASCII code, which is an integer between 0 and 255. A character is represented in memory by this ASCII code and therefore occupies exactly one byte. For example, here is how the string *"This is a test."* is stored in memory:

T	*h*	*i*	*s*		*i*	*s*		*a*		*t*	*e*	*s*	*t*	*.*
84	*104*	*105*	*115*	*32*	*105*	*115*	*32*	*97*	*32*	*116*	*101*	*115*	*116*	*46*

Decimal

54	*68*	*69*	*73*	*20*	*69*	*73*	*20*	*61*	*20*	*7 4*	*65*	*73*	*74*	*2E*

Hexadecimal

So the given string is stored in memory as the consecutive bytes

54,68,69,73,20,69,73,20,61,20,74,65,73,74,2E

TEST YOUR UNDERSTANDING 5 (answer on page 372)
How is this display stored in memory?

Line 1

Line 2

Line 3

Single-Precision Numbers and Variables

A single-precision number is stored in a "scientific notation" requiring four bytes, regardless of the size of the number. The actual algorithm used for the storage is rather complicated and is designed for efficiency in carrying out computations rather than the convenience of the programmer. One of the four bytes is used to store an exponent, which is used as a scaling factor. The other three bytes are used to store a scaled version of the number, called the **mantissa**. We will omit a precise description of the storage algorithm until Appendix A of this chapter.

Double-Precision Numbers

Double-precision numbers are stored using eight bytes. The first byte is the exponent, exactly as for single-precision numbers. The next seven bytes are used for the mantissa. The fact that 56 bits are used for the mantissa rather than 24 allows for the greater number of digit precision in double-precision numbers.

ANSWERS TO TEST YOUR UNDERSTANDINGS 1, 2, 3, 4, and 5

1: *6719*

2: *-1540*

3: a. *0111 1111 1111 1111*
   b. *1000 0000 0000 0001*

4: a. **POKE -15,3000**
   b. What you see is the decimal equivalent of the two's-complement of -15.

5: In decimal, the list of ASCII codes is

76, 105, 110, 101, 32, 49, 13,
76, 105, 110, 101, 32, 50, 13,
76, 105, 110, 101, 32, 51, 13

15.4 Operations on Bytes

In many applications (we shall see a few shortly) it is necessary to perform operations directly on the bits of a byte. In this section, we will introduce you to these operations.

Shift and Truncate Operations

It is often required to move all the bits of a byte to the left or to the right. Such operations are called, respectively, a left shift and a right shift. For example, consider this byte:

1101 0110

If we apply a left shift, we obtain the byte

1010 1100

Note that the rightmost bit is a zero and the original leftmost bit has been "pushed off the end."

Similarly, a right shift applied to the original byte yields

0110 1011

Note that the leftmost bit is replaced by a zero and the original rightmost bit is "pushed off the end."

How may operations such as those just described be carried out in BASIC? Before we describe a method, let's recall that the binary number system is based on powers of two. If we multiply a decimal number by 10, we shift all the digits to the left one place. Similarly, in the binary number system, if we multiply a number by two, we shift the bits to the left one place. Moreover, if we divide a binary number by two (integer division), then we shift the digits to the right by one bit.

In the case of multiplication by two, there may be a bit shifted into bit position nine. We may rid ourselves of this bit by using *mod 256*. (The remainder of division by 256 is exactly the rightmost eight bits.)

Here is how to perform shifts on the value of the integer variable A%:

Left Shift: *2*A% MOD 256*

Right Shift: *A%\2*

The above use of the *mod* operation may be generalized. The remainder on dividing by 2^N is precisely the rightmost N bits. The bits beyond N are replaced by zeros. This process is called **truncation**.

TEST YOUR UNDERSTANDING 1 (answer on page 376)
Write an instruction that shifts the value of A% to the right three bits.

TEST YOUR UNDERSTANDING 2 (answer on page 376)
Write an instruction that truncates the most significant three bits of the value of B%.

Logical Operations on Words

BASIC has a number of built-in operations that you may perform on 16-bit quantities (integers).

NOT. The NOT operation reverses all the bits of a number. For example, consider the number

NOT 0000 1010 1111 0101

We may compute this number by changing every 0 to a 1 and every 1 to a zero. The result is

1111 0101 0000 1010

In BASIC, we may apply the NOT operation to any integer, written in either decimal or hexadecimal form. The NOT operation converts the number to binary form, performs the above computation, and reconverts the number to decimal form. For example, let's compute *NOT 18*. We have

  18 decimal = 0000 0000 0001 0001 binary

so that

  NOT 18 = 1111 1111 1110 1110 binary
  = -19 decimal

AND.   The operation *A AND B* produces a 16-bit number from the 16-bit numbers *A and B*. More precisely, if *A* and *B* are 16-bit quantities, then

  A AND B

is the 16-bit number obtained as follows: compare *A* and *B* bit by bit. For a given bit position, if both *A* and *B* have a one, then the corresponding bit of *A* and *B* is a one. If either *A* or *B* has a zero, the corresponding bit of *A AND B* is a zero. For example, consider the 16-bit quantities

  A = 1101 1011 1000 0000
  B = 1001 0001 0011 1111

Then

  A AND B = 1001 0001 0000 0000

If *A* and *B* are integers given in decimal form, we may also apply the operation AND. The answer will be a decimal number that is obtained by computing *A* and *B* using the respective binary representations of *A* and *B*. (In using these binary representations, remember that a negative number is represented in two's-complement form.) For instance, suppose that *A = 3* and *B = 5*. Then

  A = 0000 0000 0000 0011
  B = 0000 0000 0000 0101
  A AND B = 0000 0000 0000 0001

That is,

  5 AND 3 = 1

OR.   The operation *A OR B* produces a 16-bit number from the two 16-bit numbers *A* and *B*. More precisely, if *A* and *B* are 16-bit quantities, then

  A OR B

is the 16-bit number obtained as follows: Compare *A* and *B* bit by bit. For a given bit position, if either *A* or *B* have a one, then the corresponding bit of *A OR B* is a one. If both A and B have a zero, the corresponding bit of *A OR B* is a zero. For example, consider the 16-bit quantities

A = *1101 1011 1000 0000*

B = *1001 0001 0011 1111*

Then

A OR B = *1101 1011 1011 1111*

If *A* and *B* are integers given in decimal form, we may also apply the operation OR. The answer will be a decimal number that is obtained by computing *A* and *B* using the respective binary representations of *A* and *B*. (Again, in using these binary representations, remember that a negative number is represented in two's-complement form.) For instance, suppose that *A* = *3* and *B* = *5*. Then

A = *0000 0000 0000 0011*

B = *0000 0000 0000 0101*

A OR B = *0000 0000 0000 0111*

That is

5 OR 3 = *7*

XOR.   The operation *A XOR B* is called the **exclusive OR of A and B** and produces a 16-bit result from the two 16-bit numbers *A* and *B*. If *A* and *B* are 16-bit quantities, then

A XOR B

is the 16-bit number obtained by comparing *A* and *B* bit by bit. For a given bit position, if *A* and *B* have different bits, then the corresponding bit of *A* and *B* is a one. If *A* and *B* have the same bits, the corresponding bit of *A XOR B* is a zero. For example, consider the 16-bit quantities

A = *1101 1011 1000 0000*

B = *1001 0001 0011 1111*

then

A XOR B = *0100 1010 1011 1111*

If *A* and *B* are integers given in decimal form, we may also apply the operation XOR. The procedure is similar to that described in our discussion of AND and OR.

Caution: Do not confuse the use of AND, NOT, OR, and XOR within numerical operations and the use of the corresponding words to construct statements in conditional (IF-THEN) instructions. For example, note the use of AND in the expression

A > 1 AND B < 3

In this case, the AND serves as a logical connector. The statement given is true only if both of the statements *A > 1* and *B < 3* are true. In a similar fashion, we may consider statements of the form

NOT (A > 1)

(A > 1) OR (B < 3)

(A > 1) XOR (B < 3)

The first of these statements is true provided that the statement *A > 1* is not true. The second of the statements is true if either of the statements *A > 1* or *B < 3* is true. The third statement is true provided that the statements *A > 1* and *B < 3* are both not true or are both not false.

ANSWERS TO TEST YOUR UNDERSTANDINGS 1 and 2

1: $A\% = A\% \backslash 8$

2: $A\% = (A\% * 8) \backslash 8$

15.5 Some Applications of Byte Operations

In this section, we will apply some of what we have learned about binary numbers and bytes. We will present three applications:

1. We will construct a capitalization function.

2. We will present some advanced graphics tricks using GET and PUT. These tricks will aid in displaying animations.

3. We will explain the mechanics of designing custom characters for screen display.

A Capitalization Function

You may have noticed that BASIC turns alphabetic characters within a program listing into capital letters. For example, if you type a program statement containing the letter *a*, a subsequent listing of the statement will display the letter as *A*. Let's write a program to perform such a conversion.

Of course, we may convert lowercase letters into capital letters using a series of IF...THEN statements of the form

```
IF A$="a" THEN A$="A"
```

(Here *A$* is a string variable containing the letter to be capitalized.) However, such a program would contain many statements, occupy a great deal of memory, and run very slowly. There is a much better way.

To discover the secret relationship between uppercase and lowercase letters, let's look at their respective ASCII codes. Here is a portion of the ASCII table.

Letter	ASCII Code	Letter	ASCII Code
A	65	a	97
B	66	b	98
C	67	c	99
.	.	.	.
.	.	.	.
.	.	.	.
Z	90	z	122

What is the relationship between a letter and its corresponding capital? Well, a quick look at the table shows that the ASCII code of a uppercase letter is 32 less than the ASCII code of the corresponding lowercase letter. And 32 corresponds to one of the bit positions in a byte, namely bit 5. This is no accident, but a result of good planning! Consider the binary equivalents of the ASCII codes for *A* and *a*:

65 decimal = 00000000 01000001 binary

97 decimal = 00000000 01100001 binary

Note that they differ only in the 32's place, namely bit 5. Similarly, consider the ASCII codes for *B* and *b*:

66 decimal = 00000000 01000010 binary

98 decimal = 00000000 01100010 binary

Again the only difference is in bit 5. By subsequent examination of the other letter pairs, we come up with the following rule:

To Convert a Letter From Lowercase To Uppercase:

Change bit 5 in its ASCII code from 1 to 0.

And the change in bit 5 may be accomplished by ANDing the ASCII code with *00000000 11011111 = 223 decimal*. Here's why. For all bits except bit 5, we are ANDing with a 1. If the ASCII code has a 1, the ANDing will have a 1; if the ASCII code has a 0, the ANDing will have a 0. In other words, all bits other than bit 5 will remain unchanged. On the other hand, bit 5 is ANDed with a 0 so it will certainly result in a 0. In particular, if bit 5 is a 1 (lowercase), it is converted to a 0 (uppercase).

On the basis of our discussion, we may finally construct a function FNA$(X$), which converts the character X$ into a uppercase letter if it was lowercase and otherwise leaves X$ alone:

```
DEF FNA(X$) = CHR$(ASC(X$) AND 223)
```

This function starts with a string X$ (any string will do) and computes the ASCII code of its first character. (This is the ASC(X$) part.) The ASCII code is then ANDed with 223 and the resulting ASCII code is converted back into a character. You should test this function out with some examples of characters X$. Here is a program to carry out the tests.

```
1  '*****************************************
2  'This program tests the capitalization
3  'function FNA$(X)
4  '*****************************************
10 DEF FNA$(X$) = CHR$(ASC(X$) AND 223)
20 INPUT "CHARACTER=";X$
30 Z$=FNA$(X$)
40 PRINT "THE CONVERTED CHARACTER IS "; Z$
50 INPUT "TRY ANOTHER CHARACTER (Y/N)";REPLY$
60 IF FNA$(REPLY$)= "Y" THEN 20
70 END
```

This program is interesting in several respects. First, it allows you to try out the capitalization function FNA(X$). Second, it shows you how the function may be used in practice. Observe the instructions in lines 50-70. Line 50 asks if you wish to type another character. It asks for a reply of *Y* or *N*. Most people will not even think much about it and respond with *y* or *n*. Good program design should allow for such responses. One way of doing this is to ask separately if *REPLY$ = Y* or if *REPLY$ = y*. A much cleaner approach is the one taken in line 60. We replace *REPLY$* by *FNA$(REPLY$)*. This converts a reply of *y* into *Y*. Then a single question suffices in line 70.

TEST YOUR UNDERSTANDING 1

Modify the above program so that it leaves *X$* unchanged if it begins with a non-letter character (*A-Z, a-z*).

Some Further Tricks with GET and PUT

In Chapter 12 we introduced the GET and PUT statements, which can be used for transporting images from place to place on the screen. There are several features of these commands which we have yet to discuss.

Recall that GET has the format

`GET (x1,y1)-(x2,y2), <array>`

where *(x1,y1)* and *(x2,y2)* are opposite corners of the rectangle to be stored, and *<array>* is an array that has been dimensioned of a sufficient size to hold the rectangular image. (See our preceding discussion for determining the size of the array.)

Recall that the PUT statement has the form

`PUT (x,y), <array>`

This statement puts the image stored in *<array>* on the screen, with its upper-left corner at the point with coordinates *(x,y)*. Actually, the PUT command offers five modes of displaying the image on the screen. These five modes are indicated by the words

```
PSET
PRESET
XOR
OR
AND
```

The last words should be familiar from our discussion of them earlier in this chapter. Their function in connection with the PUT command is similar to their use in the operations we described.

PUT with the PSET option displays the image in exactly the form in which it was stored. This is done independently of the data that was on the screen. This option is invoked with the command

`PUT (x,y), <array>, PSET`

PUT with the PRESET option displays the image in the array, but in inverse color. A pixel that was stored in color 3 will be displayed in color 0 (background color); color 2 will be displayed in color 1; color 1 will be displayed in color 2; and color 0 will be displayed in color 3. On a monochrome display, the PRESET option will simply reverse the roles of background and foreground. The PRESET option is invoked with the command

`PUT (x,y) <array>, PRESET`

PUT with the AND option displays the recorded image by ANDing it with the image already at the indicated position on the screen. This ANDing takes place pixel by pixel. A pixel is displayed only if the pixel was previously displayed. The AND option is invoked with the command

`PUT (x,y), <array>, AND`

PUT with the OR option displays the recorded image by ORing it with the image already at the indicated position on the screen. This ORing takes place pixel by pixel. A pixel is displayed if either the pixel was previously displayed or the array has the pixel displayed. The OR option is invoked with the command

```
PUT (x,y), <array>, OR
```

PUT with the XOR option displays the recorded image by XORing it with the image already at the indicated position on the screen. This XORing takes place pixel by pixel. In the XOR option, a pixel is displayed provided that it is displayed in **exactly** one of the original screen images and the display image. In particular, a pixel currently displayed on the screen and displayed in the current image will not be displayed. If you PUT the same image twice using the XOR option, then you will restore the screen to its original state. This property of the XOR option is especially useful for animations, since you may move an image across the screen and restore the background to its original state. The XOR option is invoked with either of the commands

```
PUT (x,y), <array>, XOR
PUT (x,y), <array>
```

(The XOR option is the default option. That is, if you use PUT without specifying an option, then the XOR option is assumed.)

The precise color assignments used with the AND, OR, and XOR options are rather complicated and are summarized in the following charts.

AND Color Assignment

Current Color	0	1	2	3
PUT Color				
0	0	0	0	0
1	0	1	0	1
2	0	0	2	2
3	0	1	2	3

OR Color Assignment

Current Color	0	1	2	3
PUT Color				
0	0	1	2	3
1	1	1	3	3
2	2	3	2	3
3	3	3	3	3

XOR Color Assignment

Current Color	0	1	2	3
PUT Color				
0	0	1	2	3
1	1	0	3	2
2	2	3	0	1
3	3	2	1	0

Let's illustrate the action of each of the options PSET, PRESET, AND, OR, and XOR using the following example. Suppose that A% is an 8-pixel by 8-pixel array that contains the letter **A**, obtained from a previous GET operation. (See Figure 15-2) Further, suppose that we use a PUT to place this image on a portion of the screen, which currently has the image in Figure 15-3. The results of each of the various options is described in Figure 15-4.

Figure 15-2. **The contents of A%.**

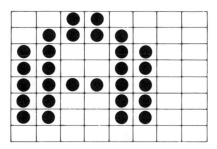

Figure 15-3. **The background.**

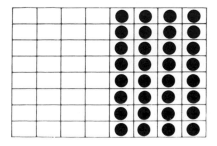

Figure 15-4. **The results of PUT with various options.**

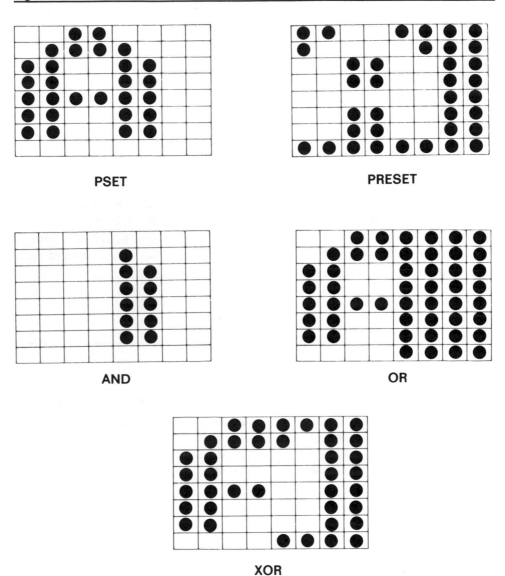

PSET

PRESET

AND

OR

XOR

Designing Custom Characters

We may combine our recently acquired knowledge of bytes and binary numbers with the PUT command to design custom characters for the screen. Here's how.

A character in graphics mode is displayed in a rectangle 8 pixels wide and 8 pixels high. Note that it does not matter whether the character is displayed in medium-resolution or high-resolution mode. The rectangle is always 8 x 8. For example, Figure 15-5 contains the pixels displayed for the letter A.

Figure 15-5. **The letter A.**

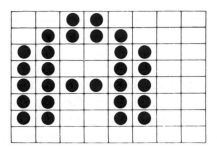

Each character may be described by a series of bytes, corresponding to the various rows of the rectangle. This description is simplest in high-resolution graphics mode. In this case, each pixel corresponds to a single bit, proceeding from left to right. For example, Figure 15-6 shows the bits corresponding to the letter A.

Figure 15-6. **The bits corresponding to the letter A.**

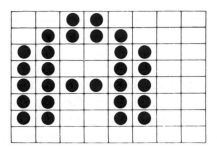

Note that each row of the rectangle corresponds to a single byte, or two hexadecimal digits. In hexadecimal, the letter *A* may be represented by the bytes

&H03, &H78, &HCC, &HCC, &HFC, &HCC, &HCC, &H00

When you perform a GET, the bytes are arranged in the array as follows:

- *A%(0)* = the width of the rectangle
- *A%(1)* = the height of the rectangle
- *A%(2)*, *A%(3)*,... contain the bytes corresponding to the pixels, with two bytes per array element.

For example, the results of GETing the letter *A* to the array *A%* yield the following array contents:

A%(0) = 8

A%(1) = 8

A%(2) = &H7803

A%(3) = &HCCCC

A%(4) = &HCCFC

A%(5) = &H00CC

Note the order in which the bytes appear. As usual, the byte to the left (the one containing the higher-order bits) is the byte **after** the byte to the right.

The above discussion applies to high-resolution graphics mode, in which each pixel corresponds to one bit. In medium-resolution graphics mode, a pixel may be in any one of four colors, numbered 0, 1, 2, 3. In binary, these choices are coded using two bits:

00 = color 0

01 = color 1

10 = color 2

11 = color 3

Each row of the rectangle now contains two bits per pixel, or 16 bits. That is, each row of the rectangle corresponds to one 16-bit integer. In terms of the array, the first row will now completely fill *A%(2)*, the second *A%(3)* and so forth.

We have just described how the GET statement fills an array. With this information, we may omit the GET statement entirely. We may fill an array with the data corresponding to a display without first creating the display on the screen. To do this:

1. Use graph paper to draw the pixels of the display.

2. Convert the rows of the display into binary.

3. Convert the binary numbers into hexadecimal.

4. Fill the 0th array element with the display width, the 1st array element with the display height.

5. Fill the array elements beginning with the 2nd with the hexadecimal numbers of step 3. (Be sure to put the later hexadecimal digits on the left of a 16-bit word.)

6. The array is now ready for PUTing.

Let's illustrate this procedure by creating an array that displays the capital Greek letter *phi*.

We begin by reducing the letter to pixels, as shown in Figure 15-7.

Figure 15-7.   **Pixel representation of the Greek letter** *phi*.

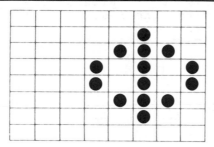

Next, we code the various rows into binary and then hexadecimal form:

row #	binary number	hexadecimal number	array element
1	0000 0000	00	0
2	0010 0000	20	32
3	0111 0000	70	112
4	1010 1000	C8	200
5	1010 1000	C8	200
6	0111 0000	70	112
7	0010 0000	20	32
8	0000 0000	00	0

We may summarize our results in this BASIC program:

```
1  '*********************************
2  ' Create and display at position
3  ' (100,100) the letter "PHI", formed
4  ' from pixels stored in an array.
5  '*********************************
10 DIM A%(9)
20 A%(0)=8: A%(1)=8: A%(2)=0
30 A%(3)=32: A%(4)=112: A%(5)=200
40 A%(6)=200:A%(7)=112: A%(8)=32: A%(9)=0
50 SCREEN 2:CLS
60 PUT (100,100), A%
70 END
```

Replacing the Graphics Character Set

The ASCII character set (ASCII codes 0-127) is stored in ROM, coded in exactly the fashion we have described above for high-resolution graphics mode. That is, each character is described by a sequence of eight bytes. This table of bytes begins at memory location *F000:FA6E*. Here is a program that fills the array A% with the appropriate data from the table for any character you specify.

```
1   '*****************************************
2   'This program looks up the pixels for a
3   'character and stores the resulting
4   'bytes in an array.
5   '*****************************************
100 'Main Program
110 DIM A%(10)
120 A%(0)=8
130 A%(1)=8
140 DEF SEG = &HF000
150 INPUT "CHARACTER TO LOAD";C$
160 OFFSET=8*ASC(C$)+&HFA6E
170 FOR J=0 TO 7
180     B$(J)=HEX$(PEEK(OFFSET+J))
190     IF LEN(B$(J))=1 THEN B$(J)="0"+B$(J)
200 NEXT J
210 FOR J=0 TO 3
220     A%(J+2) = VAL("&H" + B$(2*J+1) + B$(2*J))
230 NEXT J
240 DEF SEG
250 END
```

The above program may be used as a subroutine in various character alteration operations. For example, you may create characters that are vertically enlarged by including duplicates of the bytes corresponding to the various display lines. Here is a program that enables you to load an array with a character that is the expansion of a specified character by a given factor.

```
1   '*************************************
2   'This program creates an array which
3   'contains the pixels for the enlarge-
4   'ment of a user-defined character by
5   'a user-defined factor F.
6   '*************************************
100 DIM A%(10),B%(200)
110 INPUT "FACTOR OF ENLARGEMENT";F
120 INPUT "CHARACTER";C$
130 GOSUB 300:
150 B%(0)=8
160 B%(1)=8*F
170 FOR J=0 TO 7
180    FOR K=0 TO F-1
190        B%(F*J+K+2)=A%(J+2)
200    NEXT K
210 NEXT J
220 END
300 'Load character into array
320 A%(0)=8
330 A%(1)=8
340 DEF SEG = &HF000
360 OFFSET=8*ASC(C$)+&HFA6E
370 FOR J=0 TO 7
380    B$(J)=HEX$(PEEK(OFFSET+J))
390    IF LEN(B$(J)=1 THEN B$(J)="0"+B$(J)
400 NEXT J
```

```
410 FOR J=0 TO 3
420    A$(J+2) = VAL("&H" + B$(2*J+1) + B$(2*J))
430 NEXT J
440 DEF SEG
450 RETURN
```

You may print out the character in the array *B%( )* by using a PUT statement.

TEST YOUR UNDERSTANDING 2
Use the above program to display a letter A that is three times the usual height.

15.6   Some Graphics Tricks

In this section, we discuss various enhancements to the LINE and PAINT statements that require knowing something about binary and hexadecimal numbers.

Enhancements to LINE

Recall the format of the LINE statement:

`LINE (x1,y1)-(x2,y2),color,box`

Here *color* is one of the colors 0-3, *box* is either the letter *B* (= open box) or the letters *BF* (= filled box), and *(x1,y1)* and *(x2,y2)* are the coordinates of the endpoints of the line. After the box parameter, you may add the parameter *style*, which determines the line style. Using this option, you may draw an incredible variety of line styles, including dotted and dashed lines. Figure 15-8 shows some of the possibilities.

Figure 15-8. **Various line styles.**

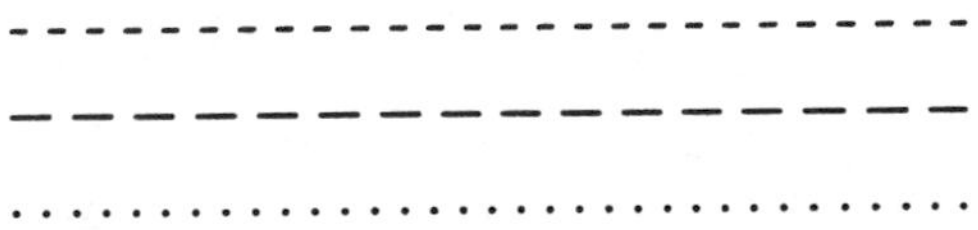

If you make use of the style option, you must code the style as a 16-bit number, input to the program as a hexadecimal number. The **LINE** command refers to this style designation as it plots the pixels of the line. It starts with the left-most bit. If it is a one, it plots the pixel. If it is a zero, then it does not plot the pixel. For the next pixel, LINE looks at the second bit of the style designation, and so forth. After 16 pixels, LINE begins over with the left-most bit. For example, here is a style designator for a dashed line with eight pixels plotted, followed by eight pixels not plotted.

11111111 00000000

In hexadecimal, this style designation is denoted $HFF00. Here is a line that contains a long dash (11 pixels) followed by a one-pixel space, followed by a dot and another space (see Figure 15-9):

binary style designation = 11111111 11111010

hexadecimal style designation = &HFFFA

Figure 15-9. **A line of style** *&HFFFA.*

To connect the points *(50,75)* and *(100,100)* with a line of style *&HFFA*, use the statement

```
LINE (50,75),,,,&HFFFA
```

Note that you must use the correct number of commas as placeholders for the color and box parameters.

TEST YOUR UNDERSTANDING 1 (answer on page 390)
Describe the line with style designation &HAAAA.

You may use the style designation with the *B* parameter, in which case, the required rectangle is drawn with its sides in the requested style. However, you may not use the style designation with the *BF* parameter. If you do, you will generate a syntax error.

Enhancements to PAINT

As you will recall, the PAINT statement allows you to paint a region of the screen with a particular color. In many graphics applications, you may wish to "crosshatch" the region with a particular pattern rather than a solid color. For example, you may wish to shade a region with horizontal lines, with vertical lines, or with a rectangular mesh. BASIC allows you to accomplish such shading with ease.

Recall that the format for PAINT is

PAINT (x,y), paint, boundary

Here *(x,y)* is a point in the region to be painted, *paint* is the color the region is to be painted, and *boundary* is the color of the boundary of the region.

The PAINT enhancement allows the paint parameter to be a string expression describing the figures to be used in shading the region. The string expression may contain as many as 64 bytes. The entire string describes one shading figure. To determine the shading figure, we convert the bytes of the string into binary to obtain an array of the form

1 0 0 1 0 1 1 0   *byte 1*

0 0 1 1 0 0 0 1   *byte 2*

1 0 0 1 0 1 1 0   *byte 3*

These bytes are translated into pixels in the usual way: in high-resolution, the bits are translated into pixels on a one-to-one basis. A one means that the pixel is displayed and a zero means that the pixel is not displayed. In medium-resolution two bits represent one pixel, with the two-bit combination representing one of the four possible colors for the pixel. For example, in high-resolution, the above array stands for the shading character

Figure 15-10.
_____

If this shading character is used, then the region to be painted will be filled with shapes of this sort, starting at the point *(x,y)* and working out to the boundaries.

The above three bytes are specified in hexadecimal as

&H96

&H31

&H96

To construct the corresponding *paint* string, we must convert these bytes into string form using the *CHR$* function. That is, the desired *paint* string is

```
CHR$(&H96) + CHR$(&H31) + CHR$(&H96)
```

The *paint* string option is extremely powerful. For example, we may shade a region using horizontal lines two pixels apart as follows:

1111 1111   *byte 1 = &HFF*

0000 0000   *byte 2 = &H00*

0000 0000   *byte 3 = &H00*

paint string = CHR$(&HFF) + CHR$(0) + CHR$(0)

Here is a short program that draws a circle and paints the interior using the last *paint* string.

```
1 '********************************************
2 'This program draws a circle and paints the
3 'interior using a specified paint string.
4 '********************************************
10 KEY OFF
20 SCREEN 2,0
30 CIRCLE (100,100),75
40 PAINT (100,100), CHR$(&HFF) + CHR$(0) + CHR$(0)
50 LOCATE 1,1
60 END
```

TEST YOUR UNDERSTANDING 2 (answer on page 390)

Write a paint string that will allow shading with vertical lines spaced with one pixel apart.

ANSWERS TO TEST YOUR UNDERSTANDINGS 1 and 2

1: The hexadecimal digit A equals 10, which in binary is 1010. So the given line style consists of dot-space-dot-space-dot-space-dot-space-dot-space-dot-space-dot-space-dot-space.

2: `CHR$(&HAA)`

15.7   Plotting Characters in Graphics Mode

My first business graphics program required me to draw a coordinate system. That was a simple enough task using the LINE statement. I calibrated the axes using tick marks, just as I was accustomed to do in lecturing my calculus students. Still no problem. However, next came the job of labeling the various tick marks. The results were very unsatisfying because I couldn't center the labels on the tick marks.

For example, if I wished to label a vertical tick mark as *4.00*, I could rarely get the label exactly centered on the tick mark! The reason was that the tick mark was drawn using graphics coordinates and the labels were being plotted with text coordinates. Each character is eight pixels wide. And BASIC automatically starts characters at positions whose x-coordinate (graphics coordinate) is divisible by eight. If that placement happens to result in a chart that looks good, fine. If not, too bad!

In response to my frustration, I developed the routine **PLOTSTRING**, which places a string at a particular graphics coordinate. In the following routine, the string is *s$*. I allow for two types of placement: point and center. In the first type, you specify a set of graphics coordinates *(x1,y1)*. The routine will plot *s$*, with the upper-left corner of the first character of *s$* at the point *(x1,y1)*. For center placement, you specify two points, *(x1,y1)* and *(x2,y2)*. The routine then centers s$ within the rectangle *(x1,y1)-(x2,y2)*.

I had so much fun with this routine that I decided to allow for vertical display of strings. There are four possible options, specified by the parameter *c%*:

c% = 1: place at point, horizontal

c% = 2: place at point, vertical

c% = 3: center, horizontal

c% = 4: center, vertical

PLOTSTRING uses the subroutine of the preceding section to read the pixels of a character into an array A%, using the table in ROM.

Here is a listing of the routine PLOTSTRING.

```
28000 '**************PLOTSTRING*******************
28005 'This routine allows precise placement of a string
28010 ' in graphics mode.
28015 ' (x1,y1),(x1,y2) are graphics coordinates
28020 ' s$=string to be placed
28025 ' c%=1:place string horizontally, with left corner of
28030 '      1st character at (x1,y1)
28035 ' c%=2:place string vertically, with left corner of
28040 '      1st character at (x1,y1)
28045 ' c%=3:center string horizontally in the
28050 '      field (x1,y1)-(x2,y2)
28055 ' c%=4:center string vertically in the
28060 '      field (x1,y1)-(x2,y2)
28065 'Maxwidth = largest allowable x-coordinate
28070 'Maxheight = largest allowable y-coordinate
28075 '*****************MAIN ROUTINE*****************
28080    IF C%=1 OR C%=2 THEN X=X1:Y=Y1
28085    ON C% GOSUB 28195,28275,28245,28320
28090    RETURN
28095 *****************SUBROUTINES*****************
28100 'Load character into array
28105    A%(0)=8
28110    A%(1)=8
28115    DEF SEG = &HF000
```

```
28120      OFFSET=8*ASC(C$)+&HFA6E
28125      FOR J=0 TO 7
28130        B$(J)=HEX$(PEEK(OFFSET+J))
28135        IF LEN(B$(J))=1 THEN B$(J)="0"+B$(J)
28140      NEXT J
28145      FOR J=0 TO 3
28150        A%(J+2) = VAL("&H" + B$(2*J+1) + B$(2*J))
28155      NEXT J
28160      DEF SEG
28165      RETURN
28170 'Place character at particular coordinates
28175 'Character =c$, coordinates (x,y)
28180      GOSUB 28100
28185      PUT (X,Y), A%
28190      RETURN
28195 'Place string in field beginning at particular
       coordinates
28200 'Field begins at (x,y), string in S$
28205      WHILE S$ <> ""
28210              IF X>MAXWIDTH THEN 28235
28215              C$=LEFT$(S$,1):S$=MID$(S$,2)
28220              GOSUB 28170: 'place character
28225              IF X<0 THEN 28235
28230                X=X+8
28235      WEND
28240      RETURN
28245 'Center string s$ in field defined by coordinates
       (x1,y1)-(x2,y2)
28250      IF X1>X2 THEN SWAP X1,X2: IF Y1>Y2 THEN SWAP Y1,Y2
28255      L=LEN(S$): C=INT((X2-X1)/8): IF L>C THEN
                                        S$=LEFT$(S$,C)
28260      X=X1+(X2-X1+1)/2-8*LEN(S$)/2+4:Y=Y1+(Y2-Y1+1)/2-4
28265      GOSUB 28195
28270      RETURN
28275 'Display string s$ vertically beginning at
       coordinate (x,y)
28280      WHILE S$ <> ""
28285              IF Y+7>MAXHEIGHT THEN 28315
28290              C$=LEFT$(S$,1):S$=MID$(S$,2)
28295              IF Y<0 THEN 28305
28300              GOSUB 28170: 'place character
28305                Y=Y+8
28310      WEND
28315      RETURN
28320 'Center string s$ vertically in field (x1,y1)-(x2,y2)
28325      IF X1>X2 THEN SWAP X1,X2: IF Y1>Y2 THEN SWAP Y1,Y2
28330      L=LEN(S$): C=INT((Y2-Y1)/8): IF L>C THEN
                                        S$=LEFT$(S$,C)
28335      Y=Y1+(Y2-Y1+1)/2-8*LEN(S$)/2:X=X1+(X2-X1+1)/2-4
28340      IF X<0 THEN X=0 : IF Y<0 THEN Y=0
28345      GOSUB 28275
28350      RETURN
```

PLOTSTRING gives you very precise control of text display in graphics mode. However, you will notice that characters are displayed somewhat more slowly than if you use the PRINT statement. This perceptible difference in speed disappears if PLOTSTRING is used in a compiled program. However, even using the BASIC interpreter, the difference in the appearance of your graphics is worth the slight delay.

You may test PLOTSTRING with a program of the form

```
100 INPUT "S$";S$
110 INPUT "C%";C%
130 INPUT "x1,y1";x1,y1
140 IF C%=3 OR C%=4 THEN INPUT "x2,y2";x2,y2
150 CLS
160 GOSUB 28000
170 END
```

15.8   Extending the PC's Character Set

In text mode, the PC has 255 characters available. The first 128 ASCII codes 0-127 correspond to the usual displayable characters and control codes. ASCII codes 128 through 255 correspond to the graphics characters. The graphics characters are available only in text mode, however. If you try to print CHR$(175), say, when in SCREEN 1 or SCREEN 2, you will get garbage. However, IBM allows you to define your own character set corresponding to the unused ASCII codes. Here's how.

1.   Define the characters in terms of bytes as we have already described. Write them in a list, with eight bytes to a character.

2.   Find a section of memory that is unused. (See below for a way to do this.)

3.   Use POKE to store the list of bytes in consecutive memory locations.

4.   POKE into memory locations *0000:7C* through *0000:7F* the offset and segment address of the first location you used.

5.   The first character in your list now corresponds to ASCII 32 + 128 = 161, the second to ASCII 33 + 128 = 162, and so forth.

For example, let's duplicate the ordinary displayable characters in ASCII codes 161-255. The ROM character table begins at *F000:FA6E*. So we poke *6E* into *0000:007C*, *FA* into *0000:007D*, *00* into *0000:007E*, and *F0* into *0000:007F*. Now ASCII code 161 is a space (= the same as ASCII code 32), ASCII code 193 is an A, and so forth.

Of course, the real power of the above procedure is that you may design your own character sets. It doesn't matter whether you wish to display Russian, Hebrew, or a set of scientific symbols. Your IBM allows you to customize your character set to your needs.

15.9   Some Useful Memory Locations

In a preceding discussion of this chapter, we outlined the layout of memory when BASIC is running. Here are several memory locations useful in working with BASIC.

Location	Contents
0000:007C- *0000:007F*	Beginning address of graphics character generator
0000:0500- *0000:0511*	Beginning segment address of BASIC interpreter

In the following addresses, the segment portion is the start of the BASIC interpreter, contained in the addresses given above.

:002E-:002F	Number of line currently being executed
:0347-:0348	Number of line generating last error
:0030-:0031	Offset into current segment of start of program
:0358-:0359	Offset into current segment of start of variables
:006A	Keyboard buffer indicator (non-zero contents means that there are characters waiting to be read).

15.10   How BASIC Stores Single- and Double-Precision Numbers

We have mentioned that BASIC uses four bytes to store a single-precision number and eight bytes to store a double-precision number. In this section, we will describe the exact method used to code each of these sorts of numbers.

Some Mathematical Preliminaries

We have already learned to convert decimal numbers to binary and binary numbers to decimal, but we discussed this process only in the case of integers. However, it is necessary to deal with numbers with non-zero decimal parts, such as .5, .125, and so forth. Each of these numbers has a representation as a **binary decimal**.

In order to discuss binary decimals, it is necessary to use powers of two that are negative as well as positive. So let's review this notion. Recall that

$$2^{(-1)} = 1/2, \ 2^{(-2)} = 1/2^2 = 1/4,$$

$$2^{(-3)} = 1/2^3 = 1/8, \ \ldots$$

We used the powers *2^0, 2^1, 2^2*, ... to represent the various places in a binary decimal. In a similar fashion, we use the negative powers of two to represent the places to the right of the decimal point in a binary decimal. For example,

.5 = 2^(-1) = .1 binary

.125 = 2^(-3) = .001 binary

TEST YOUR UNDERSTANDING 1 (answer on page 399)

What is the decimal number corresponding to the binary decimal 1.101 ?

To convert a decimal to a binary decimal, we proceed as follows:

1. Convert the integer portion just as described previously.

2. Subtract the integer portion, so that you are left only with the decimal part of the number.

3. Subtract the negative power of two, which leaves a positive remainder that is as small as possible. Put a 1 in the corresponding position of the binary decimal.

4. Repeat step 3 as long as there is a non-zero remainder.

For example, consider the decimal 5.23. The integer portion is 5, corresponding to binary 101. So the integer part of the binary decimal is 101. We subtract off the 5 and are left with .23. We try to subtract off negative powers of two. Clearly 2^-1 = .5 is too big. So we put a zero in the first binary decimal place. Now we try 2^(-2)=.25. Again too big, so we add another zero. Next we try .125. This leaves a positive remainder of .105. So we place a one in the binary decimal and repeat the procedure. Our binary decimal so far is

5.23 decimal = 101.001...

The next negative power of 2 is 2^(-4) = .0625. This leaves a positive remainder of .0425. So we include another one in the binary decimal expansion:

5.23 decimal = 101.0011...

We continue in this fashion. The binary decimal expansion of 5.23 never terminates. (It's like the decimal expansion of 1/3 = .33333...). But we may obtain as many binary places in the expansion as we like.

TEST YOUR UNDERSTANDING 2 (answer on page 399)

Convert the decimal number .875 to a binary decimal.

Single-Precision Numbers

A single-precision number occupies 32 bits, divided into three parts: exponent, sign, and mantissa (see Figure 5-11). The exponent occupies eight bits, the sign one, and the mantissa 23.

Figure 15-11.

```
byte 4          byte 3          byte 2          byte 1

31 ... 24       23  22 ... 17    16 ... 9        8 ...  0
exponent       sign   mantissa    mantissa       mantissa
```

The exponent refers to a power of two by which the mantissa is multiplied. To obtain the exponent byte, take the actual exponent and add 128. For example, if the mantissa is to be multiplied by 2^3, then the exponent byte is $128 + 3 = 131$. This method of coding exponents allows for representation of negative exponents as positive exponent bytes. For example, to multiply the mantissa by $2^{(-8)}$, the exponent byte is $128 + (-8) = 120$. Actual exponents from -128 to +127 (corresponding to exponent bytes of 0 through 255) are allowed.

The sign bit is zero in case of a positive number and one in case of a negative number.

The mantissa portion of a number needs some explaining. Let's take an example. Consider the decimal number 458. In binary, this number equals

1 1100 1010

($458 = 256 + 128 + 64 + 8 + 2 = 2^8 + 2^7 + 2^6 + 2^3 + 2^1$)

Note that if we suppress leading zeros, all binary numbers except zero start out with a one. So it's not really necessary to include the leading one. It may be implied. And to make the number 23 bits long, we add the appropriate number of zeros on the right. So we represent the number by the 23-bit mantissa:

110 0101 0000 0000 0000 0000

To determine the exponent, represent the number in the form of a binary decimal:

.111001010

To obtain this form, it is necessary to move the decimal point to the left nine places. That is,

458 decimal = .111001010 × 2^9

So the exponent in this case in nine, and the exponent byte is 137 decimal, or 1000 1001 binary. In our example, the sign bit is zero since 458 is positive. Finally, we have the result that 458 is represented in memory in the form

1000 1001 0110 0101 0000 0000 0000 0000

TEST YOUR UNDERSTANDING 3 (answer on page 399)

Determine the exponent corresponding to the number 256.

TEST YOUR UNDERSTANDING 4 (answer on page 399)

Determine the representation of the number -832.

Non-integer numbers are handled in a similar fashion. Just make sure to use the binary decimal expansion of the number. For example, the binary decimal

101.1011 0010 0000 1111

corresponds to mantissa

011 0110 0100 0001 1110 0000

and exponent

128 + 3 = 131 = 1000 0011 binary

So the given binary decimal is represented in the form

100 0011 0011 0110 0100 0001 1110 0000

TEST YOUR UNDERSTANDING 5 (answer on page 399)

Determine the way in which the number 5840.75 is stored in memory.

If the binary decimal equivalent of a number goes on for more than 24 bits (including the leading one, which is assumed), then only the leading 24 bits are used. The remaining bits are just thrown away. This is what is responsible for some of the arithmetic anomalies you may observe in the arithmetic of the PC. Certain fractions that are perfectly natural to use happen to have binary decimal expansions that have bits thrown away. When these numbers are then used in arithmetic, the answers may not be exactly what you expect!

Here is an interesting experiment. Place your PC in BASIC and obtain the BASIC prompt *Ok*. In immediate mode, type

X = 5 <ENTER>

This action creates a single-precision variable X and sets it equal to the number 5. Let's test what we have just learned by examining what's stored in memory under the variable X. To determine the location of the beginning of the storage area containing X, type

```
PRINT VARPTR(X) <ENTER>
```

BASIC will respond with a memory location, such as 4161. (Your location may be different, depending on the particular release you are using.) This means that the four bytes corresponding to X are at locations *4161, 4162, 4163*, and *4164*. Let's retrieve the contents of these memory locations using the PEEK instruction. Here are the results:

```
PRINT PEEK(4161)
0
Ok
PRINT PEEK(4162)
0
Ok
PRINT PEEK(4163)
32
Ok
PRINT PEEK(4164)
131
Ok
```

We can see the exponent byte appearing in location *4164*. It's 131, corresponding to an exponent of 3. How about the other bytes? In binary, they correspond to

0 010 0000 0000 0000 0000 0000

So the sign bit is zero and the binary decimal corresponding to the mantissa is

.[1]010 0000 0000 0000 0000 0000

To obtain the actual number, we move the decimal point three places to the right (recall that three is the exponent), to obtain

101.0 0000 0000 0000 0000 0000

That is the number 5. Our description of the internal storage procedure really works.

Double-Precision Numbers

Double-precision numbers work in much the same fashion as single-precision numbers, except that the mantissa is longer, namely 55 bits. The exponent is now in byte eight and the sign bit is in bit seven of byte seven.

ANSWERS TO TEST YOUR UNDERSTANDINGS 1, 2, 3, 4, and 5

1:   *1 5/8*

2:   *.111*

3:   *136*

4:   *1000 1010 1101 0000 0000 0000 0000 0000*

5:   *1000 1101 0011 0110 1000 0110 0000 0000*

16

Using a Printer from BASIC

16.0   Chapter Objectives

UNTIL NOW, WE HAVE USED THE PRINTER in a rather simple fashion, for listing programs and for printing output. In this chapter, we discuss some of the fine points of printer usage, including:

- Printer command sequences.
- An introduction to printer graphics.
- A graphics screen dump that prints the contents of the screen in either of the two graphics modes.

Each printer is different. Printer capabilities and the techniques for accessing them vary widely among manufacturers and even among models by a single manufacturer. The discussion of this chapter applies only to the following printers:

IBM 80 character per second Matrix Printer

IBM 80 character per second Graphics Printer

IBM Color Printer

EPSON MX/80 or MX/100 with either GRAFTRAX-80 or GRAFTRAX-PLUS

EPSON FX/80 or FX/100

EPSON LX/80

EPSON LQ 1500

16.1   Printing Fundamentals

The IBM/EPSON printers accomplish printing by means of a print head with nine wires arranged vertically. A character is sent to the printer as an ASCII code, which is an integer from 0 to 255. Some ASCII codes represent printable characters and some represent commands. In response to a printable ASCII character, the electronics of the printer cause the wires of the print head to ''fire'' in particular combinations that have been pre-programmed. For a given character, the print wires fire 12 times. After each firing, the print head is advanced by 1/12 of a character (1/120 inch). The result is a set of dot patterns arranged within a rectangular grid 9 dots high and 12 dots wide. For example, in Figure 16-1, we show the dot pattern corresponding to the letter A.

Figure 16-1. **The letter A.**

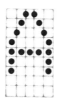

The above sequence of print-head firings happens extraordinarily fast; too fast, in fact, for the eye to observe. Because the print head prints a set of dots within a rectangular matrix, this type of printer is called a **dot-matrix printer**. One advantage of a dot-matrix printer is its great speed. The IBM Dot-Matrix Printer, the IBM Graphics Printer, and the EPSON MX/80, MX/100, and LX/80 are all capable of printing 80 characters per second. The EPSON FX/80 and FX/100 are capable of 160 characters per second. The EPSON LQ 1500 has both a high-quality and draft mode. In draft mode, it can print at 200 characters per second.

However, speed is not the only virtue of these printers. They are capable of some incredibly sophisticated printing assignments. Before we begin to tell you about the various possibilities, let's discuss the way in which the printer receives and interprets information.

Printer Communications

The IBM PC communicates with the printer through a **parallel port**, which is cabled to a connector at the rear of the system unit. If you have a monochrome display interface, then the parallel port is mounted on the monochrome display interface card. If you are using the color/graphics interface, then you must get your parallel port on some other card. The parallel port of the PC is connected to the rear of the printer via a rather heavy cable, which you may purchase from your local computer dealer. (The same cable works for all the printers we are discussing.)

When you send data to the printer (say via an LPRINT statement), here is what happens:

1. The data, in the form of a sequence of one-byte ASCII codes, is deposited in a section of the PC's memory called the **printer buffer**. This is a holding area for data awaiting transmission to the printer.

2. At intervals, the printer requests data. (Don't worry about how it does this.)

3. In response, the computer sends a number of bytes from the printer buffer, taking care to note which bytes were sent.

4. When the printer receives the bytes, it deposits them in its own buffer, to await printing.

5. Whenever the print mechanism needs a character to print, the printer looks to the buffer for a byte.

6. If the buffer is not empty, the printer takes the next byte in line.

7. The byte is decoded. It may correspond to a command or to a printable character.

8. The printer takes action on the byte. Either the command is executed or the character is printed.

9. Steps 5-8 are repeated until the printer's buffer becomes almost empty.

10. The printer then tells the computer to transmit more data and the process begins again with step 3.

The above procedure happens so quickly that you are unlikely to be aware of it. However, it is helpful to understand what is happening "under the hood" if you are to understand the operation (or non-operation) of the printer commands.

Some Elementary Printer Commands

The most rudimentary printer command is the **carriage return-line feed sequence**. A carriage return is a command to return the print head to the left-most end of the print line. A line feed advances the paper by one line. The carriage return-line feed sequence is used at the ends of most lines to reposition the print head for the beginning of the next line. In fact, the statements LPRINT and LPRINT USING automatically insert the carriage return-line feed sequence, unless you suppress it by using a semicolon at the end of the statement, as in

```
LPRINT A$;
LPRINT USING "##.##";A,B,C;
```

A carriage return is indicated by ASCII code 13 or ASCII code 141. A line feed is indicated by ASCII code 10. In theory, then, a carriage return-line feed sequence should be generated by the string

```
CHR$(13)+CHR$(10)
```

However, there is a slight catch. IBM PC BASIC automatically adds the *CHR$(10)* whenever it sees *CHR$(13)*. So the carriage return-line feed sequence may be generated with the command

```
LPRINT CHR$(13);
```

If you wish to send a carriage return without a line feed, you must use ASCII code 141.

You may use the carriage return without the line feed to produce some interesting print effects. For example, you may backspace and then overprint some characters. Here is a program that prints the string "BASIC", then backspaces to the beginning of the string and overprints each letter with a /.

```
1  '*****************************************
2  'This program prints the word BASIC and
3  'then overprints it with slashes.
4  '*****************************************
10 LPRINT "BASIC";
20 LPRINT CHR$(141); :'Carriage return, no line feed
30 LPRINT "/////"    :'Overprint and carriage return-
                      line feed
```

In the above example, we used the carriage return to go back to the beginning of the line. However, in some overprint operations, you may wish to go back only a single space. This may be accomplished with the backspace command. You may backspace the print head one character with ASCII code *8*:

```
LPRINT CHR$(8);
```

Here is a program that prints the string *BASIC* and overprints the *C* with a /, then prints *PASCAL* in character position 30 on the same line.

```
10 LPRINT "BASIC";
20 LPRINT CHR$(8);
30 LPRINT "/";
40 LPRINT TAB(30) "PASCAL"
50 END
```

A word of caution: try this program:

```
10 LPRINT "BASIC";
```

When you try to run it, nothing seems to happen. Actually, the string *BASIC* is sent to the printer's buffer. However, it is held there, until the buffer fills up. (Printing partial buffers is inefficient.) You may force release of the printer buffer by giving a carriage return-line feed sequence. For example, the program

```
10 LPRINT "BASIC"
```

will result in immediately printing the string *BASIC*, since the automatic carriage return-line feed sequence has not been suppressed.

Just as the line feed command allows you to advance the paper by one line, the form feed command allows you to advance the paper to the beginning of the next page. Form feed is indicated by ASCII code 12.

Printing Mailing Labels.   You may use your printer to print mailing address labels. Here's how. You can buy peel-off labels on continuous form backing. These labels are available in several layouts, including one and three labels across. Let's assume that we are dealing with labels 3 inches wide and 15/16 inches high, with a 1/16-inch vertical space between labels. At six lines to the inch vertical spacing, each label has room for five lines. The sixth line spaces to the beginning of the next label. The layout of two consecutive labels is shown in Figure 16-2. (Of course, one or more of the lines can be blank.)

Figure 16-2.   **2 Two consecutive labels.**

```
Line 1
Line 2
Line 3
Line 4
Line 5

Line 1
Line 2
Line 3
Line 4
Line 5
```

I usually use labels three inches wide. Since the print on the printer is 10 characters to the inch, this allows up to 30 characters per line. When I use labels that are two across, the first label begins in print column 1, and the second begins in print column 50. (These numbers depend on the particular label.)

Below are three programs that do various label printing tasks. The first program allows printing multiple copies of a single label, using forms containing only one label across. The second program performs the same task for forms containing two labels across. I use these programs for generating address labels for people I communicate with often. I also use such labels when I travel. I address the labels to my home address and regularly mail papers home, rather than carry them with me for the duration of the trip.

The third program takes addresses from a mailing list and prints a set of corresponding labels on forms containing one label across. It is assumed that the file containing the addresses is a random access file in which each record contains five fields (one per label line) each containing 20 characters.

Here are the three programs.

1. Copies of a single label, one across

```
10    DIM L$(6)
20    INPUT "NUMBER OF COPIES";NUMBER
30    FOR J=1 TO 5
40      PRINT "LINE";J;
50      INPUT L$(J)
60    NEXT J
70    FOR K=1 TO NUMBER
80      FOR J=1 TO 6
90        LPRINT L$(J)
100     NEXT J
110   NEXT K
120   END
```

2. Copies of a single label, two across

```
10    DIM L$(6)
20    INPUT "NUMBER OF COPIES";NUMBER
30    FOR J=1 TO 5
40      PRINT "LINE";J;
50      INPUT L$(J)
60    NEXT J
70    FOR K=1 TO NUMBER
80      FOR J=1 TO 6
90        LPRINT L$(J) TAB(50) L$(J)
100     NEXT J
110   NEXT K
120   END
```

3. Print Labels from a Mailing List

```
10    DIM L$(6)
20    INPUT "FILE NAME OF MAILING LIST";FILENAME$
30    OPEN FILENAME$ AS #1
40    FIELD #1, 20 AS L$(1), 20 AS L$(2), 20 AS L$(3),
                20 AS L$(4), 20 AS L$(5)
50    WHILE NOT EOF(1)
60      GET #1
70      FOR K=1 TO 6
80        LPRINT L$(K)
90      NEXT K
100   WEND
110   CLOSE
120   END
```

16.2   Printer Command Sequences

Your printer is capable of a great many options with regard to type style, print spacing, page length, and so forth. This section presents an organized look at the various command sequences available to you.

Certain printer commands are given by means of a single ASCII code. For example, a carriage return is given with ASCII code 13. However, certain printer commands are given as a sequence of ASCII codes. For such commands, the sequence of codes begins with ASCII code 27 (= Escape). This ASCII code tells the printer that the following ASCII codes are to be interpreted as part of a command rather than as printable characters. For example, consider the sequence of ASCII codes

27, 78, 3

It instructs the printer to skip three lines at the end of the page. This allows you to skip over the perforation between consecutive sheets of paper. You may communicate this sequence of ASCII codes to the printer as you would any other ASCII codes, using the LPRINT statement

```
LPRINT CHR$(27);CHR$(78);CHR$(3);
```

Line Spacing

The following commands are available for adjusting the vertical line spacing:

Action	Command Sequence
Set line spacing to 1/6 inch	27, 50
Set line spacing to 1/8 inch	27, 48
Set line spacing to 7/72 inch	27, 49
Set line spacing to n/72 inch	27, 65, n, 27, 50[1]
	27, 65, n[2]
Set line spacing to n/216 inch[1]	27, 51, n
Set line spacing to n/216 inch[1] for current line only.	27, 74, n
Default setting: line spacing = 1/6 inch	

Figure 16-3 shows some samples of various vertical line spacings.

Page Length and Layout

This group of commands allows you to set the length of the page and the amount of space to skip in order to avoid the perforations in continuous forms.

Set page length to n lines	27, 67, n
Set page length to n inches[1]	27, 67, n, 0
Leave n lines blank at bottom of page (= skip perforation)[1]	27, 78, n

---

[1]IBM printers only.
[2]Non-IBM printers only.

Cancel skip perforation[1]   27, 79

Default setting: Page length = 66 lines = 11 inches

Notes:

a.   You must set the page length before giving the *Skip Perforation* command.

b.   The *Skip Perforation* command causes the number of printed lines to be decreased by the specified skip. For example, a skip of 10 lines and standard page length will cause pages to consist of 56 lines followed by 10 blank lines.

c.   You may wish to adjust the paper so that any skip is evenly distributed between the bottom of a page and the top of the following one.

d.   The beginning of the page is set when the printer is turned on. Any form feed commands make reference to the latest vertical line spacing and the latest page length information in spacing to the top of the next page.

Figure 16-3.   **Examples of vertical line spacing.**

```
LINE SPACING 8 /72 INCHES
LINE SPACING 10 /72 INCHES
LINE SPACING 12 /72 INCHES
LINE SPACING 14 /72 INCHES

LINE SPACING 16 /72 INCHES

LINE SPACING 18 /72 INCHES

LINE SPACING 20 /72 INCHES

LINE SPACING 22 /72 INCHES

LINE SPACING 24 /72 INCHES
```

Print Style

The IBM/EPSON printers are capable of a number of print styles, including emphasized, double strike, double width, compressed, underlined, and subscript/superscript. We may group these attributes as follows:

Group A: Normal
   Compressed
   Emphasized

---

[1]IBM printers only.

Group B: Double Strike
   Subscript
   Superscript

Group C: Double Width

Group D: Underline

You may combine attributes by selecting at most one attribute from each group. For example, you may select print that is simultaneously compressed, subscript, and double width. However, you may not select print simultaneously compressed and emphasized.

Figure 16-4 shows some samples of the various print styles possible with your printer.

Here are the print commands that govern the various print styles:

Emphasized print ON	27, 69
Emphasized print OFF	27, 70
Double strike ON	27, 71
Double strike OFF	27, 72
Subscript ON[1]	27, 83, 1
Superscript ON[1]	27, 83, 0
Subscript/Superscript OFF[1]	27, 84
Compressed ON	15
Compressed OFF	18
Double-width ON (current line only)	14
Double-width OFF	20
Underline ON[1]	27, 45, 1
Underline OFF[1]	27, 45, 0

Notes:

a.   The double-width style prints five characters to the inch, but is the same height as standard print.

b.   The compressed print style prints 132 characters per 8-inch line.

---

[1]Not available with the IBM dot-matrix printer or EPSON MX/80.

Figure 16-4. **Various print styles.**

```
This is the standard type font.
This line is emphasized.
This line is double-struck.
This line is double width.
This line is condensed.
This line is italics.
```

Tabs

Set horizontal tabs at columns n1,n2,...,nk	27, 68, n1, n2,...,nk,0
Horizontal tab	9
Cancel horizontal tabs	27, 68, 0
Set vertical tabs at columns n1,n2,...,nk	27, 66, n1, n2, ...,nk, 0
Vertical tab	11
Cancel vertical tabs	27, 66, 0

16.3   Printer Graphics

In this section, we will discuss the graphics capabilities of the IBM/EPSON printers. Our discussion will not apply to the IBM Matrix Printer, unless you have equipped it with GRAFTRAX-80 or GRAFTRAX-PLUS.

As we have mentioned, the print head has nine wires arranged vertically. In the graphics mode, only the top eight of these wires are used. Figure 16-5 shows the eight wires used in the graphics modes and numbers them, from bottom to top with the numbers 0 through 7.

Each print wire corresponds to a single printed dot. You may request the print head to print any combination of dots, corresponding to the eight wires used in graphics mode. Figure 16-6 shows a number of typical dot patterns.

A dot pattern is specified as a single byte, with wire 0 corresponding to bit 0, wire 1 corresponding to bit 1, and so forth. The most significant bit corresponds to the top print wire. Figure 16-6 indicates the bytes corresponding to each of the given bit patterns.

Figure 16-5.   **The print head wires.**

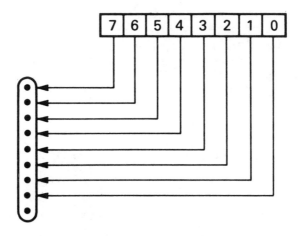

Figure 16-6.   **Some typical dot patterns.**

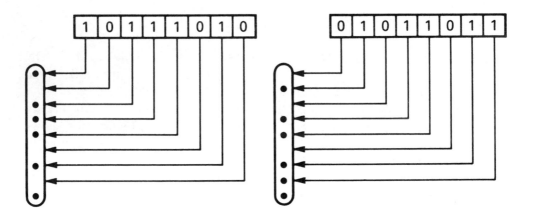

TEST YOUR UNDERSTANDING 1 (answer on page 416)

Determine the bytes corresponding to the following dot patterns:

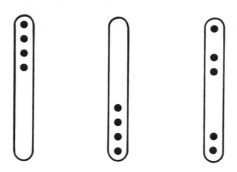

TEST YOUR UNDERSTANDING 2 (answers on page 416)

Determine the dot patterns corresponding to the following bytes:

a.   *&HFF*

b.   *&H0F*

c.   *&H1A*

You may specify more complex dot patterns by representing them in terms of a number of 8-dot vertical patterns like those above. For example, consider the following dot pattern that forms the letter *A* in Figure 16-7.

Figure 16-7.

It is formed of a grid 11 × 8 and may be represented as 11 vertical 8-bit dot patterns. Figure 16-8 shows the dot patterns with their corresponding byte representations.

Figure 16-8.

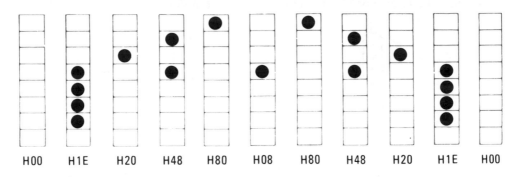

H00 H1E H20 H48 H80 H08 H80 H48 H20 H1E H00

TEST YOUR UNDERSTANDING 3 (answer on page 416)

Determine the dot configuration determined by the bytes

&HFE, &H01, &H00, &H01, &H00, &H01, &H00, &HFE

TEST YOUR UNDERSTANDING 4 (answer on page 416)

Determine the bytes corresponding to the following dot configuration (a mathematical symbol meaning ''sum''):

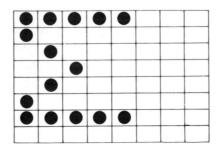

Horizontal Dot Placement

There are three graphics modes, with the following horizontal dot densities:

Medium-Resolution: 480 dots per 8-inch line

High-Resolution: 960 dots per 8-inch line

Ultra-High Resolution[1]:   1920 dots per 8-inch line

In medium-resolution, adjacent dots have a noticeable horizontal space between them. In high-resolution, this space is eliminated. In ultra-high resolu-

---

[1]IBM Graphics Printer or EPSON with GRATRAX-PLUS.

tion, adjacent dots actually overlap. For each density, you may, in principle, print any 8-dot vertical pattern in each of the horizontal dot positions on a line. (See below for an exception.) For example, in medium-resolution mode, you may print 480 vertical 8-bit patterns per 8-inch line.

Actually, it is possible to mix graphics patterns with text. For example, you might print a line consisting of 50 standard printed characters (at 10 characters to the inch = 5 inches), followed by 120 graphics patterns (at 60 per inch = 2 inches), followed by 10 standard printed characters.

As with most things in life, increasing the resolution comes at a price. If you wish to use high-resolution without any restrictions in dot placement, you can print only at half the speed of medium-resolution. A similar statement goes for ultra-high resolution. If you wish to retain the speed, you must live with some restrictions in dot placement. In order for high-resolution to run at full printer speed, you cannot print two dots that are horizontally adjacent to one another. In ultra-high resolution, you can print dots only in every third horizontal dot position.

In order to initiate a printer graphics mode, it is necessary to give an escape sequence that tells the computer:

1. The graphics mode.
2. The speed.
3. The number of vertical 8-bit graphics patterns forthcoming.

These three data items are expressed by a four-byte code:

27 m n1 n2

where *m* is a byte denoting the graphics mode/speed and *n1* and *n2* are bytes that, together, indicate the number of vertical 8-bit graphics patterns to come. Here are the meanings of *m, n1,* and *n2:*

$m = 75:$ 480 dots per 8-inch line

$m = 76:$ 960 dots per 8-inch line, half speed

$m = 89:$ 960 dots per 8-inch line, full speed, no adjacent dots

$m = 90:$ 1920 dots per 8-inch line, full speed; can print only every third dot (not available with GRAFTRAX-80)

$n1 =$ the remainder obtained when the number of graphics patterns is divided by 256

$n2 =$ the number of graphics patterns divided by 256 (integer part)

Thus, *n1* and *n2* satisfy this relationship:

<number of graphics patterns> $= 256*n2 + n1$

For example, suppose that you wish to print 400 graphics patterns in medium-resolution mode. Divide 400 by 256. The quotient is 1 and the remainder is 144. That is,

$400 = 256*1 + 144$

Therefore, $n2 = 1$ and $n1 = 144$. The command that specifies 400 graphics patterns in medium-resolution mode is then given by the sequence of bytes

27, 75, 144, 1

As a second example, suppose that we wish to print the letter *A*, given as the sequence of nine graphics patterns, as specified in the hexadecimal bytes

&H1E   &H20   &H48   &H80   &H08   &H80   &H48   &H20   &H1E

Further, suppose that we wish to use low speed, high-resolution mode. Since

$9 = 0*256 + 9$

we have $n1 = 9$ and $n2 = 0$. We initiate the desired printing pattern with the sequence of bytes

27, 76, 9, 0

We follow these bytes with the bytes representing the nine graphics patterns. Here is a program that prints the desired nine graphics patterns.

```
10 LPRINT CHR$(27);CHR$(76);CHR$(9);CHR$(0);
20 LPRINT CHR$(&H1E);CHR$(&H20);CHR$(&H48);CHR$(&H80);
30 LPRINT CHR$(&H08);CHR$(&H80);CHR$(&H48);CHR$(&H20);
40 LPRINT CHR$(&H1E);
50 END
```

Note that we did not allow any carriage returns in any of the LPRINT statements. Furthermore, note that we specified the graphics patterns in hexadecimal rather than decimal. This is because it is easier to go from the actual dot pattern to hexadecimal. Translating the hexadecimal into decimal would provide room for errors. Finally note that we sent each hexadecimal byte to the printer via a CHR$ statement. You might wonder why we don't just LPRINT the hexadecimal bytes directly, as in, say

```
LPRINT &H1E
```

This approach will not work, however, for it sends the printer the number &H1E. BASIC automatically translates this number into its decimal equivalent 31. BASIC then sends the printer the decimal digits 3 and 1, coded as ASCII codes. What gets sent are the two bytes *&H33* and *&H31*. This is not the same thing as sending the hexadecimal byte *&H1E*.

The above program is extremely hard to read. A better approach is as follows:

```
10 INIT$= CHR$(27)+CHR$(76)+CHR$(9)+CHR$(0)
20 A$ = CHR$(&H1E)+CHR$(&H20)+CHR$(&H48)
        +CHR$(&H80)+CHR$(&H08)+CHR$(&H80)
        +CHR$(&H48)+CHR$(&H20)+CHR$(&H1E)
30 LPRINT INIT$;
40 LPRINT A$;
50 END
```

Figure 16-9.
_____

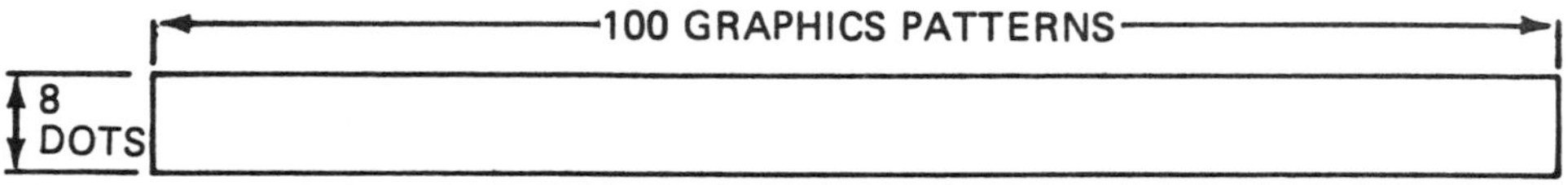

As a further example, let's draw a box as shown in Figure 16-9. The box is 100 graphics patterns wide in high-resolution. The bottom of the box is drawn by print wire 0 and the top by print wire 7. We may draw this box out of two graphics patterns, one consisting of all eight dots (for both ends) and a second consisting of only the top and bottom dot. The hexadecimal equivalents for these dots are, respectively, *&HFF* and *&H81*. (Check this!) Here is a program that draws the box.

```
10 INIT$=CHR$(27)+CHR$(76)+CHR$(100)+CHR$(0)
20 SIDE$=CHR$(&HFF)
30 MIDDLE$=CHR$(&H81)
40 LPRINT INIT$;
50 LPRINT SIDE$;
60 FOR J=1 TO 98
70   LPRINT MIDDLE$;
80 NEXT J
90 LPRINT SIDE$;
100 END
```

Note that you may mix ordinary text and graphics. For example, let's print the phrase *WRITE YOUR ANSWER IN THE BOX.* immediately to the left of the box, and the phrase *STOP* immediately to the right. Our printed line should look like the one shown in Figure 16-10.

Figure 16-10.

WRITE YOUR ANSWER IN THE BOX [============================] STOP

Here is a program to print this line.

```
10  LPRINT "WRITE YOUR ANSWER IN THE BOX.";
20  INIT$=CHR$(27)+CHR$(76)+CHR$(100)+CHR$(0)
30  SIDE$=CHR$(&HFF)
40  MIDDLE$=CHR$(&H81)
50  LPRINT INIT$;
60  LPRINT SIDE$;
70  FOR J=1 TO 98
80    LPRINT MIDDLE$;
90  NEXT J
100 LPRINT SIDE$;
110 LPRINT "STOP"
120 END
```

This program prints the desired line and does a carriage return to the next line. (There is no semicolon on line 110.)

Note that line 10 prints in ordinary text, and lines 40-100 in high-resolution graphics mode. Line 110 returns to ordinary text. It is not necessary to give any special command to return to text mode. After the specified number of graphics patterns, the printer automatically reverts to ordinary text. Any special print modes (emphasized, subscript, compressed, etc.) in effect before entry into graphics mode remain in effect on return to text mode.

If you print two consecutive lines of graphics with default line spacing (1/8 inch), you will notice that there is a small blank area between them. You may eliminate this space making a continuous graphics pattern. The secret is to use 8/72-inch spacing. (This corresponds to nine lines to the inch as opposed to the default eight lines per inch.) You may set this spacing using the command

```
LPRINT CHR$(27);CHR$(65);CHR$(8);CHR$(27);CHR$(50);
    (IBM Graphics Printer)
LPRINT CHR$(27);CHR$(65);CHR$(8);
    (others)
```

You may print as many consecutive graphics lines as you wish. However, if you then wish to return to printing text, remember to reset the vertical line spacing.

ANSWERS TO TEST YOUR UNDERSTANDINGS 1, 2, 3, and 4

1: a. &H11
    b. &H0F
    c. &HFA

2:

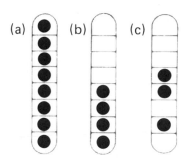

3:

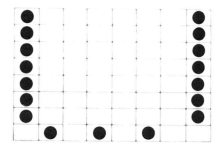

4: *&HC6, &HAA, &H92, &H8s, &H82, &H99, &H00, &H00*

16.4 A Graphics Screen Dump

Let's use what we have learned to write a program that prints the contents of the screen in either medium- or high-resolution graphics mode. Our program is designed as a subroutine to be called within another program. Once you have the desired image on the screen, just call this subroutine and it will print the contents of the screen, pixel by pixel.

To start, let's assume that we are dealing with an image in high-resolution graphics mode. The image is then 640 pixels wide and 200 pixels high. We don't wish to impose any restrictions on printing of adjacent dots, so we are stuck with printing in medium-resolution graphics mode. Of course, this allows us only 480 dots across a line, not enough to print a line of the screen. The solution to this dilemma is to print the screen sideways. The lower left corner of the screen will be printed at the upper left side of the paper. The upper left corner of the screen will correspond to the upper right corner of the paper. (See Figure 16-11.)

Our basic idea is to use the GET statement to read pixels of the screen, from bottom to top, in columns eight pixels wide. (See Figure 16-12.)

Each GET statement will yield a single byte, one bit for each of the eight pixels. This byte will be sent to the printer and printed as a graphics pattern. Each row of graphics patterns on the printer will correspond to a single column

Figure 16-11.

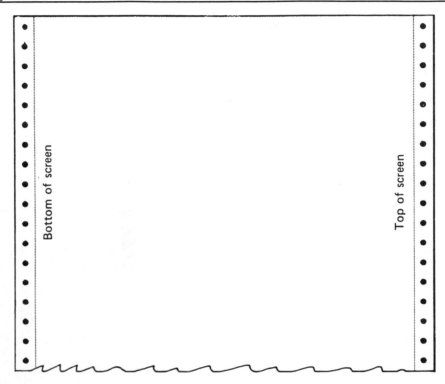

of eight pixels. Since the screen is 640 pixels wide, we will need to break the screen into 80 columns.

At 1/9 inch per column, the screen will print as 80/9 = 8.9 inches down the page. On the other hand, the width of the printed image is 200 dots, or 200/60 = 3.3 inches. As you can see, the perspective is quite distorted. The image is almost three times as long as it is high. To make up for this deficiency, let's print each graphics pattern twice. This will expand the printed image across the page to 400 dots = 400/60 = 6.7 inches. This is close to the usual 4 to 3 ratio between the horizontal and vertical measurements of the screen.

To center the image vertically on the page, we begin with one inch of space at the top of the page. Since the image will be approximately 8.9 inches down the page, this leaves about a 1-inch space at the bottom, which centers the image. Across each printed line, we are using 6.67 inches. To center the image, we must have a space of approximately .9 inches on each side of a line. Since there are 10 characters to the inch, we leave a 9-character space at the beginning of the line.

One last problem before we write our program: BASIC automatically inserts carriage returns at the end of every line. In fact, unless you tell it otherwise, it assumes that a line has ended after 80 characters and sends a carriage return-line feed sequence. In our graphics screen dump, we will be sending several hundred

Figure 16-12.

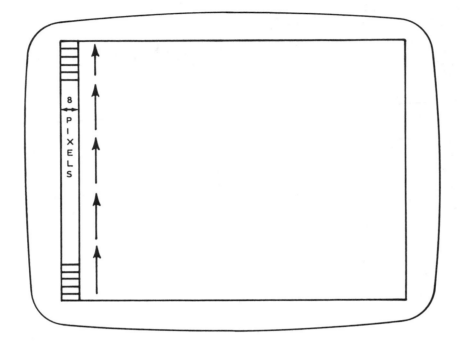

"characters" per line. (As far as BASIC is concerned, each byte sent is a "character.") We must somehow disable this automatic feature. This may be done using the *WIDTH* instruction. The statement

```
WIDTH "LPT1:",255
```

tells BASIC to assume an infinite line width for the printer. This statement disables the automatic carriage return-line feed.

After all these considerable preliminaries, here is our screen dump program.

```
1  '**************************************************
2  'This program is a subroutine which can be
3  'incorporated into a program to print the
4  'contents of a graphics screen (SCREEN 1 or
5  'SCREEN 2).
6  '**************************************************
1000 'IBM GRAPHICS PRINTER VERSION
1010 'Initialization
1020 DIM Z%(2)
1030 WIDTH "LPT1:",255
1040 'Print Screen
1050 LINESPACE9$=CHR$(27)+CHR$(65)+CHR$(8)
1060 LINESPACE6$=CHR$(27)+CHR$(65)+CHR$(12)
1070 GRAPH400$=CHR$(27)+CHR$(75)+CHR$(144)+CHR$(1)
1080 LPRINT LINESPACE9$;
1090 FOR J%=1 TO 9
1100     LPRINT
```

```
1110 NEXT J%
1120 FOR COL%=0 TO 79
1130      LPRINT SPACE$(9);
1140      LPRINT GRAPH400$;
1150      FOR ROW%=199 TO 0 STEP -1
1160           GET (8*COL%+7,ROW%)-(8*COL%,ROW%),Z%
1170           LPRINT CHR$(Z%(2))+CHR$(Z%(2));
1180      NEXT ROW%
1190      LPRINT
1200 NEXT COL%
1210 FOR J%=1 TO 10
1220      LPRINT
1230 NEXT J%
1240 LPRINT LINESPACE6$;
1250 RETURN
```

We have explained the reason behind most of the program already. However, lines 1130 and 1140 deserve some comment. The pixels corresponding to *(COL%+7,ROW%)-(COL%,ROW%)* go across the column *COL%* at row *ROW%*, proceeding from right to left. These pixels are stored in the array *Z%*. Recall the manner in which GET stores this information. *Z%(0)* contains the width of the rectangle being stored, in this case eight; *Z%(1)* contains the height of the rectangle being stored, namely 1; *Z%(2)* contains the first eight pixels of the first row of the rectangle. In this case, the entire rectangle has only eight pixels. Z%(2) contains precisely the information we want, and the information is stored with the most-significant bit corresponding to the right-most pixel. (The order of storage is guaranteed by the order in which we have stated the endpoints of the rectangle in line 1130.)

A few further comments.

1. The above program is written for the IBM Graphics Printer. To use the program on the EPSON printers, replace lines 1050-1060 with

    ```
    1050 LINESPACE9$=CHR$(27)+CHR$(65)+CHR$(8)
    1060 LINESPACE6$=CHR$(27)+CHR$(65)+CHR$(12)
    ```

2. The above program is written to be used in high-resolution graphics mode (SCREEN 2). We leave the modifications necessary to print the screen in medium-resolution graphics mode for the exercises.

17
Input the Professional Way

17.0 Chapter Objectives

In this chapter, we take a closer look at the input process and develop routines to allow for "bullet-proof" input of data. In particular, we develop routines to:

- Input a character restricted to a particular set.
- Input a string of limited length.
- Input a number of particular type and within an allowable range.

17.1 Why You Need an INPUT Routine

When you saw the title of this chapter, you probably thought: "I know about input. I can use INPUT and LINE INPUT to handle my programs' input needs." Well, I have some bad news. If you want to write professional-level programs, the BASIC input statements INPUT and LINE INPUT leave much to be desired.

For example, suppose that your program has just set up a menu with choices to be input by the user, and suppose that INPUT is used to accept the user response. BASIC responds to a type mismatch (string instead of number) with the prompt

```
Redo from start?
```

This usually wrecks the carefully planned screen layout you have just created.

INPUT accepts as numerical input any number legal in BASIC, such as *1.7839E-18*. For each input to your program, it is your responsibility to check that numbers are of the required type (say, positive or an integer between 1 and 10). But how do you prevent the program user from inputting a number such as *1E40*, which is beyond the limits allowed by BASIC? Before you can analyze the input, BASIC declares an overflow error. And you can't RESUME after an overflow!

As for string input, you usually must control the length of input. (Say, a name cannot have more than 20 characters.) Or, suppose that a question calls for a Y or N response. Your program should also accept *y* or *n* and reject all other letters.

As you can see from the above recitation, input is a complicated business. And, if you wish to write professional level programs, you must be able to control your input so that you force the user to provide input the program can use. That's the purpose of an input routine.

In this chapter, I'll describe an input routine I've developed that avoids all the problems mentioned above. It is a complex routine, but you'll have no trouble understanding it. It was more complicated to build than it is to comprehend. And now that the work's done, you can use it in your own programs.

Our input program is called *INPUT* and is composed of three main routines, called *KEYIN, SCREENIN*, and *NUMBERCK*.

KEYIN reads the keyboard, one character at a time. On the basis of user supplied information, *KEYIN* accepts certain characters and rejects others. You may request *KEYIN* to change input to all uppercase letters.

SCREENIN is a screen entry routine, which displays input characters in a specific field on the screen. *SCREENIN* allows some character editing and passes on extended ASCII codes for further analysis.

NUMBERCK is a routine that analyzes a string to determine if it is in an acceptable format to be converted into a number. If possible, *NUMBERCK* performs the conversion and passes the number back to the main program. *NUMBERCK* also determines whether the converted number is an integer.

Together, these three routines allow you to input data to your program knowing that you are in total control.

17.2   Inputting Characters

As the first part of our professional input package, let's build the routine *KEYIN*, which inputs characters from the keyboard. *KEYIN* continually inspects the keyboard buffer to determine if a key has been pressed. If so, the keyboard buffer is read via INKEY$ and the result is put into the variable *C$*. Next, *KEYIN* determines if the key corresponds to an extended ASCII code. (Is the length of *C$* two?) If so, *C$* is replaced by its second byte.

After reading the keyboard buffer, *KEYIN* goes to one of two analysis sections to determine whether the character is acceptable. There is one analysis section for ordinary ASCII codes and one for extended ASCII codes.

In general, the acceptable characters will vary with the section of the program. For one input you may wish to accept only the characters *Y, y, n*, or *N*; for another, you may wish to accept only the digits *1, 2, 3, 4, 5*; and so forth. There is a variable *CALLER* that identifies a set of acceptable characters. For each value of *CALLER* used, you must define six values:

```
MINKEY(CALLER), MAXKEY(CALLER),
SPECIALKEY$(CALLER)
EXTMINKEY(CALLER), EXTMAXKEY(CALLER),
EXTSPECIALKEY$(CALLER)
```

The first three values correspond to ordinary ASCII codes and the second three to extended ASCII codes. For example, suppose that *CALLER = 1* and

```
MINKEY(1)=32, MAXKEY(1)=127,
SPECIALKEY$(1)=CHR$(8)+CHR(13)+CHR$(27)
```

then *KEYIN* will accept any character with an ASCII code from 32 to 127 inclusive (these are the displayable, non-graphics characters), as well as the special characters *CHR$(8)* (backspace), *CHR$(13)* (carriage return), and *CHR$(27)* (Esc). Further, suppose that

```
EXTMINKEY(1)=59, EXTMAXKEY(1)=68,
EXTSPECIALKEY$(1)=""
```

Then *KEYIN* will accept extended ASCII codes 59 through 68 (function keys F1 through F10) and no other extended ASCII codes.

TEST YOUR UNDERSTANDING 1 (answer on page 425)
What are the values of the six variables if *KEYIN* is to accept all displayable, non-graphics characters, as well as the four cursor motion keys?

Actually, there is a seventh variable that can depend on the particular *CALLER*, namely *CAPSON(CALLER)*. If *CAPSON = -1* then *KEYIN* converts letters to uppercase; if *CAPSON = 0* then *KEYIN* returns the character as input. If conversion to uppercase is requested, then it is performed in line 26195. This uses the function for uppercase conversion, which we developed in the preceding chapter.

TEST YOUR UNDERSTANDING 2 (answer on page 425)
What are the values of the seven variables if *KEYIN* is to accept numerical input and all extended ASCII codes?

TEST YOUR UNDERSTANDING 3 (answer on page 425)
What are the values of the seven variables if *KEYIN* is to accept the two responses *Yes* and *No* (as indicated by the characters *Y* and *N*)?

If you type an unacceptable character, *KEYIN* beeps the speaker and waits for another character.

We have made certain assumptions in writing *KEYIN*. First, we assume that the arrays *MINKEY(), MAXKEY(), SPECIALKEY$, EXTMINKEY(), EXTMAXKEY()*, and *EXTSPECIALKEY$()* are dimensioned in the main program. Their size should be dictated by the number of different types of input required by the program.

Second, the variables *TRUE = -1* and *FALSE = 0* are assumed to be assigned in the main program. Using *TRUE* and *FALSE*, we can write statements such as

```
IF EXTENDED=TRUE THEN ...
IF MENUEND=FALSE THEN ...
```

Using *TRUE* and *FALSE* makes programs so much more readable that I include these definitions at the beginning of every program that I write.

Here is the routine KEYIN.

```
26000 '*****************KEYIN*******************
26005 '
26010 'This routine reads a character from the keyboard
26011 'and accepts or rejects it based on the caller's
26012 ' specifications.
26020 'Subroutine variables:
26025 '     CALLER = number of caller
26030 '     MINKEY(CALLER)=minimum ASCII code for CALLER
26035 '     MAXKEY(CALLER)=maximum ASCII code for CALLER
26040 '     CAPSON(CALLER)=Convert to CAPITALS?
26045 '     SPECIALKEYS$(CALLER)=String containing any
26050 '              special acceptable keys for CALLER
26055 '     EXTMINKEY(CALLER)=minimum extended ASCII
26056 '              code for CALLER
26060 '     EXTMAXKEY(CALLER)=maximum extended ASCII
26061 '              code for CALLER
26065 '     EXTSPECIALKEY$(CALLER)=special extended
26066 '                 ASCII codes for CALLER
26070 ' The above arrays must be dimensioned in the
26075 ' main program. The array values must be assigned
26080 ' in the main program. The values of TRUE and
26085 ' FALSE must also be assigned in the main
26090 ' program.
26095 '     C$=the character returned
26100 '     EXTENDED=-1 if C$ is the second byte of an
26101 '                      extended ASCII code,
26105 '              = 0 otherwise
26110 'Input character string from INKEY$
26115    C$=INKEY$
26120    IF C$="" THEN 26115: 'Wait for input
26125    C=ASC(C$)
26130    IF LEN(C$)=2 THEN EXTENDED=TRUE
                         ELSE EXTENDED=FALSE
26135    IF EXTENDED=FALSE THEN 26155
26140    C$=RIGHT$(C$,1)
26145    C=ASC(C$)
26150    GOTO 26205
26155 'Ordinary ASCII Codes
26160 '  Test for range
26165       IF C>=MINKEY(CALLER) AND C<=MAXKEY(CALLER)
                 THEN 26185
26170 '  Handle special characters
26175       IF SPECIALKEY$(CALLER)="" THEN 26240 :
                 'No special characters
```

```
26180           IF INSTR(SPECIALKEY$(CALLER),C$)=0 THEN
                26240
26185 '  Convert to capitals if necessary
26190           IF CAPSON(CALLER)=FALSE THEN 26255
26195           IF C>96 AND C<123 THEN C$=CHR$(C AND 223)
26200           GOTO 26255
26205 ' Extended ASCII codes
26210 '  Test for range
26215           IF C>=EXTMINKEY(CALLER) AND
                C>=EXTMINKEY(CALLER) THEN 26255
26220 '  Handle special characters
26225           IF EXTSPECIALKEY$(CALLER)="" THEN 26240
26230           IF INSTR(EXTSPECIALKEY$(CALLER),C$)=0
                THEN 26240
26235           GOTO 26255
26240 ' Illegal character
26245             BEEP
26250             GOTO 26115: 'Try again
26255 RETURN
```

To try out KEYIN, use a program of this type:

```
10  TRUE=-1:FALSE=0
20  DIM MINKEY(5),MAXKEY(5),EXTMINKEY(5),EXTMAXKEY(5)
30  DIM SPECIALKEY$(5),EXTSPECIALKEY$(5),CAPSON(5)
40  MINKEY(1)=0:MAXKEY(1)=0
50  SPECIALKEY$(1)= "1234567890-+E "
60  EXTMINKEY(1)=0:EXTMAXKEY(1)=0
70  EXTSPECIALKEY$(1)=CHR$(59)+CHR$(60)
80  CAPSON(1)=TRUE:CALLER=1
90  KEY OFF:FOR J=1 TO 10:KEY J,"":NEXT J
100 GOSUB 26000
110 IF EXTENDED=TRUE THEN PRINT "EXTENDED ASCII CODE"
120 PRINT ASC(C$),C$
130 INPUT "Again (Y or N)";A$
140 IF A$="Y" OR A$="y" THEN 80
150 END
```

This program allows for five different callers (only one is actually used). The acceptable characters for *CALLER 1* are the digits *0-9*, and the characters *+*, *-*, *E, space*, and the extended ASCII codes 59 and 60 (functions keys F1 and F2). Note that if you type *e*, it is converted to *E* since *CAPSON(1)=TRUE*. The program prints out the ASCII code of the character and the character itself and then awaits another character. You should run this program to convince yourself that *KEYIN* does, in fact, work.

ANSWERS TO TEST YOUR UNDERSTANDINGS 1, 2, and 3

```
1:  MINKEY(1)=32:MAXKEY(1)=127:SPECIALKEY$(1)=""
    EXTMINKEY(1)=0:EXTMAXKEY(1)=0:EXTSPECIALKEY$(1)=
    CHR$(72)+CHR$(75)+CHR$(77)+CHR$(80)
```

```
2:   MINKEY(1)=0:MAXKEY(1)=0:SPECIALKEY$(1)="1234567890-+E."
     EXTMINKEY(1)=0:EXTMAXKEY(1)=127:EXTSPECIALKEY$(1)=""
     CAPSON=-1

3:   MINKEY(1)=0:MAXKEY(1)=0:SPECIALKEY$(1)="YN"
     EXTMINKEY(1)=0:EXTMAXKEY(1)=127:EXTSPECIALKEY$(1)=""
     CAPSON=-1
```

17.3   Inputting Strings and Numbers

Now that we have a character input routine, let's extend our sights and build routines that input strings and numbers.

The routine *SCREENIN* uses *KEYIN* to accept input from the keyboard and displays it at a specified position on the screen. When you call *SCREENIN*, you must specify, in addition to the values needed by *KEYIN*, the values

XFLD = column position where output is to begin

YFLD = row where output is to be displayed

LNGTH = maximum number of characters allowed

By specifying the allowable characters for *KEYIN*, you may control the characters that are allowed in your display. You may use the backspace key to erase a character, just as in the BASIC editor. ENTER signifies the end of output, and Esc causes the display field to be erased and the cursor to be positioned at the beginning of the field. (In order for these keys to have the functions indicated, however, you must define the corresponding keys to be acceptable to *KEYIN*.)

Any extended ASCII code automatically ends input.

The end of input is indicated by setting the variable *INPUTEND* = *TRUE*. When input has ended, *SCREENIN* reads the display field using the *SCREEN* function. *SCREEN(row,column)* equals the ASCII code of the character at position *(row,column)*. The resulting string is stored in the variable *S$*. If input was ended by an extended ASCII code, then *EXTENDED* is set equal to true and *E$* contains the second character of the extended code. Note that *S$* does not include any reference to an extended ASCII code.

You will note in several places the statements

LOCATE ,,0

LOCATE ,,1

The first turns the cursor off and the second turns the cursor on. I have found that watching the cursor motion is very annoying, especially when using *SCREEN*. In order to preserve my sanity while using *SCREENIN*, I turned off the cursor whenever cursor motion proved annoying.

Here is the code for *SCREENIN*. Note that the code for *KEYIN* is required to operate SCREENIN. (We numbered *KEYIN* beginning with 26000 with this in mind.)

```
25000 '***************SCREENIN*********************
25005 'This routine inputs data as a string S$ from
       the keyboard.
25010 'It allows input to have the following
       parameters:
25015 'LNGTH = maximum length of input string
25020 'XFLD = cursor column for beginning of input
       field
25025 'YFLD = cursor row for input field
25030 'CALLER = number of caller
25035 'CAPSON(CALLER) = -1 if letters are to be
       capitalized for CALLER
25040 '              =  0 otherwise
25045 'FLDBEG = first character position in field
25050 'FLDEND = last character position in field
       (calculated)
25055 'S$=Contents of the field from beginning up to
       space before cursor
25060 'T$=contents of the field from the cursor to the
       end of the field
25065 'At end of routine, the contents of the field
       are returned in S$
25070 'LASTPOS=position currently occupied by last
       character
25075 'If a key with an extended ASCII code is pressed,
25080 'it ends processing the current field. The
25085 'contents of the field are returned in S$ and
25090 'the second byte of the extended ASCII code in
       E$.
25095 'CSR keeps track of the current column of the
       cursor
25097 '*******************************************
25100 '
25105 '******MAIN ROUTINE******
25110 '
25115     S$="":INPUTEND=FALSE:KEYHIT=FALSE
25120     FLDEND=XFLD+LNGTH-1
25125     CSR=XFLD
25130     GOSUB 25450:'Compute initial LASTPOS
25135     LOCATE YFLD,XFLD
25140     WHILE INPUTEND=FALSE
25145         GOSUB 26000:'Input character
25150         IF EXTENDED=TRUE THEN 25225
              ELSE 25195:'Analyze character
25155     WEND
25160     GOSUB 25365:'Read screen
25165     S$=S$+T$
25170     RETURN
25175 '*********************************************
25180 '
25185 '****** Subroutines ******
```

```
25190 '
25195 'Handle ordinary ASCII codes
25200    KEYHIT=TRUE
25205    IF C$=CHR$(8) THEN   25260: 'Backspace
25210    IF C$=CHR$(13) THEN 25295: 'ENTER
25215    IF C$=CHR$(27) THEN 25310: 'Esc
25220    IF C$>=CHR$(32) THEN
                     GOTO 25340:'Handle displayable character
25225 'Handle extended ASCII codes
25230    E$=C$
25235    INPUTEND=TRUE
25240    GOTO 25155
25245 'Reject character
25250    BEEP
25255    GOTO 25155
25260 'Handle Backspace
25265    IF LASTPOS<XFLD THEN 25245
25270    GOSUB 25365:'Read field
25275    IF CSR<>XFLD THEN CSR=CSR-1:
                PRINT CHR$(29)+T$+CHR$(32); ELSE PRINT T$;
25280    LOCATE YFLD,CSR
25285    LASTPOS=LASTPOS-1
25290    GOTO 25155
25295 'Handle ENTER
25300    INPUTEND=TRUE
25305    GOTO 25155
25310 'Handle ESC (Erase field)
25315    LOCATE YFLD,XFLD
25320    PRINT STRING$(LNGTH,32);
25325    LASTPOS=0:CSR=XFLD
25330    LOCATE YFLD,XFLD
25335    GOTO 25155
25340 'Display character
25345    PRINT C$;
25350    IF LASTPOS<CSR THEN LASTPOS=CSR
25355    IF CSR=FLDEND THEN
                     PRINT CHR$(29); ELSE CSR=CSR+1
25360    GOTO 25155
25365 'Read field from screen
25370    LOCATE ,,0
25375    S$="": T$=""
25380    IF LASTPOS=0 THEN 25420
25385    FOR J%=XFLD TO CSR-1
25390            S$=S$+CHR$(SCREEN(YFLD,J%))
25395    NEXT J%
25400    FOR J%=CSR TO LASTPOS
25405            T$=T$+CHR$(SCREEN(YFLD,J%))
25410    NEXT J%
25415    LOCATE ,,1
25420    RETURN
25425 'Erase field
25430    LOCATE YFLD,XFLD:CSR=XFLD:LASTPOS=0
25435    PRINT STRING$(LNGTH,32);
25440    LOCATE YFLD,XFLD
25445    RETURN
```

```
25450 'Compute LASTPOS (For initial non-blank field)
25455    LASTPOS=FLDEND:CSR=XFLD
25460    GOSUB 25365:'Read field
25465    WHILE RIGHT$(T$,1)=CHR$(32)
25470         T$=LEFT$(T$,LEN(T$)-1)
25475         LASTPOS=LASTPOS-1
25480    WEND
25485    RETURN
25490 'Clear keyboard buffer
25495    DEF SEG=0:POKE1050,PEEK(1052)
25500    DEF SEG:'Clear keyboard buffer
25510    RETURN
```

You may test *SCREENIN* using a program of the following sort.

```
1 TRUE=-1:FALSE=0
2 DIM MINKEY(5),MAXKEY(5),EXTMINKEY(5),EXTMAXKEY(5)
3 DIM SPECIALKEY$(5), EXTSPECIALKEY$(5),CAPSON(5)
4 MINKEY(1)=0:MAXKEY(1)=127
5 SPECIALKEY$(1)= ""
6 EXTMINKEY(1)=0:EXTMAXKEY(1)=0
7 EXTSPECIALKEY$(1)=CHR$(59)+CHR$(60)
8 CAPSON(1)=TRUE:CALLER=1
9 FOR J=1 TO 10:KEY J,"":NEXT J
20 CLS
21 XFLD=5:YFLD=10:LNGTH=20
30 GOSUB 25000
40 INPUT "Again (Y or N)";A$
50 IF A$="Y" OR A$="y" THEN 8
60 END
```

This program allows input of any ordinary ASCII codes and F1 and F2.

Note that *SCREENIN* returns all input in string form. But suppose that your input is a number? You can, of course, convert a string such as *"1234"* to the number *1234* using the VAL function; i.e., *VAL("1234")* is equal to *1234*. However, some care must be exercised. *VAL* accepts any string at all. It scans the string to determine the first character that shouldn't be in a number, ignores all characters from there on, and converts the initial string into a number. Thus, for example,

```
VAL("1NUMBER")=1
VAL("NUMBER")=0
```
(the null string is converted into 0)

Using *KEYIN*, we can set up a *CALLER* that allows our string to contain only the characters

1,2,3,4,5,6,7,8,9,0, + ,E, and *space*

This goes a long way toward disallowing incorrect input. However, what about the following strings?

"1.2.3", *"1EEE"*, *"1.0E + +"*, *"1.783E.78-"*

All contain only characters acceptable to *KEYIN* with the above *CALLER*. Clearly, we need a routine that checks whether a string is in proper format to be converted to a number. This is the routine *NUMBERCK*.

NUMBERCK starts with the string *S$*, which is an output of *SCREENIN*, and determines whether *S$* may be converted to a number. If so, the variable *NUMBERCK* is set equal to a negative value. If *S$* is not in correct numerical format, *NUMBERCK* is set equal to 0. If *S$* may be converted, then *NUMBERCK* converts it via the statement

```
S=VAL(S$)
```

So *S* holds the converted number, which is passed back to the calling program. The routine then sets the value of *NUMBERCK* as follows:

NUMBERCK = -3 if *S* is an integer (decimal part = 0,
$$-32768 <= S <= 32767)$$

NUMBERCK = -2 if *S* has 0 decimal part

NUMBERCK = -1 if *S* has a non-zero decimal part

The routine *NUMBERCK* takes no action if *S$* cannot be converted, other than to set the value of *NUMBERCK* equal to 0. It is up to the calling program to take any action, such as requesting the user to repeat the input.

Here is the code for the routine *NUMBERCK*.

```
27000 '**********NUMBERCK*********
27005 'This routine checks the format
27006 'of the string S$ to determine if it may
27007 'successfully be converted to a number.
27008 'It returns the result of the check in
27020 'NUMBERCK = 0: S$ not in numerical format
27025 '         =-1: S$ may be converted into a single-
                     precision real
27030 '         =-2: S$ may be converted with 0
                     fractional part
27035 '         =-3: S$ may be converted to an integer
27040 'If conversion is possible, S contains the
27045 'converted real,S$ the corresponding string.
27050 '*************MAIN ROUTINE***************
27055 'Initialize and handle leading sign
27060     N$="":NUMBERCK=TRUE:DIGIT$="1234567890."
27065     DECPT=FALSE:EXPNT=FALSE:SIGN=FALSE
27070     IF S$="" THEN 27210
27075     T$=LEFT$(S$,1)
27080     IF T$="+" OR T$="-" THEN N$=T$:S$=MID$(S$,2)
27085     IF S$="" THEN NUMBERCK=FALSE:GOTO 27210
27090     IF INSTR(DIGIT$,LEFT$(S$,1))=0
          THEN NUMBERCK=FALSE:GOTO 27135
27095 WHILE S$ <> ""  :'Loop strips spaces
                        and checks format.Result in N$
27100     T$=LEFT$(S$,1):S$=MID$(S$,2)
27105     IF T$=" " THEN 27135: 'Delete space
```

```
27110      IF (T$="+" OR T$="-") AND RIGHT$(N$,1)<>"E"
           THEN NUMBERCK=FALSE:GOTO 27135
27115      IF T$="." THEN IF DECPT=TRUE  OR EXPNT=TRUE
           THEN NUMBERCK=FALSE ELSE N$=N$+T$:DECPT=TRUE
27120      IF T$="+" OR T$="-" THEN
               IF SIGN=TRUE OR EXPNT=FALSE
                   THEN NUMBERCK=FALSE
                   ELSE N$=N$+T$:SIGN=TRUE
27125      IF T$="E" THEN
               IF EXPNT=TRUE THEN NUMBERCK=FALSE
               ELSE N$=N$+T$:EXPNT=TRUE:DECPT=TRUE
27130      IF T$<>"." AND T$<>"+" AND T$<>"-"
           AND  T$<>"E" THEN N$=N$+T$
27135 WEND
27140 'Check for overflow(<10^-38 or >10^38)
27145      N%=INSTR(N$,"E")
27150      IF N%=0 THEN 27190
27155      IF N%=1 THEN NUMBERCK=FALSE:GOTO 27210
27160      S$=LEFT$(N$,N%-1):S1$=MID$(N$,N%+1)
27165      S=VAL(S$)
27170      IF S=0 THEN D=0
               ELSE D=INT(LOG(ABS(S))/LOG(10))
27175      IF S1$<>"" THEN D=D+VAL(S1$)
27180      IF D<-37 OR D>37 THEN NUMBERCK=FALSE
27185 'Perform the conversion
27190      IF NUMBERCK=TRUE THEN S=VAL(N$)
27195      IF NUMBERCK=TRUE AND S=INT(S) THEN
           NUMBERCK=-2
27200      IF NUMBERCK=-2 AND S>=-32768! AND S<=32767
           THEN NUMBERCK=-3
27205      S$=N$
27210 RETURN
```

You may test NUMBERCK using a program such as

```
1 INPUT S$
2 GOSUB 27000
3 PRINT NUMBERCK
4 IF NUMBERCK<0 THEN PRINT "NUMBER ACCEPTED":PRINT S
5 INPUT "Again (Y or N)";A$
6 IF A$="Y" OR A$="y" THEN 1
7 END
```

The three routines *KEYIN, SCREENIN,* and *NUMBERCK* allow you to put your input on a professional basis: to control what comes in to your program and to deal with it in a totally controlled manner.

IMPORTANT NOTE: Although the three input routines give you control over your input, they do not totally lift the responsibility from your shoulders. When calling for numerical input, you must still check the returned values to determine that they are in the proper range (positive, less than 10, more than 20, and so forth). The input routines can guarantee that string input is the correct length and contains only predetermined characters. However, you must still check that string input is valid in a particular context. (Did the user type *NEP* instead of *PEN*?)

18

Planning and Developing Large Programs

18.0   Chapter Objectives

In the early parts of this introduction to BASIC, you learned the syntax of the most rudimentary BASIC statements and how to combine such statements into programs. Our first programs were reasonably short and their logic fairly simple. This chapter provides some tips on building larger programs. We will center our discussion on a concrete program, a bar chart generator, such as is found in many business graphics packages. In this chapter, we will design and implement this program and learn something about handling large programs in the process.

18.1   Planning the Bar Chart Generator

In developing a large scale program, above all else, careful attention to program design is essential. You must have a clear idea of what you want your program to do: What outputs will it produce? From what inputs?

One of the principle defects in BASIC is that it allows you to sit down and start writing a program without much thought or planning. (And I'll bet many of you thought that was an advantage!) You may be able to get away without planning if you are writing a small program. But as soon as the program requires the interplay of a number of different subroutines, producing differing outputs and affecting various program variables, program planning becomes a necessity.

Let's outline the planning process for THE BAR CHART GENERATOR.

What is the Program to Do?

A Bit About Bar Charts.   Examine the graph in Figure 18-1. It is a typical bar chart. You should note the following features of the graph. The chart graphically depicts three sets of data, with one set of bars corresponding to each set of data. We distinguish among the different data sets by the shading of the bars.

432

The bars are set in a **coordinate system**, a rectangular box whose edges are labeled with information necessary to read the chart. The bottom horizontal edge of the coordinate system is called the **x-axis**. Just below this axis are labels that describe the various bars.

The vertical, left edge of the coordinate system is called the **y-axis**. Along the y-axis is a numerical scale that allows you to determine the numerical heights of the bars.

The *x*-axis and *y*-axis are labeled with titles, as is the entire graph. Note that the *y*-axis title is arranged vertically to the left of the scale, centered vertically on the coordinate system. The *x*-axis title is centered under the coordinate system, just below the *x*-axis labels. The chart title is centered above the coordinate system.

Each of the three sets of data has a title, displayed to the right of the coordinate system. To the left of each title is a square containing a sample of the shading type corresponding to the particular data set.

Figure 18-1. **A typical bar chart.**

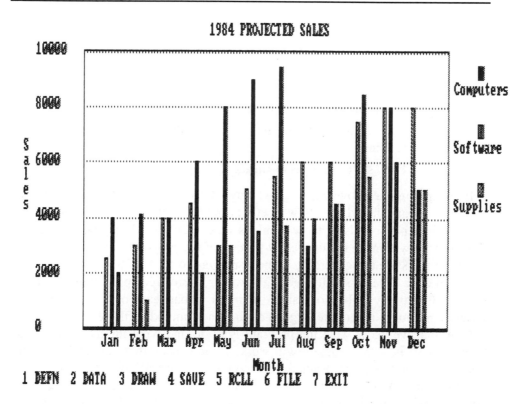

We have just taken a quick tour of a bar chart. Now we can state

GOAL: Construct a program, called THE BAR CHART GENERATOR, which displays bar charts corresponding to user-supplied data.

Before we can achieve our goal, we need to learn a great deal about programming. However, let's proceed with the first step in program development: Program Planning.

To plan our program, we begin by making a list of the specific functions that the program is to perform. This is our list of **program requirements**:

R1.   Draw bar charts on the screen.

R2.   Save on diskette the data corresponding to a bar chart so that it may be reproduced at a later date.

R3.   Recall bar chart data from diskette.

R4.   Read numerical data items from a diskette data file.

R5.   Edit bar chart data to make changes and corrections.

Once we have drawn up the above list of requirements, let's see what inputs our program will need. Examine Figure 18-1. Each visual element of the chart corresponds to an input:

I1. Chart title

I2. x- and y-axis titles

I3. x- and y-axis labels

I4. Bars

      a.   Provision for several sets of bars, reflecting different data series.

      b.   Bars of different data series need to be distinguished by different shading.

      c.   Each set of bars needs an identifying title.

In examining the above list, we ask: How many sets of bars should we allow? How many bars should we allow? Let's allow up to three sets of bars, with at most 20 bars per set. Using these numbers we can display all the data on a single screen. This will make the data entry portion of the program easier. In any case, these numbers are too generous. There is no way to fit 3 x 20 = 60 bars on the screen at once. The bars will overlap. However, there are applications where you want to display say 20 bars of a single series or 12 bars each of a set of three data series. And our numbers are large enough to accommodate these choices.

Now that we know what the program is to do and what inputs are required, let's think of how the program will work. I don't mean that you should sit and start to code at this point. Rather, you should ask yourself how the user will use this program. Actually picture the user sitting down at the computer and ask yourself: What does he or she do to use this program? When I thought about this question, I pictured the user choosing from a menu of various actions, as displayed on a function key display. This leads us to define a sequence of actions that corresponds to the function keys.

F1—Define bar chart parameters

F2—Enter x-axis labels and numerical data

F3—Draw the chart based on current data

F4—Save chart

F5—Recall chart

F6—Enter data from a data file

F7—Exit

At this point, we start to see the structure of the program emerging. There must be seven main routines, one corresponding to each of the seven function keys. Note that the requirement R5 (Editing capability) does not appear as a routine. As we'll see, it's easiest to build the editing directly into data entry routines, F1 and F2.

In addition to the seven basic routines, we will need a **control routine**, which allows us to choose from among the various functions by pressing the appropriate function key. Our program will need a number of arrays and many of the variables will require particular initial values. It is convenient to have a particular part of the program, called the **initialization**, which handles all such definitions.

Based on our discussion, we may now sketch out our program:

```
100  'Initialization
900  'Control Routine
1000 'Define Bar Chart Parameters
2000 'Input Data
3000 'Draw Chart
4000 'Save Chart
5000 'Recall Chart
6000 'Read Data File
7000 'Exit
```

Well, there's the program plan! We've left plenty of room to fill in the various program lines. And, as we'll see, there are several other routines that are required by the seven fundamental routines. However, the above sketch will be our guide.

18.2 The Initialization and Control Routines

In various sections, we have developed a number of routines that perform particular tasks for the bar chart generator. In order for these routines to work together, we need a control routine that allows us to select among them. When we planned the program, we designated seven main functions for the bar chart generator:

Define Bar Chart Parameters—Specify the coordinate system and its various labels and the number of series of data.

Input Data—Input the numerical data corresponding to the various bar heights, and string data naming the various bars.

Draw Bar Chart—Use the graphics capabilities of the PC to draw the bar chart.

Save Bar Chart—Save in a diskette data file the parameters and data corresponding to a particular bar chart.

Recall Bar Chart—Recall a bar chart that has been saved on diskette.

Read Data File—Read numerical bar chart data that has been saved in a diskette data file produced by another program.

Exit—Stop executing the program and return to BASIC.

Each of these seven functions corresponds to a routine. The code for the first routine begins in line 1000, for the second in line 2000, and so forth. We call a particular function by pressing a function key: The *n*th function is called by pressing function key *n*. Our control routine calls *KEYIN*, the character input routine, and allows only function keys F1-F7 as input. The control routine responds to an allowable function key by performing the requested function. Note that each of the function routines ends by sending control back to the control routine.

Here is the code for the control routine.

```
900  '***************CONTROL ROUTINE*******************
905  'E$ is returned by the input routine, = the second
910  'character of extended ASCII code
915  KEY OFF:CLS
920  IF E$<>"" THEN 945
925  LOCATE 25,1
930  PRINT FKEY$;
935  CALLER=5:GOSUB 25000
940  GOTO 920
945  C=ASC(E$):EXTENDED=FALSE
950  IF C=59 THEN 1000 :'Bar Chart Definition
955  IF C=60 THEN 2000 :'Data Input
960  IF C=61 THEN 3000 :'Draw Bar Chart
965  IF C=62 THEN 4000 :'Save Bar Chart
970  IF C=63 THEN 5000 :'Recall Bar Chart
975  IF C=64 THEN 6000 :'Read Data File
980  IF C=65 THEN 7000 :'Exit
985  CALLER=5:GOSUB 25000:'Await instructions
```

This routine presupposes that the function keys are disabled as soft keys and that the function key line *fkey$* has been specified somewhere. And this brings me to the subject of program organization.

I like to organize my programs (especially the large ones) in a particular order. You may have noticed that the program fragments often had what seemed like "dangling lines" at the beginning, before the documentation. This is because those lines, while necessary to run the particular fragment, really belong in another section of the program, the *INITIALIZATION*. Here is my *INITIALIZATION* for the bar chart generator.

```
10  '**********INITIALIZATION ROUTINE**********
100 'Dimension Statements
200 'Data Statements
300 'Common Statements
400 'Error Trapping Line
500 'DEF statements
600 'Define parameters for input routine
700 'Initialization of variables
702     TRUE=-1:FALSE=0
704     FOR J%=1 TO 10
706           KEY J%,"" :'Disable Function Key
708     NEXT J%
710     FKEY$="1 DEFN  2 DATA  3 DRAW  4 SAVE  5 RCLL
              6 FILE  7 EXIT"
712     XFLD=1:YFLD=1:LNGTH=0
714     MENU$(1)="BAR CHART DEFINITION"
716     MENU$(2)="TITLE? "
718     MENU$(3)="DATA SERIES 1 TITLE? "
720     MENU$(4)="DATA SERIES 2 TITLE? "
722     MENU$(5)="DATA SERIES 3 TITLE? "
724     MENU$(6)="Y AXIS RANGE:MINIMUM? "
726     MENU$(7)="Y AXIS RANGE:MAXIMUM? "
728     MENU$(8)="Y AXIS STEP? "
730     MENU$(9)="X AXIS TITLE? "
732     MENU$(10)="Y AXIS TITLE? "
734     MAXHEIGHT=199
736     MAXWIDTH=639
```

Note that *INITIALIZATION* begins with five categories of statements (not all used): *DIM, DATA, COMMON, ON ERROR,* and *DEF.* These are the "non-executable" statements of the program. When the program encounters these statements, it merely makes a definition or sets aside space or makes a note of a fact to be used later. It is a good idea to put all these statements in one part of the program. For one thing, they are easy to find if, say, you want to increase the size of an array or to insert a new function definition. A second, more compelling reason for grouping these statements together is that the BASIC Compiler requires that all non-executable statements precede all executable statements. Rather than try to rearrange the statements after the program is written, you should develop the discipline to create the *INITIALIZATION* portion of the program as you go along by placing any statements that belong to the *INITIALIZATION* at the start of a module. After all the modules are constructed, you may assemble the initial statements into the *INITIALIZATION*.

Note that, in addition to non-executable statements, *INITIALIZATION* contains variable initializations. You should get in the habit of initializing all variables. I know it's easy to get lazy, especially when dimensioning small arrays. However, if you only need an array with three elements, why use ten? Memory is precious. Conserve it. Also, give your variables descriptive names. It is true that they will take up more space in the BASIC interpreter. However, if you plan to compile your program, a descriptive name will lead to no longer a program than a single-letter name. (I assume that most larger programs will ultimately be compiled.)

To each function key corresponds a routine of the program. Each of the routines is constructed pretty much like the main program. Start with lists of requirements (outputs) and inputs. From these describe the routine in a series of steps. Each step becomes a subroutine. In each routine, you will note a "main routine," which is really like an outline of the routine. Then there are subroutines that carry out the details of the routine. The process of designing a program consists of starting from a main outline then proceeding to subroutines containing the next level of detail, and then to sub-subroutines containing the next level of detail, and so forth. This procedure is called **top-down design**.

I construct each subroutine separately and test it with sample data. It's a good idea to debug the small routines first. That way, when a bug arises at the next level, you may usually assume that the trouble is that the output from one subroutine isn't the proper input to another. (That's not always the problem, but in a surprising number of instances, it is!)

After you are sure that the subroutines are working properly, assemble them into a routine and follow the same test procedure again.

When you develop subroutines, don't worry about line numbers. Start all subroutines with line 10 (or 100 or 1000). Add and delete lines at will. After the subroutine is debugged, use the RENUM command to adjust the line numbers so that the subroutine will fit into its intended routine.

When all the main routines are debugged, assemble them into the main program and combine miscellaneous lines to form the *INITIALIZATION* section. That's all there is to it!

I don't mean to say that the above approach is the only one that can be used to sucessfully develop large programs. But it's one that works for me. Why not try it? I'm sure that you'll discover convenient variations and improvements. Programming is as much an art as a science. And there is room for artists of all schools.

18.3 The DRAW BAR CHART Module

Our bar chart program will be built from a number of separate pieces, collected as subroutines and sequenced by a controlling program. In this section, let's concentrate on the design of the portion of the program that actually draws the bar chart from the data. (We'll worry about data input later.)

Let's assign variables to some of the important quantities which our program must reference.

Our requirements, drawn up in Section 18.1, state that the program should allow for display of up to three separate sets of data. The number of different sets (or series) of data will be contained in the variable $SER\%$. $SER\%$ will equal either 1, 2, or 3. Each set of the data may contain as many as 20 data items. (This will allow up to 3 x 20 or 60 sets of bars. This is the maximum that our screen layout can accommodate.)

The data for the bar chart will be contained in an array $DTA\$(N\%,J\%)$. Here $N\%$ is the number of the data set and $J\%$ is the number of the data item within the particular data set. Here is a typical set of data:

Data Series 1	Data Series 2	Data Series 3
Jan 1580	38.35	48.55
Feb 1312.11	1450.00	12.11

For example, $DTA\$(2,1) = ``38.35''$. The month designations on the left are called **labels** and will be stored as the zero elements in the array. For example, $DTA\$(1,0) = ``Jan''$.

You may wonder why we are using a string array to store the data rather than a numerical array. There are two good reasons. First, a string array allows us to store the labels in the same array as the data. Second (and more important), a numerical array makes BASIC reformat our numbers. For example, *1450.00* is converted to the number *1450*. Of course, we can reformat our numbers on output with PRINT USING, but it is by far easier not to keep track of formats and simply store the data as a string, exactly as it was input. When we use the data for numerical purposes, we will convert it to numerical form using the VAL function.

Let's draw our bar chart in high-resolution graphics (*SCREEN 2*). We will confine our bar chart to the portion of the screen *(16,80)-(169,559)*. This gives us a 152 × 480 region for our chart. It also leaves the top two lines and the bottom four lines of the screen for titles. Also, we have room for labels eight characters wide on either side of the graph.

The problem of displaying the labels involves the precise placement of text in graphics mode, which we solved in the preceding chapter using the routine *PLOTSTRING*. Let's include *PLOTSTRING* as part of our program and use it to display the various titles.

The coordinate system for the bar chart will be described by the following parameters.

$YMIN$ = the beginning y-value on the y-axis

$YMAX$ = the final y-value on the y-axis

$XMAX$ = maximum number of data items in a data series

GRID$ = *Y* if horizontal grid lines are to be displayed

= *N* otherwise

Our program begins by defining the above screen area as a viewport. Next, we use *WINDOW* to define the coordinate system *(0,YMIN)-(XMAX + 1,YMAX)* on the viewport. Note that we use *XMAX + 1* (rather than *XMAX*) so that the value *XMAX* is within the viewport, leaving space for the last bar.

The width of the bars will be *(XMAX + 1)/120*. This makes each bar four pixels wide. (The viewport is 480 pixels wide.) We will store half of this number, or *(XMAX + 1)/240*, in the variable *BW* (=bar width). We will draw a bar by locating the center of the lower edge and drawing the sides of the bar at a distance of *BW* on either side of the center. At each of the integer positions along the x-axis, we will center the bar corresponding to data series 2. We will place the bar for data series 2, eight pixels to the left and the bar for data series 3, eight pixels to the right. We store this data in the array *ADJ()*:

```
ADJ(1) = -(XMAX+1)/60 (8 pixels to the leftt)
ADJ(2) = 0 (center)
ADJ(3) = (XMAX+1)/60 (8 pixels to the right)
```

Here is the program.

```
1 YMIN=-500:YMAX=500:XMAX=5:YSTEP=100
5 SER%=3
100 'Dimension statements
110 DIM DTA$(3,20)
120 DATA 150,175,300,400,450,-300,-200,500,125,175,
    -200,-100,425,120,-200
200 'Variable initialization
240 FOR J%=1 TO 5
250  FOR N%=1 TO 3
260   READ DTA$(N%,J%)
270  NEXT N%
280 NEXT J%
3000 '**************DRAWBAR ROUTINE***************
3005    CLS
3010    KEY OFF
3015    SCREEN 2:SER%=3
3020    YMIN=VAL(YMIN$)
3025    YMAX=VAL(YMAX$)
3030    YSTEP=VAL(YSTEP$)
3035    IF YMIN>YMAX THEN SWAP YMIN,YMAX
3040    IF YMIN=YMAX THEN 3095
3045    IF YSTEP=0 THEN 3095
3050    GOSUB 3105:'Compute SER%
3055    STYLE$(1)=CHR$(&HFF):STYLE$(2)=CHR$(&HAA):
        STYLE$(3)=CHR$(&H99)+CHR$(&H55)
3060    BW=(XMAX+1)/240
3065    ADJ(1)=-(XMAX+1)/60:ADJ(2)=0:ADJ(3)=(XMAX+1)/60
3070    GOSUB 3195:'Write Titles
3075    GOSUB 3305:'Write x-axis labels
3080    GOSUB 3360:'Write y-axis labels
```

```
3085      GOSUB 3415:'Draw coordinate system
3090      GOSUB 3435:'Draw bars
3092      GOSUB 3480:'Draw grid lines
3095      E$="":GOTO 920:'Return to control routine
3100 ***************SUBROUTINES****************
3105 'Compute SER%
3110      FOR N%=3 TO 1 STEP -1
3115              XMAX(N%)=20:J%=0
3120              DATAEND=FALSE
3125              WHILE DATAEND=FALSE
3130                      IF DTA$(N%,20-J%)<>"" THEN
                          DATAEND=TRUE:
                          XMAX(N%)=XMAX(N%)+1
3135                      XMAX(N%)=XMAX(N%)-1:J%=J%+1
3140                      IF J%=21 THEN DATAEND=TRUE
3145              WEND
3150      NEXT N%
3155      IF XMAX(3)<=0 THEN SER%=2
3160      IF SER%=2 AND XMAX(2)<=0 THEN SER%=1
3165      IF SER%=1 AND XMAX(1)<=0 THEN SER%=0
3170      XMAX=XMAX(1)
3175      FOR J%=1 TO 3
3180              IF XMAX< XMAX(J%) THEN XMAX=XMAX(J%)
3185      NEXT J%
3190      RETURN
3195 'Write titles
3200      LOCATE 5,72:PRINT SER1TITLE$;
3205 IF SER%=1 THEN 3225
3210      LOCATE 9,72:PRINT SER2TITLE$;
3215 IF SER%=2 THEN 3225
3220      LOCATE 13,72:PRINT SER3TITLE$;
3225      LINE (599,23)-(606,30),,B
3230      PAINT (603,27),STYLE$(1)
3235      IF SER%=1 THEN 3265
3240      LINE (599,55)-(606,62),,B
3245      PAINT (603,60),STYLE$(2)
3250      IF SER%=2 THEN 3265
3255      LINE (599,87)-(606,94),,B
3260      PAINT (603,93),STYLE$(3)
3265      X1=80:X2=559:Y1=0:Y2=7:C%=3:S$=TITLE$
3270      GOSUB 28000
3275      Y1=191:Y2=184:S$=XTITLE$
3280      GOSUB 28000
3285      X1=0:X2=7:Y1=16:Y2=167:C%=4
3290      S$=YTITLE$
3295      GOSUB 28000
3300      RETURN
3305 'Write x-axis labels
3310      K=480/(XMAX+1)
3315      FOR J%=1 TO XMAX
3320          L=79+K*J%
3325          M%=4*LEN(DTA$(0,J%))
3330          LINE (L,167)-(L,170):'Tick marks
3335          X1=L-M%:X2=L+M%-1:Y1=171:Y2=178:C%=1
3340          S$=DTA$(0,J%)
```

```
3345          GOSUB 28000
3350      NEXT J%
3355      RETURN
3360 'Write y-axis labels
3365      IF YSTEP=0 THEN 3410
3370      M=(YMAX-YMIN)/YSTEP
3375      FOR J%=0 TO M
3380          S$=STR$(YMIN+J%*YSTEP)
3385          X1=8:X2=79
3390          Y1=167-J%*152/M-4
3395          Y2=Y1-7:C%=1
3400          GOSUB 28000
3405      NEXT J%
3410      RETURN
3415 'Draw coordinate system
3420      VIEW (80,16)-(559,167),,3
3425      WINDOW (0,YMIN)-(XMAX+1,YMAX)
3430      LINE (0,0)-(XMAX+1,0):'Draw x-axis
3432      RETURN
3435 'Draw bars
3440      FOR N%=1 TO SER%
3445          FOR J%=1 TO XMAX(N%)
3450              IF DTA$(N%,J%)="" THEN 3470
3455              HT=VAL(DTA$(N%,J%))
3460              LINE (J%+ADJ(N%)-BW,0)
                       -(J%+ADJ(N%)+BW,HT),,B
3465              PAINT (J%+ADJ(N%),HT/2),STYLE$(N%)
3470          NEXT J%
3475      NEXT N%
3477      RETURN
3480 'Draw grid lines
3485      FOR J%=0 TO (YMAX-YMIN)/YSTEP
3490          H=YMIN+J%*YSTEP
3495          LINE (0,H)-(XMAX+1,H),,,&H8888
3500      NEXT J%
3505      RETURN
```

Note that the initial lines (below line 3000) provide some data you may use to test the program. Note also that we have indicated subroutines to insert titles, but we'll work out those routines in the next section.

One further point. Note the array *STYLE$()*. It defines the various shading types for the bars. *STYLE$()* is used in the *PAINT* statement in line 3465. *STYLE$()* is the style string that produces the various shadings in the bars of Figure 18-1.

18.4   Defining a Bar Chart

Our bar chart program has two program modules that require keyboard input—the chart definition module and the data entry module. Let's now build these two modules using the input routines developed in Chapter 17.

The Define Bar Chart Parameters Module

By pressing a function key, you will be able to start the bar chart definition module. This part of the bar chart program allows you to enter the bar chart parameters into predetermined fields on the screen. When you start the chart definition module, the screen is cleared and the program creates a display like the one in Figure 18-2.

Figure 18-2. **Bar chart definition menu.**

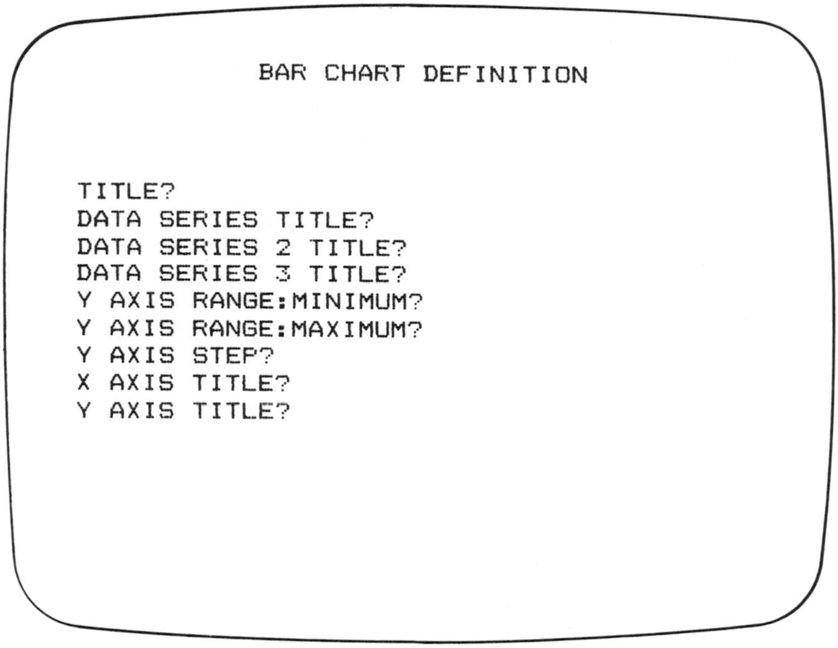

```
                  BAR CHART DEFINITION



      TITLE?
      DATA SERIES TITLE?
      DATA SERIES 2 TITLE?
      DATA SERIES 3 TITLE?
      Y AXIS RANGE:MINIMUM?
      Y AXIS RANGE:MAXIMUM?
      Y AXIS STEP?
      X AXIS TITLE?
      Y AXIS TITLE?
```

The program is requesting the following pieces of data:

TITLE$ = chart title (at most 50 characters)

SER1TITLE$ = data series 1 title (at most 10 characters)

SER2TITLE$ = data series 2 title (at most 10 characters)

SER3TITLE$ = data series 3 title (at most 10 characters)

YMIN$ = minimum displayable y-value in string form

YMAX$ = maximum displayable y-value in string form

YSTEP$ = value of each subdivision along the y-axis in string form

XTITLE$ = Title for x-axis (at most 10 characters)

YTITLE$ = Title for y-axis (at most 10 characters)

The program allows you to use the cursor up and down keys to move from line to line of the menu. In each line, the cursor is positioned in the first position of the input field. You may type your input into the field, using the backspace and Esc keys for editing. When an extended ASCII code (cursor motion key or function key) is detected, the program reads the field at the current cursor position and assigns the value *S$*, returned by the input routine, to the appropriate program variable. In the case of inputs to be converted into numbers, the program calls on *NUMBERCK* to check for numerical format. If the format test fails, then the value of *S$* is not assigned to the program variable and the field is erased. If a function key is pressed, then it causes the program to read the current field, assign the program variable, if possible, and then to *GOTO* the main control program, which we assume begins in line 900.

Here is our program.

```
5  '**********INITIALIZATION ROUTINE**********
10 'Dimension Statements
15      DIM MINKEY(5),MAXKEY(5),EXTMINKEY(5),
        EXTMAXKEY(5)
20      DIM CAPSON(5),SPECIALKEY$(5),EXTSPECIALKEY$(5)
        DTA$(3,20)
25      DIM MENU$(11)
30 'Define parameters for input routine
35      MOTION$=CHR$(71)+CHR$(72)
40      FUNCTION$=CHR$(59)+CHR$(60)+CHR$(61)+CHR$(62)
                  +CHR$(63)+CHR$(64)+CHR$(65)
45 '    **Text input(CALLER=1)**
50      MINKEY(1)=32:MAXKEY(1)=127:
        SPECIALKEY$(1)=CHR$(8)+CHR$(27)
55      CAPSON(1)=0
60      EXTMINKEY(1)=59:EXTMAXKEY(1)=68
65      EXTSPECIALKEY$(1)=MOTION$+FUNCTION$
70 '    **Numerical input (CALLER=2)**
75      MINKEY(2)=0:MAXKEY(2)=0
80      CAPSON(2)=-1:SPECIALKEY$(2)=CHR$(8)+CHR$(27)
85      EXTMINKEY(2)=59:EXTMAXKEY(2)=68
90      EXTSPECIALKEY$(2)=MOTION$+FUNCTION$
95 'Variable initialization
100     TRUE=-1:FALSE=0
105     MENU$(1)="BAR CHART DEFINITION"
110     MENU$(2)="TITLE? "
115     MENU$(3)="DATA SERIES 1 TITLE? "
120     MENU$(4)="DATA SERIES 2 TITLE? "
125     MENU$(5)="DATA SERIES 3 TITLE? "
130     MENU$(6)="Y AXIS RANGE:MINIMUM? "
135     MENU$(7)="Y AXIS RANGE:MAXIMUM? "
140     MENU$(8)="Y AXIS STEP? "
```

```
145      MENU$(9)="X AXIS TITLE? "
150      MENU$(10)="Y AXIS TITLE? "
1000 '**********BAR CHART PARAMETERS INPUT*************
1005 SCREEN 0:CLS:LOCATE 25,1:PRINT FKEY$;
1010 'Display template
1015 LOCATE 1,27:PRINT MENU$(1);
1017 LOCATE 2,23:
     PRINT "(Follow each entry with a ";CHR$(25);" )";
1020 FOR J%=2 TO 10
1025     LOCATE J%+2,1
1030     PRINT MENU$(J%);
1035 NEXT J%
1040 MENUEND=FALSE
1045 GOSUB 1170:'Display current parameter values
1050 XFLD=25:YFLD=4
1055 WHILE MENUEND=FALSE
1060     LOCATE YFLD,XFLD
1065     IF YFLD=4 THEN CALLER=1:LNGTH=50
1070     IF YFLD>4 AND YFLD<7 THEN CALLER=1:LNGTH=10
1075     IF YFLD>7 AND YFLD<11 THEN CALLER=2:LNGTH=10
1080     IF YFLD>10 THEN CALLER=1:LNGTH=10
1085     GOSUB 25000: 'Call input routine
1090     IF YFLD>7 AND YFLD<11 THEN
                 GOSUB 27000:'Numberck
1095     IF YFLD>7 AND YFLD<11 AND NUMBERCK=FALSE
                 THEN GOSUB 25425:GOTO 1085
1100     IF YFLD=4 THEN TITLE$=S$
1105     IF YFLD=5 THEN SER1TITLE$=S$
1110     IF YFLD=6 THEN SER2TITLE$=S$
1115     IF YFLD=7 THEN SER3TITLE$=S$
1120     IF YFLD=8 THEN YMIN$=S$
1125     IF YFLD=9 THEN YMAX$=S$
1130     IF YFLD=10 THEN YSTEP$=S$
1135     IF YFLD=11 THEN XTITLE$=S$
1140     IF YFLD=12 THEN YTITLE$=S$
1145     IF E$=CHR$(80) THEN IF YFLD<12 THEN YFLD=YFLD+1
1150     IF E$=CHR$(72) THEN IF YFLD>4 THEN YFLD=YFLD-1
1155     IF INSTR(FUNCTION$,E$)>0 THEN MENUEND=TRUE
1160 WEND
1165 GOTO 900: 'Return to control routine
1170 'Display current parameter values
1175     LOCATE 4,25:PRINT TITLE$
1180     LOCATE 5,25:PRINT SER1TITLE$
1185     LOCATE 6,25:PRINT SER2TITLE$
1190     LOCATE 7,25:PRINT SER3TITLE$
1195     LOCATE 8,25:PRINT YMIN$
1200     LOCATE 9,25:PRINT YMAX$
1205     LOCATE 10,25:PRINT YSTEP$
1210     LOCATE 11,25:PRINT XTITLE$
1215     LOCATE 12,25:PRINT YTITLE$
1220     RETURN
```

Note that we have defined *CALLER*s 1 and 2 to correspond to the text input
and numerical input, respectively. The only extended ASCII codes allowed are
Cursor Up *(E$ = CHR$(72))* and Cursor Down *(E$ = CHR$(80))* and the function
keys F1-F7, which return you to the main control routine in line 900.

The Data Input Module

The **data input module** is the part of the program in which you enter the numerical values for the various bars and the corresponding identifying labels, which will be displayed below the bars. This module is very similar to the bar chart definition module. When it is called, it clears the screen and creates a display like the one in Figure 18-3.

Figure 18-3.   **The data input matrix.**

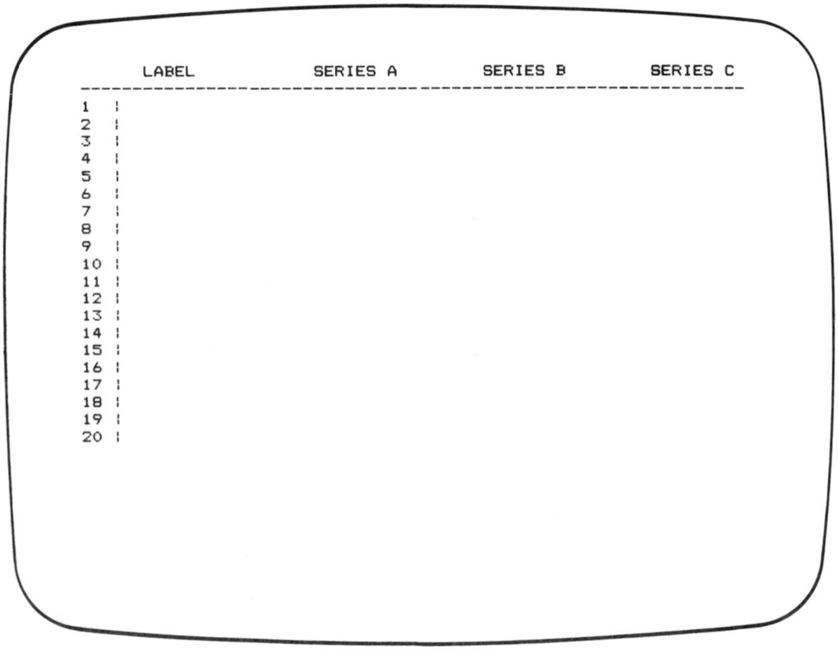

```
          LABEL          SERIES A        SERIES B       SERIES C
         -------------------------------------------------------------
      1  :
      2  :
      3  :
      4  :
      5  :
      6  :
      7  :
      8  :
      9  :
     10  :
     11  :
     12  :
     13  :
     14  :
     15  :
     16  :
     17  :
     18  :
     19  :
     20  :
```

You type your data into the various positions in the matrix. The cursor motion keys move you around within the matrix. Function keys F1-F7 return you to the main control routine in line 900.

Here is the code for the data input module.

```
2000 '**********DATA INPUT ROUTINE**********
2005 SCREEN 0
2010 GOSUB 2055:'Display spreadsheet
2015 ROW%=1:COL%=0
2020 DATAEND=FALSE
2025 WHILE DATAEND=FALSE
2030     GOSUB 2335:'Locate cursor
2035     GOSUB 2150:'Input data
2040 WEND
2045 GOTO 900:'Return to control routine
```

```
2050  ***************SUBROUTINES******************
2055  'Display spreadsheet
2060  CLS
2065  LOCATE 1,34
2070  PRINT "DATA VALUES"
2075  PRINT TAB(20) "(Move the cursor with
                        direction arrows)"
2080  PRINT TAB(8) "LABEL" TAB(26);
2081  IF SER1TITLE$<>"" THEN PRINT SER1TITLE$;
                        ELSE PRINT "SERIES 1";
2082  IF SER2TITLE$<>"" THEN PRINT TAB(44) SER2TITLE$;
                        ELSE PRINT TAB(44) "SERIES 2";
2083  IF SER3TITLE$<>"" THEN PRINT TAB(62) SER3TITLE$
                        ELSE PRINT TAB(62) "SERIES 3"
2085  PRINT STRING$(80,45);
2090  FOR J%=1 TO 20
2095      LOCATE J%+4,1
2100      PRINT J%; TAB(5) "|";
2105  NEXT J%
2110  FOR ROW%=1 TO 20
2115     FOR COL%=0 TO 3
2120             GOSUB 2335:'Convert to
                              screen coordinates
2130             PRINT DTA$(COL%,ROW%);
2135     NEXT COL%
2140  NEXT ROW%
2145  RETURN
2150  'Input data
2155  IF COL%=0 THEN CALLER=3 ELSE CALLER=4
2160  XFLD=C%:YFLD=R%:LNGTH=10
2165  GOSUB 25000
2170  IF S$="" THEN 2195
2175  IF CALLER=3 THEN NUMBERCK=TRUE
2180  IF CALLER=4 THEN GOSUB 27000
2185  IF NUMBERCK<0 THEN DTA$(COL%,ROW%)=S$
2190  IF NUMBERCK=FALSE THEN GOSUB 25425:GOTO 2330
2195  IF INSTR(FUNCTION$,E$)>0 THEN
      DATAEND=TRUE:GOTO 2330
2200  IF E$=CHR$(72) THEN 2230:'Cursor up
2205  IF E$=CHR$(75) THEN 2245:'Cursor left
2210  IF E$=CHR$(77) THEN 2260:'Cursor right
2215  IF E$=CHR$(80) THEN 2275:'Cursor down
2220  IF E$=CHR$(71) THEN 2290:'Home (To position 1,0)
2225  IF E$=CHR$(79) THEN 2310:'End (To position 20,3)
2230  'Cursor up
2235      IF ROW%>1 THEN ROW%=ROW%-1 ELSE GOTO 2290
2240      GOTO 2330
2245  'Cursor left
2250      IF COL%>0 THEN COL%=COL%-1
                        ELSE COL%=3:GOTO 2230
2255      GOTO 2330
2260  'Cursor right
2265      IF COL%<3 THEN COL%=COL%+1
                        ELSE COL%=0:GOTO 2275
2270      GOTO 2330
```

```
2275 'Cursor down
2280     IF ROW%<20 THEN ROW%=ROW%+1 ELSE GOTO 2310
2285     GOTO 2330
2290 'Home (To position 1,0)
2295     COL%=0
2300     ROW%=1
2305     GOTO 2330
2310 'End (To position 20,3)
2315     COL%=3
2320     ROW%=20
2325     GOTO 2330
2330 RETURN
2335 'Compute screen coordinates
2340 R%=ROW%+4
2345 C%=18*COL%+8
2350 LOCATE R%,C%
2355 RETURN
```

Note that it was necessary to define two new *CALLER*s, *CALLER 3* and *CALLER 4*, since this module allows you to use all six cursor motion keys, whereas the bar chart definition module only allows you to use Cursor Up and Cursor Down.

Note how easy it was to force the program user to give correct input. That's the whole point of using an input routine rather than BASIC's prepackaged input statements.

18.5   The Other Modules

Let's now describe the other modules of the program.

Save Bar Chart Module

This module saves the titles and data corresponding to a bar chart using a sequential data file.

```
4000 '**********SAVE BAR CHART*************
4005 CLS:SCREEN 0
4010 PRINT "SAVE BAR CHART"
4015 INPUT "NAME OF FILE";FILENAME$
4020 OPEN FILENAME$ FOR OUTPUT AS #1
4025 WRITE #1, TITLE$
4030 WRITE #1, SER1TITLE$
4035 WRITE #1, SER2TITLE$
4040 WRITE #1, SER3TITLE$
4045 WRITE #1, YMIN$
4050 WRITE #1, YMAX$
4055 WRITE #1, YSTEP$
4060 WRITE #1, XTITLE$
4065 WRITE #1, YTITLE$
4070 FOR N%=0 TO 3
```

```
4075     FOR J%=1 TO 20
4080             WRITE #1, DTA$(N%,J%)
4085     NEXT J%
4090 NEXT N%
4095 CLOSE #1
4100 LOCATE 25,1:PRINT FKEY$;
4105 E$=""
4110 GOTO 900
```

Recall Bar Chart Module

This module recalls from a sequential file the titles and data for a bar chart. It is assumed that the file has been created using the format specified by the *SAVE BAR CHART* module.

```
5000 '**********RECALL BAR CHART**************
5005 CLS:SCREEN 0
5010 PRINT "RECALL BAR CHAR"
5015 INPUT "NAME OF FILE";FILENAME$
5020 OPEN FILENAME$ FOR INPUT AS #1
5025 INPUT #1, TITLE$
5030 INPUT #1, SER1TITLE$
5035 INPUT #1, SER2TITLE$
5040 INPUT #1, SER3TITLE$
5045 INPUT #1, YMIN$
5050 INPUT #1, YMAX$
5055 INPUT #1, YSTEP$
5060 INPUT #1, XTITLE$
5065 INPUT #1, YTITLE$
5070 FOR N%=0 TO 3
5075     FOR J%=1 TO 20
5080             INPUT #1, DTA$(N%,J%)
5085     NEXT J%
5090 NEXT N%
5095 CLOSE #1
5100 GOTO 3000: 'Display bar chart
```

Read From Data File Module

This module allows the user to import data items from a sequential data file into a part of the bar chart input matrix.

```
6000 '**********READ DATA FILE**********
6005 CLS:SCREEN 0:ROW%=0
6010 PRINT "READ DATA FILE"
6015 INPUT "NAME OF FILE";FILENAME$
6020 OPEN FILENAME$ FOR INPUT AS #1
6025 PRINT:PRINT "Which data item does the
                  data file begin with?"
6030 INPUT "          Which label (1 to 20) ";S$
```

```
6045 GOSUB 27000:IF NUMBERCK>-3 THEN 6500
6050 IF S<1 OR S>20 THEN 6500
6055 ROW% = S
6100 INPUT "          Which series (1 to 3) ";S$
6115 GOSUB 27000:IF NUMBERCK>-3 THEN 6500
6120 IF S<1 OR S>3 THEN 6500
6125 COL% = S
6200 WHILE ROW<=20 AND NOT EOF(1)
6205     WHILE COL%<=3 AND NOT EOF(1)
6210         INPUT #1, DTA$(COL%,ROW%)
6215         COL% = COL% + 1
6220     WEND
6225     COL%=1:ROW%=ROW%+1
6230 WEND
6235 CLOSE #1
6240 GOTO 2000 :'Display the data and prompt for more
6500 'Error in input
6505 PRINT "IMPROPER INPUT"
6510 IF ROW%>0 THEN 6100 ELSE 6030
```

Error-Trapping Routine

Here is the error-trapping routine for the program.

```
10000 'Error trapping routine
10002     IF ERR=13 THEN PRINT "Type mismatch (bad
          file name?)":GOTO 10100
10005     IF ERR=53 THEN PRINT "File not found":
          GOTO 10100
10010     IF ERR=61 THEN PRINT "Disk full":GOTO 10100
10015     IF ERR=62 THEN PRINT "Input past end of
          file":GOTO 10100
10020     IF ERR=67 THEN PRINT "Too many files":
          GOTO 10100
10025     IF ERR=68 THEN PRINT "Device unavailable":
          GOTO 10100
10030     IF ERR=70 THEN PRINT "Disk Write Protect":
          GOTO 10100
10035     IF ERR=71 THEN PRINT "Disk not ready":
          GOTO 10100
10040     IF ERR=72 THEN PRINT "Disk media area":
          GOTO 10100
10045     IF ERR=75 THEN PRINT "Path/file access
          error":GOTO 10100
10050     IF ERR=76 THEN PRINT "Path not found":
          GOTO 10100
10055     IF ERR=99 THEN PRINT "Improper input":
          GOTO 10100
10060     ON ERROR GOTO 0:'Unrecoverable error
10100     PRINT "Hit <ENTER> to try again, ESC to
          abort attempt, or Q to Quit the program:";
10105     A$ = INKEY$
10110     IF A$="" THEN 10105
```

```
10115       A = ASC(A$)
10120       IF A=13 THEN RESUME
10125       IF A=27 THEN E$="":RESUME 920
10130       IF A=81 OR A=113 THEN RESUME 7000
10135       GOTO 10105
```

18.6   Conclusion

We have now constructed all of the routines of the BAR CHART GENERA-
TOR. In order to achieve a running program, it is only necessary to collect all of
the pieces into one program and the standard subroutines (*KEYIN, SCREENIN,
PLOTSTRING*, etc.). This is a straightforward affair. If you have created the
pieces in separate files, you may unite them using BASIC's MERGE command.
The only snag is to collect the various pieces of the *INITIALIZATION* routine,
which occurs at the beginning of the program. For your reference, we include a
completed listing of lines 1-899.

```
10 '***********INITIALIZATION ROUTINE**********
100 'Dimension Statements
105       DIM MINKEY(5),MAXKEY(5),
          EXTMINKEY(5),EXTMAXKEY(5)
110       DIM CAPSON(5),SPECIALKEY$(5),
          EXTSPECIALKEY$(5),DTA$(3,20)
115       DIM MENU$(11),A%(10),B$(10),XMAX(3)
200 'Data Statements
300 'Common Statements
400 'Error Trapping Line
410       ON ERROR GOTO 10000
500 'DEF statements
600 'Define parameters for input routine
602       MOTION$=CHR$(71)+CHR$(72)+CHR$(75)
          +CHR$(77)+CHR$(79)+CHR$(80)
604       MOTION1$=CHR$(72)+CHR$(80)
606       FUNCTION$=CHR$(59)+CHR$(60)+CHR$(61)
          +CHR$(62)+CHR$(63)+CHR$(64)+CHR$(65)
608 '     **Text input(CALLER=1)**
610       MINKEY(1)=32:MAXKEY(1)=127:
          SPECIALKEY$(1)=CHR$(8)+CHR$(27)
612       CAPSON(1)=0
614       EXTMINKEY(1)=0:EXTMAXKEY(1)=0
616       EXTSPECIALKEY$(1)=MOTION1$+FUNCTION$
618 '     **Numerical input (CALLER=2)**
620       MINKEY(2)=0:MAXKEY(2)=0:SPECIALKEY$(2)
          ="1234567890-+ E."+CHR$(8)+CHR$(27)
622       CAPSON(2)=-1
624       EXTMINKEY(2)=0:EXTMAXKEY(2)=0
626       EXTSPECIALKEY$(2)=MOTION1$+FUNCTION$
628 '     **Text input(CALLER=3)**
630       MINKEY(3)=0:MAXKEY(3)=127:SPECIALKEY$(3)=""
632       CAPSON(3)=0
634       EXTMINKEY(3)=0:EXTMAXKEY(3)=0
```

```
636        EXTSPECIALKEY$(3)=MOTION$+FUNCTION$
638 '      **Numerical input (CALLER=4)**
640        MINKEY(4)=0:MAXKEY(4)=31:
           SPECIALKEY$(4)="1234567890-+ E."
642        CAPSON(4)=-1
644        EXTMINKEY(4)=0:EXTMAXKEY(4)=0
646        EXTSPECIALKEY$(4)=MOTION$+FUNCTION$
648 '      **Control Routine(CALLER=5)**
650        MINKEY(5)=0:MAXKEY(5)=0
652        CAPSON(5)=0
654        EXTMINKEY(5)=0:EXTMAXKEY(5)=0
656        EXTSPECIALKEY$(5)=FUNCTION$
700 'Initialization of variables
702        TRUE=-1:FALSE=0
703        KEY OFF
704        FOR J%=1 TO 10
706              KEY J%,""
708        NEXT J%
710        FKEY$="1 DEFN   2 DATA   3 DRAW   4 SAVE
                  5 RCLL   6 FILE   7 EXIT"
712        XFLD=1:YFLD=1:LNGTH=0
714        MENU$(1)="BAR CHART DEFINITION"
716        MENU$(2)="TITLE? "
718        MENU$(3)="DATA SERIES 1 TITLE? "
720        MENU$(4)="DATA SERIES 2 TITLE? "
722        MENU$(5)="DATA SERIES 3 TITLE? "
724        MENU$(6)="Y AXIS RANGE:MINIMUM? "
726        MENU$(7)="Y AXIS RANGE:MAXIMUM? "
728        MENU$(8)="Y AXIS STEP? "
730        MENU$(9)="X AXIS TITLE? "
732        MENU$(10)="Y AXIS TITLE? "
734        MAXHEIGHT=199
736        MAXWIDTH=639
740 'Set up screen to start with a
    user-friendly message
742        CLS
744        LOCATE 23,1
746        PRINT "Choose one of the following function
                  keys to start off:";
```

In this chapter, we presented an approach to the development of large BASIC programs. It has the virtue of being an organized approach, which you can follow to develop even the most complex programs. With experience, you will surely develop refinements of your own.

Index

Documentation for Optional Program Diskette

NINETY-FOUR OF THE MAJOR PROGRAMS in this book are available on diskette. You may order this diskette at your local bookseller or via the attached order envelope. Using the diskette, you may use the programs in the book without going through the somewhat painful tasks of typing and debugging.

Using the Program Diskette

1. If you are using the Program Diskette for the first time, make a backup copy just as you would for any master diskette. (Follow the backup procedure outlined on pages 27-28.)

2. Start your computer, load BASIC by inserting the DOS diskette (version 2.00 or above) into the current drive, typing BASICA and obtaining the BASIC Ok prompt. Note that the Program Diskette does not contain DOS.

3. The programs on the diskette are listed below by program name and page number. To run a program, first insert the Program Diskette. You may use either disk drive. If you insert the Program Diskette into the current drive, type:

   `RUN "<program name>"`

   and press ENTER. For example, to run the program TICTAC type:

   `RUN "TICTAC"`

   and press ENTER.

4. When the program is finished, BASIC will redisplay the Ok prompt. You may then rerun the same program by typing RUN and pressing ENTER or you may run another program by giving a command as described in 3.

5. To interrupt a program, simultaneously press Ctrl and Break.

Program Diskette Contents

Now Fully Revised and Expanded to Include
All Versions of BASIC through 3.1!

"This book is the most comprehensive BASIC reference manual available! It sets a new standard for the documentation of BASIC. . . . no other book compares in format, completeness, or level of detail!"

—Larry Joel Goldstein
author of the best-selling
**IBM PC: Introduction to the Operating System,
BASIC Programming and Applications**

". . . 580 pages of solid-gold information. . . . I can recommend Schneider's Handbook *without reservation to everyone, whether you're a beginner, semi-professional, or professional programmer. . . . a very valuable reference."*

—Richard Aarons, *PC Magazine*

"Our overall reaction is one of unbridled enthusiasm!"

—San Diego Computer Society

**Handbook of BASIC for the IBM PC
 Revised and Expanded**
David I. Schneider

If you're programming in BASIC, you need this book by your side! Unlike the BASIC reference manual that accompanies the IBM PC, this handy tool assumes very little knowledge of BASIC—yet covers all the material from the original manual to accommodate experienced users.

In it you'll find:

- BASIC statements organized alphabetically
- Several examples of using each BASIC command
- Discussion of the subtleties and variations of each command
- Plus—applications to illustrate further uses of each function

1985/590pp/paper/D5106-2/$22.95

TO ORDER, simply clip or photocopy this entire page and complete the coupon below. Enclose a check or money order for $22.95. (Please add $2.00 for postage and handling, plus local sales tax).

Mail to: **Brady Computer Books, Simon&Schuster, Box 500, Englewood Cliffs, NJ 07632.** To order by Phone, call (800) 624-0023. (In New Jersey, call (800) 624-0024.)

Name _____

Address _____

City _____ State _____ Zip _____

Charge my credit card instead: ☐ MasterCard ☐ Visa

Account # _____ Expires on _____

Signature as it appears on card _____
Dept. Y   D620X
Prices subject to change without notice.